Lecture Notes in Computer Science

Lecture Notes in Computer Science

Lecture Notes in Computer Science

Edited by G. Goos and J. Hartmanis

134

Program Specification

Proceedings of a Workshop
Aarhus, Denmark, August 1981

Edited by J. Staunstrup

Springer-Verlag
Berlin Heidelberg New York 1982

Editor

Jørgen Staunstrup
Computer Science Department, Aarhus University
Ny Munkegade, 8000 Aarhus C, Denmark

CR Subject Classifications (1979): 4.2, 5.20, 5.21, 5.24

ISBN 3-540-11490-4 Springer-Verlag Berlin Heidelberg New York
ISBN 0-387-11490-4 Springer-Verlag New York Heidelberg Berlin

© by Springer-Verlag Berlin Heidelberg 1982
Printed in Germany

Printing and binding: Beltz Offsetdruck, Hemsbach/Bergstr.
2145/3140-543210

TABLE OF CONTENTS

CHAPTER 1

INTRODUCTION

This is a selection of the papers presented at the Workshop on Program Specification held at the Computer Science Department, Aarhus University, Denmark, from the 4th to the 7th of August, 1981.

By looking at the literature on program specification one gets the impression that a number of different schools e.g. algebraic, axiomatic, operational and their sub-schools struggle to show the superiority of their technique. But at a closer look many problems and achievements are the same in several of the techniques. It was the intention of the workshop to bring together representatives from the different schools to try to compare and contrast, hopefully to the benefit of everybody.

Two major trends emerged at the workshop

- the different techniques are not alternatives, but rather supplements to each other. Several participants presented work on how to fit what was before disparate techniques into the same framework e.g. the papers by Gallimore and Coleman, Goguen, and Guttag in these proceedings;

- the field currently called program specification spans very widely. At the workshop there were serious and interesting discussions of topics as different as: the mathematical foundations of set theory, pragmatic considerations of how an interactive specification editor should work, and sociological and psychological investigations of human communication. It is unlikely that there are very many common concepts, techniques, and goals in such a disperse area. A major issue at the workshop was therefore attempts to distinguish more well-defined subproblems e.g. the paper by Guttag in these proceedings.

The organization of the workshop

A conscious effort was made to prevent the workshop from dissolving into a number of committees each discussing their own technique in their own jargon. One such effort was the distribution of three informally specified examples to all participants six months before the workshop. Everybody was asked to provide their own specifications of each of the examples and present them at the workshop. This provided us with a number of different specifications of the same example using different techniques. Chapters 2, 3 and 4 contain most of these specifications.

Furthermore, all participants were asked to present their view on a number of topics: formal models, combining specifications, verification and implementation techniques and concurrency. In chapter 5 there is a selection of papers describing some of the work which was presented in the sessions. The next section contains the complete program of the workshop.

Jim Horning, Xerox, Palo Alto, was invited to the workshop to try to pick out the major trends and to give his personal summary of the workshop. In addition to this he conducted a survey of the participants' experience using their techniques on "real" systems. These two contributions are collected in chapter 1.

Acknowledgement.

The workshop was supported financially by the Danish Research Council "Det naturvidenskabelige Forskningsråd" and the Computer Science Department, Aarhus University.
Workshops such as this has become a tradition at the Computer Science Department, Aarhus University. One of the reasons for this is Karen Møller. She deserves a special thank you for making it an easy job to arrange such workshops and for creating a friendly cooperative and relaxed atmosphere during the workshop.

Aarhus, December 1981.

PROGRAM FOR

WORKSHOP ON PROGRAM SPECIFICATION

Tuesday, August 4

9.00-9.15   Welcome

9.15-10.00   Use of specification
             - J. Guttag

10.30-12.30 EXAMPLE 2, KWIC-index generation
             - H. Ehrig & H.-J. Kreowski
             - J. Steensgaard-Madsen
             - R. Gallimore
             - L. Sandegaard Nielsen

14.00-15.00 The Tactics of Algorithm and Program Design
             - J. Nievergelt

Wednesday, August 5

9.00-10.30   Formal Models
             - I. Sørensen & B. Sufrin
             - H. Klaeren

11.00-12.30 Combining Specifications
             - J. Steensgaard-Madsen
             - H. Ehrig & H.-J. Kreowski

14.00-15.30 Combining Specifications
             - J. Goguen
             - D. Musser

16.00-16.30 - F. Cristian

Thursday, August 6

9.00-10.30   Testing and Validation Systems
             - P. Mosses
             - H. Klaeren
             - J. Guttag

11.00-12.00 Verification and Implementation Techniques
             - R. Gallimore
             - H. Ehrig & H.-J. Kreowski

12.00-12.30 Program Development, a personal view
             - P. Naur

14.00-15.00 Ordinary
             - J. Goguen

15.30-16.30 Z
             - I. Sørensen & B. Sufrin

9.00-9.30	On the Structure of Application Systems - D. Bjørner
9.30-10.30	Concurrency - M. Powell & J. Hughes
11.00-12.00	Concurrency - H. Barringer & A. Wills
12.00-12.30	Proceedings - discussion
14.00-15.30	Communication Network - D. Musser - L. Sandegaard-Nielsen - I. Sørensen & B. Sufrin

PROGRAM SPECIFICATION:

ISSUES AND OBSERVATIONS

J.J. Horning
Computer Science Laboratory
Xerox Palo Alto Research Centers

INTRODUCTION

As will be clear from the papers included in this volume, one
of the principal characteristics of this workshop was variety:
we came with widely differing motivations for working on program specifications, which had led us to address different
issues using many different approaches and notations. It is
not the purpose of this brief note to impose a uniform conceptual
framework on this variety, to summarize the material presented
(the papers themselves do that), nor even to record the content
of our discussions. Rather, I have taken the opportunity to
set down personal reflections on some themes that recurred
during the workshop. I chose some because I sensed a surprising
degree of consensus, others, because they represent important
unresolved issues.

In good workshops, the best ideas arise through interactions,
rather than from individual contributions. Thus, I have not
generally attempted to allocate credit for the ideas we discussed.
A statement that I have attributed to someone may represent only
a reformulation or summary that caught my fancy. Although I have
not intentionally misrepresented anyone's position, there are
undoubtedly errors of quotation and interpretation.

USES OF PROGRAM SPECIFICATIONS

Almost from the outset, it was apparent that the term "program specifications" meant widely different things to different participants. Many differences arose from the various uses we intended for our specifications. Just about the only things that we all had in common were an interest in computer programs, and the notion that a specification somehow made something "more specific".

In the opening presentation, J. Guttag introduced a classification of specifications as "local", "system", or "structural" that we frequently (if not always consistently) used thereafter.

Local specifications apply to a single program unit (procedure, module, cluster, ...). They are used to expose and document local decisions in a program's design by defining an interface. They may contain both mathematical and programming-language dependent concepts. This is a relatively well understood area; most of our techniques can produce useful local specifications. Perhaps we should be more concerned with promoting their use than with further refining our techniques in this area.

System specifications indicate requirements on the "externally observable behavior" of an entire system, generally a complex system. They define the interface between the system and its environment, using concepts that are relevant in that environment. To limit the amount of detail that must be considered at one time, a system specification is usually constructed by combining subspecifications, but this structure need not (and perhaps should not) bear any particular relation to the structure of the system's implementation.

Unlike local specifications, system specifications should probably be written by specification specialists. To ensure that they represent the client's intent, however, they must be easily checkable by specialists in the application domain. Whereas local specifications are intended to be complete, many uses of system specifications occur while they are in the process of development. It is thus important to be able to answer questions about an incompletely specified system, and to determine what decisions remain to be made.

Structural specifications are a tool that system designers can use to record a high-level description of some aspects of a design. They typically consist of behavioral specifications of subsystems, plus some relations among them. Although they take the same form as system specifications, the intent is that their structure indicate the structure of the system's implementation. Thus a structural specification can both guide the implementation process and provide a basis for early analysis of the design. Subsystem specifications may themselves be system specifications; at the bottom level they will be local specifications.

As our discussions progressed, a somewhat more detailed classification of the uses of specifications emerged. Although they all involve some form of communication, these different uses lead to rather different requirements for program specifications; there is no reason to expect any single form to be optimal for all of them.

Clarification. Our various efforts to develop formal specifications corresponding to the three examples (see   ) revealed several incompletenesses and ambiguities.(E.g., in the KWIC program, should duplicate lines be printed? How is punctuation treated?) One advantage of the specification process is that it causes these questions to be posed early in the system development cycle, and may improve the chances of their being answered by the client, rather than decided by the whims of the lowest-level programmers. J. Goguen pointed out that there is a big difference between an unnoticed ambiguity and a parameter that allows the answer to some question to be delayed. A specification should document both the decisions that have been made and those that have been postponed.

Contract. When the client and the implementor belong to distinct organizations, the understanding between them should be documented in a form adequate to enable a third party to determine whether it is fulfilled.

Design. As the design of a system progresses, various alternatives are proposed, evaluated, and accepted or rejected. Successive decisions lead to increasing specificity. It is important to record these decisions in a form useful to (at least) the designers and the implementors. (B. Sufrin noted that it is sometimes difficult to distinguish between specifications and designs.) Some specification systems make it easier to evaluate alternative designs, or even to conceive new ones.

Construction. Specification is generally seen as falling somewhere between the client's informal desire for a system to solve some problem and the programmer's development of a running program that solves a problem that is (ideally) not very different from the original problem. There is little agreement, however, on where (or even whether) to place boundaries in this spectrum. Even the rubric that "specification should say _what_, not _how_" was challenged. (P. Naur: "Programs are specifications." J. Goguen: "Programming is a special case of specification.") Several variations of stepwise refinement were presented for use in developing specifications that could be evolved into implementations. Conversely, it was argued (notably by D. Musser and J. Goguen) that the major tools of specification (theories, abstraction, ...) were too useful to be excluded from the programmer's toolkit.

Validation. If "a program is its own specification", and there is no other, then programs cannot be "incorrect" (merely "surprising"). In order to check, formally or informally, that a program does what it is supposed to do, we need some redundant indication of its intended behavior. Several approaches to program specification are motivated by the desire to make it easier to ensure (or demonstrate) that a program is consistent with its specification.

The assistance may come from the technique's suitability for a formal proof system, a particular programming language (or its semantic definition language), a program development methodology, or any combination of these factors.

Maintenance. When a program must be changed to remove a latent error, enhance its behavior, or respond to a change in its environment), it can be very helpful to have careful documentation of what it (and each of its components) was intended to do. Furthermore, the problems of validation generally increase as a system is modified.

Generalization. Concepts developed for a particular system and lessons learned through its construction and use are often more general than the system itself. Our ability to communicate and to reuse such concepts depends on abstracting and specifying their essential characteristics. New specifications and new designs should not start from scratch, but should incorporate and refine the best previous work.

ABSTRACTIONS

Abstraction is a means of suppressing details without being less
precise. We agreed that it is our most powerful tool for mastering
the complexities of real systems - some would say that it is
practically our only tool. We need abstraction not only to suppress
implementation details at levels where they are irrelevant, but
to organize our understanding of the concepts involved.

Naming. The fundamental abstraction mechanism underlying all
others is the ability to use a name to stand for something. For
example, we see this twice in the procedure mechanism: the procedure's name can be used to stand for an invocation of its body;
within its body, the name of a formal parameter can be used to
stand for the actual parameter(s) supplied at the point(s) of call.
In both cases, this suppresses detail that is irrelevant for some
purposes.

Parameterization. Much of our discussion focussed on parameter
mechanisms and related issues. We talked about parameterized
specifications, parameterized parameters, specification of parameters, how to check whether parameters are being passed consistently, and even how to pass specification languages as parameters. The
power and generality of a specification language will largely
depend on its parameterization mechanisms. We saw that there
are deep and subtle semantic traps here for the unwary, that considerable progress is being made in developing adequate theoretical
foundations, and that much research remains to be done. This is
the area where the communication gap between theoreticians and
practitioners is widest.

Constraints vs. refinements. A specification may supply either
properties or a constructive definition of its "specificand";
both styles were advocated. A constraint consisting of only required properties ("what", "intent", "implicit specification") is
generally more abstract than a refinement consisting of an explicit definition ("how", "model", "abstract implementation").
This should make it easier for the reader to separate the specificand from the "incidental scaffolding" in the specification,
but may make it harder to visualize the specificand or to determine

the consistency of the specification. Fortunately, a consensus
emerged that either style can in principle be extended to include the other; future systems may allow the specifier to
choose on a case-by-case basis, depending on his application
and intended use.

Specification language. J. Goguen made a strong case that an
adequate language for system and structural specifications must
itself abstract from the language(s) used for local specifications.
Only thus can we make our specification system independent of the
application domains of the systems we wish to specify. CLEAR is
a language for "putting theories together", parameterized with
respect to the language(s) in which those theories are written.
The concept of "institution" formalizes the requirements that
such a language must satisfy.

THE SPECIFICATION PROCESS

"Specification" is both a noun and a verb. Correspondingly,
we discussed issues related to the process of specification
and issues related to specification documents. Although we spent
more time on the latter, we seemed better able to focus on matters
of substance in the former area.

Multiple views (1). A good specification will be put to many
different uses in its lifetime; no single form of presentation
is likely to be well-suited for all of them. Rather than developing different forms independently, and attempting to ensure
their consistency, it would be highly desirable to maintain a
single form (perhaps a specification data base) that could be
viewed in many different ways, with appropriate external forms
generated on demand.

Multiple views (2). If a system is specified by constraints on
its behavior, it may be much more effective to express different
constraints in terms of concepts appropriate to different views
of the system. For example, some aspects of a cash dispenser are
best stated from the customer's viewpoint, others from the teller's,
others from the auditor's, and still others from the maintenance
engineer's.

Multiple views (3). As we begin using more general concepts from
"specification libraries", we will need to specialize them for
particular uses. There will be many common patterns to these
specializations. In the CLEAR language, "views" provide default
fittings (coercions), by which a theory can be used as a parameter
in contexts where the requirement specifies a simpler theory.

User dialog. "Specification is a problem-oriented excercise".
(I. Sørensen). Whatever a specification is to be used for, it is
important that the specifier and the client engage in dialog to
ensure that the result satisfies the client's needs. Even if the

specifier is well-trained in a particular technique, it is unlikely that the client will be, which is the principal reason why readability by novices cannot be dismissed as an issue of "mere notation".

Design. Although specification may extend beyond the "design phase" of a project (in both directions), specification (albeit mostly informal specification) is surely ubiquituous in the design process. We noted that formal specification, in addition to recording a design, could assist the process in various ways. It encourages the paradigm "Generalize by developing a theory; then particularize" (I. Sørensen); this can lead to a more systematic exploration of the design space. The decomposition of a specification into subspecifications is generally not unique; in a structural specification we advance the design by making (and validating) such choices (R. Gallimore).

Problems of scale. Implicit in much of our discussion was the belief that specification of large systems is non-linearly more difficult than specification of small ones. But of course we only had time to illustrate our various techniques using small examples, where the overhead of the "putting together" mechanisms often dwarfed the content of the specification. There was a clear consensus that we should be focussing our research on tools for managing the complexity of large systems, but substantial divergence on the issue of whether the greatest profit would come from better mental tools for understanding and organizing specifications or from better "metal tools" (hardware/software systems).

Libraries. Everyone is in favor of libraries of reusable specification components. Several of the presentations addressed issues important to the content of such libraries. However, no one seemed to have any good ideas about how to structure a large library so that relevant entries could be easily located.

<u>Incremental development.</u> Most of the techniques presented
allowed complex systems to be specified by adding details a few
at a time, starting from a relatively simple top-level specification. However, there was considerable variation in the extent
to which they controlled the amount of detail relevant when
considering lower-level components of the specification. Some
seemed to yield large "programs" that would have to be understood
<u>in</u> <u>toto</u>, while others carefully ensured that each unit of the
specification could be understood and validated separately.
Although this correlation may not be necessary, it seemed that
the latter group were the methods that distinguished between constraints and refinements at each level; local verification is the
process of showing for each refinement that the constraints on
components are strong enough to imply that it satisfies its own
requirements.

<u>Testing.</u> As specifications get larger, so does the potential for
errors. In addition to the usual issues of program verification,
we kept returning to issues related to checking specifications
themselves: Are they consistent? Do they really reflect (enough of)
the client's intent? Do the structural specifications satisfy
the system specifications?

Experience with several systems for executing specifications
indicates that most specifications that are written contain
errors, ranging from "typos" to blunders to deep misunderstandings.
Again, it seems important to exploit some form of redundancy to
detect them; this might be a collection of intended theorems, an
abstract program, or another form of specification.

<u>Tools.</u> A recurrent theme was that the set of available tools
strongly influences what it is reasonable to attempt in program
specification. J. Guttag identified several uses for "metal tools"
that would complement our mental tools: guide novices into effective use of mental tools; remove drudgery from the expert's use;
ease the task of filing, updating, and retrieving current versions
of the components of large specifications; make it easy to

"browse" specialized views on demand and avoid "the tyranny of paper", where the author must choose the form of presentation; keep track of the interrelations among multiple levels of abstraction, multiple levels of formality, and multiple kinds of information; automate some kinds of testing, using theorem provers and direct execution; answer questions about both the specification and the specificand.

J. Goguen presented a set of tough problems that should be dealt with to develop a good set of tools: modularization; definitions vs. constraints; application domain independence; effectiveness (direct implementability and checkability of specifications); integration into the total programming environment, including use as a communication tool and incorporation of informal specifications; programming system and programming language independence; a sound theoretical basis that explains the relations among theories, models and specifications.

Others worried about excessive dependence on mechanical aids. "Don't let your tools trap you into suboptimal ways of doing things." (D. Bjørner) "Sometimes the discipline of paper is useful. Avoid the tyranny of anything!" (I. Sørensen)

THE FORM OF SPECIFICATIONS

To the frustration of many of us, who had hoped to focus on
"deeper" issues, much of our time was spent dealing with issues
of the concrete syntax of various specification languages.
In retrospect, this was perhaps unavoidable, given the plan to
compare methods through common examples. ("I gotta use words
when I talk to you.") It is also symptomatic of a larger problem
for the field of program specification: When the notation used
in a small example requires more explanation than the implementing
program would, too many potential clients will fail to see the
point of specification.

Syntactic sugar. Although a workshop is hardly the place to
thrash out such details, in the privacy of our own research centers
we should be worrying more about the interfaces seen by clients
and by specifiers. As with other formal languages, there is a
tension between the desire for a simple, elegant, uniform formal
basis and the desire to make commonly occurring idioms clear and
concise. We still have much to learn from programming language
designers in this area.

Many surface details that can greatly affect readability and
writability of specifications are "trivial" at the level of theoretical foundations and implementation. The only bar to getting them
right is deciding what that means. Although there is no substitute
for good taste in design, useful clues about where it should be
applied can be gleaned by observing where people ask for more explanation than seems to be appropriate. "Once you get it right,
you can stop explaining it".

Formal basis. A beautiful facade is no substitute for a sound
foundation. A specification language without a precise semantics
may serve to obscure imprecision, rather than to remove it.
Fortunately, it appears that each of the major styles of specification can be given a rigorous formal basis (although this has
sometimes come after the fact). It was not always clear that the

practitioners understood the pratical implications of work
on theoretical underpinnings or that theoreticians knew how
their work would be applied in practice. However, our communication improved as the workshop progressed, as did our understanding of how the various formalisms can be related to each
other.

Structures. Several presentations dealt with some aspect of
"the algebra of theories". But a large specification also has
many implicit structures. Two units may be related (directly
or transitively) because one is used in the specification (or
the refinement) of the other, or because it is a specialization (subclass, instance) or an abstraction (generalization),
or because it provides an analogous function, or because it is
a newer version, or perhaps simply because some of its text
was copied. Depending on the purpose, any of these structures
could provide a reasonable basis for organizing a display of the
specification. Several people made the point that a specification
document should explicitly record the history of the specification process. (Some wanted an expurgated version, with the mis-
taken paths removed; others argued that the reasons for rejection
of these paths could be invaluable during maintenance.)

AFTERWORD

I hope that these reflections will inspire you to read the papers in this volume in a spirit of quest, seeking the evidence on all sides of the contentious issues, as well as the basis for my optimism in areas where I have proclaimed consensus.

The survey which follows should give you a better idea of our collective view of the practical applications of this work.

I am sure that I have not been able to convey a sense of all that we accomplished at this workshop, and I apologise to all those whose contribution or favorite topic I neglected, be it on the difference between specification and programming, the rôle and limits of formalism in achieving precise communication of intent, the treatment of errors, exceptional conditions, reliability and timing constraints, or the specification of concurrency.

A Survey on Applications of Specification Techniques

The following is the result of a survey conducted at the
workshop on the participants' practical use of specification
techniques. Everybody was asked to answer the following three
questions:

A)   What is the largest running system that has been
        specified by your techniques?

B)   How many people (outside your own group) are using
        your technique to design systems they are intending to
        build?

C)   Where is the bottleneck? Why aren't more systems
        carefully specified?

A)   What is the largest running system that has been
        specified by your techniques?

        _____

D. Bjørner   (VDM/META-IV).
        After the implementation was complete, we produced
        a complete VDM specification for IBM's System/R database
        system, as seen from the PL/I programmer's view. This
        specification is 80 typed pages in length, and includes
        multi-user facilities, locking, transaction control,
        and backout.

        We have also specified a full compiler for CHILL, the
        CCITT standard implementation language for telecommuni-
        cation systems, which is "about as complex" as Ada.
        Several implementations are in progress. We participated
        in the formal specification of Ada.

Oxford group   (Z).
        We have formally specified a medium-scale (2,000 lines
        of code) data base system, a screen editor, and the Unix filing
        system.

J. Staunstrup (axiomatic).
        I specified approximately half of the SOLO
        operating system - the parts for handling the terminal
        and the file system.

J. Goguen   (CLEAR and OBJ).
        We have specified modest programming languages, simple
        data bases, AI problem solvers, and list processing with
        garbage collection.

D. Musser   (Affirm).

        We specified simple communication protocols and the
file updating module of a message system.

J. Guttag   (algebraic axioms).

        We have specified a window package for the Alto
(not presently being used, however) and a backgammon
playing program.

H. Ehrig and H.-J. Kreowski

        We have specified small experimental data base systems
(airport schedule, parts system, library).

M.S. Powell   (DTL).

        DTL has been used to specify its own virtual machine
implementation.

H. Barringer   (modified META-IV).

        We specified a message-based run-time system for
support of some features (at present) of Ada tasks.

H. Klaeren

        We have specified a compiler for Meyer and Ritchie's
LOOP language, producing code for an idealized random
access machine, and proved correctness of the compiler,
but of course nobody wanted to implement it.

J. Steensgaard-Madsen

        The module tree technique has been used to design
a 10,000 line PASCAL program to phototypeset documents.

B)   How many people (outside your own group) are using your techniques to design systems they are intending to build?

D. Bjørner   (VDM/META-IV).
        Several groups: SZKI and SZAMKI (Budapest), CSELT (research division of Italian Telegraph), University of Kiel, Chr. Rovsing, Inc.

Oxford group   (Z).
        Four in industry and one in a university. We are also aware of several experiments, and every year five to ten students who are going to industry are trained in our techniques.

J. Goguen   (CLEAR and OBJ).
        Groups at the University of Massachusetts, Ballistic Missile Defense Command, and Digital Equipment Corporation.

D. Musser   (Affirm).
        The internet Project at ISI (University of Southern California), a group at MITRE Corp.

H. Ehrig and H.-J. Kreowski
        The algebraic approach in general is used in several German universities: Aachen, Berlin, Bonn, Dortmund, München.

M.S. Powell   (DTL).
        None, but an automotive manufacturer is preparing to use our method to design a large industrial press-line monitoring system.

C)   Where is the bottleneck? Why aren't more systems
      carefully specified?

D. Bjørner

    Lack of properly educated people, industrial inertia,
    requirement for higher level of more formally trained
    people, inadequacies of past languages and methods,
    lack of computer-aided support tools.

Oxford group

    Lack of real-life examples, insufficient documentation
    of techniques.

J. Staunstrup

    A specification language frequently becomes a strait
    jacket. The notation doesn't seem to be adequate to
    describe the domains needed in realistic systems.
    It is hard to decompose/structure a specification to
    make it manageable.

J. Goguen

    Theorem proving, user expertise, system support, etc.

D. Musser

    Theorem proving, resource limitations on large proofs
    (time, memory, user comprehension), limited form of
    abstraction, incompatibility between main specification
    method (algebraic) and programming language (PASCAL),
    lack of facilities for combining specifications.

J. Guttag

    Lack of appreciation of the utility of writing and
    reading formal specifications, lack of tools to support
    the construction and reading of large specifications.

H. Ehrig and H.-J. Kreowski

Lack of education in the methods outside of university and research centers, widespread belief that careful specifications and correctness proofs are too time-consuming and expensive, lack of appropriate tools.

M.S. Powell

Most people working in the area are more interested in refining their techniques than in finding ways of making them palatable for real world users.

H. Barringer

Not enough education, many systems are not practical for industrial use.

H. Klaeren

Complexity of real specifications, especially the number of details, exceptions, if's and when's.

J. Horning

Lack of practical demonstrations, inability to manage complexity of real specifications.

A. Wills

Many people are convinced that no practical method exists and doubtful that one can exist.

R.M. Gallimore

Educational: general users do not have the necessary skills. Methods and support tools are not sufficiently developed to make their application attractive.

J. Rushby

For most applications, the cost of failure is not yet high enough!

Example 1: Geometrical Constructions

Consider a program which performs a number of classical (Euclidian) geometrical constructions. Assume that the following three kinds of figures are needed: points, lines and circles.

A number of different operations are necessary: construct a line from two points, check if two circles intersect, construct a line from two intersecting circles, construct a point from two crossing lines etc. Different variations of these operations can be considered, here we concentrate on the following set of operations which must be specified:

operation same_point (p1, p2: point): boolean;

operation new_line (p1, p2: point): line;

operation crossing (l1, l2: line): boolean;

operation meet (l1, l2: line): point;
      (* returns the intersection of two crossing lines *)

operation new_circle (p1, p2, p3: point): circle;
      (* construct the circle which passes through the three
        points p1, p2 and p3 *)

operation intersect (c1, c2: circle): point x point;
      (* return the pair of points where two circles intersect *)

operation concentric (c1, c2: circle): boolean;
      (* true if the two circles c1 and c2 are concentric *)

operation tangent (p: point; c: circle): line;
      (* return the line which is a tangent of the circle c at the
        point p *)

Jørgen Staunstrup
Computer Science Department
Aarhus University

The Technique

The operations for performing geometrical constructions are
specified axiomatically. That is by giving <u>a set of valid pairs</u>.
Each valid pair is two values, one is interpreted as the value
before the operation, the other as the value after the operation.
These pairs are specified implicitly by giving predicates which
they must satisfy. Such predicates are usually called pre and post
conditions.

<u>Operations</u> map values into other values, but this mapping need
not be one to one, i.e. functional. It can be many to one or one
to many. Therefore the term operation is used rather than function.
An operation takes one value and yields a value (<u>application</u> of the
operation), but a value may consist of many components (<u>cartesian
product</u>).

A <u>data type</u> is a set of values with some common properties, namely
that they can be applied in the same operations. Each value of a
type has a distinct name and each type has a distinct name. Any two
values of the same type can be compared (=).

The Notation

The notation is explained by the following example of an operation
which computes the square root of a real number:

> <u>operation</u> sqrt(x: real): real
> <u>if</u> x > 0 <u>and</u> y' * y' = x → sqrt = y' <u>end</u>

The operation can only be applied if x > 0 and if there exists
a value y, such that y' * y' = x. If this is the case, the value
of y' is the square root of x. Note, that this is an example of
a one to many relation since both $(x, \sqrt{x})$ and $(x, -\sqrt{x})$ are
valid pairs of arguments and results for this operation.

The Example

The geometrical constructions are assumed to take place in a usual two-dimensional coordinate system:

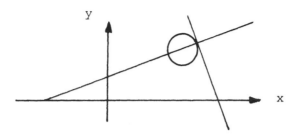

A point is denoted by its coordinates, a line by the equation ax + b = y, and a circle by its centre and radius.

```
point  =  (x,y: real);
line   =  (a,b: real);
circle =  (p: point; r: real);
```

For simplicity we assume that none of the lines in the construction are parallel with the y-axis. This restriction could be avoided by a slightly more complex specification.

The following is a specification of the operation newline.

```
operation newline (p1,p2: point): line
if
    (a' * p1.x + b' = p1.y) and (a' * p2.x + b' = p2.y)
            → newline = (a',b')
end
```

The new line is determined by the value (a',b') which satisfies the equation a' * x + b'= y for both points p1 and p2. To avoid lines parallel with the y-axis an additional restriction, p1.x ≠ p2.x is included:

```
      operation newline (p1,p2: point): line
      if
         (a' * p1.x + b'= p1.y) and (a' * p2.x + b' = p2.y)
         and (p1.x ≠ p2.x)
                → newline = (a',b')
      end
```

The following two predicates are useful in the remaining part of
the specification:

$$p \in l \equiv l.a * p.x + l.b = p.y$$

i.e. the point p is on the line l

$$p \in c \equiv (c.p.x - p.x)^2 + (c.p.y - p.y)^2 = c.r^2$$

i.e. the point p is on the circle c

```
operation crossing(l1,l2: line): boolean
if true → p' ∈ l1 and p' ∈ l2 = crossing end

operation meet(l1,l2: line): point
if p' ∈ l1 and p' ∈ l2 → meet = p' end

operation new_circle(p1,p2,p3: point): circle
if p1 ∈ c' and p2 ∈ c' and p3 ∈ c' → new_circle = c' end

operation intersect (c1,c2: circle): point x point
if p' ∈ c1 and p' ∈ c2 and p" ∈ c1 and p" ∈ c2
      and p' ≠ p" → intersect = (p',p") end

operation concentric (c1,c2: circle): boolean
if true → concentric = (c1.p = c2.p) end
```

So far, the only quantifier used is the implicit existential
quantifier used for all the primed values e.g. p' and p". In the
specification of tangent a universal quantifier is necessary.

```
      operation tangent (p: point; c: circle): line
      if p ∈ c and p ∈ l' and (∀x: x ∈ c and x ∈ l' ⇒ x = p)
            → tangent = l'  end
```

Splitting up the Specification

Specifications and programs share the danger of becoming
complex and intertwined. This should clearly be avoided
for specifications as it should for programs. The specification of the operations for doing geometrical constructions
given above has the germ for such complexity. If, for
example, lines parallel with the y-axis are allowed, it
should not be necessary to change the entire specification.
If such global changes are necessary it is a sign that
the specification is difficult to use. Because at each point
of the specification it is necessary to be aware of many details.

In the example, it is the details of the abstract values
point, line and circle which should be localized as much as
possible. Many other abstract representations of these values
could be used, e.g. representing the lines and circles as
infinite sets of points. Therefore the representation
should be concealed as much as possible. Since the details of
the representation present such a problem, one should ask
the question: Why not avoid the explicit representation and
choose some implicit characterization of the values e.g.
Euclid's axioms? I can only find pragmatic answers to this.
The implicit characterizations can be very hard to find. The
Peano or Euclid axioms are the conclusion of a long abstraction
process. Furthermore, an explicit representation as for example
a pair of coordinates can be easier to grasp than an implicit
characterization like the Euclidian axioms.

So an abstract representation can be a necessary evil but the
contamination should be reduced as much as possible. A solution
would be syntactic restrictions on the scope of names. But what
should these scope rules be? One solution that has been proposed is the class concept where a number of operations form
a block whose internal structure is not visible from the outside.

Considering the above example the class concept is not
sufficient. Each of the geometrical figures point, line and
circle should be a separate class, but then the encapsulation
prevents us from defining such operations as tangent. Which
class should it belong to?

A small improvement of the above specification would be a
specification where one was forced to explicitly state when
details of the representation are referred to. For example,
in the specification of the predicate: p $\in$ l, both the representation of points and lines are referred to. This could
be specified as follows

$$\text{operation } \in \text{ (p:point; l: line): boolean}$$
$$\text{line, point } \underline{if} \text{ true} \rightarrow \in \; = \text{ (l.a * p.x + l.b = p.y) } \underline{end}$$

the notation is the SIMULA prefix notation where one block, A,
can be prefixed by another, B, thereby making the internal declarations of B visible in A. Without such a prefix the specification of an operation should not be allowed to refer to
the details of the abstract representation of a value, but
only be allowed to manipulate the value as a whole.

Joseph A. Goguen
Computer Science Laboratory
SRI International

1. Introduction

The geometrical construction problem posed for this workshop raises a number
of issues which may be of some general interest for program specification.
Assuming, as seems natural at first thought, that standard representations
from analytical geometry are to be used*, we are required to encode what
amounts to a small textbook (e.g., much of the first 160 pages of [Morrill et
al 72]) on the subject in a language which is much more rigorous than that
usually found in textbooks. The following points can be identified as
particular difficulties for specification techniques of the kinds with which I
am familiar:

1. Analytic geometry is based on the real numbers. How can we specify
   this particular structure?

2. Alternative representations are sometimes required. For example,
   if we choose to represent lines in "slope-intercept form," i.e.,
   as pairs (m,b) which determine the points (x,y) such that y = mx+b,
   then we need a separate representation for vertical lines, such as
   their x-intercept, (a), determining the points (x,y) such that x =
   a.

3. Under certain conditions, some of these constructions fail. For
   example, two lines fail to meet if they are parallel. This means
   that we need to consider exceptions or errors.

4. Under certain conditions, some constructions yield elements of a
   type other than that which is usually expected. For example,
   square root (in SQFIELD below) yields a postive element (of sort

---

*One could also consider using the axioms for plane geometry given by
Euclid, or by Hilbert.

"poselt"), satisfying the equation $(\ x)^2 = x$, whereas the
operation $\_^2$ expects sort "elt". But fortunately, poselt is a
<u>subsort</u> of elt (see OFIELD, which specifies ordered fields), so
that the given equation makes sense.

5. This is a fairly complex problem, and therefore we would like to
   break its specification into a number of parts, much as a textbook
   on analytic geometry is broken into chapters. Insofar as is
   reasonable, these parts should be hierarchically organized, and
   should make use of parameterization, so as to permit building up
   and using a library of useful and reusable general specifications.

6. [Staunstrup 81] points out that some constructions, for example,
   the tangent to a circle through a point, require access to
   previously defined representations. Unfortunately, this seems to
   be in conflict with the desire to structure specifications into
   separate clusters each having its representations hidden from all
   other clusters.

These last two points concern the structuring of complex specification, as is
also desirable to enhance their readability, writability, and modifiability.
To do this while providing a rigorous semantics for all of the constructions
involved may be one of the most important problems of contemporary computer
science.

The first six subsections below briefly discuss how each of these issues was
approached. This geometrical constructions specification is written in
ORDINARY, a specification language still in its design stage, and not yet well
documented (there is only a draft SRI report at this time [Goguen & Burstall
80]). Indeed, this is the first public exposure of our thoughts on ORDINARY.
Working on this problem has suggested some new features for ORDINARY, and
these features may not survive in the form in which they are presented here.
A major design consideration for of ORDINARY has been that it should be as
"ordinary" as possible, in the sense that specifications written in it be
close to the way that ordinary programmers talk about their problems.

I would like to thank Jurgen Staunstrup for posing this problem, and to
acknowledge the collaboration of Rod Burstall in many of the ideas presented

here. I would also like to thank Karl Levitt, Michael Melliar-Smith, and David Elliott who are members of the SRI ORDINARY team, Brad Silverberg who was, and Pepe Meseguer, who contributed many important corrections to this document.

1.1 The Reals

The reals are an uncountable structure, and therefore cannot be specified with standard initial algebra semantics. Perhaps they can be specified with continuous initial algebra semantics [Goguen, Thatcher, Wagner & Wright 77], but I have chosen to dodge this problem by parameterizing all constructions over an arbitrary field having square roots of positive elements. Of course, any implementation of these geometrical constructions on a computer will have to use a set of approximations to the reals which is not only not uncountable, but is actually finite.

The specification of this "requirement" theory for a parameter to the geometrical constructions specification is given in Section 2, and illustrates some further interesting points. For example, it is not possible to specify fields purely equationally, or even with conditional equations having a conjunction of equations as condition, because the axiom

$$x \bullet (y/x) = y \text{ if } x \neq 0$$

has the inequation "$x \neq 0$" as its condition. However, because we aren't trying to specify a particular structure, there is no need to restrict ourselves to pure equational logic, or even to its generalization to conditional equations. Thus we shall permit the use of arbitrary first order logical axioms for the specification of theories which express requirements. Similarly, we permit clusters to declare relns (relations) as well as sorts and ops (operations) in their interfaces. [Theoretical justification is given in [Burstall & Goguen 81] and [Goguen & Burstall 80], under the heading of "duplex institutions".]*

1.2 Alternative Representations

The problem here is similar to that addressed in PASCAL under the heading of

---

*Occasional technical remarks are enclosed in square brackets. It is not necessary to follow these to understand the main flow of ideas.

"variant records" [Jensen & Wirth 78]. Our syntax for ORDINARY is also
similar. This is illustrated in the specification LINE, where two
representations are given for lines.

1.3 Exception Handling

Most specification techniques do not deal with exceptions in an adequate
manner. The most common formal approach is to use partial operations, which
are undefined under the exceptional conditions, e.g. [Kaphengst & Reichel
77, Reichel & Hupbach & Kaphengst 80]. Many specification techniques do not
provide a formal treatment of errors at all. Our treatment of exceptions in
this example follows the "error algebra" approach of [Goguen 77] which permits
explicit and informative error messages to be given for exceptional
conditions. [There are still some unresolved theoretical problems with error
algebras, but our extensive practical experience with OBJT [Goguen & Tardo 79]
suggests that it will be possible to resolve these.]

1.4 Coercions

In order to handle cases where things of one sort are also of another sort --
for example, natural numbers are rational numbers -- and cases where something
may be of one of several sorts -- for example, the intersection of two circles
can be zero, one, or two points, or else a circle* -- we shall use "order
sorted algebra" [Goguen 78]. In this approach, a partial ordering relation is
given on the set of sorts, e.g. nat $\leq$ rat. Hopefully, our specification can
be understood without any technical knowledge of this theory. Indeed, its
purpose is only to provide a foundation for notions which are already
intuitively understood.

1.5 Structured Specification

Many specification techniques fail to provide any methods for structuring
specifications except for placing comments at appropriate places, while other

----

*In fact, the specification given below does not use "union types" as
suggested here to resolve this difficulty, but rather considers the case where
the circles coincide to be an exception, and otherwise returns the finite,
possibly empty, set of points in common.

specification techniques provide only purely syntactic methods, such as
conventions for indentation, or for drawing lines in certain places, or a
macro-expansion facility. The challenge is to provide structuring methods
which have well-defined semantics and whose syntax is also intuitively
suggestive. Parameterized specifications and local definitions (e.g., given
inside a block) are two of the more important of these. We would like,
insofar as possible, to make use of a library of pre-defined parameterized
specifications. Parts of such a library are given in Sections 2 and 3 below.

The basic unit for abstract data type specification and encapsulation in
ORDINARY is the cluster*. Parameterized clusters have requirement clusters,
describing conditions which must be satisfied in order for an instance of the
cluster to be meaningful as an actual parameter. For example, if the cluster
DET3[R:: RING] specifies 3-dimensional determinants over an arbitrary ring R,
its requirement cluster is RING; this just says that any R which is used as an
actual parameter for DET3 must be a ring. Or, STACK[X:: TRIV] might be a
parameterized cluster for specifying stacks of X's, where the only requirement
on X is the "trivial" one, that it have a designated sort, i.e., that it
provide a set of elements. TRIV is built into ORDINARY, but if it were not,
it could be specified as follows (this example also shows the basic syntax for
clusters):

        cluster TRIV
            sorts elt endcl

If we want to apply DET3 and STACK to INT, the integers, we will have to say
how INT is to be viewed as a ring, and as a set. In ORDINARY as in CLEAR
[Burstall & Goguen 77, Burstall & Goguen 81], this is done by giving a
"binding" of the sorts and operations in the requirement cluster to those in
the actual parameter. We now call such bindings views. It is often
convenient to provide them when the actual parameter is defined, rather than
later when the application is to be performed. Thus we can write just
DET3[INT] and STACK[INT]. If the sorts of RING and TRIV were ring and elt,

---

*ORDINARY also provides modules for specifications involving states, after
the style of HDM [Levitt, Robinson & Silverberg 79]. We intend to give these
a semantics similar to so-called "final algebra semantics" [Wand 77].
However, the present specification does not require the use of states.

respectively, then the views are denoted [ring is int] and [elt is int] respectively; we do not need to write "+ is +," "0 is 0" etc., because ORDINARY permits omitting components of the binding which are the same in the two specifications. Every cluster has a principal sort*, which can be indicated by saying "view as TRIV by [elt is ...]", or else is the first new sort introduced (if any are), or (if both of the above fail) is the principal sort of the parameter. In the case where a cluster is defined as an enrichment of another, say A is "enrich B by ..." then A is automatically given a view as B, and the principal sort of B is also that of A. For example, FIELD is defined as an enrichment of RING; therefore, every field is a ring, and the principal sort of FIELD is the same as that of RING, namely elt. [More technically, these views are theory morphisms, and they define forgetful functors on the corresponding categories of algebras. A view as TRIV (i.e., a principal sort) always determines a forgetful functor to the category of sets, i.e., determines an underlying set functor.]

1.6 Information Hiding

The definition of abstract interfaces -- i.e., of which sorts and operations that have aready been defined can be exported and which are for internal use only (i.e., are "hidden") -- presents some particular difficulties in this specification exercise. ORDINARY provides conventions for exporting from a cluster all sorts and operations except a few which may be labelled "hidden"; or for hiding all except a few which are labelled "visible". The default option in ORDINARY for operations provided when a representation is defined, is that they are hidden outside the cluster in which they are introduced. However, we permit the sorts and operations associated with representations to be visible within the same block. This addresses the problem of constructions which require access to previously defined representations [Staunstrup 81], but I am not sure that this approach is adequate for more complicated cases which might arise.

1.7 General Discussion

---

*In roughly the sense of [Guttag 75]. Incidentally, the concept of views appears to be similar to the ideas of perspective advocated by Guttag and Horning at this workshop.

I have chosen to specify these geometrical constructions using standard
representations from analytic geometry, giving explicit algebraic
representations for all operations and exceptions. Of course, this approach
is particularly tempting and convenient when using an algebraic specification
technique. However, it seems clear that it would be simpler in many ways to
use an implicit set theoretic approach as in [Staunstrup 81]. One difficulty
would be that one still should prove, for example, that the intersection of
two lines is one point, unless the lines are either parallel or identical;
however, such proofs will be most conveniently carried out using the algebraic
representations of analytic geometry.

It should be noted that these ORDINARY specifications are completely
self-contained, in the sense that all of the concepts that they use are
defined by other ORDINARY specifications. On the other hand, a good deal of
machinery is needed in order to give semantics for these specifications.
However, our proposed strategy of defining ORDINARY through translation into
CLEAR relegates some of the more esoteric topics to the semantics of CLEAR.

Of course, the main interest in this specification exercise, at least for me,
is not in the equations themselves, but rather in the various techniques by
which specifications are structured and are built up from other
specifications.

2. Fields

The minimal structure required to carry out these geometrical constructions is
that of an ordered field in which all non-negative elements have square roots.
This structure is not entirely trivial to specify; to do so amounts to giving
key excerpts from a few chapters of a modern algebra textbook. Of course, the
real numbers are the model used in ordinary Cartesian geometry; but there are
other models, such as that formed by closing the rational numbers under square
roots of positive elements. [This alternative is particularly attractive
because this field is computable in the sense of [Rabin 60].]

The following structured specification is a block which begins with Abelian
groups, and then goes on to rings, fields, partially ordered sets, ordered
fields, and finally what we want, SQTFIELD. Many, perhaps all but the last,
of these specifications could be expected to be in the "algebra book" of a

comprehensive ORDINARY library.

An operation can be declared binary infix associative of sort s by writing
"_•_ : s,s -> s (assoc)"; this means that associative syntax (such as x•y•z)
can be used in expressions, and also that an associative equation is asserted
for •. More general "mixfix" syntax among several sorts is declared in a
similar manner, and an expression will be considered well-formed iff it has a
unique parse; these conventions follow those of OBJ [Goguen & Tardo 79].
Similarly, but going beyond OBJ, variables do not need to be declared if their
sorts can be deduced. Comments appear between the delimiters <* and *>.

  block ALGEBRA

    cluster ABGP
      sorts elt
      ops 0: elt
        _+_ : elt,elt -> elt (assoc)
        -_: elt -> elt, _-_: elt,elt -> elt
      eqns x+y = y+x, x+0 = x, x+(-x) = 0, x-y = x+(-y)   endcl

    cluster RING is extend ABGP by
      ops 1: elt
        _•_ : elt,elt -> elt (assoc)
      eqns x•1 = 1•x = x, x•(y+z) = (x•y)+(x•z)   endcl

  <* The following is a parameterized enrichment: given any ring R, we
  can enrich it with the concepts of three dimensional vectors and
  determinants. The notation "rep r3 by ..." says that we are going to
  construct the theory of 3-dimensional vectors using some previously
  given standard constrution, in this case, record, which is actually
  built into ORDINARY. The constructor for these records is (_,_,_),
  with each of the three components being of sort "elt" from the ring,
  and with selectors 1,2,3 for the three components (thus, for example,
  2(r1,r2,r3) = r2). *>

  cluster DET3 [R:: RING]
    sorts r3   <* This will be 3-dimensional vectors from R *>
    ops det3: r3,r3,r3 -> elt, one: r3
    rep r3 by record (_,_,_) with 1: elt, 2: elt, 3: elt

    eqns det3(p1,p2,p3) = (1(p1)•2(p2)•3(p3)) - (2(p1)•1(p2)•3(p3))
              + (2(p1)•3(p2)•1(p3)) - (3(p1)•2(p2)•1(p3))
              + (1(p1)•3(p2)•2(p3)) + (3(p1)•1(p2)•2(p3))
         one = (1,1,1)   endcl

```
cluster FIELD is extend RING by
    ops _⁻¹: elt -> elt, _/_: elt,elt -> elt
    err-ops overflow: elt

    eqns x●y = y●x, x/y = x●(y⁻¹)
    axioms x●x⁻¹ = 1 if x ≠ 0
    err-eqns 0⁻¹ = overflow    endcl


    <* We now prepare to define ordered fields *>
cluster POSET
    sorts elt
    relns _>_, _≥_ : elt,elt
    axioms x > y and y > z implies x > z
      not x > x, x ≥ y iff x > y or x == y    endcl


cluster OFIELD is combine FIELD and POSET over TRIV extended by
    sorts noneg < elt
    axioms x == 0 or x > 0 or -x > 0
      x > 0 and y > 0 implies x+y > 0 and x●y > 0
      noneg(x) iff x ≥ 0    endcl


cluster SQTFIELD is extend OFIELD by
    ops _²: elt -> elt,√_ : noneg -> noneg
    eqns x² = x●x, (√x)² = x    endcl

endblock ALGEBRA
```

The combine...and...over... construction assumes that the first two (or n)
mentioned clusters all have a common view as the last mentioned cluster, in
this case TRIV. [The semantics of this construction is given by taking the
pushout of all these views, taking account of any shared subtheories, much as
in CLEAR [Burstall & Goguen 80].] The extend (or, in this case, extended by)
construction is the same as CLEAR's enrich construction, except that we
explicitly require that the enrichment should be a consistent extension, i.e.,
that the old theory is "protected", or is a subtheory of the new.

The new sort poselt of OFIELD is introduced as a subsort of the old sort elt
of FIELD, and is later defined by an associated predicate of the same name to
be the non-negative elements.

3. A Library of Standard Constructions

This section gives a block containing a few standard constructions which are used in the geometrical constructions specification. Whereas the specifications of the previous section (except DET3) were used to define classes [more technically called varieties] of algebras (such as partially ordered sets, or Abelian groups), the specifications in this section are parameterized (except BOOL), and are used to define new particular structures (i.e., abstract data types), given particular values for their parameters, (e.g., given a parameter with a view as TRIV, such as INT, we can form SET[INT]). Note that if a formal parameter is named X, and its requirement theory has a principal sort, then the principal sort of X can be denoted x. Parameterized cluster specifications are often defined using representations constructed from other previously defined clusters. [In the terminology used by CLEAR, a rep is a derive from an enrich, leaving the original constructors hidden.] One of these specifications, MAP, uses what may seem an excessively clever trick, namely giving a recipe for constructing new functions from expressions which can denote such functions. [This is used to provide a comprehension scheme for sets. A more detailed discussion is given with the specifications.] The infix operation == denotes the equality assumed to be provided with every concrete structure, including any actuals supplied to parameterized specifications. Every sort is also assumed to come with an equationally defined conditional, with mixfix syntax "if_then_else_fi" where the first may be filled with either a boolean valued expression or a predicate.

block CONSTRUCTIONS

```
    <* Booleans are actually built into ORDINARY, but they could have been
    defined in it, and if they had been, the definition would be as
    follows. [The word data preceeding sorts indicates that the initial
    algebra interpretation is to be taken.] *>

  cluster BOOL
     data sorts bool
     ops true, false: bool
       _and_ , _or_ : bool,bool -> bool (assoc)
       not_: bool -> bool

     eqns true and b = b, false and b = false
        true or b = true, false or b = b
        not true = false, not false = true    endcl
```

40

```
cluster MAP[X:: TRIV, T:: TRIV]
    data sorts map
    ops empty: map, constfn: y -> map
        _[_]: map,x -> y, update: x,y,map -> map
    err-ops undef: x -> y
    meta-ops lambda_._: (var v: x),(exp: (var v: x) -> y) -> map

    eqns constfn(y)[x] = y
        update(x,y,f)[x'] = if x == x' then y else f[x'] fi
        (lambda v. E)[x] = E[x]
        f = f' if (∀x)f[x] == f'[x]
    err-eqns empty[x] = undef(x)     endcl


cluster SET [X:: TRIV]
    uses MAP,BOOL
    sorts set
    ops ∅: set, {_}: x -> set
        _∪_, _∩_: set,set -> set (assoc)
        ~_: set -> set
        {_|_}: (var v: x),(exp: (var v: x) -> bool) -> set
    relns _in_: x,set

    rep set by MAP[X,BOOL]

    eqns ∅ = constfn(false), {x} = update(x,true,∅)
        (S∪S') = lambda x.(S[x] or S'[x])
        (S∩S') = lambda x.(S[x] and S'[x])
        (~S) = lambda x.(not S[x])
        {v | E} = lambda v. E
    axioms x in S iff S[x] == true     endcl
```

endblock CONSTRUCTIONS

Lambda in MAP is a "meta-operation" which given a variable v of sort x and an
expression of sort y, E, in the variable v, forms a new constant of sort map,
denoted "lambda v. E". Expressions of the form "(lambda v. E)[x]" can be
reduced to the (built in) evaluation of expression E at argument x, by the
last eqn of MAP. The use of this facility is illustrated in SET. A
disadvantage is that it can be difficult to check equality for maps defined
with lambda, since initial algebra semantics gives f1 == f2 iff f1[x] == f2[x]
for all x. [It is easy to provide a semantics for meta-operations taking
advantage of the fact that ORDINARY semantics is defined by giving a
translation in CLEAR, which already has a formal semantics. This is done by
adding definitions of instances to the appropriate theories.]

It is important to distinguish the empty map from the empty set: the empty
map, empty, is the completely undefined partial function; while the empty set,
∅, like all sets, is represented by a total boolean valued function, in this
case, the constant function with value false.

4. Geometrical Constructions

This section contains the "meat" of the specification, consisting of about
fifty lines. There are certain new features which arise here. The first is
the renamed by construction used in defining PTSET; this is just a re-viewing
which changes the names of some sorts and operators of the preceding
specification. The second is the "variant record" syntax required for the two
representations which are used for lines. Each representation is a case, with
its own name (either "general" or "vertical"); this construction also also
supplies predicates having the same names as the cases, which are used in
expressions which say different things, depending on which representation is
used. For example, one could say "... if vertical(l)" or "... = case(general
l) is ... or case(vertical l) is ..." where l is a line. The third feature is
the "... where ... = ... and ..." construction which permits the introduction
of names for subexpressions, local to a single equation. (A similar effect
could be achieved with the use of hidden operations.) Some further
constructions (not needed here) are discussed in [Goguen 81].

```
block GEOM[F:: SQTFIELD]
   uses ALGEBRA,CONSTRUCTIONS

   cluster D3 is DET3[F]   endcl

   cluster 2POINT
      sorts point
      ops d: point,point -> noneg   <* distance *>
      rep point by record (_,_) with x: elt, y: elt
         <* Cartesian coordinates *>
      eqns d(p,q) =√((x(p)-x(q))²+(y(p)-y(q))²)   endcl

   cluster PTSET is SET[2POINT] renamed by [set is ptset]   endcl

   cluster LINE
      uses BOOL,2POINT,PTSET
      sorts line
      ops line: point,point -> line
         _crosses_: line,line -> bool
         meet: line, line -> point
      err-ops no-line: line, no-meet: point, same-line: line -> point
```

```
rep line by case general record ( , ) with m: elt, b: elt
         or by case vertical record ( ) with a: elt
    <* Alternative representations: either slope-intercept form, called
       "general"; or else "vertical", represented by the x-intercept *>

eqns line(p1,p2) = case general(not x1 == x2) is
            ((y1-y2)/(x1-x2),((y2*x1)-(y1*x2)/(x1-x2))
         or case vertical(x1 == x2) is (x1)
            where x1 = x(p1) and y1 = y(p1) and x2 = x(p1) and y2 = y(p2)
    l1 crosses l2 = not m(l1) == m(l2)
    meet(l1,l2) = case(general l1,l2) is
                  ((b2-b1)/(m1-m2),((m1•b2)-(m2•b1))/(m1-m2))
         or case(general l1,vertical l2) is (a(l2),(a(l2)-b2)/m2)
         or case(vertical l1,general l2) is (a(l1),(a(l1)-b1)/m1))
            where m1 = m(l1) and b1 = b(l1) and m2 = m(l2) and b2 = b(l2)
err-eqns line(p1,p2) = no-line if p1 == p2
    meet(l1,l2) = no-meet if case(general l1,l2) m(l1) == m(l2)
                            and not l1 == l2
    meet(l1,l2) = same-line(l2) if l1 == l2        endcl


cluster CIRCLE
     uses BOOL,2POINT,LINE,PTSET,D3
     sorts circle
     ops circle: point,point,point -> circle
         _[_]: circle,point -> elt (hidden)
         intersect: circle,circle -> ptset
         concentric: circle,circle -> bool
         tangent: point,circle -> line
     err-ops no-circle: circle, circles-coincide: ptset, no-tangent: line

     rep circle by record ( , ) with center: point, radius: noneg
            <* center-radius form *>

eqns circle(p1,p2,p3) = ((D,E),D²+E²+F)
            where D = det3(c,y,one)/det and E = det3(x,c,one)/det
            and F = det3(x,y,one)/det and det = det3(x,y,one)
            and x = (x(p1),x(p2),x(p3)) and y = (y(p1),y(p2),y(p3))
            and c = (x(p1)²+y(p1)²,x(p2)²+y(p2)²,x(p3)²+y(p3)²)
        c[p] = d(p,center(c))²-radius(c)²
        intersect(c1,c2) = {p ¦ c1[p] == 0 and c2[p] == 0}
        concentric(c1,c2) = (center(c1) == center(c2))
        tangent(p,c) = case general(d(p,center(c)) > radius(c)) is (m,B-mA)
            or case vertical(d(p,center(c)) = radius(c)) is (a-A)
                where m = (((a-A)•(b-B))+r(•√(c[p])))/((a-A)²-r²)
                and a = x(center(c)) and b = y(center(c)) and r = radius(c)
                and A = x(p) and B = y(p)

     err-eqns
        circle(p1,p2,p3) = no-circle if det3(x,y,one) == 0
            where x = (x(p1),x(p2),x(p3)) and y = (y(p1),y(p2),y(p3))
        intersect(c1,c2) = circles-coincide if c1 == c2
        tangent(p,c) = no-tangent if d(p,center(c)) < radius(c)    endcl
```

<u>endblock</u> GEOM

Justification for the determinant formula for circle(p1,p2,p3) can be found
for example in [Morrill <u>et</u> <u>al</u> 72].   The other formulae used above are more
straightforward.

REFERENCES

[Burstall & Goguen 77]
Burstall, R. M. and Goguen, J. A.
Putting Theories together to Make Specifications.
Proc. 5th Int. Joint Confr. on Artificial Intelligence , 1977.

[Burstall & Goguen 80]
Burstall, R. M., and Goguen, J. A.
The Semantics of CLEAR, a Specification Language.
In Proceedings of the 1979 Copenhagen Winter School on Abstract
Software Specification, pages 292-332. Springer-Verlag,
1980.
Lecture Notes in Computer Science, volume 86.

[Burstall & Goguen 81]
Burstall, R. M. and Goguen, J. A.
An Informal Introduction to CLEAR, a Specification Language.
In Boyer, R. and Moore, J, editor, The Correctness Problem in
Computer Science, . Academic Press, 1981.

[Goguen & Burstall 80]
Goguen, J. A. and Burstall, R. M.
An Ordinary Design.
Technical Report, SRI International, 1980.
Draft report.

[Goguen & Tardo 79]
Goguen, J. A. and Tardo, J.
An Introduction to OBJ-T.
In Specification of Reliable Software, pages 170-189. IEEE
(Cambridge, Mass.), 1979.

[Goguen, Thatcher, Wagner & Wright 77]
Goguen, J. A. , Thatcher, J. W., Wagner, E. and Wright, J. B.
Initial Algebra Semantics and Continuous Algebras.
Journal of the Association for Computing Machinery 24(1),
January, 1977.

[Goguen 77]
Goguen, J. A.
Abstract Errors for Abstract Data Types.
In Working Conference on Formal Description of Programming
Concepts. IFIP, 1977.
Also published by North-Holland, 1979, edited by P. Neuhold.

[Goguen 78]
Goguen, J. A.
Order Sorted Algebra.
Technical Report, UCLA Computer Science Department, 1978.
Semantics and Theory of Computation Report No. 14; to appear in
Journal of Computer and System Science.

[Goguen 81]
Goguen, J.
ORDINARY Specification of KWIC Index Generation.
In , . Springer-Verlag, 1981.
these proceedings, Lecture Notes in Computer Science.

[Guttag 75]
>Guttag, J. V.
The Specification and Application to Programming of Abstract
Data Types.
PhD thesis, Univ. of Toronto, 1975.
Computer Science Department, Report CSRG-59.

[Jensen & Wirth 78]
Jensen, K. and Wirth, N.
Pascal User Manual and Report.
Springer-Verlag, 1978.
second edition.

[Kaphengst & Reichel 77]
Kaphengst, H. and Reichel, H.
Initial Algebraic Semantics for Non-Context-Free Languages.
In Springer-Verlag Lecture Notes in Computer Science, vol. 56,
pages 120-126. Springer-Verlag, 1977.

[Levitt, Robinson & Silverberg 79]
Levitt, K., Robinson, L. and Silverberg, B.
The HDM Handbook.
Technical Report, SRI, International, Computer Science Lab,
1979.
vols. I,II,III.

[Morrill et al 72]
Morrill, W. K., Selby, S. M. and Johnson, W. G.
Modern Analytic Geometry.
Intext (Scranton Penn.), 1972.

[Rabin 60]
Rabin, M.
Computable Algebra: General Theory and Theory of Computable
Fields.
Transactions of the American Mathematical Society 95:341-360,
1960.

[Reichel & Hupbach & Kaphengst 80]
Reichel, H., Hupbach, U. R., and Kaphengst, H.
Initial Algebraic Specifications of Data Types, Parameterized
Data Types, and Algorithms.
Technical Report, VEB Robotron, Zentrum fur Forschung und
Technik, 1980.

[Staunstrup 81]
Staunstrup, J.
Geometrical Constructions.
In , . Springer-Verlag, 1981.
these proceedings, Lecture Notes in Computer Science.

[Wand 77]
Wand, M.
Final Algebra Semantics and Data Type Extensions.
Technical Report, Indiana University, Computer Science
Department, 1977.

Example 2: KWIC – index generation

Consider a program which generates a KWIC index (keyword in context).
A title is a list of words which are either significant or non-significant.
A rotation of a list is a cyclic shift of the words in the list, and a significant
rotation is a rotation in which the first word is significant. Given a set of
titles and a set of non-significant words, the program should produce an
alphabetically sorted list of the significant rotations of the titles.

   titles

        THE THREE LITTLE PIGS.
        SNOW WHITE AND THE SEVEN DWARVES.

   non-significant words

        THE, THREE, AND, SEVEN

   should produce:

        DWARVES. SNOW WHITE AND THE SEVEN
        LITTLE PIGS. THE THREE
        PIGS. THE THREE LITTLE
        SNOW WHITE AND THE SEVEN DWARVES
        WHITE AND THE SEVEN DWARVES. SNOW

J. Steensgaard-Madsen
Computer Science Institute
University of Copenhagen

In a sequence of steps a KWIC-index generation program is specified. With each new step details are added. The emphasis is put on program structure. This means that the program is broken into interactive parts (modules), and that the specification of interaction is considered more important than anything else.

The overall structure is as follows, where arcs indicate flow of data

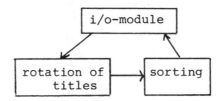

The three parts are interconnected by a main program. Data flow between the modules without any of the three parts being aware of the internal type structure defined by the other two. Also the main program is completely independent of such definitions. For example, only the i/o-module depends on whether a "word" is a sequence of characters or a reference to such a sequence.

First the main program is shown. Its phrase structure can be expanded to the following "natural language" specification:

Within a WORD_CONTEXT we shall PROCESS_ROTATED_LINES of
WORDS by PRINT_ALL_LINES; lines to be printed are obtained
by SORTING of LINES using a function LESS_THAN to decide
whether a line A must precede a line B in the final sequence; the decision is based on the FIRST_WORD of lines
A and B. FOR_EACH_LINE, available after rotation, we
RELEASE the current line L to the sort module, such that
it later may be printed. When the lines have been sorted
each will be passed to the i/o-module by PRINT_ONE_LINE;
actual printing is controlled by SCANNING the current
line Y and the execution of PRINT_WORD for every word W
in Y.

    Not every word may appear as first word of a line.
The i/o-module must read a list of insignificant words
and these affect the generation of rotated lines. FOR-
_ALL_DUMMY_WORDS_READ it is necessary to REMEMBER the
current word W for the rotation.

    Lines are built from titles. We may GET_ALL_TITLES
from the i/o-module and for each BUILD_ONE_LINE for rotation. A line is initially blank, but FOR_EACH_WORD_READ
we may INCLUDE one word W in the line.

The phrase structure is described in three *module trees* following the main program text. The one with DEFINE_WORD_CONTEXT
as the root corresponds to the i/o-module; the PROCESS_ROTATED-
_LINES, to the rotation. The simplest tree is SORTING, which
is shown along with an informal outline of its internal struc-

ture. The following more detailed version of SORTING constitutes the complete specification of this part. It is required of the reader to disregard the apparent statement of how the sorted sequence is obtained, much the same as is required when reading an algebraic type specification.

The description of the sorting module includes a specification of the type (SEQ) on which the description depends. A pattern of a module description followed by a specification of the types needed is used for the two more complicated modules. Finally an even more detailed specification of one of the more complicated modules is given in a Pascal like language. From this a final program is obtained by replacing the type specifications with Pascal type definitions and implementing the primitive functions described by the type specification.

The specification of the entire program is not yet complete. A more detailed version of the i/o-module is required. Some problems that must be considered in a refinement step are

1. It will be most convenient if input data is organized such that the list of insignificant words precedes the titles. If this is not acceptable, a buffer for titles is needed somewhere in the program. The present specification assumes that such a buffer, if needed, is defined in the i/o-module. There seems to be no advantage by any other decision.

2. What appears as WORDS outside the i/o-module is inside identified as TOKENS. Whether TOKENS are character strings, or references to character strings, is not specified. The proper choice may depend on estimates of statistics describing input data.

3. A TITLE is considered a sequence of TOKENS. This means that punctuation symbols should be represented as TOKENS also. A punctuation symbol should probably be considered an insignificant symbol. As soon as TOKENS are fully specified it is easy to modify the specification of DUMMYLIST to include a set of unavoidable insignificant symbols.

4. At present, empty TITLES are accepted as well as TITLES with insignificant symbols only. Such TITLES will not appear on output however.

```
DEFINE_WORD_CONTEXT

-- providing access to i/o by WORDS within:
  (PROCESS_ROTATED_LINES of WORDS

    -- processing the lines by means of FOR_EACH_LINE in:
      (PRINT_ALL_LINES      -- as defined in the word context

        -- by use of PRINT_ONE_LINE in
          (SORTING of LINES
            KEY:
              (LESS_THAN (FIRST_WORD(A), FIRST_WORD(B)))
            PRODUCER_OF_LINES:
              (FOR_EACH_LINE (RELEASE(L)))
            RECEIVER_OF_LINES:
              (PRINT_ONE_LINE
                  (SCANNING (E) BY: (PRINT_WORD(W)))
              )
          )
      )

  -- where insignificant words are obtained by REMEMBER in:
    (FOR_ALL_DUMMY_WORDS_READ (REMEMBER(W))

  -- and where lines are build from titles in:
    (GET_ALL_TITLES      -- as defined in the word context

      -- handling each title by
        (BUILD_ONE_LINE(FOR_EACH_WORD_READ(INCLUDE(W))))
    )
  )
```

Main program

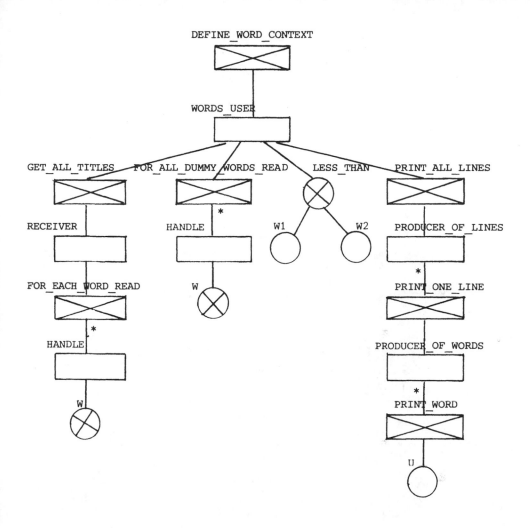

WORD_USER:

      FOR_ALL_DUMMY_WORDS_READ must be used only once and the
      use must be completed prior to the use of GET_ALL_TITLES

      GET_ALL_TITLES must be used only once

An edge marked with an asterisk denotes a right that may be
exercised iteratively

DEFINE_WORD_CONTEXT module tree

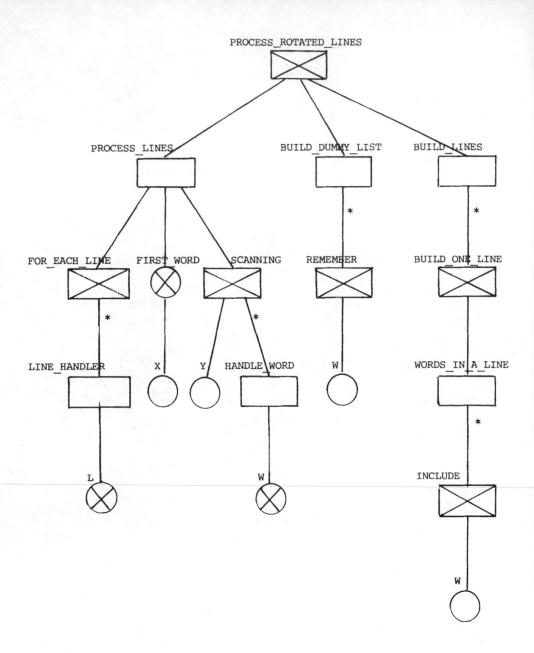

BUILD_LINES:

    The use of this part may be deferred until FOR_EACH_LINE
is used in PROCESS_LINES. It will be an acceptable restriction if no part of the above may be used recursively.

        GENERATE_ROTATED_LINES module

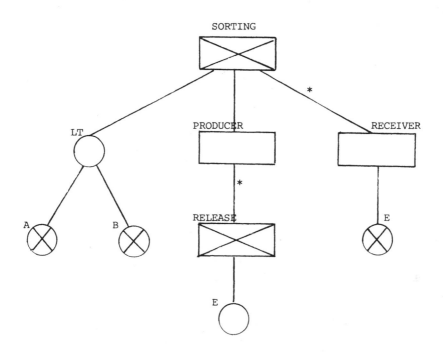

```
SORTING of ITEMS
   (LT (A, B: ITEMS): BOOLEAN,
    PRODUCER (RELEASE (E: ITEMS)),
    RECEIVER (E: ITEMS)
   )
```

```
    "let D be a sequence of ITEMS, initially empty"

    PRODUCER ("enter E into D, possibly in proper order")

    "do whatever neccessary to obtain a properly ordered D"

    WHILE ("D is not empty")
     DO:
       (RECEIVER ("first item in D"),
        "remove first item from D"
       )
```

SORTING module tree and module outline

```
SORTING of ITEMS
  (LT(A:ITEMS,B:ITEMS):BOOLEAN,
   PRODUCER(RELEASE(E:ITEMS)),
   RECEIVER(E:ITEMS)
  )
```

```
    type SEQ = empty | append(SEQ,ITEMS).
    with
       SEQ = concat(SEQ,SEQ) | rem(SEQ).
       ITEMS = first(SEQ).
    for S1, S2: SEQ; I: ITEMS let
       concat(S1,empty) => S1,
       concat(S1,append(S2,I)) => append(concat(S1,S2),I),
       rem(append(S1,I)) =>
          if S1=empty then empty else append(rem(S1),I),
       first(append(S1,I)) => if S1=empty then I else first(S1),
          tabu rem(S1), first(S1) if S1=empty
    end;

    def SIFT(L:SEQ;X:ITEMS;R:SEQ):SEQ =>
          if R=empty then append(L,X)
          else if LT(X,first(R)) then concat(append(L,X),R)
               else SIFT(append(L,first(R)),X,rem(R));

    var D: SEQ;

D:= empty; PRODUCER (D:= SIFT(empty,E,D));

WHILE (D≠empty) DO: (RECEIVER (first(D)); D:= rem(D))
```

Definition of the SORTING module.

```
DEFINE_WORD_CONTEXT
  (WORDS_USER of WORDS
     (GET_ALL_TITLES
        (RECEIVER(FOR_EACH_WORD_READ(HANDLE(W:WORDS))))),
      FOR_ALL_DUMMY_WORDS_READ(HANDLE(W:WORDS)),
      LESS_THAN(W1:WORDS,W2:WORDS):BOOLEAN,
      PRINT_ALL_LINES
        (PRODUCER_OF·LINES
           (PRINT_ONE_LINE
              (PRODUCER_OF_WORDS(PRINT_WORD(U:WORDS)))
  )  )  )   )
```

```
-- types: TOKEN, TITLE, TITLELIST, DUNNYLIST, and LINELIST
     var INP: DUMMYLIST;
   INP:= INPUT;
   WORDS_USER of TOKEN
     (  var TL: TITLELIST; var T: TITLE;
      IF (not eod(INP)) THEN: (ABORT)
      ELSE: (TL:= get_list(INP);
              WHILE (TL≠eof)
                 DO: (T:= get_title(TL); TL:= cut(TL);
                      RECEIVER (WHILE (T≠.)
                                  DO: (HANDLE (get_word(T));
                                       T:= cut_title(T)
      )      )      )            )          )

      (WHILE (not eod(INP))
          DO: (HANDLE (get_dummy(INP)); INP:= rem(INP)
      )      )

      (W1 < W2)   -- Token must allow <

      (OUT:= heading;
       PRODUCER_OF_LINES
          (PRODUCER_OF_WORDS (OUT:= OUT & U);
          OUT:= OUT & newline
      )  )
```

Definition of the DEFINE_WORD_CONTEXT module

<u>type</u>

    TITLE = "." | TOKEN TITLE.

    TITLELIST = eof | TITLE TITLELIST.

    DUMMYLIST = : TITLELIST | TOKEN DUMMYLIST.

    LINELIST = heading | LINELIST & TOKEN | LINELIST & newline.

<u>with</u>

    TOKEN   = get_dummy (DUMMYLIST) | get_word (TITLE).

    TITLE   = get_title (TITLELIST) | cut_title (TITLE).

    TITLELIST = get_list (DUMMYLIST) | cut (TITLELIST).

    DUMMYLIST = rem (DUMMYLIST).

    BOOLEAN   = eod (DUMMYLIST).

<u>for</u> U,W: TOKEN; L: TITLELIST; D: DUMMYLIST; S,T: TITLE <u>let</u>

   get_dummy (W D) $\Rightarrow$ W,

     <u>tabu</u> get_dummy (D) <u>if</u> eod (D),

   get_word (W T) $\Rightarrow$ W

     <u>tabu</u> get_word (T) <u>if</u> T = . ,

   cut_title (W T) $\Rightarrow$ T,

     <u>tabu</u> cut_title (T) <u>if</u> T = . ,

   get_title (T L) $\Rightarrow$ T,

     <u>tabu</u> get_title (L) <u>if</u> L = eof,

   get_list (: L) $\Rightarrow$ L,

     <u>tabu</u> get_list (D) <u>if</u> not eod (D),

   cut (T L) $\Rightarrow$ L,

     <u>tabu</u> cut (L) <u>if</u> L = eof,

   rem (W D) $\Rightarrow$ D,

     <u>tabu</u> rem (D) <u>if</u> eod (D),

   eod (: L) $\Rightarrow$ true,

   eod (W D) $\Rightarrow$ false,

<u>end</u>

Specification of types for DEFINE_WORD_CONTEXT

```
PROCESS_ROTATED_LINES of WORDS
   (PROCESS_LINES of LINES
      (FOR_EACH_LINE(LINE_HANDLER(L:LINES)),
       FIRST_WORD(X:LINES):WORDS,
       SCANNING(Y:LINES;HANDLE_WORD(W:WORD))
      ),
   BUILD_DUMMY_LIST(REMEMBER(W:WORDS)),
   BUILD_LINES
      (BUILD_ONE_LINE(WORDS_IN_A_LINE(INCLUDE(W:WORDS)))
   )  )
```

```
-- define the types LIST and RINGS from WORDS


     var D: LIST;


  D:= empty; BUILD_DUMMY_LIST (D:= append(D,W));


  PROCESS_LINES of RINGS
    (BUILD_LINES
        ( var J, L: RINGS;
         L:= blank; WORDS_IN_A_LINE (L:= extend(L,W));
         J:= L;
         WHILE (J≠blank)
           DO: (IF (first(J) in D) THEN: (SKIP)
               ELSE: (LINE_HANDLER (L));
               J:= cut(J); L:= extend(cut(L),first(L))
    )  )       )


    (first(X))


    (L:= Y;
     WHILE (L≠blank) DO: (HANDLE_WORD (first(L)); L:= cut(L))
    )
```

Definition of the PROCESS_ROTATED_LINES module

type

   LIST = empty | append (LIST, WORDS).

with

   BOOLEAN = WORDS in LIST

for   U,W: WORDS; S: LIST **let**

  W in empty $\Rightarrow$ false

  W in append (S, U) $\Rightarrow$ if (W = U) then true else (W in S)

end

type

   RINGS = blank | extend (RINGS, WORDS).

with

   RINGS = cut (RINGS).

   WORDS = first (RINGS).

for W: WORDS; L: RINGS **let**

  cut (extend (L,W)) $\Rightarrow$ if L = blank then blank else extend (cut(L),W),

  first(extend (L,W)) $\Rightarrow$ if L = blank then W else first (L)

    tabu cut (L), first (L) **if** L = blank

end

Specification of types used in PROCESS_ROTATED_LINES

```
procedure PROCESS_ROTATED_LINES of WORDS
    (procedure PROCESS_LINES of LINES
        (procedure FOR_EACH_LINE (procedure LINE_HANDLER(L: LINES));
         function FIRST_WORD(X: LINES): WORDS;
         procedure SCANNING(Y: LINES; procedure HANDLE_WORD(W: WORDS))
        );
     procedure BUILD_DUMMY_LIST (procedure REMEMBER(W: WORDS));
     procedure BUILD_LINES
        (procedure BUILD_ONE_LINE
            (procedure WORDS_IN_A_LINE (procedure INCLUDE(W: WORDS)))
);
type
    LIST = empty | append(LIST, WORDS).
with
    BOOLEAN = WORDS in LIST.
for U, W: WORDS; S: LIST let
        W in empty ⇒ false,
        W in append(S, U) ⇒ if (U = W) then true else (W in S)
end;
type
    RINGS = blank | extend (RINGS, WORDS).
with
    RINGS = cut (RINGS).
    WORDS = first (RINGS).
for W: WORDS; L: RINGS let
        cut (extend(L,W)) ⇒ if L = blank then blank else extend (cut(L), W),
        first (extend(L,W)) ⇒ if L – blank then W else first(L),
        tabu cut(L), first(L) if L = blank
end;
```

```
{body of PROCESS_ROTATED_LINES}

      var D: LIST;

begin
   D := empty;
   BUILD_DUMMY_LIST (begin D := append (D,W) end);

   PROCESS_LINES of RINGS
     {FOR_EACH_LINE:}
     (begin
        BUILD_LINES
          (   var J,L: RINGS;
            begin
              L := blank;
              WORDS_IN_A_LINE (begin L := extend (L,W) end);

              J := L;
              while J <> blank do begin
                 if not first (J) in D then LINE_HANDLER (L);
                 J := cut (J); L := extend (cut (L), first (L))
              end
            end)
     end)

     {FIRST_WORD:}
     (first (X))
     {SCANNING:}
     (  var  L: RINGS;
       begin
         L := Y;
         while L <> blank do begin
            HANDLE_WORD (first (L)); L := cut (L)
         end
       end)

end   {PROCESS_ROTATED_LINES};
```

J. W. Hughes and M. S. Powell

Department of Computation,
UMIST

Abstract

A method of program specification is described which leads naturally to the expression of a program as a network of simple processes. Starting with the problem statement the valid inputs and outputs of the system are specified by grammars which represent the structure of the input and output streams of a "black-box" which can be decomposed hierarchically into a structured network of processes which performs the required transformations. Three forms of network structure are described, analagous to the three forms of control in sequential programs. The leaves of the hierarchical description are sequential processes described by a form of attributed translation grammar which permits the specification of semantic as well as syntactic transformations. The notation can be used to specify programs which may be implemented either in conventional programming languages or by direct compilation of the DTL notation. The method is illustrated by application to the KWIC index workshop example.

1. INTRODUCTION

The concept of abstraction in program specification and design originated ten years ago in Wirth's Stepwise Refinement Method [9] and Dijkstra's Structured Programming [1]. The distinction between procedural abstractions for encapsulating the details of algorithms, and data abstractions, to abstract from storage representation was developed by Liskov [7] and Parnas [8]. Programs designed using these methods have an organised hierarchical structure, and are consequently easier to understand than unstructured programs. In practice, however, these methods of program abstraction are only really effective for smaller programs. Large programs often have an unduly complex hierarchical structure. Each additional abstraction increases both the size of the hierarchy and the potential interactions between components. Each new member and interaction has to be verified and understood. The larger and more complex the program, the greater is the temptation for the programmer to optimise prematurely and thus undermine the benefits of structured programs.

The methods above allow the specification of a solution to a problem only as a sequential algorithm. They lack any concepts for expressing concurrency and force the designer to specify operations as sequential when they have no natural order dependency. Thus, they introduce into the design constraints which are not inherent in the problem

being solved and force arbitrary decisions which need never be made. More recently,
with the development of multiprocessor computers, the possibility of implementing
systems as a large number of small programs has become viable. At the same time,
the concept of process abstraction has emerged in the work of Hoare [3], Kahn and
McQueen [5] and Jackson [4]. By means of process abstraction a system can be described as a network of concurrent processes each of which proceeds sequentially and
communicates with its neighbours in the network. Such a description is readily understood providing :

 (i)   the structure of the network can be understood;
(ii)   each sequential process is simple.

All previous work has shown that a system is more readily understood if it can be
decomposed hierarchically into simpler independent components. Design methods using
process abstraction, therefore, must allow hierarchical decomposition of both the
network and the sequential processes within it.

Distributed Translation Language (DTL) is a notation developed at UMIST for the design
of systems using the concept of process abstraction. Its use is illustrated here by
application to workshop example 2 : KWIC Index generation.

2. DTL STRUCTURE

A system specified in DTL can be regarded as a structured network in which each node
is a sequential process and each directed edge connecting two processes is a stream
along which data items, communicated between the processes, flow. The sequence of
data items communicated on a stream is regarded as a string from a language, so the
structure of the data items which can be transmitted on a stream can be specified
hierarchically by means of a grammar. Stream communication is considered to be fully
synchronised.

Each sequential process can be regarded as translating its inputs into its outputs
and is specified by means of an attributed translation grammar [6]. The translation
grammar specifies the relationship between the input and output streams of the process.
Each sequential process thus has a hierarchical structure, determined by the productions in its translation grammar, which stems from the structure of the data it communicates.

Although networks of sequential translations could be constructed as in CSP, simply
by specifying the neighbours with which they communicate, this would not give a very
clear view of the overall structure of the network. Furthermore, it would allow arbitrary unstructured networks to be specified and thus create hazards similar to those
caused by the unstructured use of goto statements in sequential programming languages. A hierarchical structure is, therefore, imposed by the provision
of three network construction operators. These represent the concurrent counterparts
of the sequential structuring devices for sequence, selection, and iteration. They

allow pipeline, disjoint parallel and cyclic network structures to be composed from
sequential translations and concurrent translations which may, themselves, be specified by (possibly recursive) network structures. It is likely that as in sequential
languages, explicit definition of program structure will have beneficial effects on
both language definition and efficient implementation as well as the more obvious
benefit of improved program clarity.

3.   The DESIGN PROCESS

3.1 Stream Specification

The design process starts with a specification of a "black-box" which is required to
transform the provided inputs to the system into the required outputs. The informal
description of the KWIC system suggests the structure shown in Figure 1. Next the
internal structures of the input and output streams are specified by grammars, as
shown in Figure 2, in accordance with the informal specification. The notation is
essentially an extension of BNF. * denotes optional iteration of the following
bracketed expression and the only terminal symbol used is ch which has one attribute
of type char. The optional | following the attribute names in the stream grammar
definitions introduces a Boolean guard expression which is used to locally restrict
the values of the attribute which are acceptable in a particular definition. The
alphabets of all three streams can therefore be defined as follows :

   titles,non-significant words, sorted significant rotated titles= ch(c:char)

Notice that the stream grammars specify the stream structures at many different levels
but that there is no reason at this stage in the design process why the lower levels
should be completely specified. For example, the definitions of <character>, <eow>,
<eot>, <end> and <eort> could be considered to specify a concrete representation for
words and punctuation which should not fundamentally affect the design of the system.
Definitions such as <titles> and <word> give a more abstract view of the data objects
involved.

Further notice that the grammar specifies the structure of the data items within the
streams but does not specify the relationship between the streams or between the attribute values of different items within the same stream. Such relationships are specified by the translations which produce and consume them.

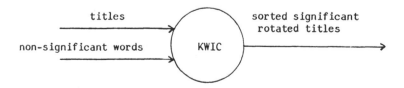

Figure 1

65

```
<titles>  ::= *(<title>) <end>
<title>   ::= *(<word>) <eot>
<word>    ::= <character> *(<character>) <eow>
<character> ::= ch(c | not (c in [' ', '.',eof]))
<eow> ::= ch(c|c=' ') | <empty>
<eot> ::= ch(c|c='.')
<end> ::= ch(c|c=eof)

<non-significant words> ::= *(<word>) <end>

<sorted significant rotated titles> ::= *(<rotated title>)<end>
<rotated title> ::= <word>*(<word>)<eot>*(<word>)<eort>
<eort> ::= ch(c|c=nl)
```

Figure 2

3.2 Network Decomposition

Once the streams have been specified, the translation required to generate the output from the input is designed. In the initial design stages, this is a node-splitting exercise which identifies subprocesses which can be used together to achieve the
desired translation.

As has already been mentioned, it would be desirable to be able to think about the
KWIC index system in isolation from the concrete representations of its data streams.
This implies that a process KWIC' which operates on a concrete representation independent pair of input streams should be a component of the existing KWIC translation.
This is possible provided that a deformatter process can be specified which will
translate the input streams of KWIC into streams suitable for input to KWIC'. The
first stage in refining KWIC is, therefore, to apply a pipeline decomposition to
produce the structure shown in Figure 3a. A further pipeline decomposition can now
be applied to KWIC' to produce a totally abstract KWIC and a formatter process which
translates the output of abstract KWIC into the concrete representation required by
KWIC. This produces the structure shown in Figure 3b. Finally, as the titles and
non-significant word streams can be deformatted independently a disjoint parallel
decomposition can be applied to the deformatter to produce the structure shown in
Figure 3c. This is specified in DTL by the concurrent translation shown in Figure
3d. The pipeline operator , >>, connects two translations such that all the outputs
from the first are inputs to the second and all the inputs to the second are outputs
to the first. The pipeline operator is associative so it is permissible to write
expressions of the form a>>b>>c without the use of brackets. A translation constructed as a pipeline has the property that all inputs from its external environment are
inputs to the first translation and all outputs from the last translation are outputs
to the environment.

66

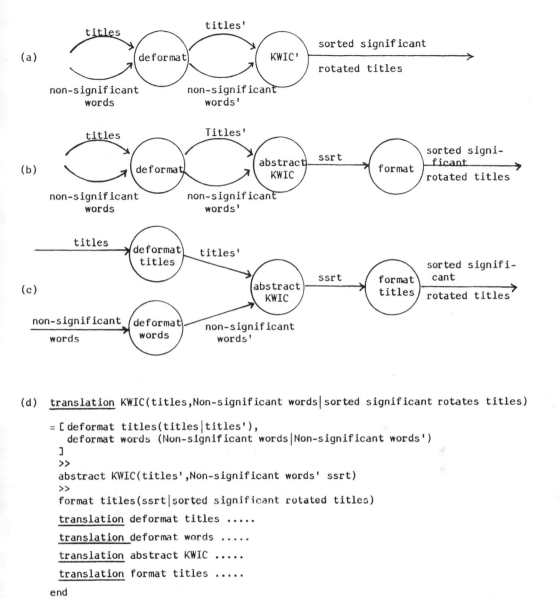

(d) translation KWIC(titles,Non-significant words|sorted significant rotates titles)

   = [deformat titles(titles|titles'),
       deformat words (Non-significant words|Non-significant words')
     ]
     >>
     abstract KWIC(titles',Non-significant words' ssrt)
     >>
     format titles(ssrt|sorted significant rotated titles)

     translation deformat titles .....

     translation deformat words .....

     translation abstract KWIC .....

     translation format titles .....

   end

(e) <titles'> ::= *(<title'>) end
     <title'> ::= *(<word'>) eot
     <word'>   ::= ch(c_1) *(ch(c_i)) eow

     <Non-significant words'> ::= *(<word'>) end

     <ssrt> ::= *(<rotated title'>) end
     <rotated title'> ::=< word'> *(<word'>)eot *(<word'>) eort

Figure 3

Notice that the node-splitting refinement leads to the creation of new streams internal to the structure. Their specification may be chosen to suit the needs of the components which they connect and are independent of the external environment with which the translation as a whole communicates.

Grammars to define the new streams created by this first stage refinement of KWIC are shown in Figure 3c. They introduce the new terminal symbols end, eot, eow and eort, to replace the non-terminals with the same names which specified concrete punctuation conventions in the input and output streams of KWIC.

The notation $[e_1....e_n]$ used in the definition of abstract KWIC denotes DTL's disjoint parallel operator. Any number of translations may be composed in parallel providing that they have no streams in common.

The KWIC system can be completely specified using only these two network operators to decompose translations hierarchically, therefore the remaining description of the decomposition process will proceed apace, stopping only to admire the more interesting features of the design method along the way.

Figure 4a shows the result of applying a pipeline decomposition to abstract KWIC. This new pipeline structure separates the issues of generating the significant rotated titles and ordering the result. It demonstrates perhaps more clearly than the previous example that pipeline composition is merely an expression of the functional composition of the translation functions of its components.

Generating significant rotations can be viewed as the process of generating all rotations of the original titles and then selecting the significant ones. Pipeline decomposition of generate significant rotations separates these two processes, as shown in Figure 4b. However, the non-significant word information is not relevant to the rotation of titles, therefore a disjoint parallel decomposition can be applied to rotate titles to decompose it into a process which rotates titles and the identity translation applied to the non-significant words.

Figure 4c shows the resulting network structure from which, by convention, the standard identity translation I is omitted. The DTL specification of this structure is shown in Figure 4d. The identity translation must be explicit in the network expression in order to conform to the strict definition of pipeline composition. The third network structuring device is the cycle operator which is applied to a translation to denote that some output from the translation is used as input to it. The three operators allow complex components to be regarded in the same way as sequential translations with a well defined set of input and output streams and permit hierarchical refinement of the specification by node-splitting.

3.3 Recursive Definition

Recursive networks are specifiable by using the name of the defined translation in its defining expression. Figure 5a shows a network which is a refinement of the

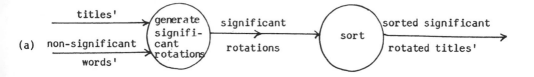

(a)

titles'
non-significant words'
→ generate significant rotations
significant rotations →
sort
sorted significant rotated titles' →

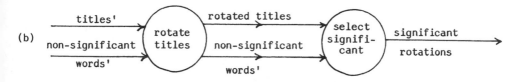

(b)

titles'
non-significant words'
→ rotate titles
rotated titles
non-significant words'
→ select significant
significant rotations →

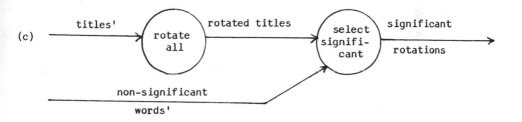

(c)

titles'
→ rotate all
rotated titles
→ select significant
significant rotations →

non-significant words'

(d) <u>Translation</u> generate significant rotations

        (titles,non-significant words|significant rotations)=

   [rotate all(titles|rotated titles), I(non-significant words)]

    >>

   select significant (rotated titles,non-significant words|significant rotations)

   <u>translation</u> rotateall .....

   <u>translation</u> select significant .....

  <u>end</u>

Figure 4

rotateall translation and Figure 5b its DTL definition. The refinement stems from the observation that the order of the titles in the sequence is not significant and each title can be rotated independently. The effect of the network, therefore, is to separate each title in the sequence, generate all rotations for each title and merge together the results.

(a)

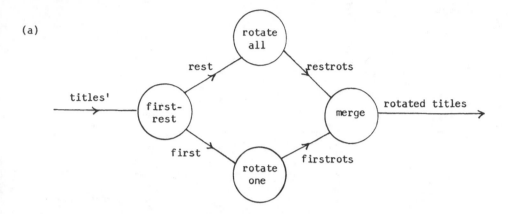

(b) <u>translation</u> rotateall (titles|rotated titles)

      firstrest (titles|first,rest)
      >>[rotateall(rest|restrots),rotateone(first|firstrots)]

      >> merge (firstrots,restrots|rotated titles)

      .
      .
      .

    <u>end</u>

<u>Figure 5</u>

Of the new streams created by this decomposition, rest has the same grammar as titles', restrots and firstrots have the same grammar as rotated titles which is the same as sorted significant rotated titles', and first has the same grammar as <title'> which is a nonterminal sub-structure of titles'.

From a functional point of view, a recursive network can be considered to be unbounded. However, from an implementation point of view, a translation need never be created unless some existing translation in a network requires to communicate with it. This simple form of lazy evaluation ensures that in the above example the recursion terminates when there are no more titles to send along the stream labelled rest in Figure 5.

A further use of a recursive network can be found in the decomposition of the translation rotateone. This is first decomposed into a pipeline as defined in Figure 6.

The translation appendeort appends an <u>end</u> <u>of</u> <u>rotated</u> <u>titie</u> symbol to the end of the input title. The translation is, therefore, from <title'> to <rotated title'>. This is necessary as the existing <u>end</u> <u>of</u> <u>title</u> symbol is significant and must be rotated with the rest of the words in the title.   Translation rotate title generates

all the rotations of the title recursively as shown in Figure 7, by firstrotate
generating the unchanged title on one stream and the title rotated one position
on its other output stream.

Translation rotateone(title|rotated title)=
      appendeort(title|newtitle)
      >>
      rotatetitle(newtitle|rotated title)

      translation appendeort .....
      translation rotatetitle .....

end

Figure 6

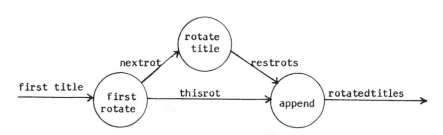

translation rotatetitle(firsttitle|rotated titles)=
      firstrotate(firsttitle|thisrot,nextrot)
   >>[rotatetitle(nextrot|restrots), I(thisrot)]
   >> append(thisrot,restrots|rotatedtitles)
end

Figure 7

The translation firstrotate clearly has two functions. Providing the input does not
start with an eot, it needs to transmit its input to thisrot and transmit to nextrot
the input with the first word removed and appended before the eort symbol. This is
specified as shown in Figure 8, by duplicating the input, sending one copy to the
thisrot stream and the other to a translation which performs the shift.

The translation shift is of interest because in order to move first word in the rotated title to the end, an unbounded buffer is required to hold the characters in the
word. The description is shown in Figure 9.

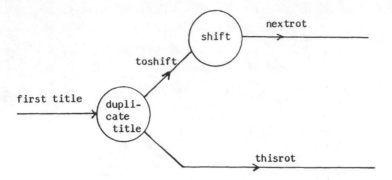

translation firstrotate(firsttitle|thisrot,nextrot)=
    duplicatetitle (firstrot|thisrot,toshift)
  >>[(toshift|nextrot), I(thisrot)]
end

Figure 8

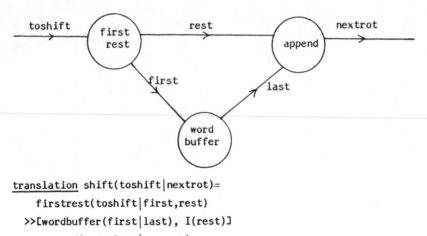

translation shift(toshift|nextrot)=
    firstrest(toshift|first,rest)
  >>[wordbuffer(first|last), I(rest)]
  >> append(rest,last|nextrot)

    .
    .
    .

end

Figure 9

The translations firstrest and append have the same function applied to words as those used previously applied to titles and, like them, must be sequential. Wordbuffer is decomposed into a recursive network where the depth of recursion depends on the length

of the word to be buffered. It can be implemented by the translation shown in
Figure 10, where the component firstrest separates the first character from the rest,
the component singlebuffer buffers the first character, the component wordbuffer
buffers the rest and append reforms the word for output. In this case, the singlebuffer is not essential and could be replaced by I, since the single character is
stored in the adjacent pipelined translations. However, if a more complex structure
such as a title were to be buffered, the analogous singlebuffer would be a wordbuffer
which is not replaceable by I because it needs indefinite character storage; this
is described in Figure 10 and is implemented by a network of translations.

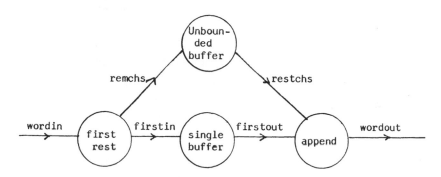

translation unboundedbuffer(wordin|wordout)=
    firstrest(wordin|firstin,remchs)
   >>[unboundedbuffer(remchs|restchs),singlebuffer(firstin|firstout)]
   >> append(firstout,restchs|wordout)
   .
   .
   .

end

Figure 10

3.4 Summary of Decomposition

The examples in this section have shown how the KWIC' example can be decomposed into
a pipeline of two components, the first which generates all significant rotations
and the second which sorts them. The first component was in turn decomposed into a
pipeline with two components of which the first component was a parallel decomposition
of two translations, one generating all rotations, the other merely transmitting non-
significant words. The second pipeline component uses these to transmit only significant rotations. The description of the rotateall component has been refined to
the stage where all its leaf components are sequential translations.

3.5 Sequential Translations

A point is reached in the decomposition of networks where some translations need to

73

be performed sequentially. This is generally due to some order dependent property
of the overall translation being specified. As a rule, premature sequentialisation
of a translation will decrease the potential parallelism inherent in the specification and introduce the need for alternative data structure representations for distributed objects which are already mapped onto streams. The latter requirement
carries with it the danger of overly restrictive specification. For example, in the
KWIC example, premature sequentialisation of operations on words might tempt the
programmer to use a bounded array representation for words, whereas the current specification allows both words and titles to be of any length.

In order to demonstrate the specification of sequential translations, examples from
the previous sub-section will be used. Many of the translations which have sequential decompositions in the previous sub-section can be derived directly from standard
pro-forma translations (functional forms). Duplicate and append are two good examples
of this. Their high-level structures would be the same regardless of the stream
structures they operate on. Their detailed structures can be derived by substituting
specific stream grammars into a standard framework. A program development environment
might facilitate this part of the design process.

Not all sequential translations can be provided 'off the peg' and the format and de-
format translations used to define KWIC in Figure 3 fall into this category. A DTL
sequential translation which translates a stream with the format specified by
<non-significant words> in Figure 2 into a stream with the structure specified by
<non-significant words'> in Figure 3(e) is shown in Figure 11.

Translation deformatwords(in|out)
        in = ch(c:char);
        out = ch(c:char), eow, end

        <deformatwords> ::= *(<word>)<end>;
        <word> ::= <character>*(<character>)<eow>;
        <character> ::= ch(c|not (c in[' ','.',eof]))[ch(c)];
        <eow> ::= (ch(c|c=' ')|<empty>)[eow];
        <end> ::= ch(c|c='.')[end]
end

Figure 11

A DTL translation definition has a heading, which specifies its name and identifies
formal streams by which it communicates, and a body which specifies the transformation required. In a sequential translation the body finally specifies the stream
alphabets assumed in earlier refinements. In the example above, the input stream in
consists only of ch data items, each with a single attribute of type char. The alphabet of the output stream out is that of in augmented by the two data items eow and end.

Alphabet definitions are followed by an attributed translation grammar whose root
production defines a non-terminal symbol identified by the name of the translation.
The notation for the productions of this grammar is similar to that used previously
for specifying the structure of streams, with additions which will be described in
this section. Output terminal symbols are distinguished from input terminal symbols
by enclosing them in [ ]. Thus, if all output symbols are deleted the grammar describes the input language of the translation. Conversely, if all input symbols are
deleted the grammar specifies the output language of the translation.

The overall sequential translation specification describes the relation between its
input streams and its output streams. The translation grammar can, therefore, be
thought of as specifying the sequences of communication events in which the translation process may participate. A translation terminates when it has completed its
translation or failed. Thereafter, no communication can take place on any of its
streams. Such termination is referred to as open circuit termination and can be
visualised as a gap in the network of which the translation was part.

A translation fails if :

  (i)   It is placed in an environment which generates a sequence of communication
         events which do not conform to its defining translation grammar.
  (ii)   It must communicate with a translation which has terminated.
 (iii)   Some internal catastrophe occurs.

A further form of termination, called short circuit termination, is possible. A
common class of translation grammar has been identified which has the form :

    <root> ::= <complex translation> <identity>
    <identity> ::= *(item[item])

where item stands for any data item with any attributes, i.e. it transforms an initial
substring of its input and transmits the remainder unchanged. The identity non-
terminal is, therefore, provided as a predefined production in DTL. Its behaviour is
exactly that of the standard identity translation I, which has been described in
Section 3.2, a translation which is performing the identity translation has effective-
ly short circuited itself and can be regarded as terminated. In practice, it is necessary to specify which pairs of input and output streams are to be shorted together.

Figure 12 shows a specific instance of an append translation which uses this facility.
This is the append translation used in the specification of the word buffer in Figure
10.

    <u>Translation</u> append(first,rest|out)
        first,rest,out = ch(c:char),eow
        <append> ::= first.eow [eow]
               | <u>Figure 12</u>
            first.ch(c) [ch(c)] <identity(rest|out)>
    <u>end</u>

After copying one ch item from the stream called first to the output stream, this
translation terminates by short circuiting the stream called rest to the stream
called out. The notation stream.item is used to associate terminal symbols with
specific streams. Conventionally, such explicit stream identification is omitted if
no ambiguity arises.

4. DISCUSSION

This paper has described a program design methodology which is a successor to the
abstraction methods of Liskov [7] and Parnas [8] in that it utilises the concept of
process abstraction.

The methodology results in an operational specification of a program which is readily
implementable on a variety of computer architectures. Guttag [2] has claimed that
whilst operational specifications are easier for programmers to understand they have
two main drawbacks. Firstly, the effect of sequences of operations upon a data structure is not easy to deduce and secondly, operational specifications lead to over-
specification. These two drawbacks need not occur when designing programs using DTL.

The effects of sequences of operations are closely related to sequences of data and
are explicitly specified in DTL by attributed translation grammars. An attributed
translation grammar specifies clearly and ambiguously the structure of both sequences
of data items transmitted between processes and sequences of operations upon this data.

Although a tendency to overspecify or not is dependent upon the talents of the specifier, DTL provides the means to avoid making unncessary or premature decisions about,
for example, the sequencing of operations until the structure of the problem being
solved necessitates a particular sequencing.

The specification of structured data as streams or collections of streams facilitates
the specification both of order dependent (sequential) and order independent (concurrent) recursive structures. The temptation to choose bounded storage representations for naturally unbounded data structures is avoided so that the generality of
the resulting solution is increased and unnatural constraints are not introduced.
For example, the specification of the KWIC system given in earlier sections avoids
imposing any bounds on words or titles. The premature choice of storage structure
which often results from the need to specify data shared between modules of a hierarchical decomposition does not occur because no data is shared between translations.
Instead, atomic components of a data structure are passed between translations on the
streams. This makes it a simple matter for one translation to impose one structure
upon the items it consumes or generates and for an adjacent translation to see a
different structure. This is because different equivalent stream grammars can specify
the same sequences of data items.

Work on the DTL notation to date has concentrated mainly on refining the design methodology to the point where it can be used by system designers and programmers in a

conventional programming environment. It is hoped that use of the method could result in better structured, inherently self documenting systems which can either explicitly or implicitly take advantage of the parallel nature of current and future hardware developments. The method is based on a technique which has found favour in the commercial programming world [4] but also draws heavily on more formal methods. It is hoped that these latter foundations will facilitate the development of correctness techniques, but more work is required before this can be established.

Acknowledgements

The research described in this paper was supported by Science Engineering Research Council grants Nos. GR/A 74678 and GR/B 35062.

REFERENCES

1. Dijkstra, E. W. "Notes on Structured Programming"
             APIC Studies on Data Processing No. 8, Academic Press, NY.1972,pp 1-81

2. Guttag, J. "Notes on Data Abstraction"
             Nato Summer School.   26 July - 6 August 1978.

3. Hoare, C. A. R. "Communicating Sequential Processes"
             CACM, Vol.21, No. 8 (August 1978) pp. 666-677

4. Jackson, M.A. "Information Systems : Modelling, Sequencing and Transformations"
             IEEE Proc. International Conference on Software Engineering 1978

5. Kahn, G. and McQueen, D.B. "Coroutines and Networks of Parallel Processes"
             IFIP Conference on Information Processing 1977.

6. Lewis, P. M. and Stearns, R.E. "Syntax Directed Transductions"
             JACM, Vol.15 No. 3 (July 1968) pp 465-488

7. Liskov,B. "Modular Program Construction using Abstractions"
             Lecture Notes in Computer Science, No. 86, Springer Verlag 1980,
             pp 354-389

8. Parnas, D.L. "Information Distribution Aspects of Design Methodology"
             Information Processing 71, Vol. 1 North Holland Publishing Co. 1972
             pp 339-344

9. Wirth, N. "Program Development by Stepwise Refinement"
             Comm. ACM, Vol.14 No. 1 (April 1971).

H. Ehrig and H.J. Kreowski
TU Berlin
Fachbereich Informatik

This note presents an algebraic specification of a KWIC index generation
(keyword in context). Given a list of titles (tlist) and a list of
non-significant words (wlist), the program KWIC returns an alphabetically
sorted list of significant rotations of the titles (again a tlist). A significant
rotation of a title is a cyclic shift of some words of the title in which
the first word is significant.

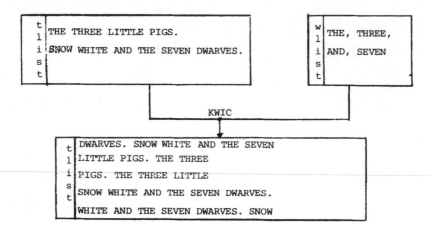

The design of KWIC is displayd in an top-down like fashion. The main modul
kwic shows the declaration and divides the task of KWIC into the generation
of rotations by KWICO and a back-end sorting of the resulting titletist by
tSORT. Both operations belong to the submodul kwicO.

kwic =

  kwic0 +

  opns: KWIC: tlist wlist ———→ tlist
  eqns: KWIC(tl,nonsign)=tSORT(KWIC0(tl,nonsign))

KWIC0 generates the rotated titles of a titlelist concatenating the significant
rotations for the first title (which are generated using KWIC1) and the result
of KWIC0 applied to the rest of the titlelist. This recursive definition is
initialized by the empty list of titles tEMPTY.

  kwic0 =

  kwic1 +

  opns: KWIC0: tlist wlist ———→ tlist
  eqns: KWIC0(tEMPTY, nonsign)=tEMPTY
       KWIC0(tLADD(title,tl),nonsign)=
          tCONCAT(KWIC1(title,wEMPTY,nonsign),KWIC0(tl,nonsign))

The main work ist left to KWIC1. It has to rotate the titles, which are
considered as lists of words (wlist), as well as to check significance.

  kwic1 =

  list(list(list(data),w),t)+

  opns: KWIC1: wlist^3 ———→ tlist
  eqns: KWIC1(wEMPTY,part2,nonsign)=tEMPTY
       KWIC1(wLADD(word,restpart1),,part2,nonsign)=
       if wIS-IN(word,nonsign)
       then KWIC1(restpart1,wRADD(part2,word),nonsign)
       else tLADD(wCONCAT(wLADD(word,restpart1),part2),
            KWIC1(restpart1,wRADD(part2,word),nonsign))

The third argument of KWIC1 gives the non-significant words. The concatenation
of the first and second arguments represents the working title. It is split
into two pieces to obtain a simple termination condition: The first part is
subject fo futher cyclic shifts whereas the second one is assumed to be properly
rotated already. (Hence when KWIC0 calls KWIC1, the second argument is chosen
empty.) So the procedure can stop if the first argument is empty.

Otherwise another cyclic shift is possible, and KWIC1 has to check the
significance of this und procede in any case (therefore the term
KWIC1(restpart1,wRADD(part2,word),nonsign) occurs within the then - as well
as the else - part of the second equation). But whether the current title
wCONCAT(wLADD(word,restpart1),part2) is added to the output list or not,
depends on the significance of its first word: wIS-IN(word,nonsign).

The rest of the story is only list handling on three levels: list of titles,
which are lists of words, which are lists of something. All this list handling
ist provided by the parameterized specification list(data).
On the first level list(data) represents words over an arbitary alphabet data

where data is a formal parameter. Actualizing data by words with parameter
passing morphism w:data $\longrightarrow$ list(data) leads on the second level to list
of words, formally given by list(list(data),w). Finally, data can be actualized
by lists of words (i.e. titles) using t:data $\longrightarrow$ list(list(data),w). This
leads to lists of titles, formally given by list(list(list(data),w),t),
which are used in modul kwic1. The parameterized specification list(data),
the corresponding parameter passing morphisms w and t, and the notation for
sorts and operations in the corresponding actualized specifications is
explained in the appendix in more detail.

APPENDIX:

The parameterized specification list(data) ist given by

list(data) =

    data +

    sorts: list

    opns: EMPTY: $\longrightarrow$ list

         DATA: data $\longrightarrow$ list

         CONCAT: $list^2 \longrightarrow$ list

         LADD: data list $\longrightarrow$ list

         RADD: list data $\longrightarrow$ list

         JOIN: $list\ data^2\ list \longrightarrow$ list

         IS-IN: data list $\longrightarrow$ bool

         LE,EQ: $list^2 \longrightarrow$ bool

         IS-SORTED: list $\longrightarrow$ bool

         SORT: list $\longrightarrow$ list

         if-then-else: $bool\ list^2 \longrightarrow$ list

eqns: CONCAT(EMPTY,l)=l

CONCAT(l,EMPTY)=l

CONCAT(CONCAT(l,l'),l'')=

    CONCAT(l,CONCAT(l',l''))

LADD(x,l)=CONCAT(DATA(x),l)

RADD(l,x)=CONCAT(l,DATA(x))

JOIN(u,x,y,v)=CONCAT(u,CONCAT(DATA(x),CONCAT(DATA(y),v)))

IS-IN(x,EMPTY)=F

IS-IN(x,LADD(x',l))=(x$\equiv$x')OR IS-IN(x,l)

LE(EMPTY,l)=T

LE(LADD(x,l),EMPTY)=F

LE(LADD(x,l),LADD(x',l'))=

  $\left[(x \preccurlyeq x') \text{ AND NON}(x\equiv x')\right]$ OR

  $\left[(x\equiv x') \text{ AND LE } (l,l')\right]$

EQ(l,l')=LE(l,l') AND LE(l',l)

IS-SORTED(EMPTY)=T

IS-SORTED(DATA(x))=T

IS-SORTED(JOIN(u,x,y,v))=

    IS-SORTED(RADD(u,x))AND(x$\preccurlyeq$y)AND IS-SORTED(LADD(y,v))

SORT(u)= if IS-SORTED(u) then u else SORT(u)

SORT(JOIN(u,x,y,v))= if   x$\preccurlyeq$y

                then SORT(JOIN(u,x,y,v))

                else SORT(JOIN(u,y,x,v))

if T then l else l' = l

if F then l else l' =l'

The operation EMPTY, DATA and CONCAT are generating lists of data with associative concatenation. The list manipulating operations LADD, RADD and JOIN are derived from DATA and CONCAT. The predicate IS-IN(x,l) is true if x is an element of l, LE is alphabetic order of words resp. lists, EQ ist equality, IS-SORTED(l) is true if l is alphabetically sorted and SORT(l) is the sorted list derived from l.

The formal parameter data is an extension of the well-known specififcation for bool with sort bool, constants T(true) and F(false) and the logical operations NON, AND and OR.

data =

bool +

sorts: data

opns: $\_\leqslant\_$:data^2 $\longrightarrow$ bool

$\_\equiv\_$:data^2 $\longrightarrow$ bool

requ: initial(bool),

$x \leqslant x$	(reflexive)
$(x \leqslant y) \wedge (y \leqslant z) \Rightarrow (x \leqslant z)$	(transitive)
$(x \leqslant y) \wedge (y \leqslant x) \Leftrightarrow (x \equiv y)$	(antisymmetric)
$(x \leqslant y) \vee (y \leqslant x)$	(total)
$x = y \Leftrightarrow x \equiv y$	(equality)

The formal parameter data has a total order relation $\leqslant$ and an equality $\equiv$ on the sort data. Instead of equations we have requirements in the sense of /Eh 81/. The requirement (requ) initial (bool) makes sure that in each actualization actual of the formal parameter data the bool-part is the initial bool-algebra with values T and F. The logical requirements make sure that $\leqslant$ is reflexive , transitive, antisymmetric and totally ordered (i.e. an total order relation) while the equality requirement implies that $\equiv$ is the semantical equality.

Parameter passing is done in the sense of /Ehr 81/ which ist based on /ADJ 80-81/. Given a parameter passing morphism h:data $\longrightarrow$ actual the actualization of list(data) by actual is called list(actual,h) where all sorts and operations from the body part of list(data) are labeled with prefix h, i.e. hlist, hEMPTY, hCONCAT, hLADD, hRADD or hSORT.

In our parameterized specification kwic1 we first have used the parameter passing morphisms w:data $\longrightarrow$ list(data) where bool ist bool, data is list, $\leqslant$ is LE and $\equiv$ ist EQ, leading to the parameterized specification list(list(data),w), short wlist, with sort wlist and wLADD:list wlist $\longrightarrow$ wlist. Then we have used the parameter passing morphism t:data $\longrightarrow$ wlist where bool is bool, data is wlist, $\leqslant$ is wLE and $\equiv$ is wEQ, leading to the parameterized specification list(wlist,t), short tlist, with sort tlist and tLADD:wlist tlist $\longrightarrow$ tlist.

In all our specifications we still have the formal parameter <u>data</u> such that we have to take the semantics of parameterized specifications with requirements (see/Ehr81/). In order to be able to use the well-known initial algebra semantics we could actualize <u>data</u> by the following actual parameter.

<u>alphabet</u> =

    <u>bool</u> +

    sorts: alphabet

    opns: a1,...,an: $\longrightarrow$ alphabet

          _ $\leqslant$ _ :alphabet^2 $\longrightarrow$ bool

          _ $\equiv$ _ :alphabet^2 $\longrightarrow$ bool

    eqns: (ai $\leqslant$ aj)=T   for i $\leqslant$ j

          (ai $\leqslant$ aj)=F   for i $>$ j

          (ai $\equiv$ aj)=(ai $\leqslant$ aj) AND (aj $\leqslant$ ai)

Taking a: <u>data</u> $\longrightarrow$ <u>alphabet</u> to be the obvious parameter passing morphism with "data is alphabet" we can actualize all our parameterized specification where e.g. <u>list</u>(<u>list</u>(<u>list</u>(<u>data</u>),w),t) becomes <u>list</u>(<u>list</u>(<u>list</u>(<u>alphabet</u>,a),w),t).

For each specification we have now the usual initial algebra semantics (quotient term algebra) in the sense of /ADJ 76 - 78/.

REFERENCES

/ADJ 76 - 78/   Goguen, J.A.-Thatcher, J.W.-Wagner,E.G.: An initial algebra approach to the specification, correctness and implementation of abstract data types, IBM Research Report RC-6487, Oct. 76. Current Trends in Programming Methodology, IV: Data Structuring (R.T.Yeh,Ed.) Prentice Hall, New Jersey (1978), pp. 80 - 149

/ADJ 80 - 81/   Ehrig,H. - Kreowski, H.-J. - Thatcher, J.W. - Wagner, E.G. - Wrigth, J.B.: Parameterized data types in algebraic specification languages, LNCS 85 (1980),pp. 157 - 168, long version to appear 1981

/Ehr 81/   Ehrig, H.: Algebraic theory of parameterized specifications with requirements, LNCS 112(1981), pp. 1 - 24

Leif Sandegaard Nielsen
Computer Science Department
Aarhus University

The Path Processes specification [1] is a concurrent solution
to a non-concurrent problem. This operational specification
may be used as the basis for programming the solution in an
available programming language.

The problem and the first decomposition of the solution is
given by the following sequence of activities. The described
system is a pipe-line of three processes in the presented order.

ROTATE:
Input: A set of titles. A title is a list of words.
Output: The set of all rotations of the input titles.
        A rotation of a list is a cyclic shift of the words
        in the list.

FILTER:
Input: A set of titles.
Output: The set of significant input titles. A significant
        title is a title in which the first word is signifi-
        cant. The non-significant words are known by FILTER.

SORT:
Input: A set of titles.
Output: The alphabetically sorted list of input titles.

The program produces an alphabetically sorted list of the significant rotations of a given set of titles.

The rotate activity is done by a single process. Titles are
received by the entry-operation "put" and shifted by the local
operation "shift" (a single shift). Each shifted title is forwarded to the first filter process.

```
PROCESS rotate
(* OPERATION PART *)
ENTRY-OP put(IN t: title) END
OP shift(IN-OUT t: title) ... END


(* CONTROL PART *)
VAR
   t: title
   l: length

INIT l:=0 END
PATH (l=0 → put=>t; l:=t.l
      □ l>0 → filter1.put(t); shift(t); l:=l-1
      )*
END
END "rotate"
```

The type "title" has a length field "l". The control part describes the restrictions on the sequence of actions of the
process by a regular expression in conditional statements.
The rotate process explicitly allows the execution of the
entry-operation by an operation permission "put=>t". The titles
are produced outside the described system and entered from a
producer process by its execution of an external operation
call "rotate.put(t)". A synchronous communication between the
two partner processes is the result.

The filter activity is done by a list of processes. Each process checks a single non-significant word.

```
(PROCESS filteri(my: word)
(* OPERATION PART *)
ENTRY-OP put(IN t: title) END

(* CONTROL PART *)
VAR
   t: title
```

```
      PATH (put=>t; (t.first<>my → filter<i+1>.put(t)
                   □ t.first=my → dummy) )* END
      END "filteri" □) i=1..m
```

The macro notation can be expanded statically (e.g. "filter<3+1>"
is "filter4"). The type "title" has a word field "first". The
number of non-significant words is m. "filter<m+1>" should be
interpreted as "sort1".

The sort activity is done by a list of processes. If k titles
are given to "sort1", then after a while the k first processes
will each hold one of the k titles and the order of the titles
will be sorted with the "smallest" title in "sort1". If a new
title is given to "sort1" it will flow through the "sorting
array" and find its place. If a title is removed from "sort1"
the list of titles will shift downwards. Inserting and deleting may be done in an interchangeable way.

```
      (PROCESS sorti
      (* OPERATION PART *)
      ENTRY-OP put(IN t: title) END
      ENTRY-OP get(OUT t: title) END


      (* CONTROL PART *)
      VAR
        x,y: title

      PATH (put=>x;
              (put=>y; (x>y → sort<i+1>.put(x); x:=y
                       □ x≤y → sort<i+1>.put(y))
              □ put.r-get.r>1 → get<=x; sort<i+1>.get(x)
              )*;
              put.r-get.r=1 → get<=x)*
      END
      END "sorti" □) i=1..n
```

Each operation "op" has a return counter "op.r" (number of completed executions). The difference "put.r-get.r" in "sorti"

is the number of titles in the suffix of the sorting array
starting at "sorti".

The meaning of the control part is given by the graph:

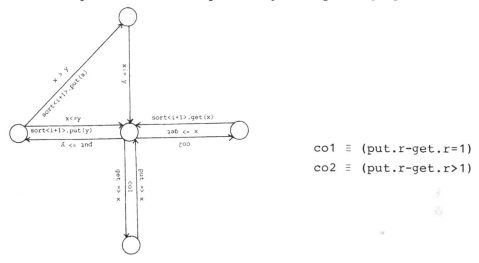

$$co1 \equiv (put.r\text{-}get.r=1)$$
$$co2 \equiv (put.r\text{-}get.r>1)$$

The nodes represent the states and the arcs represent the actions. To chose an action the condition on the arc has to be
true. If the action is an external operation call (e.g
"sort2.put(x)") or an operation permission (e.g. "put=>x")
there must be a partner willing to do the corresponding communication action.

The two possible classes of communication statements (operation calls and permissions) must always be explicitly mentioned in the control part.

The total system leaves the sorted list of significant titles
in the sorting array. If the result should be presented it
might be done by changing the last filter process to check
for a special closing title and then start an output process.

This concurrent solution with a high degree of decomposition
catches the essence of the three main activities: The rotations
of the input titles, the exclusion of the non-significant titles and the comparison of the significant titles.

Reference

[1] Concurrency, Leif Sandegaard Nielsen (these proceedings)

J.R. Abrial and I.H. Sørensen
Programming Research Group
Oxford University Comp. Lab.

1. INTRODUCTION.

This paper gives a formal specification of a program for generating a KWIC (KeyWord in Context) Index.

The specification itself is not very complicated, but it serves to illustrate how a specification can be divided up into several parts, each of which formalises a single aspect of the total problem. In this paper problems such as *sequence rotation*, *sorting of sequences* and *lexicografic ordering* will be treated in isolation, and then used in the final specification of the KWIC index generation program.

2. INFORMAL SPECIFICATION.

Consider a program to generate a KWIC index. A *title* is a list of words which are either *significant* or *non-significant*. A *rotation* of a list is a cyclic shift of the words in the list, and a *significant rotation* is a rotation in which the first word is significant. Given a set of titles and a set of non-significant words, the program should produce an alphabetically sorted list of significant rotations of the titles.

Example:
With the following set of titles

    THE THREE LITTLE PIGS
    SNOW WHITE AND THE SEVEN DWARVES

and the non-significant words

    THE, THREE, AND, SEVEN

the program should produce:

    DWARVES SNOW WHITE AND THE SEVEN
    LITTLE PIGS THE THREE
    PIGS THE THREE LITTLE
    SNOW WHITE AND THE SEVEN DWARVES
    WHITE AND THE SEVEN DWARVES SNOW

3. FORMAL SPECIFICATION.

In this section we will formalise the following:

"... Given a set of titles and a set of non-significant words, the program should produce an alphabetically sorted list of significant rotations of the titles."

Assume we are given an abstract set –

$$T$$

which represents the set of all possible *titles* (note that we have abstracted the fact that titles are lists of words at this level of description).

The problem involves the concept *'rotations'* of titles, hence we can assume that there exists a function–

$$\text{rotations} : T \rightarrow F(T)$$

which maps a given title into a finite set of titles, i.e. its rotations.

The problem also refers to *significant* rotations, hence we are interested in a subset of titles, the elements of which are all considered to be significant–

$$\text{significant\_titles} : P(T)$$

As the problem statement involves the additional notion of *alphabetically sorted* lists of titles, we shall also be interested in a set of all alphabetically sorted sequences of titles–

$$\text{alphabetically\_sorted} : P(\text{seq}[T])$$

Thus, given a finite set of titles –

$$\text{set\_of\_titles} : F(T)$$

the program that we wish to specify should produce a *result* which is a list of titles –

$$\text{result} : \text{seq}[T]$$

which is alphabetically sorted, i.e.

$$\text{result} \in \text{alphabetically\_sorted}$$

and which is composed of significant rotations of the given titles:

```
ran(result) =
    U{rotations(t) ∩ significant_titles | t:set_of_titles}
```

(Note that the result is finite.)

The discussion above can be summarised by the following schema:

```
SPEC_1 _____ T _____
    │
    │   rotations             : T → F(T);
    │   significant_titles    : P(T);
    │   alphabetically_sorted : P(seq[T]);
    │
    │   set_titles            : F(T);
    │   result               : seq[T]
    │_____
    │
    │   result ε alphabetically_sorted;
    │   ran(result) =
    │        ∪{rotations(t) ∩ significant_titles | t:set_of_titles}
    │
```

The given specification is incomplete as we have not yet given a definition of the concepts 'rotations', 'significant_titles' and 'alphabetically_sorted'. In the following three sections these concepts will be described in isolation and the descriptions will be used in the last section of this paper to give a final formal specification of the desired KWIC program.

4. ROTATIONS OF SEQUENCES.

According to the informal specification '...A *title* is a list of words...', hence we can 'instantiate' the specification as introduced in the previous section with the set of non-empty sequences for **T**:

$$SPEC\_1[seq1[W]]$$

where **W** denotes an abstract set of words.

The function rotations will in this section be formally defined in terms of a more primitive concept, as explained in the informal specification: '...A *rotation* of a list is a cyclic shift of the words in the list...'.

Thus we shall first formalise 'cyclic shift' in a straightforward way.

Given a sequence

$$⟨a \ b \ c \ d⟩$$

we get by shifting it once

$$⟨b \ c \ d \ a⟩$$

by shifting it twice we get the sequence

$$⟨c \ d \ a \ b⟩$$

The subsequent cyclic shifts are

$$\langle d\ a\ b\ c \rangle$$

and

$$\langle a\ b\ c\ d \rangle$$

In the following definition of the cyclic shift we adopt the convention that the cyclic shift of an empty sequence again is the empty sequence.

$$\underline{}\ X\ \underline{}\ \text{DEF}\ (1)$$

```
    cyclic_shift : seq[X] → seq[X]

    cyclic_shift(⟨⟩) = ⟨⟩;
    (∀ s:seq[X]; x:X) (cyclic_shift(⟨x⟩*s) = s*⟨x⟩)
```

From this definition and the definition of the transitive closure (see [1]) we may deduce the following 'expected' properties for cyclic_shift.

```
                         X

    s:seq[X]    ⊢ ran(cyclic_shift(s)) = ran(s) ∧
                   #(cyclic_shift(s)) = #(s) ;

    s:seq1[X]; i:N1; j:N
                ⊢ cyclic_shift^j(s)(i) = s( (i+j-1)mod#(s) + 1);

    s:seq[X]    ⊢ cyclic_shift*({s}) = {cyclic_shift^i(s) | i:0..#(s)};

    S:P(seq[X]) ⊢ cyclic_shift*(S) = ∪{cyclic_shift*({s}) | s:S}
```

The introduced definition (DEF (1)) can then be used to refine SPEC_1 as follows:

SPEC_2 $\underline{}$ W $\underline{}$

```
    SPEC_1[seq1[W]]

    (∀ title : seq1[W])
        ( rotations(title) = cyclic_shift*({title}) )
```

5. SIGNIFICANT ROTATIONS.

In the informal specification the expression '...significant rotation...' is explained in terms of a more primitive notion, namely that of significant words. Given the set

significant_words : $\mathbb{P}(\mathbf{W})$

a significant title is a sequence of words '...in which the first word is significant...'. This definition implies that the sequences in question are non-empty. Hence we can further refine our specification as follows:

SPEC_3 _____ **W** _____

> SPEC_2[**W**];
> significant_words : $\mathbb{P}(\mathbf{W})$
>
> _____
>
> significant_titles =
>   { s:seql[**W**] | first(s) ∈ significant_words}

Note that

_____ **W** _____

> SPEC_3[**W**];
> t ∈ ran(result) ⊢ first(t) ∈ significant_words

6. ALPHABETICAL ORDERING.

In this section we shall formalise the notion of '...alphabetically sorted list...', since the list produced by the program must be sorted according to the alphabetical ordering.

In general, a sequence can be sorted according to any total order relation defined over the elements of such sequences.

For example, the sequence-

⟨ 2 4 6 6 13 17 ⟩

is sorted according to the relation ≤: $\mathbf{N} \times \mathbf{N}$ because all pairs of adjacent elements belong to the relation, i.e.

{(2,4), (4,6),.. ..,(13,17)} ⊂ ≤

or

2≤4, 4≤6,.. ..,13≤17

Generally, for a given relation the set of sequences which are sorted according to that relation are those sequences whose 'neighbour' elements are included into that relation. Using the definition of the next function from [1] we get-

```
     sorted_according_to : (X⟷X)  →  P(seq[X])

  (∀ R : X⟷X)
  sorted_according_to(R) = {s : seq[X] | next(s) ⊂ R}
```

The relation in question for the KWIC example is the *alphabetical ordering*. We know, intuitively, what the alphabetical order is, e.g. we know that the alphabetical ordering of the set of words-

        { SNOW, PIGS, SEVEN, DWARVES, LITTLE }

is the sequence

        ⟨ DWARVES LITTLE PIGS SEVEN SNOW ⟩

Such an ordering relies on the basic ordering of letters and the *lexicographical* ordering of sequences of letters, e.g.

        DWARVES 'is_less_than' LITTLE

because

        D 'is_less_than' L

and

        SEVEN 'is_less_than' SNOW

because

        (S - S) 'and' (EVEN 'is_less_than' NOW)

The concept of lexicographical ordering can be generalised. Given a relation R and a set X we can define a new relation, Lexicographical(R) between sequences of X. This relation has the following properties-
Given a sequence s then

        (⟨⟩) Lexicographical(R) (s)

and given two sequences s1 and s2, and two elements x1 and x2 then

        (⟨x1⟩ * s1) Lexicographical(R) (⟨x2⟩ * s2)

if and only if

```
        (x1 = x2) ∧ (s1 Lexicographical(R) s2)
or

        x1 ≠ x2 ∧ (x1 R x2)
```

For example, we have

```
        ⟨3 4 2⟩ Lexicographical(⟨) ⟨3 6⟩
```

because

```
        (3 = 3) ∧ (4⟨6)
```

The dicussion above lead to the following definition–

X _____ DEF (3)

```
    Lexicographical : (X ↔ X) → (seq[X] ↔ seq[X])


    (∀ R:X↔X; s1,s2:seq[X]; x1,x2:X )
      ( ⟨⟩ Lexicographical(R) s2 ) ∧
      ( (⟨x1⟩ * s1) Lexicographical(R) (⟨x2⟩ * s2) ⟺
        ( x1=x2 ∧ s1 Lexicographical(R) s2 ∨
          x1≠ x2 ∧ x1 R x2 )
```

Given a character set **C** we may select a finite subset

```
        letters : 𝔽(C)
```

and define a total relation between these letters

```
        ⟨_let : letters ↔ letters
```

This ordering induces a relation on sequences of letters (e.g. words) which is

```
        Lexicographical(⟨_let)
```

Likewise this relation induces a relation between sequences of words (i.e. titles) which is

```
        Lexicographical(Lexicographical(⟨_let))
```

In the following schema we summarise (using DEF (3)) this definition of alphabetical ordering–

```
ALPHA _____ C _____
|
|    letters  : F(C);
|    words    : P(seq[C]);
|    titles   : P(seq[seq[C]])
|
|    <let      : C ↔ C;
|    <word     : seq[C] ↔ seq[C];
|    <title    : seq[seq[C]] ↔ seq[seq[C]]
|_____
|
|    words = seql[letters];
|    titles= seql[words];
|
|    <word   = Lexicographical(<let);
|    <title  = Lexicographical(<word)
|_____
```

7. THE FORMAL SPECIFICATION.

The set of alphabetically sorted titles is the set of sequences of words which are ordered according to the order ($<_{title}$) given in ALPHA. Using the definitions in ALPHA and the definitions given in the extensions DEF(1) and DEF(2) we can give the final specification of the KWIC program. Note that we have simplified the description by eliminating the notion of rotations, significant_titles and alphabetically_sorted.

```
KWIC _____ C _____
|
|    ALPHA[C];
|
|    set_of_titles         : F[titles];
|    significant_words     : P(words);
|    result                : seq[titles]
|_____
|
|    result ε sorted_according_to(<title);
|    ran(result) =
|    {s:cyclic_shift*(set_of_titles) | first(s) ε significant_words }
|_____
```

List of References.

[1]   I.H. Sørensen:
       'A Specification Language'
       Included paper.

R.M. Gallimore and D. Coleman[*]
Department of Computation
UMIST

1. INTRODUCTION

The functional specification of a KWIC index generation program is
developed by a process of refinement and the possibility of verifying design
decisions is demonstrated.   We begin by repeating the informal problem
description:

"A title is a list of words which are either significant or
non-siginificant. A rotation of a list is a cyclic shift of the words in
the list, and a significant rotation is a rotation in which the first word
is significant. Given a set of titles and a set of non-siginificant words,
the program should produce an alphabetically sorted list of the significant
rotations of the titles".

The first decision is to denote the sets of titles and work by
lists or sequences. Based on the problem description and this decision
we can supply an abstract syntax and corresponding domain definitions
for the values to be manipulated.   The definitions are presented in figures 1
and 2:

```
<titles>::={<titles>}

<title> ::={<word>}⁺ eot

<word>  ::={<alphanum>}⁺

<words> ::={<word>}

<rotations>::={<rotation>}

<rotation> ::={<word>}⁺ eot {<word>}

              |

           eot{<word>}⁺

<alphanum>::=A|B| ...          |0|1|  ... |9
```

Figure 1: Abstract Syntax for kwic inputs and outputs

---

[*]
 This work was undertaken by the authors while D. Coleman
 was on study leave at the University of California, Berkeley

```
        alphanum =  A, B, ... Z, a, b, ... z, 0, 1, ... 9

        eot      = null

        word     = *(alphanum)
        word     = *(word)
        token    = word @ eot

        title    = *(token)

        titles   = *(title)

        rotation = *(token)

    rotations = *(rotation)
```

Figure 2: Domains of values manipulated by kwic

2.   Kwic

2.1.   Implicit Specification for Kwic

        kwic : titles x words → rotations

where kwic denotes a function satisfying

kwic.1   : ordered(kwic(s, ns))   ∀s : titles; ns : words

kwic.2   : perm(kwic(s, ns), allsigrotations(s, ns)) ∀s : titles; ns : words

        Now, ordered is a predicate that is satisfied iff lessr (a
lexicographic ordering relation) holds between every successive
pair of rotations in its argument. Ordered and lessr are defined as
follows:

function ordered : rotations → boolean

r, s : rotation; t : rotations

cases

    ordered(λ)   = true

    ordered(r)   = true

    ordered(r::s::t) = if lessr(r, s) then ordered(s::t)

                                       else false

end
```
```

```
function lessr : rotation x rotation → boolean

v, w : t ken; r, s : rotation

cases

    lessr(λ, s)        = true

    lessr(v::r, λ)     = false

    lessr(v::r, w::s) = if kind(v) = eot then lessr(r, w::s)

                          else if kind(w) = eot then lessr(v::r, s)

                              else if =_w(val(v), val(w)) then lessr(r, s)

                                  else <_w(val(v), val(w))

end

where =_w and <_w are defined as:

function =_w : word x word → boolean

v, w : alphanum; r, s : word

cases

=_w(λ, λ)          = true

=_w(λ, w::s)       = false

=_w(v::r, λ)       = false

=_w(v::r, w::s) = if v = w then =_w(r, s)

                              else false

end

function <_w : word x word → boolean

v, w : alphanum; r, s : word

cases

<_w(λ, λ)

<_w(λ, w::s)

<_w(v::r. λ)

<_w(v::r, w::s) = if v = w then <_w(r, s)

                              else v < w

end
```

2.2. Function Definition for Kwic

We now propose a function definition for kwic:

function kwic : titles x words → rotations

s : titles; ns : words

cases

   kwic(s, ns) = sort(allsigrotations(s, ns))

end

The two functions sort, allsigrotations must satisfy the following implicit specifications:

sort : rotations → rotations

Properties

sort.1: ordered(sort(s))   ∀s : rotations

sort.2: perm(sort(s), s)   ∀s : rotations

allsigrotations : titles x words → rotations

asr.1: member(r, allsigrotations(s, ns))

               ⟺ member(r, everyrotation(s)) **and**

                 issignificant(r, ns)

                     ∀r : rotation; s : titles; ns : words

where member, and issignificant are defined as follows:

function member : rotation x rotations → boolean

r, s : rotation; t : rotations

cases

   member(r, λ)   = false

   member(r, s::t) = **if** r = s **then** true

                          else member(r, t)

end

```
function issignificant : rotation x words → boolean

w : token; s : rotation; ns : words

cases

   issignificant(λ, ns)     = false
   issignificant(w::s, ns) = if kind(w) = eot then false

                                   else if member(val(w), ns) then false

                                                           else  true

end
```

The truth of theorems kwic.1 and kwic.2 follows directly from
the implicit specification of sort and the definition supplied for
function kwic. We now consider each of the subproblems in turn.

3.   The Sort Subproblem

3.1   Refinement of the Specification

The function sort is defined as follows:

```
function sort : rotations → rotations

s : rotations

cases

   sort(λ) =  λ
   sort(s) = m(asc(s), sort(rest(s)))

end
```

It defines a recursive sort function in terms of sort, and
subsidiary functions m, asc, rest. The functions asc and rest decompose
the sequence s such that

(i)   asc(s) defines an embedded sequence of rotations whose
elements are weakly ascending under lessr. Asc must satisfy the
implicit specification:

```
      asc : rotations → rotations
      asc.1 : ordered(asc(s))              ∀ : rotations
```

(ii)   rest(s) identifies the remaining sequence of rotations when the elements of asc(s) have been removed from s.

rest : rotations → rotations

rest.1 : members(asc(s)) U members(rest(s)) = members(s) ∀s : rotations

where 'members' collects together the elements of a sequence into a bag of the appropriate type - in this case a bag of rotations, and U denotes bag-union.

    The function m applied to two sequences of rotations defines the sequence value resulting from merging the two input sequence values together such that if the two input sequences s, t are ordered, then the value m(s, t) will also be ordered.

m : rotations x rotations → rotations

Properties

m.1 : ordered(s) and ordered(t) ⇒ ordered(m(s, t))

m.2 : members(s) U members(t) = members(m(s, t))

Functions asc, rest, and m are defined as follows.

function asc : rotations → rotations

r, s : rotation; t : rotations

cases

    asc(λ)   = λ

    asc(r)   = r

    asc(r::s::t) = if lessr(r, s) then r::asc(s::t)

                                 else asc (r::t)

end

<u>function</u> rest : rotations → rotations

r, s : rotation; t : rotations

<u>cases</u>

    rest(λ) = λ

    rest(r) = λ

    rest(r::s::t) = <u>if</u> lessr(r, s) <u>then</u> rest(s::t)

                                 <u>else</u> s::rest(r::t)

<u>end</u>

<u>function</u> m : rotations x rotations → rotations

x, y : rotation; s, t : rotations

<u>cases</u>

    m(λ, λ) = λ

    m(λ, y::t) = y::m(λ, t)

    m(x::s, λ) = x::m(s, λ)

    m(x::s, y::t) = <u>if</u> lessr(y, x) <u>then</u> y::m(x::s, t)

                               <u>else</u> x::m(s, y::t)

<u>end</u>

3.2   Proofs of Properties of the Specification Functions

We are now able to treat the function definitions as systems
of rewrite rules in constructing proofs that the specification
functions satisfy their implicit specifications in the sort subproblems.
Before we begin let us define the function 'members' which collects
together in a bag all the items contained in a sequence. Let D denote
some domain of data items then

```
function members : *(D) → B(D)

i : D; s : *(D)

cases

    members(λ)=[ ]

    members(i::s) = [i] U members(s)

end
```

THEOREM asc.1   ordered(asc(s))   s : rotations.

Proof

        By induction on rotations where s < t iff

length(s) < length(t)   s, t : rotations.

Bssis s = λ and asc(λ) = λ and ordered(λ) ⇒ ordered(asc(s))

Induction step Assume theorem true ∀ s' < s. Consider s = r::s'

case(i) s'= = x::s"

case(a) lessr(r, x) then

        ordered(asc(s))

    = ordered(asc(r::x::s"))

    = ordered(r::asc(x::s"))   defn of asc.

    = true   defn of ordered and the induction
                                    hyphothesis

case(b) not less(r, x) then

        ordered(asc(s))

    =   ordered(asc(r::x::s"))

    =   ordered(asc(r::s"))   defn of asc.

    =   true   induction hypothesis

case(ii) s' = λ

    =   ordered(asc(s))

    =   ordered(asc(r))

    =   ordered(r)   defn of asc

    =   true   defn of ordered

THEOREM rest.1 members(asc(s)) U members(rest(s)) = members(s) s : rotations

Proof Induction on the length of s.

Basis s =   s : rotations

    members(asc(λ)) U members(rest(λ)) = members(λ)

    trivially true.

Induction Step Assume theorem rest.1 true for all s' < s

and consider s = j::s'   j : rotation; s, s' : rotations

case(i) s' = λ

l.h.s. members(s) = members(j)

r.h.s. members(asc(s)) U members(rest(s))

    = members(asc(j)) U members(rest(j))

    = members(j) U members(λ)

    = members(j)

case(ii) s' = k::s"

   case(a) not lessr(j, k)

r.h.s. members(asc(s)) U members(rest(s))

    = members(asc(j::k::s")) U members(rest(j::k::s"))

    = members(asc(j::s")) U members(k::rest(j::s")

    = members(asc(j::s")) U members(rest(j::s")) U [k]

    = members(j::s") U [k]   (induction hypothesis)

    = members(j::k::s")

    = members(s)

   case(b) lessr(j, k)

r.h.s. members(asc(s)) U members(rest(s))

    = members(asc(j::k::s")) U members(rest(j::k::s"))

    = members(j::asc(k::s")) U members(rest(k::s"))

    = [j] U members(asc(k::s")) U members(rest(k::s"))

    = [j] U members(k::s")   (induction hypothesis)

    = members(j::k::s")

    = members(s)

By similar reasoning we can prove theorems m.1, m.2 for function 'm'.
The details of these proofs are left to the interested reader. These
proven theorems may then be used to show that sort processes the
desired properties.

THEOREM   sort.1   ordered(sort(s))   s : rotations

Proof: Induction on the length of s

Basic s = λ

    ordered(sort(λ))

  = ordered(λ)

  = true

Induction Step   Assume theorem sort.1 true Ψ s' < s and

                                        j : rotation; s, s' : rotations

    ordered(sort(j::s')

= ordered(m(asc(j::s'), sort(rest(j::s'))))

Now ordered(asc(j::s')) follows from Theorem asc.1

and ordered(sort(rest(j::s'))) is true from the induction hypothesis

    since rest(j::s') < (j::s')   from the definition of rest.

Consequently

    ordered(m(asc(j::s'), sort(rest(j::s')))) from theorem m.1

THEOREM   sort.2 members(sort(s)) = members(s)   s : rotation

Proof Left to the reader.

We have shown that the value defined by sort (and thus by kwic)
is an alphabetically ordered sequence of rotations. In addition
sort permutes the sequence of rotations that is its argument. We can
now refine and prove the specification for allsigrotations independently.

4.   All Significant Rotations

4.1   Refinement of the Specification

Given a sequence of titles the function allsigrotations must identify for each title every rotation beginning with significant word.

allsigrotations : titles x words → rotations

Properties

asr.1 : member(r,allsigrotations(s,ns)) ⟺ member(r,everyrotation(s))

$$\text{and issignificant}(r,ns)$$

asr.2 : allsigrotations(λ,ns) = λ

where r : rotation; s : titles; ns :words

and issignificant is defined as follows

function issignificant : rotation x words → boolean

w : token; s : rotation; ns : words

cases

issignificant(λ, ns)   = true

issignificant(w::s; ns) = if kind(w) = eot then false

$$\text{else if member(val(w),ns)) then false}$$

$$\text{else true}$$

end

and member is defined by the schema, letting D denote some domain of data items:

function member : D X *(D) → boolean

x, y : D; s : *(D)

cases

   member(x,λ)   = false

   member(x, y::s) = if x = y then true

$$\text{else member(x, s)}$$

end

Suppose that we choose to define allsigrotations as follows:

function allsigrotations : titles x words → rotations

t : title; s : titles; ns : words

cases

   allsigrotations(λ, ns)   = λ

   allsigrotations(t::s, ns) = signif(everyrotation(t::s), ns)

end

where 'everyrotation' defines every rotation that may be generated from every title:

everyrotation : titles → rotations

Properties:

er.1: members(everyrotation(λ)) = [ ]

er.2: members(everyrotation(t::s)) = members(allrotations(t))

$$U \text{ members(everyrotation(s))}$$

where t : title; s : titles.

     'Signif' filters out those members of a sequence of rotations whose first word is significant.

signif : rotations x words → rotations

Properties:

snf.1 : member(r, signif(s, ns)) ⟺

        member(r, s) and issignificant(r, ns)

           r : rotation; s : rotations; ns : words.

4.1.1.   Generating Everyrotation

function everyrotation : titles → rotations

t : title; s : titles

cases

   everyrotation(λ)   = λ

   everyrotation(t::s) = allrotations(t)::everyrotation(s)

end

The function allrotations must define all possible rotations of a title.

allrotations : title → rotations

Informally: members(allrotations(t))

$$= [t, rotate(t), rotate^2(t) , \ldots \quad rotate^{length(t)-1} (t)]$$

where $rotate^1(t) = rotate(t)$, $rotate^i(t) = rotate^{i-1} (rotate(t))$, $i > 1$

The property can be restated more formally using subsidiary functions:

<u>function</u> nth.member : integers x rotations → rotations

r : rotation; s : rotations; n : integer

<u>cases</u>

   nth.member(0, r::s) = r

   nth.member(n, r::s) = nth.member(n-1, s)

<u>end</u>

<u>function</u> rotate.by.n : integer x rotation → rotation

r : rotation; n : integer

<u>cases</u>

   rotate.by.n(0, r) = r

   rotate.by.n(n, r) = rotate.by.n(n - 1, rotate(r))
    <u>end</u>

    We can restate the desired property as
ar.1: allrotations(λ) = λ

ar.2: nth.member((n <u>mod</u> length(r)) , allrotations(r)) = rotate.by.n(n,r)

             r : rotation; n : integer; length(r) > 0

Define allrotations as

<u>function</u> allrotations : title → rotations

t : title

<u>cases</u>

   allsigrotations(λ) = λ

   allrotations(t) = nrotations(t, length(t))

<u>end</u>

Implicit specification for nrotations:

nrotations : rotation x integer → rotations

nr.1 : nrotations(t, 0) = λ

nr.2 : nth.member((m mod n)   , nrotations(t, n)) = rotate.by.n(m,t)

                       t : rotation; m, n : integer, m, n > 0

Function Definition for nrotations

function nrotations : rotation x integer → rotations

r : rotation; n : integer

cases

   nrotations(r, 0) = λ

   nrotations(r, n) = r::nrotations(rotate(r), n - 1)

end

where

function rotate : rotation → rotation

r : rotation; k : token

cases

   rotate(λ)   = λ

   rotate(k::r) = r::k

end

4.1.2.   Signif

function signif : rotations x words → rotations

r : rotation; s : rotations

cases

   signif(λ, ns)   = λ

   signif(r::s, ns) = sig(r, ns)::signif(s, ns)

end

Function definition for sig

```
function sig : rotation x words → rotation

k : token; r : rotation; ns : words

cases

    sig(λ, ns)    = λ

    sig(k::r, ns) = if kind(k) = eot then  λ

                    else if member(val(k), ns) then λ

                                          else k::r

end
```

4.2   Proofs of Properties

Space does not permit the inclusion of exhaustive proofs. The example proofs of the sort specification illustrate the nature and complexity of the reasoning involved.

4.3   Representation-Abstraction Functions

We illustrate these functions for the domain 'titles'. Suppose that we represent the 'eot' (representing full stop in the text) by a special word, and introduce a distinct marker 'eos' to mark the end of the titles.

Representation Function	Abstraction Function

word

$R(w) = (\text{word}, w)$ $A_w((\text{word}), w) = w$

title

$R_t(\text{eot}) = (\text{word}, \text{'eot'})$ $A_t((\text{word}, \text{'eot'}))::s = \text{eot}$

$R_t(w::t) = R_w(w)::R_t(t)$ $A_t(w::t) = A_w(w)::A_t(t)$

titles

$R_{ts}(\lambda) = \text{eos}$ $A_{ts}(\text{eos}) = \lambda$

$R_{ts}(t::s) = R_t(t)::R_{ts}(s)$ $A_{ts}(z::(\text{word}, \text{'eot'}))::s$

$\qquad\qquad\qquad\qquad\qquad\qquad = A_t(z::(\text{word}, \text{eot}))$

$\qquad\qquad\qquad\qquad\qquad\qquad\qquad ::A_{ts}(s)$

where z is a sequence of tagged words whose value does not equal 'eot'.

4.4. Realisation

For example, we can introduce a realisation for the function 'everyrotation'.

function everyrotation' : titleseq $\rightarrow$ rotationseq

t : titleseq

cases

   everyrotation'(eos) = eors

   everyrotation'(t)   = allrotations'(title(t))

                     ::everyrotation'(title^{-1}(t))

end

where title (title^{-1}) recognises (removes) the prefix of tagged words from t that corresponds to a title.

function title : titleseq $\rightarrow$ rotseq

k : word ; t : titleseq

cases

   title(k::t) = if val(k) = eot then k::eor

                            else k::title(t)

end

function title^{-1} : titleseq $\rightarrow$ titleseq

k : word ; t : titleseq

cases

title^{-1}(k::t) = if val(k) = eot then t

                      else title^{-1}(t)

end

Representations for each syntactic class (domain) can be used to produce an explicit functional realisation of an abstract function, as above, or to guide the final implementation in an imperative language.

Process Networks

The function definitions can be used to deduce the configuration of communicating processes to perform a computation. For instance the sort subprogram may consist of a recursive network of processes:

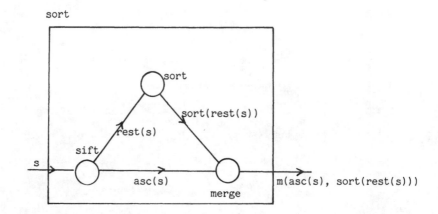

Figure 8: Scheme illustrating a recursive network of processes implementing the 'sort' function

Informally, the behaviour of the processes is as follows:

sift : inputs a sequence of data items and 'splits' the sequence. Beginning with the first item read, it sends the embedded sequence of data items whose values are weakly ascending direct to process merge, all other items are sent, in their order of arrival, to process sort.

sort : may recursively involve a new instance of the network to sort its input.

merge : accepts two input sequences and merges them to form a single output sequence : such that every item read appears in the output sequence, and if both input sequences are weakly ascending then the output sequence will be weakly ascending.

Assertions

For each process in the resulting program it is possible to deduce correctness assertions from the functional specification eg. if for each process P, $g_P{}^i$ and $h_P{}^j$ are functions defining the effect of P on its input stream i and output stream j, using this notation we might state the following propositions

$$g_{sort}(s) \quad\quad = \text{ if } good(s) \text{ then } tail(\nu(isrot,s))$$

$$h_{sort}(s,o) \quad\quad = \text{ if } good(s) \text{ then } o :: sort(s) :: (eos)$$

$$g_{sift}(s) \quad\quad = \text{ if } good(s) \text{ then } tail(\nu(isrot,s))$$

$$h^1{}_{sift}(s,a) \quad\quad = \text{ if } good(s) \text{ then } a :: asc(s) :: (eos)$$

$$h^2{}_{sift}(s,r) \quad\quad = \text{ if } good(s) \text{ then } r :: rest(s) :: (eos)$$

$$g^1{}_{merge}(a,s) \quad\quad = \text{ if } good(a) \text{ and } good(s) \text{ then } tail(\nu(isrot,a))$$

$$g^2{}_{merge}(a,s) \quad\quad = \text{ if } good(a) \text{ and } good(s) \text{ then } tail(\nu(isrot,s))$$

$$h_{merge}(a,s,o) \quad\quad = \text{ if } good(a) \text{ and } good(s) \text{ then } o :: me(a,s) :: (eos)$$

where $good(s) = (kind(head(\nu(isrot,s)))) = eors)$ specifies that the sequence transmitted on each input stream starts with a sequence of rotation valued data items followed by an eors.

The use of such assertions in the verfication of an implementation as a recursive process network is discussed in reference [2].

REFERENCES

[1] GALLIMORE, R.M. and COLEMAN, D.
    Specification of Distributed Programs.
    These proceedings.

[2] COLEMAN, D. and GALLIMORE, R.M.
    Partial Correctness of Distributed Programs.
    These proceedings.

Joseph A. Goguen
Computer Science Laboratory
SRI International

1. Introduction

This brief note presents a specification of the KWIC index generation problem
in the current draft version of SRI's specification language ORDINARY [Goguen
& Burstall 80]. No features of the language are required beyond those already
introduced for the geometrical constructions specification [Goguen 81], and
familiarity with that document, which also contains further relevant
references is assumed. However, three additional standard constructions which
we need are given in Section 2. Section 3 contains the actual KWIC spec.

Certain ORDINARY constructions appear here with somewhat different syntax than
already seen in the geometrical constructions example. The first is that the
rep section of the last cluster (called INDEX) gives representations for three
different sorts; these are connected by and. Secondly, because of the
coercion (list $\geq$ x) in the LIST cluster, several equations have variables
whose sort cannot be uniquely determined; these variables are therefore
declared in a vars section. Finally, in one case it is necessary to
explicitly define a view, rather than to rely on the trivial views which are
supplied automatically. This is done with syntax view...as...by...endview,
where the last ... contains a binding, and the first ... is optional.

This is not a difficult problem. Indeed, its very simplicity tempts one to
write algorithms rather than axioms (including equations). This algorithmic
temptation shows slightly here in the recursive definition of the function
rot(t,k), which forms the kth rotation of a given title, t, using the hidden
function shift. Another possibly interesting point about this problem is that
its statement suggests maintaining a careful distinction between sets and
lists, but the algorithmic temptation often favors lists over sets.

2. Standard Constructions

Section 3 assumes that the block CONSTRUCTIONS contains the following three standard constructions as well as SET from [Goguen 81].

    cluster NAT
        data sorts nat
        ops 0,1: nat
          inc,dec: nat -> nat
          _+_, _*_: nat,nat -> nat (assoc)
        err-ops neg: nat
        relns > : nat,nat

        eqns dec(inc(n)) = n, 1 = inc(0)
             0+n = n, inc(m)+n = inc(m+n)
             0*n = 0, inc(n)*m = (n*m)+m
        err-eqns dec(0) = neg, dec(neg) = neg
        axioms x > x, x > 0, inc(x) > x   endcl

        <*we now define simple order*>
    cluster SORDER is enrich POSET by
         axioms x > y or y > x or x == y   endcl

    cluster LIST [X:: TRIV]
         uses NAT
        data sorts list > x
        ops nil: list, __: list,list -> list (assoc)
          first: list -> elt, rest: list -> list
          length: list -> nat
        err-ops no-first: elt, no-rest: list
        relns _in_: elt,list

        vars e,e': elt, l: list
        eqns nil l = l, l nil = l
          first(e) = e, first(el) = e
          rest(e) = nil, rest(el) = l
          length(nil) = 0, length(el) = inc(length(l))
        err-eqns first(nil) = no-first, rest(nil) = no-rest
        axioms not e in nil, e in e'l iff (e == e') or e in l   endcl

3. KWIC Specification

The whole specification is parameterized by ALPH, an arbitrary simply ordered
alphabet. It will then be easy to specify and use, for example, the ASCII
alphabet with its standard ordering, or any desired other ordered alphabet.

```
block KWIC [ALPH:: SORDER]
    uses (NAT,LIST,SET) of CONSTRUCTIONS

WORD = LIST[ALPH] renamed by [list is word] extended by
    relns >_: word,word, ordered: word      <* lexicographic *>

    vars e,e': elt, w,w': word
    axioms e > nil, ew > e'w' iff (e > e' or (e == e' and w > w'))
        ordered(nil), ordered(e)
        ordered(ee'w) iff e' > e and ordered(e'w)     endcl

view WORD as SORDER by [elt is word] endview
        <* here it must be proved that lexicographic order is simple *>


cluster TITLE
        uses NAT,WORD,LIST
        sorts title
        ops shift: title -> title (hidden), rot: title,nat -> title

        rep title by LIST[WORD]

        vars w: word, t: title
        eqns shift(nil) = nil, shift(wt) = tw
            rot(t,0) = t, rot(t,inc(k)) = shift(rot(t,k))     endcl


cluster INDEX
        uses WORD,TITLE,SET,LIST
        sorts titlset,nsigset,index
        ops index: titlset,nsigset -> index

        rep titlset by SET[TITLE] and nsigset by SET[WORD]
                and index by LIST[TITLE]

        axioms ordered(index(ts,ns))
            t in index(ts,ns) iff ((∃t',k) t' in ts and t == rot(t',k))
                and not first(t) in ns     endcl

endblock KWIC
```

REFERENCES

[Goguen & Burstall 80]
  Goguen, J. A. and Burstall, R. M.
  An Ordinary Design.
  Technical Report, SRI International, 1980.
  Draft report.

[Goguen 81]
  Goguen, J. A.
  ORDINARY Specification of Some Construction in Plane Geometry.
  In Staunstrup, J., editor, Proceedings, Workshop on Program
    Specification, . Springer-Verlag, 1981.
  to appear in Lecture Notes in Computer Science.

Example 3: Communication Network

Consider a computer network consisting of a number of nodes. Each node
can communicate with a subset of the other nodes. The program to be
specified is the collection of subprograms (one in each node) which makes
the communication possible. The only entity which can be communicated
is a packet. Each packet contains a destination which is an identification
of one of the nodes. When a packet arrives at its destination it must be
consumed and it disappears from the net. The nodes can receive packets
from other nodes, these packets must either be consumed or sent to other
nodes (not necessarily the destination node). All nodes have a description
of the underlying graph. Connections are not changed dynamically. You
are free to choose a suitable representation of this description.

Leif Sandegaard Nielsen
Computer Science Department
Aarhus University

This paper describes two different communication networks.
Both specifications may be used as the basis for programming
the solution in an available programming language.

The first Path Processes specification [Sandegaard Nielsen 1981]
describes a computer network with n node processes. A packet
is described by a record type "message" with a destination
field "to". A packet is transferred as a value parameter when
a process calls an entry-operation "put" in another process
and the other process allows the execution by an operation
permission. If the receiving node is the destination of the
packet it is consumed else a route-table is used to map the
destination identification into the identification of the next
node on the route towards the destination node.

The packets are produced outside the described system and
entered from a producer process by its execution of an external operation call "nodei.put(m)". A synchronous communication
between the two partner processes is the result.

```
(PROCESS nodei(route: routeable)
(* OPERATION PART *)
ENTRY-OP put(IN m: message) END
OP consume(IN m: message) ... END

(* CONTROL PART*)
VAR
  m: message
  next: 1..n
```

```
      PATH (put=>m;   (* operation permission *)
            (m.to=i → consume(m)   (* local operation call *)
            □ m.to<>i → next:= route[m.to];   (* or *)
                ((next=j → nodej.put(m) □) j=1..n)
                                    (* external operation call *)
            )
        )*   (* repetition *)
  END
  END □) i=1..n
```

The macro notation can be expanded statically.

The control part describes the restrictions on the sequence
of actions of the process by a regular expression in conditional statements.

In this case each process behave in a very restrictive way.
One packet at a time is received and managed. A cycle of processes may deadlock if all processes simultaneously call the
entry-operation of the next process in the cycle. The net topology given by the route-tables or the actual flow of packets
must exclude this possibility.

The second specification:

```
    (PROCESS nodei(route: routeable)
    (* OPERATION PART *)
    VAR
      q: sequence(max) of message;
                (* a bounded queue of messages *)

    ENTRY-OP put(IN m: message)
      q.insert(m)
    END

    OP get(OUT m: message)
      q.remove(m)
    END
```

```
        OP consume(IN m:message) ... END


    (* CONTROL PART *)
    VAR
      m: message
      next: 1..n

    PATH (put.r-get.r<max → put )* END
    PATH (put.r-get.r>0 → get(m);
              (m.to=i → consume(m)
              □ m.to<>i   next:= route[m.to];
                          ((next=j → nodej.put(m) □) j=1..n)
              )
         )*
    END
    END "nodei" □) i=1..n
```

In the second specification of the computer network each process has a queue of packets.When a packet is removed from the
queue it is either consumed or forwarded. But in the last case
the process alternatively allows a new execution of "put".

Each operation "op" has a return counter "op.r" (number of
completed executions).

The control part consists of two paths. The meaning is given
by the graph:

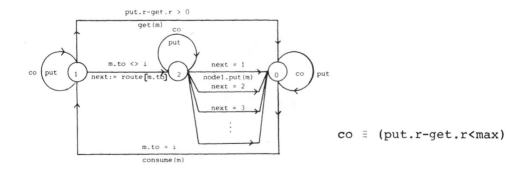

$$co \equiv (put.r-get.r<max)$$

The nodes represent the states and the arcs represent the
actions. To choose an action the condition on the arc has to
be true. If the action is an external operation call
(e.g. "node1.put(m)") or an operation permission (e.g. "put")
there must be a partner willing to do the corresponding communication action. In state 2 above the process either accepts
a "put" (if the queue is not full) or does an external call.
The process waits in state 2 until a partner process is willing
to do the communication. With the bounded queues it is still
possible that a part of the system may deadlock.

Reference
[1] Concurrency, Leif Sandegaard Nielsen (these proceedings)

Ib Holm Sørensen

Programming Research Group, Oxford University

1. INTRODUCTION.

This paper gives a formal specification of a *COMMUNICATION NETWORK*. This example illustrates an approach developed for specifying systems consisting of several independent process components.

Formal methods for developing systems which consist of modules running in isolation and having well-defined starting and stopping points are fairly well understood. These methods, in which modules can be described as mathematical functions, cannot, however, be employed in the development of systems which consist of several interacting autonomous process-components (i.e *distributed systems*). The 'function' computed by a subcomponent in such a system can at any point in time be *interrupted* and influenced by non-deterministically occurring stimuli from the environment or from other concurrently executing process-components. The component itself may interfere with computations within other components depending on some non local information.

The complexity of such systems necessitates the development of alternative formal methods. The aim of the research leading to the methods which is illustrated in this paper is to contribute to this development by providing tools for specifying, analysing and refining the designs of distributed systems.

Specifications of a system include a description of an abstract state-space and a description of the transformations of that state. The state is constrained by axioms. These constraints proscribe those 'abstract' tranformations which would violate the axioms, and allow (by definition) those which would not. In other words, an operational model in which the transformations may or may not occur whenever sufficient pre-conditions are met can be derived from the description of the abstract state and the constraints. The approach, for specifying distributed systems, presented in this paper allows for systems behaviour to be investigated using such an operational model for describing *non-deterministic systems*. Such systems are described in terms of constraints on the communications which may occur across a set of interfaces (i.e. connections). The constraints are imposed by axioms involving the *past history of communications* along one or more of the connections. A communication history along a single connection is modelled as a *sequence*.

123

The specification of a distributed system provides enough information for a non-deterministic model of the its behavior to be defined and analysed Furthermore, the inside of each process-component (an object between a set of interfaces) can be constructed from the the axioms which constrain the activities along its own *external interfaces*.

The set theoretical notation used in this paper is described informally in [1]. A complete description of the approach for specifying distributed systems which in this paper is applied to a communication network can be found in [2].

2. A COMMUNICATION NETWORK.

In this paper a specification of a communication network will be developed. The design decisions taken will be formally stated and motivated. A formal description of the behaviour of a single station (node) will be given, as well as a description of the static properties of the network as a whole. These descriptions will be used to verify that the *global behaviour* of a network, which consists of stations whose *local behaviour* complies with the given specification, agrees with some independently stated *rules* for networks.

2.1 A Discussion of a Communication Network.

A *NETWORK* consists of a collection of *STATIONS*. In this formal description the set of stations will be denoted by-

St

The value which is communicated over the NETWORK is called a *PACKET*. Packets are denoted by-

Pk

All packets have a *SOURCE* station and a *DESTINATION* station-

source, dest : Pk → St

Example:
Consider the network illustrated in Figure (1) consisting of five stations.

{ 1, 2, 3, 4, 5 }

FIGURE (1)

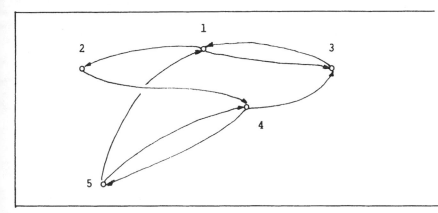

Given a set of packets,

            { a, b, c }

We might have,

            source = { (a,1), (b,5), (c,2) }
            dest   = { (a,5), (b,3), (c,5) }

The set of packets which originates in station i is

            $source^{-1}(\{i\})$

The set of packets which can be consumed by i is

            $dest^{-1}(\{i\})$

For the example above we get,

            $source^{-1}(\{1\})$ = {a}
            $dest^{-1}(\{5\})$ = {a,c}

Let us first formalise some obvious properties for stations in a network.

Stations either *consume* or *transmit* packets. In order to formalise this statement in our framework we introduce the *history* of the input performed by each station—

            In : **St** → seq[**Pk**]

and a *history* of the output performed by each station—

            Out: **St** → seq[**Pk**]

The output from station i, $\mathrm{Out}(i)$, will be written Out_i; similarly for In.
We can now state some requirements for the behaviour of a station.

a) Only packets originating in (or previously received by) a station can be transmitted along the outgoing connections for that station. We have–

$$(\forall\ i\!:\!St)\ (\mathrm{ran}(\mathrm{Out}_i)\ \subseteq\ \mathrm{source}^{-1}(\{i\})\ \cup\ \mathrm{ran}(\mathrm{In}_i))$$

b) A packet arriving at its destination must be consumed– i.e. it must not be retransmitted, therefore we strengthen a)

$$(\forall\ i\!:\!St)$$
$$(\mathrm{ran}(\mathrm{Out}_i)\ \subseteq\ (\mathrm{source}^{-1}(\{i\})\ \cup\ \mathrm{ran}(\mathrm{In}_i))\ -\ \mathrm{dest}^{-1}(\{i\}))\qquad \text{DEF }(2)$$

c) If we assume that packets are distinguishable– the fact that no packet can be transmitted from a particular station more than once can be formalised–

$$(\forall\ i\!:\!St)(\ \mathrm{Out}_i^{-1}\ \epsilon\ \mathbf{Pk}\ \twoheadrightarrow\ \mathbf{N}\ )\qquad\qquad\qquad \text{DEF }(3)$$

b) and c) record the decisions taken with respect to the behaviour of a station, ignoring the fact it may have several *input channels* and several *output channels*. We may say that a station's behaviour is like the behaviour of an *unlimited unordered buffer*, i.e. a station will always accept incoming packets, but these packets may be stored for later transmission. Such a system is called a *store and forward* system.

Alternative designs will be discussed below:

1) Limited buffering capacity.

In order to describe stations with limited buffering capacity we might have added the invariant, (for some limit L),

$$(\forall\ i\!:\!St)\ (\ \mathrm{card}(\ \mathrm{ran}(\mathrm{In}_i)\ -\ \mathrm{dest}^{-1}(\{i\})\ )\ )\ -\ \mathrm{card}(\mathrm{Out}_i)\ \leqslant\ L)$$

However, a limit on the buffer-store for a station in a network may cause the network to deadlock.

2) Scheduling.

No policy for scheduling the outgoing packets has been suggested. Hence we allow for the possibility of *unfair scheduling* where a packet within a station may be *starved* (overtaken by other packets an unreasonable number of times).

A *FIFO* scheduling might be described as follows:

For a *relay-station* i where

$$dest^{-1}(\{i\}) = source^{-1}(\{i\}) = \{\}$$

a *FIFO* ordering could be imposed as usual by requiring that the history sequence describing the output is a *prefix* of the sequence describing the input, i.e.

$$Out_i \subseteq In_i$$

For a *terminal-station* i , where

$$dest^{-1}(\{i\}) \neq \{\} \quad \vee \quad source^{-1}(\{i\}) \neq \{\}$$

the *ordering* axiom could be expressed as follows:

$$ignore(source^{-1}(\{i\}))(Out_i) \subseteq ignore(dest^{-1}(\{i\}))(In_i)$$

where

$$ignore[X] : \mathbb{P}(X) \to seq[X] \to seq[X]$$

is defined such that

$$(\forall\ S:\mathbb{P}(X);\ s:seq[X])$$
$$ran(ignore(S)(s)) = ran(s) - S \quad \wedge$$
$$(\exists\ f:Monotone)\ (ignore(S)(s) = s \bullet f)$$
where
$$Monotone = \{f:\mathbb{N}\nrightarrow\mathbb{N}\ |\ (\forall x,y:\mathbb{N})\ x\leqslant y \implies f(x)\leqslant f(y)\}$$

NB ignore removes elements from a sequence. The result is a new sequence where the order of the remaining elements is the same as the ordering between these elements in the original sequence, e.g.

$$ignore(\{a,c\})(\langle a\ b\ c\ d\ e\rangle) = \langle b\ d\ e\rangle$$

A *FIFO* scheduling policy could cause unnecessary runtime delays, because the station to which a scheduled packet is to be transmitted could be temporarily engaged in other communications. For these reasons we will not impose a *FIFO* scheduling policy.

DEF(2) and DEF(3) gave some dynamic properties for a station, without any reference to the topology of the network, i.e. so far we have only described a collection of dis-connected stations-

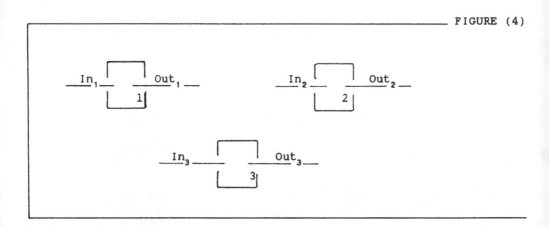

FIGURE (4)

The connections between the individual stations are described by:

$$\text{Network} \quad : \text{St} \leftrightarrow \text{St}$$

where we assume that the number of connections is finite, i.e.

$$\text{Network} \quad \epsilon \; \mathbb{F}(\; \text{St} \times \text{St} \;)$$

hence we might get:

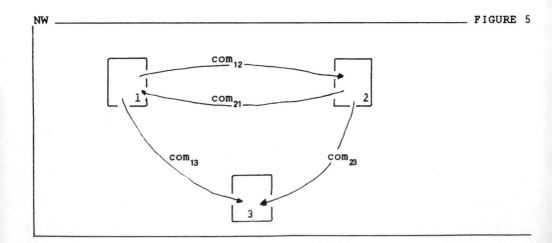

NW ——————————————————————————————— FIGURE 5

128

When packets are sent along the connections of the network, the information which changes is:

Communication_between : **St** × **St** -→ seq[**Pk**]   **where**
dom(Communication_between) = Network

that is, when a packet is sent from station i to station j, the *history sequence*

Communication_between(i,j)

will be extended.

Let com$_{ij}$ denote (as in F IGURE(5)) the

Communication_between(i,j)

The correct behaviour of a station depends on its capability to transmit each packet along a proper connection. We will in what follows discuss two possibilities for proper routing of packets.

a) A packet should not be sent to a station from which the packet's destination cannot be reached, i.e.

($\forall$ i,j:**St** | (i,j) $\in$ Network)
    ($\forall$ p:**Pk** | p $\in$ ran(com$_{ij}$)) (j,dest(p)) $\in$ Network*

NB Network* is a description of the stations which are connected through the network.
(* is the transitive closure operator see [1] section 4).

The axiom above does not prevent a packet from 'entering a loop' or 'traveling' erratically round the network without ever reaching its destination. We therefore strengthen the axiom:

($\forall$ i,j:**St** | (i,j) $\in$ Network)
    ($\forall$ p:**Pk** | p $\in$ ran(com$_{ij}$))
        ((j, dest(p)) $\in$ Network* $\wedge$
          distance(Network)(j,dest(p)) <
          distance(Network)(i,dest(p))   )
    where

$$\text{distance} \; : \; (X \leftrightarrow X) \; \rightarrow \; (X \times X \nrightarrow \mathbb{N})$$

is defined such that

$$(\forall \; r \; : \; X \leftrightarrow X)$$
$$(\forall i,j:X| \; (i,j) \in r^*)$$
$$(\; \text{distance}(r)(i,j) = \min\{n:\mathbb{N} \; | \; (i,j) \in r^n\} \;)$$

This condition insures that all packets visit a finite number of stations, and travel along a route of minimal length.

b) Condition a) does not allow a station to send a packet along a connection which is not on the shortest route for that packet. The following specification allows a station to choose a longer but possibly faster route. It is still guaranteed that all packets will reach their destinations in a finite number of steps.

We first formalise the concept of a proper route for a packet, which is a route within the network where no station is visited more than once, hence

$$\text{proper\_routes} \; : \; (X \leftrightarrow X) \; \rightarrow \; \mathbb{P}(\text{seq}[X])$$

where

$$(\forall \; r \; : \; X \leftrightarrow X \;)$$
$$\text{proper\_routes}(r) = \{rt:\text{seq}[X] \; | \; \text{next}(rt) \; \subseteq r; \; rt^{-1} \in X \nrightarrow \mathbb{N} \; \}$$

NB next is defined in [1] section 4.

for the network illustrated in FIGURE(5) we have:

$\langle 1 \; 2 \; 3 \rangle \quad \in \text{proper\_routes}(NW)$

$\langle 1 \; 3 \rangle \qquad \in \text{proper\_routes}(NW)$

$\langle 3 \; 1 \rangle \qquad \notin \text{proper\_routes}(NW)$

$\langle 1 \; 2 \; 1 \; 3 \rangle \notin \text{proper\_routes}(NW)$

The requirements for a packet router for the network,

$$\text{Packet\_router} \; : \; \mathbf{Pk} \nrightarrow \text{seq}[\mathbf{St}]$$

can now be formalised:

All routes are proper routes:

$$ran(Packet\_router) \subseteq proper\_routes[St](Network)$$

Exactly the packets which can reach their destination from their source can be given a route by the router:

$$dom(Packet\_router) = \{p:\textbf{Pk} \mid (source(p),dest(p)) \in Network^*) \}$$

A route for a packet 'starts' at its source and 'ends' at its destination:

$$dest = last \circ Packet\_router$$
$$source = first \circ Packet\_router$$

NB. separate packets sent between the same source and destination may take (or be given) different routes.

The use of output channels is determined by the packet router in the following way:

$$(\forall\ i\ :\ \textbf{St}\ )$$
$$(\forall\ j:\textbf{St}\ \mid\ (i,j) \in Network)$$
$$(\forall\ p:\textbf{Pk}\ \mid\ p \in ran(com_{ij})\ )$$
$$(i,j)\ \in\ next(Packet\_router(p))$$

2.2. A SPECIFICATION OF A NETWORK.

The decisions taken in the previous section will be summarised in this section, using the schema notation introduced in [1].

The *static* properties of the network presented are described below.
A description of source and destination (introduced above) is no longer necessary as the source and destination of packets are the first and the last stations along their route. Packets are all the packets ever processed by the Network, hence we must require that at least these packets have a route within the network. Start_in gives for each station the set of packets originating in that station. Previously we used the *inverse* of the source function to describe these packets.

```
    Network        : F(St × St) ;
    Packet_router  : Pk  ⇸ seq[St] ;
    Packets        : P(Pk) ;
    Start_in       : St  ⇸  P(Pk)
  _____

    ran(Packet_router) ⊆ proper_routes(Network);
    Packets ⊆ dom(Packet_router);
    Start_in = (first ∘ Packet_router)⁻¹   ◁ Packets
```

The *dynamic* properties are described in the schema NETWORK. The properties are described in terms of *invariant conditions* on the histories of the communications between the stations. Axioms (2) and (3) are substituted for the axioms DEF(2) and DEF(3) respectively; they have been simplified as the Packet_router, axiom (4), insures that–

a) a packet cannot 'leave' its destination,

b) a packet can 'leave' a station along only one outgoing connection.

NETWORK _____ St   Pk

```
    com  :  (St  × St)  ⇸  seq[Pk]
  _____

    dom(com)    = Network;                                      (1)
    (∀ i : St )
    (∀ j : St  | (i,j) ∈ Network )
       ( ran(com(i,j)) ⊆ Start_in(i) ∪ IN(i) ∧                  (2)
           com(i,j)⁻¹    ∈ Pk ⇸ N              ∧                (3)
           ((∀ p:Pk  | p ∈ ran(com(i,j)) )
                   (i,j) ∈ next(Packet_router(p))   ))           (4)
       where   IN(i) = ∪{ran(com(k,i) | k : Network⁻¹({i})}
```

The initial state of a network system is a system where no communication has taken place–

INITIAL_NW _____ St   Pk

```
    NETWORK[St, Pk]
  _____

    (∀ (i,j): St  × St  | (i,j) ∈ Network) (com(i,j) =⟨⟩)
```

The final state of a network system is a system where all packets have reached their destination-

<pre>
FINAL_NW _____ St Pk _____
|
| NETWORK[St, Pk]
| _____
|
| (∀ i:St | i ∈ dom(Network))
| (∀ p:Pk | p ∈ (Start_in(i) ∪ IN(i)) - OUT(i))
| (i = last(Packet_router(p)))
| where   IN(i) = ∪{ran(com(k,i) | k : Network⁻¹({i})}
| and   OUT(i) = ∪{ran(com(i,j) | j : Network({i})}
|
</pre>

2.3. AN ANALYSIS OF THE NETWORK.

The given network will be analysed with respect to *termination* and *deadlock*.
Under the assumption that a finite number of packets are being 'submitted' to the network system, i.e.

$$Packets \in F(Pk) ,$$

we will verify that
1) The operations of the system cease after the occurence of a finite number of communications (*termination*).
2) The network system only terminates in an acceptable final state – as described in FINAL-NW (*deadlock-free*).

2.3.1. Termination.

Termination is guaranteed if we can present a *decreasing variant function*.
A communication between station i and station j can be described as-

<pre>
Observations _____ Pk _____
|
| OBS_ij : Pk → {NETWORK} ⇸ {NETWORK}
| _____
|
| OBS_ij = (λ p:Pk) (λNETWORK)(μ NETWORK')
| (com' = com ⊕ {(i,j) → com(i,j) * ⟨p⟩})
|
</pre>

NB. (⊕) is the *function overriding* operator.

According to the definition above a communication will *increase* the length of the *history* of the communications along a single connection. Therefore the following function must be an *increasing variant function* –

```
Vl   : {NETWORK} → N
Vl   = (λ NETWORK) (Sigma(com, card • ran) )
```

where Sigma is defined as

$$X$$

```
   Sigma  : (F(X) × (X↦N)) ↠ N

   (∀ s:F(X); f:X↦N | s ⊆ dom(f); s ≠ {})
      Sigma(s,f) = f(τ(s)) + Sigma(s-{τ(s)},f)
      Sigma({},f) = 0
```

According to axiom (3) of NETWORK a packet can appear only once along any connection, hence

```
(∀ nw:NETWORK)   Vl(nw) ⩽ card(Packets)*card(Network)
```

Therefore the following function is a *decreasing variant function*–

```
V   : {NETWORK} → N
V = (λ nw:NETWORK) ((card(Packets)*card(Network)) - Vl(nw))
```

NB, in a termination state 's' we do not guarantee that V(s) = 0̄.

2.3.2. Deadlock.

We can describe the activity along channel (i,j) as follows:

$$Pk$$

```
   activity_along_{ij}  : {NETWORK} ↔ {NETWORK}

   activity_along_{ij}  = ∪{ OBS_{ij}(p) | p : Pk}
```

A termination state of a network is a state where no activity can take place, and can be described as:

Terminal : $\mathbb{P}(\{NETWORK\})$

Terminal =
$\{NETWORK\} - \cup\{dom(activity\_along_{ij})|(i,j) : Network\}$

A system is *deadlock-free* if it only terminates in acceptable final states.

For this network system we have:

$\vdash$ Terminal $\subseteq$ $\{FINAL\_NW\}$

The proof of THEOREM(7) is directly derivable from LEMMA(9) and LEMMA(10)

We first describe the states of the network in which a communication is expected to take place.

$$\textbf{Pk}$$
—— LEMMA (8)

$\vdash$ $dom(activity\_along_{ij})$ =
   $\{NETWORK \mid (\exists~p:\textbf{Pk})$
                $(p~\in~(Start\_in(i)\cup IN(i))-OUT(i))~\wedge$
                $(i,j)~\in~next(Packet\_router(p))~\}$

$\vdash$ $\cup\{dom(activity\_along_{ij}) \mid (i,j) : Network\}$ =
   $\{NETWORK \mid (\exists~p:\textbf{Pk})~(\exists~(i,j):Network)$
                $(p \in (Start\_in(i)\cup IN(i))-OUT(i))~\wedge$
                $(i,j)~\in~next(Packet\_router(p))~\}$

NB the functions IN and OUT are defined as in FINAL_NW.

LEMMA(9) describes the termination states:

```
                                                          _____ LEMMA (9)
 ⊢   Terminal =
        {NETWORK | (∀ (i,j):Network) (∀ p:Pk)
                       (p ∉ (Start_in(i)∪IN(i))-OUT(i)) ∨
                       (i,j) ∉ next(Packet_router(p))   }
```

LEMMA(10) states that a *termination* state is an *acceptable final* state.

```
                                                          _____ LEMMA (10)
     NETWORK;
     (∀ (i,j):Network)
      (∀ p:Pk)
      (p     ∉ (Start_in(i)∪IN(i))-OUT(i) )   ∨
      (i,j) ∉ next(Packet_router(p))
     ⊢  FINAL_NW
```

proof:

```
     (∀ i:St | i ∈ dom(Network))
        (∀·p:Pk | p ∈ (Start_in(i)∪IN(i)) - OUT(i) )
           (∀ j:St | (i,j) ∈ Network)
     we deduce from the hypothesis
(1)              (i,j) ∉ next(Packet_router(p))
     as p is 'within' the buffer, we conclude
(2)              i ∈ ran(Packet_router(p))
     from (1) , (2) we get
(3)              i = last(Packet_router(p))
     which according to the definition FINAL_NW completes the proof
```

List of References.

[1]   I.H. Sørensen:
      'A Specification Language'
      Included paper.

[2]   I.H. Sørensen:
      'Specification and design of Distributed Systems'
      D.Phil Thesis from the University of Oxford, September 1981.

CHAPTER 5

Submitted Papers

PARTIAL CORRECTNESS OF DISTRIBUTED PROGRAMS

D. Coleman[*] & R.M. Gallimore

Department of Computation

UMIST

Manchester

ENGLAND

ABSTRACT

This paper presents a notation and proof system for distributed programs. A distributed program comprises a network of communicating processes whose execution may proceed concurrently. Processes communicate via named uni-directional streams. Processes are characterised in terms of their externally observable behaviour, that is by the way their communication activities affect the sequences of values transmitted by their input and output streams. By considering only processes whose overall effect on each stream is deterministic, the externally observable behaviour of a process may be specified as a set of sequence transforming functions. The proof system deals with partial correctness and proofs are purposely limited to showing consistency with a functional specification. The approach is distinguished by the ability to prove the partial correctness of processes in isolation and the properties of networks of processes using Hoare style proof rule. An example illustrates the use of the technique.

---

[*]
This work was undertaken by the authors while D. Coleman
was un study leave at the University of California, Berkeley

1. INTRODUCTION

This paper studies the verification of distributed programs constructed as networks of communicating processes.

For distributed programs there are at least three aspects of program correctness. A proof of partial correctness shows that as long as a distributed program terminates cleanly then it computes the desired function. In addition a termination proof may be required for each process. It is also necessary to show that the communication between processes is correctly synchronised and that the system is free from potential deadlock.

Proof systems [1,5] have been proposed for distributed programs based on Hoare's CSP notation [3]. In CSP communication between processes is also used as the means of inter-process synchronisation. This results in a simple and elegant model of distributed computation. As a consequence however the proof systems in [1,5] must employ a co-operation proof, in addition to proofs about individual processes to establish the partial correctness of a program. In [5] auxiliary variables are introduced into the program text and proofs to help describe global relations by relating the program variables of one process to program variables of another. Unfortunately this results in the need for additional non-interference proofs between processes [6].

In this paper we consider the partial correctness of distributed programs based on the process network model of [4] but extended to allow non-determinism into the control structures of sequential processes. The following section defines the programming notation used. The explanation given is informal and operational in character and only the distributed skeleton of the language is described.

Section three defines the axioms and proof rules for
the constructs of the programming notation. By employing
axioms for input and output commands that make reference to
the sequences of values transmitted by named streams it is
possible to prove the partial correctness of processes in
isolation. The properties of interconnections of processes may
be inferred using a Hoare proof rule for network commands.
An example is introduced to illustrate the approach in proving
a program consistent with a mathematically defined specification
function. This example also illustrates the relationship
between program proof and the design method employed in [2]
in which the specification of a (distributed) program and proofs
of its properties are produced by stepwise refinement.

2.   DISTRIBUTED PROGRAMS

2.1   Programming Concepts

Informally we regard a program as a network of processes
which communicate via streams, as shown in figure 1, where nodes
represent processes and arcs represent streams [4]. It is
assumed that processes may proceed concurrently.

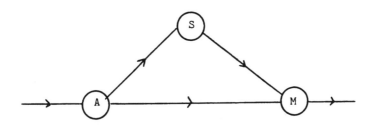

Figure 1:   a process network

Processes are independent and self contained units,
which may themselves be process networks or purely sequential.
In the final analysis however every terminating process network
is constructed from terminating sequential processes. Processes
communicate via streams. Operationally streams are undirectional
channels of unlimited capacity from a unique producer process
to a single consumer process. Streams are typed by the alphabet
of data items that may appear in them. A data-item type is a
record structure with an identifiable kind. Since streams have
unbounded capacity there is no synchronisation implicit between
the corresponding input and output commands in different
processes.

We have adopted a functional notation for the description
of process networks. Simultaneous stream equations define the
output streams of a process to be the functional application
of a process to its input streams. Any network can be conveniently
described by a set of such stream equations together with
functional composition.

(a)    $[(o) = Q(P(i))]$

(b)

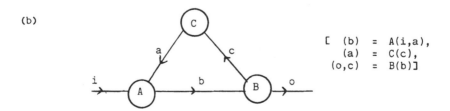

$$[(b) = A(i,a),$$
$$(a) = C(c),$$
$$(o,c) = B(b)]$$

Figure 2:   process networks and network commands

No special operators are necessary, nor we believe desirable, to describe process networks.

We use a non-deterministic CSP like notation for sequential processes   [3].   Although it is not essential, non-determinism permits an elegant description of stream processing algorithms. Our model of processing and streams makes necessary a number of differences with CSP itself. Apart from the absence of synchronous message passing the most important differences are

a) input and output takes place on the stream parameters of a
   process rather than named processes

b) input commands may test the value as well as the kind of a
   data item

c) processes may have local procedures which take the form
   of named guarded commands

d) a process may execute in parallel with a local process
   network, communicating with it via privately declared
   streams.

2.2   Programming Notation

In this section we briefly introduce the language features together with an informal, operational semantics.

2.2.1 Stream Alphabets and Data Items

A stream alphabet declaration defines the set of values that may be input from or output to a stream using that alphabet. An alphabet is defined using a list of data item definitions, where each definition specifies a distinct data item kind and the values associated with that kind. For example

alphabet integer.sequence = num (:integer), eos

specifies that only values of kind num or eos may appear in a stream based on the integer.sequence alphabet. A data item value of kind num has an associated integer component value.

The value of a data item is defined by its kind and an
ordered list of n(≥0) typed components. A stream may only
transmit values belonging to a single alphabet.

2.2.2 Skip and Assignment Commands

skip :   skip

A skip command has no effect and cannot fail.

assignment :   x := e

An assignment command causes the expression e to be evaluated
using the current values of the variables; this value is then
assigned to the variable x on the right hand side. An expression
is undefined if any of its variables is undefined; an undefined
expression causes the assignment statement to fail.

2.2.3 Input Command

input command :   in? : k

                 or in? x : k

                 or in? x : k[b]

An input command requests the input of a data-item tagged with
a specific kind, k, from an input stream, in. The kind must
be contained in the alphabet defined for that stream. A variable
of the appropriate type must be specified for each component
of the data item. If execution succeeds the component values are
assigned to these variables. A successful input command thus
affects both the internal state of the containing process and
the state of a stream.

An input command may be qualified by a boolean expression
involving the variables named in the input command. The boolean
expression is evaluated using the state of the variables that
would exist if execution of the input command succeeded. The
input command will succeed if and only if, the boolean expression
evaluates to true.

Unlike CSP synchronisation with a corresponding output command is not specified. The evaluation of an input command on an empty stream is delayed until the stream becomes non-empty.

Examples:

    input? : eos

    input? i : num

    input? j : num[j < max]

2.2.4 Output Command

    output command :   out! : k

                        out! $(e_1 \ldots e_n)$: k

Execution of an output command sends a data item to an output stream. The output command gives the kind of the data item and the values of the components of the data item (if any) are obtained by evaluating the corresponding n-tuple of expressions $(n \geq 0)$.

The output command fails if (i) the stream alphabet does not include items of the kind specified or (ii) any of the expressions evaluates to undefined or (iii) if there is a type conflict between any of the expressions and the corresponding component of the data-item.

Examples:

    out! : eos

    out! (j+20) : num

2.2.5 Alternative and Repetitive Commands

Alternative and repetitive commands are formed from sets of guarded commands.

<guarded command> ::= <guard> → <command list>

                        |

                        <implicit guarded command>

144

A guard b;c consists of boolean expressions $b \equiv b_1; \ldots.;b_n$ $(n \geq 0)$
and an input command c(optional if $n > 0$). An implicit guarded
command takes the form of a procedure call (followed by an optional
command list); its guard is that of the body of the called
procedure. A guard is executed by execution of its constituent
elements from left to right. A guarded command is executed only
if and when the execution of its guard does not fail. A guard
fails if any of the constituent boolean expressions evaluate
to false or undefined or the input command fails. An implicit
guarded command fails if the procedure call fails.

Example:

       count > 0; in? : pop → rest! : pop;

                               count := count-1

alternative command : (guarded command$_1$ ▌.....▌ guarded command$_n$)

       An alternative command specifies the execution of exactly
one of its guarded commands. Any guarded command whose guard
evaluates successfully may be chosen. An alternative command
fails if all its guards fail or if the selected guarded command
fails.

Example: ($j \leq k$ → max := k ▌ k < j → max := j)

Failure of all the guards of an alternative can be avoided by the inclusion
of an otherwise alternative as the last alternative:
($x \geq 0$;y > 0 → divide(x,y|quot,rem) ▌ otherwise → divide.error)
The otherwise guard evaluates successfully if and only if all the
other guards fail.

repetitive command: *(guarded command$_1$ ▌ ... ▌guarded command$_n$)
A repetitive command specifies that its constituent alternative command
should be executed as many times as possible. A repetitive command

terminates when all the guards of all the guarded commands fail simultaneously. Failure of an alternative command causes the program to be aborted, whereas failure of a repetitive command causes control to pass on to the next command in the containing process

Example: *(in? j : num[j > min] → out! j :: num ∎

            in? j : num[j ≤ min] → skip)

           input a sequence of num data-items from in,

           and outputs to out all those whose value exceeds

           min.

2.2.6 Procedure and Procedure Call

    procedure declaration: procedure id(input parameters|output parameters)

                   begin

                     g

                   end;

A procedure id is local to the process in which it is declared. A procedure defines a parameterised guarded command. A procedure may read or change the value of its output parameters, it may only read its input parameters.

Example: procedure div (x,y:integer|quotient,remainder:integer);

       begin

         x ≥ 0 and y > 0 → quotient := 0;

                        remainder := x;

                        *(remainder ≥ y → remainder := remainder -y;

                                     quotient := quotient +1)

       end;

This procedure can be called to perform integer division for non-negative x and positive y.

<u>procedure call :</u> proc-id (actual input parameters|actual output parameters);

      The actual parameters of a procedure call must correspond in number and type with the formal parameters of the procedure declaration. Input parameters are called by value, output parameters are called by reference. Execution of a procedure call produces the effect of executing the guarded command of the body with the appropriate parameter substitution.

<u>Example:</u> (div(x,y|quot,rem) ▌otherwise → divide.error);

2.2.7 <u>Processes</u>

      A process is an autonomous, self contained program unit, with its own local variables and procedures. The execution of a process is called an instance of a process. Process instances are created by the execution of a network command. A process instance terminates when the command list of the process body terminates.

      The network command initiating a process instance supplies actual parameters to be substituted for formal parameters identified in the heading of the process's declaration. A parameter to a process may be

  (i) <u>constant parameter</u> creating a synonym for the value of the corresponding actual parameter supplied when an instance is created.

 (ii) <u>input stream parameter</u> the corresponding actual parameter can be input from but not output to.

(iii) <u>output stream parameter</u>   the corresponding actual parameter can be output to but not input from.

Actual and formal stream parameters must use the same alphabet. It is possible for a process to both input from and output to the same stream if that stream is supplied as both an actual input stream and actual output stream parameter ("aliasing").

Example:

```
alphabet rotn  =  word(:alfa); eos

process rotate (in:seq rotn) ⇒ (out:seq rotn);

begin

   (in? : eos → out! : eos

   ▌

    in? w:word → *(in? x:word → out! x:word);

                out! w:word;

                in? : eos;

                out! : eos

   )

end;
```

Rotate consumes a sequence of words terminated by an eos and outputs
a cyclic shift of the words similarly terminated.

2.2.8 Network command

A network command denotes a network of processes by a set of
stream equations

network command : $[(\overline{0}_1) = e_1$

$$(\overline{0}_2) = e_2$$

$$\vdots$$

$$(\overline{0}_n) = e_n]$$

The notation $\overline{x}$ represents the vector $x_1, x_2 \ldots, x_n$

The stream equations of the network command denote the subnetworks
from which the network is built.

The streams on the left hand side of a stream equation specify
the output streams of the subnetwork, those appearing on the right
are the input streams. The right hand side of a stream equation
specifies the structure of the subnetwork. Input streams of a
subnetwork are connected to a process by functional application of the

process name to the streams. The output streams of a subnetwork
are connected to the output streams of the outermost process of
the right hand side stream expression. Functional composition
of two processes denotes the connection of the output streams of
the inner process to the input streams of the outer.

A set of stream equations in which a stream is both an input
and output stream denotes a cyclic subnetwork.

Subnetworks are connected together by using the output
stream of one subnetwork as an input stream to the other.

The streams in a network command are either input, output
or intermediate streams. Each <u>input</u> stream appears exactly
once as the input stream of some stream equation. Each <u>output</u>
stream appears exactly once as the output stream of some stream
equation. Each intermediate stream appears once as an output stream
of a stream equation and once as an input stream of a stream equation.
An intermediate stream has the initial value empty. The input and
output streams of a network must be the input and output streams of
the issuing process or program. The alphabet used by a stream is
determined by its context.

Execution of a network command initiates the execution of
all its components processes.

A network command terminates when all the process instances
of the network terminate.

<u>Examples</u>

(1) [(out) = less (integers(|15))]

Execute a pipeline process network in which the output
stream of the process integers (with constant parameter seed value
15) is the input stream to process less. The output stream of
less

is connected to the stream out.

    The two processes may be executed concurrently.

(2)   [(ascend, rem) = sift (input),

       (out)   = merge (ascend, sort(rem))]

    The stream input is processed by sift which sends its output on two streams ascend and rem. The stream rem is processed by sort whose output is "merged" together with stream ascend. The output stream of merge is assigned to the stream out

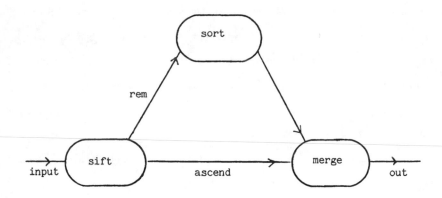

2.2.9 Local Networks

    The execution of a network command allows a process to dynamically reconfigure by invoking a subnetwork of instances of processes. The sub-network communicates with the rest of the system by means of the input and output streams of the host process, whose execution is suspended until the network command terminates. Some problems, such as the implementation of certain abstract data types, may result in the recursive reconfiguration of networks to an unacceptable degree of nesting. In some cases the excessive reconfiguration can be avoided if the host process is able to communicate via privately declared streams to a local subnetwork whose externally observable input-output behaviour is limited to the private streams. The body of the local network command, l, and the local subnetwork may execute concurrently and co-operate in a manner closely modelled by that of systems of co-routines.

local network: local in $\bar{i}$; out $\bar{o}$ [n];

                          begin

                              l

                          end;

The host process may output from within l, to the local out-streams $\bar{o}$, which must only occur as input streams to the local network denoted by [n] . Conversely the host may while executing within l, input values from the local in-streams $\bar{i}$ which may only appear as outputs of the local network. The streams named in the network command [n] may include only members of $\bar{i}$, $\bar{o}$ and intermediate streams ie. a local network can have no global side-effects.

Example:

alphabet rtnseq = word (:alfa); val; die

          rotn   = word (:alfa); eos

process sequence (in:seq rtnseq) ⇒ (out:seq rotn)

begin

  *(in?:val → out!:eos);

  (in? x:word → local in ans:seq rotn; out rest:seq rtnseq

                      [ans = sequence(rest)];

```
                    begin
                *(in?:val → out! x:word;

                        rest!:val;

                        *(ans?z:word → out!z:word);

                        ans?:eos;

                        out!:eos

                    ▌
                    in?w:word → rest!w:word
                    );
                    rest!:die
                end(*local network*)

    ▌

  in?:die → skip

  )

end;
```

Process 'sequence' stores a sequence of words by means of a recursively
defined local network, and outputs the sequence of words in response
to an input data item of kind val. The data item kind die is
introduced to enforce termination of each process in the local network.

2.2.10 Program

A program communicates with the outside world via its source
and sink streams. It may only input from sources and output to
sinks. One program body comprises a network command constructed
from process types and stream alphabets that must have been previously
declared.

```
program rotator (in:seq rotn|output:seq rotn)

const c = "number of rotations"

alphabet rotn = word(:alfa); eos

        rtnseq = word(:alfa); val; die

        rotations = word(:alfa); eor; eos

process sequence (in:seq rtnseq) ⇒ (out:seq rotn);
```

```
        begin

           ⋮

           see section 2.9

        end;

        process rotate (in:seq rotn)  ⇒ (out:seq rotn)

        begin

           ⋮

           see section 2.7

        end

        process nrotations(in:seq rotn|count:integer)  ⇒ (out:seq rotations);

        begin

           (count = 0 → out!:eos

           ▮

             otherwise → local in t:seq rotn; out s:seq rtnseq;

                         [t = sequence(s)];

                         begin

                            *(in?k:word → out!k:word; s!k:word);

                            in?:eos; out!:eor; s!:val;

                            [out = nrotations(rotate(t)|count-1)];

                            s!:die

                         end

           )

        end;

        begin

           [out = nrotations (in|c)]

        end.
```

3.   PROGRAM CORRECTNESS

A complete program may comprise a single sequential process or be composed of networks of component processes which communicate via streams. Each process in a network is similarly defined. This program structure is exploited in the development of a proof of correctness of a distributed program against a functional specification of its intended behaviour. First we present proofs for component processes which we combine as necessary using a Hoare-style proof rule for the network command. Thus we can reason about the partial correctness of a complete program, involving potential concurrency between processes, using a uniform approach. To facilitate this we must provide axioms and proof rules for all constructs used in the construction of processes and programs.

In our model of distributed computation data streams are treated explicitly. Consequently streams involved in input, output and interprocess communication in a distributed program are explicitly declared and identified in the relevant I/O commands. This represents an important distinction from CSP in which input-output commands refer to other process identifiers and the notion of communication channel is implicit in the program text.

Consequently, when we provide assertions which characterize the data sequences transmitted by particular streams, the axioms and proof rules can capture the functional meaning of individual processes considered in isolation from the whole program. It should be noted that our view of streams does not preclude any particular synchronization strategy for inter-process communication. For instance streams can be defined to use simple synchronization in order to make them behave like the capacity free channels of CSP. Alternatively they may operate as asynchronous message buffers of finite and bounded or infinite capacity. These considerations may have profound practical consequences, affect the classes of inputs for which a program will terminate cleanly, and dictate the form and complexity of total correctness proofs. However they do not significantly affect our reasoning about the functional behaviour of programs, i.e. the effect of processes on the state of streams. We require only that streams should transmit data items within finite time and preserve the order of transmission.

3.1. Assertions

An assertion is a boolean valued expression which characterises the relationships among variables at some point in a program. The basic units of assertions are therefore the boolean expressions of the programming notation (in our case the same as Pascal), extended to allow the definition of input and output on streams.

```
<atomic assertions> ::= "boolean expressions using extended variables"
<extended variable> ::= <variable>
                      |
                        <sequence expression>
<sequence expression>::= <stream identifier>
                      |
                        <function designator>
                      |
                        <sequence expression>::<sequence expression>
                      |
                        <data-item>
```

A sequence expression denotes a sequence whose value may be the value of a stream variable, the value of a sequence returning specification function, the concatenation (::) of two sequence expressions or the value of a single data item.

```
<data item> ::= <kind>
              |
                (<kind>,<expression>{,<expression>})
```

A data item value is specified in the usual way by listing its kind and components.

```
<assertion> ::= <atomic assertion>
                |
                <quantified assertion>
                |
                (<assertion><logical connective><assertion>)
                |
                not <assertion>
```

<quantified assertion> :: = $\exists$(<bound variables>) [<assertion>]

<logical connective> := or|and|$\Rightarrow$

<bound variables> ::= <identifier>{,<identifier>}

More complex assertions are built from atomic assertions using the existential quantifier and a subset of the logical connectives of the first order predicate calculus.   A quantified assertion introduces one or more existentially bound variables, whose scope is delimited by brackets [ ].

Whenever no confusion can be caused we abbreviate assertions by omitting brackets and parentheses.

Examples

(1) $\exists n$ [w = 2^n*y and n > 0]

is an abbreviated assertion which is true iff w is a positive power of 2 times y

(2) $\exists a$ [ascend = asc(a) ::(eos)]

The value of the stream ascend can be composed from the concatenation of the value of function asc applied to some sequence a and the data item eos.

[Note: care must be taken in the interpretation of assertions about the sequences of items transmitted by streams in a process network. When a process (network) is viewed in isolation such assertions can be taken as statements about the value of the input streams and output streams of the process (network). However, an assertion cannot make statements about the value of an intermediate stream within a process network since that depends on the temporal behaviour of two or more processes. In reference to an intermediate stream, an assertion makes a more general statement about the sequence of data items (which may be) transmitted by the stream ie. the history of the stream].

3.2.   The Proof System

The following axioms and proof rules determine the effect of
program execution on the state of variables, including the streams,
acted upon by processes.

The notation

$$P(\begin{smallmatrix} x \\ y \end{smallmatrix})$$

is used for the formula which is obtained by systematically substituting
y for all free occurrences of x in P.   If this introduces conflict between
free variables of y and bound variables of P, the conflict is resolved by
systematic renaming of the latter variables

$$P\left(\begin{smallmatrix} x_1,\ldots,x_n \\ y_1,\ldots,y_n \end{smallmatrix}\right)$$

denotes simultaneous substitution for all occurrences of any x_i in $x_1,\ldots,x_n$
by the corresponding y_i.   Thus occurrences of x_i within any y_i are not
replaced.   The variables x_1 , $\ldots,x_n$ must be distinct, otherwise the
simultaneous substitution is not defined.   On occasions we denote a list
of variables $x_1,\ldots,x_n$ by $\bar{x}$.

3.2.1 The Function Guardof

The assertion which must be true before some guarded command s can be selected for execution is denoted guardof (s). Guardof (s) is defined as follows:-

1. explicit guards

$$\text{guardof } (bexp_1; \ldots; bexp_n; \text{ input-command} \to \text{command-list})$$
$$= bexp_1 \text{ and } \ldots \text{ and } bexp_n \text{ and guardof (input-command)}$$

Before an explicit guarded command can be executed all of its guards must evaluate to true. The necessary and sufficient precondition for the evaluation of an input command to be successful is given by

$$\text{guardof } (i? \; \overline{vars} : k[bexp]) = \text{kind (head(i))} = k \text{ and } bexp(val(head(i)))^{\overline{vars}}$$

That is, the data item at the head of i must

1) be of kind k

2) have a list of components agreeing in type and number with the variable list $\overline{vars}$ such that bexp is true when the tuple val(head(i)) is substituted for the variables $\overline{vars}$.

2. implicit guards

Execution of a guarded command

$$P(\overline{a}\,|\,\overline{b})$$

can only be attempted if the guardof the body of P, after substitution of actual for formal parameters, evaluates to true.

$$\text{guardof } (P(\overline{a}\,|\,\overline{b}) = \text{ guardof } (S\frac{\overline{u}}{a}))$$

where procedure P has the declaration

procedure $P(\overline{u}\,|\,\overline{v})$; begin S end

Notice that if I is some stand-alone input command then the assertion guardof (I) is the necessary and sufficient condition for the execution of I to be successful (ie terminate).

3.2.2 Axioms and Proof Rules

Using the definition of guardof given above the axioms and
proof rules for the programming commands and constructs can now be given:

Simple Commands

A1 : skip

$$\{P\} \quad skip \quad \{P\}$$

A2 : assignment

$$\{P(\tfrac{x}{exp})\} \qquad x := exp\{P\}$$

A3 : input command

$$\{ \, P \left(\begin{array}{c} \overline{vars} \\ val(head(i)), \end{array} \begin{array}{c} i \\ tail(i) \end{array} \right) \underline{and} \; guardof \; (i? \; \overline{vars} : k[bexp]) \, \}$$

$$i?\overline{vars} : k[bexp]$$

$$\{P\}$$

The effect of an input command is to assign the component values
of the head data item of stream i to $\overline{vars}$ and then to remove this
item from i. The guardof precondition ensures that the input command will
always terminate successfully.

A4 : output command

$$\{ \, P\left(\begin{array}{c} 0 \\ 0::(k,\overline{exp}) \end{array} \right) \} \; 0! \; \overline{exp} : k \; \{P\}$$

An output command only affects the named output stream, its value
is updated by having the data item $(k,\overline{exp})$ appended to it.

[Note: Axioms A3 and A4 differ from those of CSP[1] in which the
output command is deemed to have no (side) effect and a preassertion P
to an input command can give rise to any arbitrary post assertion Q
when the containing process is considered in isolation. The validity
of a particular post assertion Q is not treated until co-operation
between proofs is tested to investigate the composite behaviour of
communicating CSP processes. This difference follows from our decision
to make streams explicit and allow the specification and proof of a
process in isolation from all the other processes with which it communicates].

Structured Commands

R1: alternative command

$$\frac{\forall i : 1..n \quad \{P \text{ and } guardof(Si)\} \quad Si \quad \{Q\}}{\{P\} \quad S_1 \parallel S_2 \ldots \parallel S_n \quad \{Q\}}$$

The post assertion must be established irrespective of which alternative
is selected for execution.

R2: repetitive command

$$\frac{\forall i : 1..n \{P \text{ and } guardof (Si)\} \quad Si \quad \{P\}}{\{P\} \ *(S_1 \parallel S_2 \ldots \parallel S_n) \ \{P \text{ and } \underline{not}(guardof (S_1) \ \underline{or} \ guardof (S_2) \ldots guardof (S_n))\}}$$

The invariant assertion P must be preserved by the repeated alternative
command irrespective of which path may be chosen on any iteration.

[Note: Rules R1 and R2 deal simultaneously with alternatives guarded
by either boolean expressions, input commands or procedure calls]

R3 : command list

$$\frac{\{P\} \ S_1 \ \{Q\}, \ \{Q\} \ S_2 \ \{R\}}{\{P\} \ S_1; \ S_2 \ \{R\}}$$

R4: explicit guarded command

$$\frac{\{P\} \ g \ \{Q\}, \ \{Q\} \ S \ \{R\}}{\{P\} \ g \ \rightarrow \ S \ \{R\}}$$

In an explicit guarded command the guard g can comprise a list of boolean expressions possibly followed by an input command. Axiom A3 handles the input command and the axiom for a boolean expression is

A5:   {P}   bexp {P}

Procedure declaration takes the general form

procedure $P(\overline{u}|\overline{v})$; begin S end

where $\overline{u}$ are the formal input parameters

$\quad$ $\overline{v}$ are the formal output parameters

$\quad$ S is a guarded command

Suppose we can assume that the procedure body, S, satisfies

$\quad$ {Q} S {R}

where none of the input parameters $\overline{u}$ occurs free in Q.

Providing the procedure is deterministic in effect it may be treated like a Pascal procedure   .   We may deduce the existence of functions associated with the procedure body

$\overline{f}$: the effect of executing S on the values of the formal output parameters

$\overline{g}$: the effect on the value of the input streams

$\overline{h}$: the effect on the value of the output streams

The procedure body may operate on input-output streams accessible from the process in which the procedure is declared. The functions $\overline{f}, \overline{g}, \overline{h}$ may be regarded as those which map the initial values of the variables and streams on procedure entry onto their value on procedure exit. These functions satisfy   the following implication:

$$Q \supset R \left(\frac{\overline{v}}{f(u,\overline{\imath})}, \quad \frac{\overline{\imath}}{g(u,\overline{\imath})}, \quad \frac{\overline{o}}{h(u,\overline{\imath},\overline{o})} \right)$$

for all values of the variables ($\overline{v}$) and streams ($\overline{\imath}$ and $\overline{o}$) involved in the assertion.

It is this property that may be assumed in proving assertions about calls of the procedure, including those occuring within the body, S, itself and in other declarations within the same process.

The proof rule for a procedure call (ie. implicit guarded command) with general form

$$P(\overline{a}|\overline{b}) \quad \text{where} \qquad \overline{a} \text{ are the actual input parameters}$$
$$\overline{b} \text{ are the actual output parameters}$$

is

R5:
$$\{P \left(\frac{\overline{b}}{f(\overline{a},\overline{I})}, \quad \frac{\overline{\imath}}{g(\overline{a},\overline{I})}, \quad \frac{\overline{o}}{h(\overline{a},\overline{I},\overline{o})} \right)\} \quad P(\overline{a}|\overline{b}) \quad \{P\} \;)$$

Note that $\overline{a}$ and $\overline{b}$ must all be distinct (in the sense that none can contain or be a variable which is contained in another); otherwise the effect of the procedure call is undefined.

Process Declaration

Process declaration takes the form:

process $P(\overline{I}|\overline{c}) \twoheadrightarrow (\overline{o})$; D; begin S end

where	P	is the process identifier;
	$\overline{c}$	are formal constants;
	$\overline{I}$	are the formal input streams;
	$\overline{o}$	are the formal output streams;
	D	are the local procedure declarations;
and	S	is a command list.

Our treatment of process declaration is analogous to the treatment of procedure declaration. Given the assertion $\{P\}$ $S\{Q\}$ where none of the input constants $\bar{c}$ or streams $\bar{i}$ occur free in Q, proving the process is deterministic in effect, we may deduce the existence of functions:

$\bar{g}$:   the effect on formal input streams

$\bar{h}$:   the effect on formal output streams

satisfying the following

$$P \supset Q \left(\frac{\bar{i}}{\bar{g}(\bar{i},\bar{c})}, \ \frac{\bar{o}}{\bar{h}(\bar{i},\bar{c},\bar{o})} \right)$$

for all values of the constants $(\bar{c})$ and streams $(\bar{i},\bar{o})$ involved in this assertion.

It is this property that may be assumed in proving assertions about invocations of the process, including those within S itself.

The functions $\bar{g}$, $\bar{h}$ may be regarded as those which map the initial values of $\bar{c}$, $\bar{i}$, $\bar{o}$ onto the final values of $\bar{i}$ and $\bar{o}$ on completion of the execution of S. They are used in the proof of assertions about network commands.

Network Command

A network command denotes a network of processes. Providing all the component processes of a network are deterministic in effect then the network will be deterministic in effect. Thus the value of each input stream if and when the network terminates will be some function of its initial value. Similarly the value of each output stream will be some function of its initial value and that of the input streams.

The proof rule for a network command is of the form

R6:　　　$\{P\left(\begin{array}{cc} i & o \\ i_s, & o_s \end{array}\right)\} \ S \ \{P\}$　　$\forall \ i \ \epsilon \ I, \ o \ \epsilon \ O$

where (a) I and O are the input and output streams of the network command S

　　　　(b i_s and o_s are formed from the input and output effect functions

　　　　of the network processes as described below.

<u>input streams</u>:

　　　　If a stream i is supplied as the kth input stream to a process p
then the final value is

$$g_{p.}^k \ (i, \bar{c})$$

where g_p^k is the kth component of the tuple of functions $\bar{g}_p$ which define
the input effect of process $\bar{p}$ and $\bar{c}$ are the constant parameters of p.

<u>output streams</u>:

　　　　The final value of an output stream is determined by the functional
composition of some or all of the output effects of the component processes
of the network. The final value of an output stream o is obtained as follows.
Consider a stream equation

$$\bar{o} \ = \ p(\bar{x}|\bar{c})$$

where $p(\bar{x}|\bar{c})$ is a subnetwork. Each o in $\bar{o}$ can be expressed as the application
of some component h_p^k of the tuple of output effect functions $\bar{h}_p$ for process p.

　i) if o is an intermediate stream then its value is given by

$$h_{p.}^k \ (\bar{x}, \lambda, \bar{c})$$

ii) if o is an output stream of the network then its value is given by

$$h_p^k \ (\bar{x}, o, \bar{c})$$

　　　　All subnetworks occuring in $\bar{x}$ can similarly be replaced by an application
of some component function belonging to the output effect of some process.
Intermediate streams in $\bar{x}$ can be replaced in a similar way.

Example

The proof rule applied to the network command

[out = nrotations (rotate(t) | count-1)]

gives the correctness formula

$$\{P\left(g_{rotate}^{\;\;t}(t),\; h_{nrotations}^{\;\;out}(h_{rotate}(t),out,count-1)\right)\}$$

[out = nrotations (rotate(t) | count-1)]

{P}

The above proof rule for a process network is only valid if the network is acyclic.

Local Network

We have seen for a network command that the value of an output stream is some function of its initial value and that of the input streams to the sub-netowrk. The sequence of values produced by a local network may be consumed within the local network command body of the host process at an arbitrary rate. If we employ an auxiliary variable, i^H, for each local in-stream i to record the "output from local network consumed so far", we can then deduce an invariant relation between the outputs (consumed and potential) from a local network and the inputs to the local network.

Local in-streams

The input axiom applied to local in-streams within body may be extended to include the auxiliary variable

$$\{P\left(\overline{val}^{\;\overline{vars}}(head(i)),tail(i)^{\;i},i^H \;.head(i)^{\;i^H}\right)\; \underline{and}\; guardof\; (i?\overline{vars}:k[bexp])\;\}$$

i? $\overline{vars}$:k[bexp]

{P}

Consider a local in-stream y, acted upon as an output stream
in the following stream equation of the network command

$$\overline{o} = p(\overline{x}|\overline{c}) \quad \text{where} \quad p(\overline{x}|\overline{c}) \text{ is a subnetwork}$$

$$\text{and y is the kth component of } \overline{o}$$

At any point in body the total potential communication along y,
from the local networks will be

$$h_p^{\ k}(\overline{x},\lambda,\overline{c}) \qquad \text{the kth component of the output effect tuple}$$

$$\overline{h}_p \text{ for p.}$$

We can thus deduce the following INVARIANT RELATION for each
local in-stream y within the local network command body:

$$y^H :: y = h_p^{\ k}(\overline{x},\lambda,\overline{c})$$

where y is the k component of $\overline{o}$ in $\overline{o} = p(\overline{x}|\overline{c})$

in [t], the network command defining the sub-network.

The value associated with y reflects the residual potential
communication along the stream.

Local streams are initially empty upon initiating a local network
command

Local out-streams: the output axiom applies unmodified to local
out-streams. The sequence value associated with
a local out-stream records the potential
communication from the host to the conetwork.
How much communication has actually taken place
depends on the relative speed of execution of
processes within the local network.

If a local out-stream, o, is supplied as the kth input to a process, p,
then at any point within the body of the local network command

$$g_p^{\ k}(\overline{x},\overline{c}) \quad (\overline{x} \text{ is the value associated with the n-tuple of input}$$

$$\text{streams to p).}$$

is the minimum outstanding communication via o.

$g_p^{\,k}$ is the kth component of $\overline{g}_p$, the input effect of p.

We introduce the auxiliary variable to facilitate the definition of the semantics of local-network commands. It does not occur in the program proper but may occur in assertions.

4.   USE OF THE PROOF SYSTEM

This section illustrates the use of the proof system. It outlines the steps involved in proving the consistency of a process to a functional specification (see [2] for a definition of the notation). The function defines an abstract data type 'sequence' which can be used to remember and recover a   sequence of words:

word = *(alfanum)

val = null

eos = null

rotation = *(word ⊕ eos)

commands = *(word ⊕ val)
command = word ⊕ val
__function__ sequence : commands → rotation

s : commands

__cases__

   sequence (s) = sequence' (s,λ)

__end__

__function__ sequence' : commands X commands → rotation

x : command; s,t : commands;

__cases__

   sequence' (λ,t)   = λ

   sequence' (x::s,t)   = if kind(x) = word __then__ sequence'(s,t::x)

                          else words (t::x)::(eos)::sequence'(s,t::x)

__end__

<u>function</u> words : commands → rotation

x : command; t : commands

<u>cases</u>

  words (λ) = λ

  words (x::t)   =   <u>if</u> kind(x) = word <u>then</u> x::words(t)

                                                <u>else</u> words(t)

<u>end</u>

      The process sequence defined below is specified using a generalised function 'seq' which applies the function sequence to the longest initial subsequence of valid commands from its parameter, using the operator µ(see [2]).

<u>function</u> seq : *(D) → rotation

s : *(D)

<u>cases</u>

  seq(s) = sequence (µ(iscom,s))

<u>end</u>

iscom(x) $\stackrel{\Delta}{=}$ (kind(x) = word) <u>or</u> (kind(x) = val)

     In the example the process nrotations generates an integer number of rotations of a sequence of words. It uses the process 'sequence' in a local network to store the current'rotation' before performing the next cyclic shift of words.

```
alphabet rotation  = word(:alfa), eos;
         rotations = word(:alfa), eor, eos;
         command   = word(:alfa), val, die, eos;
process nrotations (in:seq rotation|n:integer)  ⇒ (out:seq rotations)

begin
   (n = .o → out!:eos
    ▮
    otherwise → local in t:seq rotation;out s:seq command;
                      [t = sequence(s)];
                  begin
                     *(in?k:word → s!k:word; out!k:word);
                     in?:eos; out!:eor; s!:val;
                     [out = nrotations(rotate(t)|n-1)]
                  end(*local*)
   )
end;
process sequence (in:seq command)  ⇒ (out:seq rotation);

begin
   *(in?:val → out!:eos
     ▮
     in?w:word → local in ans:seq rotation; out rest:seq command;
                       [ans = sequence(rest)];
                  begin
                  *(in?v:word → rest!v:word
                    ▮
                    in?:val → out!w:word;
                              rest!:val;
                              *(ans?x:word → out!x:word);
                              ans?:eos; out!:eos
                   );
                   rest!:die
                  end(*local*)
    )
in?:die
end;
process rotate(in:seq rotation) ⇒ (out:seq rotation);
begin
   (in?w:word → *(in?x:word → out!x:word);
                   out!w:word
   );
   in?:eos;
   out!:eos
end;
```

For each process p, $g_p{}^i$ and $h_p{}^j$ are the functions defining the effect of p on its input stream i and output stream j. Using this notation we may state the following propositions about the process

$$g_{rotate}(s) \quad = \quad \text{if okrot(s) then tail } (\nu(isword,s))$$

$$h_{rotate}(s,o) \quad = \quad \text{if okrot(s) then o::rotate } (\mu(isword,s))::(eos)$$

$$g_{sequence}(s) \quad = \quad \text{if okcom(s) then tail}(\nu(iscom,s))$$

$$h_{sequence}(s,o) \quad = \quad \text{if okcom(s) then o::seq(s)}$$

$$g_{nrotations}(s,n) \quad = \quad \text{if okrot(s) then if n = 0 then s}$$
$$\text{else if n > 0 then tail}(\nu(isword,s))$$

$$h_{nrotations}(s,o,n) \quad = \quad \text{if okrot(s) then o::nrotations}(\mu(isword,s),n)::(eos)$$

where functions nrotations, rotate are appropriately defined specification functions (see [2]).

The predicates are

$$okrot(s) \quad \overset{\Delta}{=} \quad kind(head(\nu(isword,s))) = eos$$

$$okcom(s) \quad \overset{\Delta}{=} \quad kind(head(\nu(iscom,s))) \quad = die$$

$$isword(x) \quad \overset{\Delta}{=} \quad kind(x) \quad = \quad word$$

Outline Proof of Sequence

Being able to prove general properties of the specification functions [2] , we need only prove consistency of the implementation as indicated in the above propositions. For 'sequence' we must show:

process sequence(in:seq command) $\Rightarrow$ (out:seq rotation);

$\{P : in \subseteq i \text{ and } okcom(i) \text{ and } out = 0\}$

```
begin
{ P1 : ν(iscom,in) = ν(iscom,i) and out::seq(in) = o::seq(i)}

 *(in?:val → out!:eos

    ▌

    in?w:word →
                    {P2 : ν(iscom,in) = ν(iscom,i) and

                        out::seq((word,w)::in) = o::seq(i)}

                 local ...
                 ┌
                 │  S1
                 └
                 end(*local*)

  )

in?:die

end;
```

$\{Q : in = tail \ (ν(iscom,i)) \ \underline{and} \ out = o::seq(i)\}$

The control paths P → P1, P1 → Q and P1 → P2 are straightforward.

For example, consider path P1 → Q.

$\{P1 \ \underline{and} \ \underline{not} \ guardof \ *(in?:val → ... \ ▌ \ in?w:word → ...)\}$

 in ? die

$\{Q\}$

$P1 \ \underline{and} \ kind(head(in)) \neq val \ \underline{and} \ kind(head(in)) \neq word)$

        in
→ Q (tail(in)) $\underline{and}$ guardof(in?:die)

 (i) $ν(iscom,in) = ν(iscom,i)$ $\underline{and}$

 (ii) $out::seq(in) = o::seq(i)$ $\underline{and}$

(iii) $kind(head(in)) \neq val \ and \ kind(head(in)) \neq word$

 ⇒

(a) $tail(in) = tail(ν(iscom,i))$ $\underline{and}$

(b) $out = o::seq(i)$ $\underline{and}$

(c) $kind(head(in)) = die$

Proof

(a) (i) and (iii) ⇒ in = ν(iscom,i)

$$⇒ tail(in) = tail (ν(iscom,i))$$

(b) (iii) ⇒ μ(iscom,in) = λ

$$⇒ seq(in) = λ$$

Thus

out::seq(in = o::seq(i) <u>and</u> seq(in) = λ

$$⇒ out = o::seq(i)$$

(c) from (a) we know that in = ν(iscom,i) and

from the pre-condition that kind (head(ν(iscom,i))) = die)

thus kind(head(in)) = die

(b) illustrates trivially how the function definitions are used
as re-write rules when proving assertions.

In order to show that P1 is a suitable loop invariant we
must prove a theorem about the local network. The
annotated statements are:

{P : in = i $\underline{\text{and}}$ out = 0 $\underline{\text{and}}$ okcom(i)}

local in ans:seq rotation; out rest:seq command;

        [ans = sequence(rest)];

{P1 : ν(iscom,in) = ν(iscom,i) $\underline{\text{and}}$ out = o::seq((words,w)::rest)}

      $\underline{\text{and}}$ rest::in = i $\underline{\text{and}}$ ans^H = seq(rest)

*(in?v:word $\rightarrow$ rest!v:word

   ∎

  in?:val $\rightarrow$ out!w:word;

        rest!:val;

$\left\{\begin{array}{l} \text{P2 : rest::in = i } \underline{\text{and}} \ \nu(\text{iscom,in}) = \nu(\text{iscom,i}) \ \underline{\text{and}} \ \text{okrot(ans)} \ \underline{\text{and}} \\ \text{out::ans = o::seq((word,w)::rest) } \underline{\text{and}} \ \text{tail}(\nu(\text{isword,ans})) = \lambda \end{array}\right\}$

        *(ans?x:word $\rightarrow$ out!x:word);

        ans?:eos $\rightarrow$ out!:eos

 );

rest!:die

end(*local*)

{Q:in = ν(iscom,i) $\underline{\text{and}}$ out = o::seq((word,w)::i)}

The most interesting steps in the proof of the local network
involve the loop invariants P1, P2. They use the invariant
property of the local network. Stated in terms of an auxiliary
variable ans^H, it is

    ans^H::ans = seq(rest)

We use this invariant property in traversing the path P1 $\rightarrow$ P2.

{P1 $\underline{\text{and}}$ guardof(in?:val)} in?:val $\rightarrow$ out!w:word;

$$\frac{\qquad\qquad\text{rest!:val}\qquad\qquad\{P2\}}{\text{P1 } \underline{\text{and}} \text{ guardof(in?:val)} \Rightarrow \text{P2}\left(\begin{array}{ccc} \text{in} & \text{out} & \text{rest} \\ \text{tail(in)}, & \text{out::(word,w)}, & \text{rest::(val)} \end{array}\right)}$$

(i) ν(iscom,in) = ν(iscom,i) <u>and</u>

 (ii) out = o::seq((word,w)::rest) <u>and</u>

(iii) rest::in = i   <u>and</u>

 (iv) ans^H = seq(rest)

  (v) kind(head(in)) = val

$\circ$ $\Rightarrow$

(a) ν(iscom,tail(in)) = ν(iscom,i) <u>and</u>

(b) rest::(val)::tail(in) = i   <u>and</u>

(c) out::(word,w)::ans = o::seq((word,w)::rest::(val)) <u>and</u>

(d) okrot(ans) <u>and</u>

(e) tail(ν(isword,ans)) = λ

(a) and (b) are straightforward

We use ans^H = seq(rest) as an indirect way of expressing the

fact ans = λ in P1. If ans was used explicitly we would have to

perform a substitution for ans each time an output was made to rest.

To prove (c), (d), (e) we use

     ans^H = seq(rest) and ans^H::ans = seq(rest::(val))

             $\Rightarrow$ ans = words(rest)::(eos)

(d) and (e) follow directly and for (c) we are left to

show (from (ii))

o::seq((word,w)::rest)::(word,w)::words(rest)::eos = o::seq((word,w)::rest::(val))

         out   ans

which is true since

     seq (s::(val)) = seq (s)::words(s)::(eos)

can be proved as a theorem about the function seq.

Theorem about seq

seq(s::(val)) = seq(s)::words(s)::eos

Proof: Induction on s

  (i) <u>Base case</u> s = λ

l.h.s. seq((val)) = seq'(val,λ)

                  = words(val)::eos::seq'(λ,val)

                  = λ::eos::λ

                  = eos

r.h.s. seq(val)::words(val)::eos

                  = λ::λ::eos

                  = eos

  (ii) <u>Induction Step</u>   Assume theorem true $\forall$ s' < s and let s' = a::s'.

<u>Prove</u> seq(a::s'::(val)) = seq(a::s')::words(a::s')::eos

<u>case (i)</u> a = (val)

l.h.s. seq((val)::s'::(val))

  = seq'((val)::s'::(val),λ)

  = words(λ)::eos::seq'(s'::(val),val)

  =   eos::seq'(s'::(val),λ) trivial lemma

  =   eos::seq(s'::(val))

  =   eos::seq(s')::words(s')::eos induction hypothesis

  =   seq((val)::s') ::words((val)::s')::eos

  = seq(s)::words(s)::eos

<u>case (ii)</u> a = (item,z)

l.h.s. seq(a::s'::(val))

  = seq'(a::s'::(val),λ)

  = seq'(s'::(val),a)

  = seq'(s',a)::words(a::s')::eos   by lemma :1

  = seq'(a::s',λ)::words(a::s')::eos

  = seq(a::s')::words(a::s')::eos

  = seq(s)::words(s)::eos

Lemma 1 for seq'

seq'(s::(val),t) = seq'(s,t)::words(t::s)::eos

Proof:

Base case s = λ

    seq'((val),t) =   words(t::(val))::eos

                   = seq'(λ,t)::words(t)   ::eos

                   = seq'(s,t)::words(t::s)::eos

Induction Step   Assume lemma true ∀ s' < s, s = a::s'

case (i) a = (val)

    seq'(a::s'::(val),t)

  = words(t::a)::eos::seq'(s'::(val),t::a)

  = words(t::a)::eos::seq'(s',t::a)::words(t::a::s')::eos induction hypothesi

  = seq'(a::s',t)::words(t::a::s')::eos

  = seq'(s,t)::words(t::s)::eos

case (ii) a = (item, z)

l.h.s.   seq'(a::s'::(val),t)

    = seq'(s'::(val),t::a)

    = seq'(s',t::a)::words(t::a::s')::eos

    = seq'(a::s',t)::words(t::a::s')::eos

    = seq'(s,t)::words(t::s)::eos

5.   CONCLUSION

We have described a notation for distributed programs
expressed as networks of communicating processes. A command
was introduced to allow a process to communicate with a
concurrently executing local sub-network of processes. This
notation,illustrated by an example,can be used to implement
dynamic data types as recursive networks of processes.

We have presented a proof system for the partial correctness
of distributed programs in which input and output commands are
axiomatized in terms of the way in which they affect the
sequence of values transmitted by the streams operated upon.
We are consequently able to prove the partial correctness of
processes in isolation. Properties of networks of processes
can be inferred by the use of a Hoare style proof rule.

Externally a process is described in terms of the sequence
of data items transmitted by communication streams. This approach
is taken in [2] in which functions are used to specify the way
in which a process is intended to transform the value of its
input-output streams. A partial correctness proof is restricted
to verifying that a program meets a functional specification.
More general properties of the program can be proved in terms
of the functions.

REFERENCES

1.   APT, K.R. FRANCEZ, N. and de ROEVER, W.   A Proof System for
        Communicating Sequential Processes,
        ACM Transactions on Programming Languages and Systems,
        vol 2, No 3, July 1980, Page 359-385.

2.   GALLIMORE, R.M. and COLEMAN, D.   Specification of
        Distributed Programs,
        these Proceedings.

3.   HOARE, C.A.R.   Communicating Sequential Processes,
        Communications of the ACM 21, 8, 666-6777 (1978).

4.   KAHN, G. and MacQUEEN, D.B.   Coroutines and Networks of
        Parallel Processes,
        Proc. IFIP Congress, 1977, North-Holland, Amsterdam 1977,
        pp 993-998.

5.   LEVIN, G.M. and GRIES, D.   A Proof Technique for Communicating
        Sequential Processes,
        Acta Informatica 15, 281-302 (1981)

6.   OWICKI, S.S., and GRIES, D. Verifying Properties of Parallel
        Programs: An Axiomatic Approach,
        Communications of the ACM, 19, 5 (May 1976), 279-285.

SPECIFICATION OF DISTRIBUTED PROGRAMS

R.M. Gallimore & D. Coleman *

Department of Computation

UMIST

Manchester

ENGLAND

ABSTRACT

This paper describes a technique for program development by
refinement using complementary implicit and functional specifications.
The approach can be used to specify programs expressed as networks
of communicating processes. A typed functional notation is introduced
for that purpose and its use illustrated in the specification of a
kwic-index generation program.

General properties of a program can be established by proving theorems
about the functional specification. Consequently proof techniques can be
used at each stage of the development process. Proofs about the final
implementation only need to establish that it meets its functional
specification.

---

*
This work was undertaken by the authors while D. Coleman
was on study leave at the University of California, Berkeley

1. INTRODUCTION

The conventional approach to proving programs correct is to
provide a specification in the form of pre- and post-conditions,
assertions about the state of the program before and after execution
respectively. After program development an attempt is made to prove
that the implementation satisfies the specification using a variant
of the method of inductive assertions[7, 8]. Unfortunately, this
approach has certain shortcomings. Proof techniques are only used in
the final stages of program development, whereas ideally proof techniques should be used to eliminate errors as early as possible in the
life cycle of a program. Finding the right assertions is a daunting
task as the programmer is forced to view the program from a different
point of view than during its construction. The task of proving is
made more unmanageable because the assertions must be stated in terms
of variables used in the implementation and consequently may contain
a wealth of irrelevant detail.

Rigorous specification and proof techniques should be used
during every stage of a program's development from the initial design
to final implementation [10]. In fact, proofs of a design are simpler
than proofs of an implementation because a design can be stated in
abstract terms, avoiding unnecessary representation and algorithmic
details. In order to make most effective use of the proving activity
we should employ a specification technique during the design phase
which

(a)   allows the development of program and proof by a process
      of refinement,   and

(b)   facilitates the proof of properties of partially specified
      programs.

Proofs (theorems) constructed early in the life cycle will be concerned with properties of a general, abstract nature while the final proofs will concentrate on the details and idiosyncrasies of a particular implementation. The detailed proofs about an implementation should have the simplest possible objectives i.e. to display consistency between the implementation and an intermediate specification of the algorithm employed.

Specifying Distributed Programs

The need for systematic design and verification techniques is more keenly felt in the case of concurrent programs than for their sequential counterparts. Several proof systems, comprising axioms and rules of inference have been proposed for programming languages and constructs based on both the centralised (shared variable) and distributed models of concurrent computation [1 , 12 , 14].

This paper introduces an approach to the specification and proof of distributed programs. It involves the development of complementary implicit and functional specifications to facilitate the use of proof techniques from the earliest stages of the design. The implicit specification states the required properties of the system stated as assertions or theorems to be proved. On the other hand the functional specification gives an explicit definition of the transformation that the program must perform between its inputs and outputs.

The following section describes a model of concurrent computation and shows that recursively defined functions are sufficiently powerful for its description.

2.   THE MODEL OF CONCURRENT COMPUTATION

Informally we regard a program as a network of processes which communicate via streams, as shown in figure 1, where nodes represent

processes and arcs represent streams [11]. It is assumed that
processes may proceed concurrently

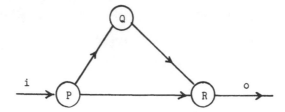

Figure 1: A Process Network

        Processes are independent, self-contained units, which may them-
selves be process networks, or purely sequential. In the final
analysis, however, every terminating process network is constructed from
the interconnection of terminating sequential processes. Processes
may only communicate via streams by means of special input-output
commands. Operationally a stream is a unidirectional channel of
unlimited capacity transmitting typed data-items from a unique
producer process to a single consumer process. A stream preserves the
order of transmission of data items. Since streams have unbounded capacity there is no strict synchronisation implicit between the corresponding input and output commands in different processes
        We allow for the possible use of non-determinism in the control
structures of the sequential processes, for non-determinism permits an
elegant description of stream processing algorithms.
However, we limit our discussion to processes whose overall, externally
observable, effect is deterministic i.e. the sequence of data items
which a process transmits on a particular stream during a computation
is uniquely determined by the sequence(s) of data values input by that
process during the computation. This restriction is necessary to
allow us to interpret the effect of a process 'denotationally' as

functional relationships between the history of communication
(sequence of data items transmitted) of its input streams and
each of its output streams [11]. For the sake of simplicity we
denote the behaviour of a process with n output streams by n functions,
each giving the relationship between the sequences of values input
by the process and the sequence of values transmitted on a particular
output stream. The source and target of such a function correspond to
the set of all finite sequences of typed data-items that may be transmitted by the input streams and output stream in question. For example,
we may describe process P of figure 2 by a function $g:S_2 \rightarrow S_4$ (where
S_i is a domain of sequences), process R by a function $h:S_3 \times S_4 \rightarrow S_5$,
while process Q is described by a pair of functions $f_1:S_1 \rightarrow S_2$, $f_2:S_1 \rightarrow S_3$.

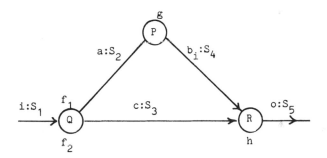

Figure 2

Within a process network the interconnection of two processes
by means of a stream corresponds to the functional composition of
the functions describing the effect of the consumer process and that
function describing the effect of the producer on the stream in
question.

Thus, for example, we may describe the effect of the process
network in figure 2 by the equation

$$0 = h(g(f_1(i)), f_2(i))$$

where i ranges over the domain of all possible input sequences S_1

0 is an element of the domain of output sequences S_5.
Alternatively, we may describe the effect by the following system of
equations:

$$a = f_1(i)$$

$$b = g(a)$$

$$c = f_2(i)$$

$$0 = h(a, b).$$

Any process which may itself give rise to an interconnection of
instances of processes to form a sub-network may be described in terms
of the functions describing the processes in the sub-network using
functional composition and recursion.

The functional abstraction may thus be used to denote the
meaning of programs constructed as recursive process networks. Such
descriptions are made possible by considering only component processes that transform input values into output values deterministically.

Turning our attention to the problem of program design, it is
therefore possible to develop an a priori specification of a program
using the techniques of function definition, composition and recursion.
By adopting a suitable programming notation to describe an algorithm
we shall be free to use recursive process networks for its implementation wherever it is found to be necessary or natural to do so.

The following section introduces a notation for the definition of
functions, and the domains of values which form their sources and
targets (domains and ranges). It is subsequently used to specify
the effect of a distributed program in terms of the sequences of
data-items transmitted by the streams of the program.

3. FUNCTIONAL SPECIFICATION LANGUAGE

3.1 Values Manipulated

The data values by a program are modelled by suitably defined sets of values in the specification language. The specification language thus provides base sets of values to denote the simple types typically occurring in a programming notation, together with standard operations for the construction of user defined sets. The language is introduced with the specific purpose of describing the intended behaviour of programs by functions and does not encompass the notion of data abstraction for the specification of complex data types.

3.1.1 Basic Sets of Values

The basic set of values of the specification language are:

   i)   integer = {... -1, 0, +1, ...}

   ii)   char   = {A .. Z, a .. z, ...}

  iii)   the boolean values, boolean = {true, false}

A specification may also utilise finite sets of values, defined by enumeration e.g.

      colour = {red, green, amber}

Set Operators

Sets of values may be constructed from existing sets using the following operators

   i)   set union (+),

   ii)   set product (X),

  iii)   disjoint union (⊕).

Disjoint union may only be applied to a set associated with an identifier. The value of a disjoint union of a series of set identifiers is the disjoint union of their values where the set identifiers are used as the distinguishing tags e.g. colour ⊕ boolean = {(colour, red), (colour, green), (colour, amber), (boolean, true), (boolean, false)}.

Two functions are defined as primitive operations in the specification language which may be used to identify the kind and value of a tagged n-tuple.

Definitions:

If $x = (k, d_1, d_2, \ldots, d_n) \in k - item$, $n \geq 0$, then

i) $kind(x) = k$

ii) $val(x) = \begin{cases} (d_1, d_2, \ldots, d_n) & n \geq 1 \\ undefined & n = 0 \end{cases}$

iv) sequence (*)

Let *D denote the set of finite sequences of elements taken from the set D. We include in *D the empty sequence, written λ. Every other element of *D may be obtained by appending to the left of an existing element from *D an element from D, using the operator ::

:: : D X *D → *D   (left append)

Thus the set *D comprises objects denoted by all finite, variable free, expressions constructed from λ, the elements of D and the left append operator :: e.g.

λ, a::λ, b ::λ, $\ldots$, a :: (a ::λ), a :: (b ::λ), $\ldots$

where a, b $\ldots$ denote elements of D. We frequently use an element identifier to denote a sequence comprising only a single element from D e.g. we may write a to denote a ::λ.

The operator :: is also used to represent 'append right' and 'concatenate' operations defined axiomatically below

:: : *D X D → *D   (append right)

A1 : λ:: x = x :: λ

A2 : (y :: s) :: x = y :: (s :: x)   ($\forall$x, y $\in$ D; s $\in$ *D

:: : *D X *D → *D   (concatenate)

A3 : λ:: s = s

A4 : (x :: t) :: s = s :: (t :: s)   ($\forall$x $\in$ D; s, t $\in$ *D)

Within an expression, ambiguity about which operator :: represents
is eliminated by defining the set from which each variable in the
expression may take its value.

We occasionally use an alternative notation for sequences as a
list of terms enclosed in angle-brackets. Thus λ

is also written <> and for instance
a :: (b :: (c :: λ)) is denoted by <a, b, c>.

The following operators operate on sequences:

head has the value of the first element in a sequence

head : *D $\rightarrow$ D

head (x :: s) = x   ($\forall x \in$ D, s $\in$ *D)

The head of an empty sequence is undefined.

tail has the value of a sequence after the first element has been
removed

tail : *D $\rightarrow$ *D

tail (λ)   = λ

tail (x :: s) = s   ($\forall x \in$ D, s $\in$ *D)

The operators :: (denoting left append, right append and concatenate)
head and tail are provided as primitive operations on objects defined
as sequences in program specifications.

Associated with any set, D say, is a predicate D which when applied
to an item x has the value true iff x $\in$ D and the value false otherwise
e.g. colour (red) = true, colour (A) = false etc.

Bags

Consider B(D) the set of bags (counted sets) of elements taken
from some set D. We include the empty bag, written ϕ. Every other bag
may be obtained using the 'put' operation

put: B(D) x D $\rightarrow$ B(D)

The set B(D) comprises objects denoted by all finite, variable free expressions constructed from ϕ, the elements of D and the operator put e.g.

ϕ, put(ϕ, a), put(ϕ, b) . . . put(put(ϕ, a), a) put(put(ϕ, b), a) . . .

We also use an alternative notation for bag values as a list of elements enclosed in square brackets. Thus ϕ is written [] and, for instance put(put(put(ϕ, a), b), a) may be denoted by [a, b, a]. No significance is attached to the order of occurrence of elements in either representation and thus we may define the equality relation on bags inductively;

    beq : B(D) x B(D) → boolean

    beq(ϕ, ϕ) = true

    beq(ϕ, put(B, b)) = false

    beq(put(A, a), ϕ) = false

    beq(put(A, a), put(B, b)) = <u>if</u> a = b then beq (AB)

                        <u>else</u> <u>if</u> isin (B, a)

                                <u>then</u> beq(A, del(put(B, b), a)

                                <u>else</u> false

where the functions isin and del are defined as follows:

    isin: B(D) x D → boolean

    isin(ϕ, a) = false

    isin(put(B, b), a) = <u>if</u> a = b <u>then</u> true

                            <u>else</u> isin (B, a)

    del : B(D) x D → B(D)

    del(ϕ, a) = ϕ

    del(put(B, b), a) = <u>if</u> a = b <u>then</u> B

                        <u>else</u> put(del(B, a), b)

The infix operator U is used to denote 'bag union'

U : B(D) x B(D) → B(D)

AUϕ = A

AUput(B, b) = put(AUB, b)

AUB = BUA

3.1.3   Semantics

Since specification functions will often be defined recursively
it is essential that the recursion be well defined. Each function
definition must mean exactly one correspondence between target and
source. As is well known this may be achieved by imposing a complete
partial order structure on all value spaces and defining the meaning
of functions to be the least fix point of the recursion [6,15]. In this
section we outline suitable cpo's corresponding to the syntactic domains
and functions of the specification language.

The base sets can be structured as discrete cpo's with a ⊥ element
corresponding to "undefined".

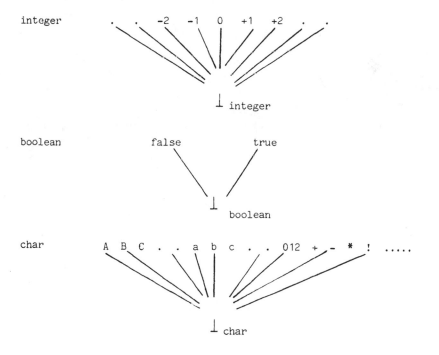

Finite sets can be structured as discrete cpo's in a similar way. The base set null corresponds to the cpo with one element.

The basic operators of the specification language are disjoint union, ⊕, union, +, and direct product, X. As long as specifications only involve the union of disjoint sets cpo's can always be constructed corresponding to each domain.

In addition to ordinary, or set, domains the specification language allows the definition of sequence domains, *D, whose elements are all the finite sequences of elements taken from some ordinary domain D. A cpo for *D can be defined by the domain equation

$$*D \equiv D^0 + D^1 + D^2 + \ldots$$

where $D^1 \equiv D$, $D^n \equiv D^{n-1} \, X \, D$ and D^0 is a one element cpo.

In domain equations the operator + represents disjoint sum

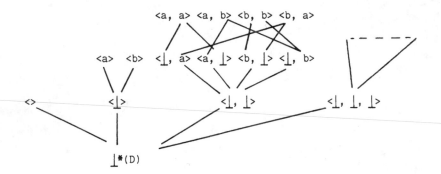

All base functions of the specification language are monotonic. All specfication functions are by definition strict (i.e. if any input parameter is undefined then the function value is undefined). Thus all specification functions are monotonic and consequently have unique least fix points. We may therefore safely assert that every specification function has a unique meaning.

A Domain for Bags

The cpo defining the structure of the bag domain defined over some set D is isomorphic to the domain of finite sequences *D.

$$B(D) \equiv D^0 + D^1 + D^2 + \ldots$$

where $D^1 \equiv D$, $D^n \equiv D^{n-1} \times D$ and D^0 is a one element cpo [ ]. Again + represents a disjoint sum.

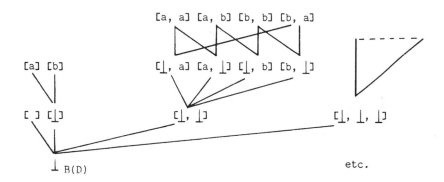

In fact the principal difference between bags and sequences is in the definition of the equality operator defined on BAGS and SEQUENCES respectively.

3.2   Functional Notation

This section gives the syntax and an informal semantics for the functional notation used in defining the intended behaviour of distributed programs.

3.2.1   The Source and Target of a Function

The source and target of a function must be defined as domains.

<domain>::=<set expression>|<bag expression>

<set expression>::=<set term>

|

(<set expression>)

|

<set expression><set operator><set expression>

<set operator>::= + | X

<bag expression>::=<bag term>{U <bag term>}

<bag term>::=<bag identifier>

|

<bag enumeration>

<bag enumeration>::=[<identifier>{,<identfier>}]

<bag equation>::=

<bag identifier> = <bag expression>

Bag values may not have a recursive definition. The infix operator
= represents bag equality and may be used in boolean expressions.

The value of a domain is defined by a set expression, or a bag
expression. A set expression denotes a set formed by a finite number
of applications of set union (+) and cross-product (X) applied to set
terms. In a set expression cross-product binds more tightly than
union.

<set term>::=<set identifier>{@<set identifier >}

|

<set enumeration>

|

<base set>

|

<sequence domain>

<set enumeration>::= {<identifier>{,<identifier>}}

<base set>   ::=integer|boolean|char|null

<sequence domain>::=*(<set expression>)

<set equation>::=<set identifier>=<set expression>

A set term may be (1) a set identifier in which case its value
is that of the set associated with the identifier in a set equation,
(2) the disjoint union of name sets, (3) a set value defined by
enumeration, (4) a base set or (5) a sequence domain denoting the set
of all finite sequences of elements taken from some domain.

Examples of domains and set equations:

word = *(char)

words = *(word)

eot   = {'eot'}

token = word @ eot

3.2.2 Function Definition

< function definition> ::= <function heading><function body>

<function heading>::=

__function__ <function identifier>: <source> →<target >

<source >::= <domain >{X <domain >}

<target >::= <domain >

A function heading defines the source and target of a function.
The function body defines the actual mapping.

<function body >::=

   <variable declarations> __cases__ <equation>{<equation>} __end__

<variable declarations>::=<declaration>{;<declaration>}

|

<empty>

<declaration>::=

   <variable identifier>{, <variable identifier>}: <domain>

<equation>::=

   <function identifier> (<formal parameters>) = <expression>

<formal parameters>::=<formal parameter>{, <formal parameter>}

<formal parameters>::= <constants >

|

```
                    <variable identifier>

                    |

                    <function application>
```

A function mapping is defined by a series of equations. Each
equation specifies the function value for that subset of the function
source determined by the formal parameters. A formal parameter may
be a constant value, a bound variable or the application of a function
to formal parameters. The scope of a bound variable is the equation
in which it occurs. A variable may only take values form the domain
with which it is associated in the variable declaration.

A function is undefined for any value in its source for which
there are no defining equations.

3.2.3 Expressions

```
<expression>::=<simple expression >

                    |

                    <conditional expression>

<simple expression>::=<constant>

                    |

                    <variable identifier>

                    |

                    <function application>

<function application>::=

        <function identifier>(<simple expression>{,<simple expression>})

<conditional expression>::=

        if <bexp> then <expression>

                    else <expression>

<bexp> ::= true|false|<variable identifier>|(<bexp>)

            |

            |not <bexp>|<bexp> and <bexp>|<bexp> or <bexp> ...
```

```
<expression><relational operator><expression>
```
|
```
<function application>
```

The expression on the right hand side of an equation specifies the value of a function in terms of

(i)   a simple expression, i.e. a constant value, the value of a bound variable, or the value of some function applied to actual parameter values specified by simple expressions, or

(ii)   a conditional expression specifying the conditional selection between two expressions.

The value of a conditional expression of the form if b then e_1 else e_2 is defined such that if b has the value

a)   true: the conditional expression has the value of e_1

b)   false: the conditional expression has the value of e_2

3.2.4   Examples

(1)   A function whose value is the sum of the values in a sequence of data items taken from

intval = {num} X integer

function sum : *(intval) → integer

s : *(intval)

cases

sum(λ) = 0

sum (s) = val (head(s)) + sum (tail(s))

end

(2)   function asc:*(intval) → *(intval)

s : *(intval)

cases

asc (λ) = λ

```
            asc (n) = n

            asc (s) = if val (head(s)) ≤ val (head(tail(s)))

                      then head(s) :: asc (tail(s))

                      else asc(head(s)::tail(tail(s)))

        end
```

For some sequence s from *(intval), asc(s) defines an embedded sequence of data items. This sequence is equal to s if the length of s is ≤ 1. In all other cases it is the embedded sequence starting with head(s) whose associated values are ordered by ≤ (defined on the integers). For example

        asc(<(num, 3), (num, 5), (num, 6), (num, 5)>)

        = <(num, 3), (num, 5), (num, 6)>

(3)   It is possible to use expressions as formal parameters to functions on the left hand side of the equations which

        a)   make the equations more readable

and   b)   make explicit the pattern matching which must be performed on the actual parameters to decide which of its defining equations is applicable [3].

This point is illustrated in the following alternative definition of the function of example (2).

```
function asc' : *(intval) → *(intval)

i, j : intval;

   s : *(intval)

cases

asc'(λ) =  λ

asc'(i) = i

asc'(i::j::s) = if val (i) ≤ val(j) then i::asc'(j::s)

                                    else asc'(i::s)

end
```

198

4. THE GENERAL APPROACH

4.1 Implicit Specification

An implicit specification states the properties that a solution must exhibit in implementation independent terms. It takes the form of relationships that must hold between the inputs and outputs of the program. We can record this information as (i) a type clause which identifies the sets of values (domains) from which the input values and output values must be selected and (ii) theorems stating the constraints and relationships that must hold.

For example, consider an implicit specification for a program kwic which must accept a set of titles and a set of non-significant words and produce an alphabetically sorted list of the significant rotations of the titles (i.e. those rotations beginning with a word that is significant).

In order to minimise the amount of detail to be considered we begin by making some simplistic assumptions about the domains of values to be manipulated. From the informal problem specification denote the sets of titles and words by sequences. This seems a reasonable device since they will ultimately form the inputs to a program. We can now supply an 'abstract syntax' for these domains using extended BNF notation.

<titles>   ::={<title>}

<title>   ::={<word>}$^+$ eot

<word>   ::={<alphanum>}$^+$

<words>   ::={<word>}

<rotations>::={<rotation>}

<rotation> ::={<word>}$^+$ eot {<word>}

             |

             eot{<word>}$^+$

< alphanum > ::=A|B ... |0|1| ... |9

Figure 3: Abstract syntax for inputs and outputs to KWIC

Curly brackets {} denotes zero or more repetitions

            and {}$^+$ denotes one or more repetitions.

We have conveniently ignored spacing and punctuation for the moment.

The domains of values that are to be manipulated are defined as follows:

alphanum = {A, B, ... Z, a, b, ... z, 0, 1, ... , 9}

eot   = null

word   = *(alphanum)
words   = *(word)
token   = word @ eot

title   = *(token)

titles   = *(title)

rotation = *(token)

rotations = *(rotation)

Figure 4: Domains of values manipulated by kwic

The informal specification may be rewritten:

kwic : titles x words → rotations

where kwic denotes a function satisfying:

    i)   the output from kwic is alphabetically ordered

    ordered(kwic(s, ns))   ,   ∀s : titles; ns words

   ii)   the output from KWIC is a permutation of all the significant rotations which may be generated from the list of titles input

    perm(kwic(s, ns), allsigrotations(s, ns))   ∀s : titles, ns : words

    This implicit specification is completed by supplying definitions for the predicates ordered, perm, and the function allsigrotations.

    The specification reflects a natural decomposition of the original problem identifying the sub-problem of generating all significant rotations of a sequence of titles. An implicit specification for this sub-problem is:

    allsigrotations : titles x words → rotations

where allsigrotations denotes a function satisfying:

    i)   if the input comprises the empty sequence of titles then the output contains no rotations.

    allsigrotations (λ, ns)= λ ∀ns: words

   ii)   member(r, allsigrotations(s, ns)) ⟺ member(r, everyrotation(s))

                                 and issignificant(r, ns)

                                    ∀r : notation, s : titles,

                                            ns : words.

    That is, the output from allsigrotations comprises every rotation that can be generated from the titles input whose initial word is not contained in the list of non-significant words.

    In general there is no unique decomposition of a problem. At each stage we introduce new functions and predicates to denote the newly identified sub-problems for which we have not yet provided a

specification. The general process is one of step-wise refinement of
the specification. The choice of functions and predicates is a form
of shorthand by which we control the amount of extra complexity to be
introduced at each step.

4.2   Functional Specification

By introducing further hypothetical function identifiers a
detailed implicit specification of the program could be completed.
However, we aim to make use of proof techniques as early in the development process as possible. We can achieve this objective if,
having postulated the existence of a function such as kwic, or
allsigrotations, we supply a definition for it. A suitable function
for kwic might be defined as follows:

function kwic : titles x word → rotations

s : titles; ns : words

cases

   kwic(s, ns) = sort(allsigrotations(s, ns))

end

The obvious purpose of the new function sort is to accept
a sequence of rotations and sort them into alphabetical order.

Sort must have the following properties:

sort : rotations → rotations

   The rotations produced by sort

   i)   must be alphabtically ordered

   ordered(sort(s))   s : rotations

   ii)   must be a permutation of the input sequence

   perm(sort(s), s)   s : rotations

If we can identify a function sort which satisfies this
specification it is a trivial matter to verify the function defined
for kwic against its specification.

Theorem kwic.1

ordered(kwic(s, ns))   s:titles, ns : words

Proof

ordered(kwic(s, ns))

⇒ ordered(sort(allsigrotations(s, ns))

⇒ true   allsigrotations(s, ns)∊rotations

                                                and property (1) of sort.

Theorem kwic.2

perm(kwic(s, ns), allsigrotations(s, ns)) s : titles; ns : words

Proof

perm(kwic(s, ns), allsigrotations(s, ns))

⇒ perm(sort(allsigrotations(s, ns)), allsigrotations(s, ns))

⇒ true

Reference [16]   contains a complete implicit/functional specification

of a solution to the kwic problem defined on the abstract domains of

figure: 4 . Informal but rigorous proofs are also presented

to verify that functions possess the required properties.

4.3   Representations, Realisations and Proofs of Consistency

4.3.1   Representation

We have so far managed to suppress the question of representation,

working with an abstract definition for input-output syntax and

domains. However, it is unlikely that a typical imperative programming

language for distributed computation can be expected to communicate

arbitrarily complex data items such as titles and rotations. It

is more reasonable to assume that the units of communication will be

much simpler and generally smaller.

In order to facilitate the construction of an implementation,

and the proof of its consistency with the specification, we can begin by deciding on a concrete representation for the data to be manipulated.

Assuming that streams in the final program will be capable of transmitting words as integral units we introduce extra 'marker' values into the data sequences which will delimit instances of syntactic objects. Such a representation is given for the kwic example below,

$\text{<titles>} ::= \{\text{<title>}\} \text{ eos}$

$\text{<title>} ::= \{\text{<word>}\}^{+} \text{ eot}$

$\text{<word>} ::= \{\text{<alphanum>}\}^{+}$

$\text{<words>} ::= \{\text{<word>}\} \text{ eows}$

$\text{<rotations>} ::= \{\text{<rotation>}\} \text{ eors}$

$\text{<rotation>} ::= \{\text{<word>}\}^{+} \text{ eot } \{\text{<word>}\}^{*} \text{ eor}$

$$|$$

$\text{eot} \{\text{<word>}\}^{+} \text{ eor}$

$\text{<alphanum>} ::= A| B| \ldots \qquad 0| 1| \ldots | 9$

Figure 5: Concrete syntax for kwic

```
alphabet = {A, B, ... , Z, a, b, ... , z, 0, 1, ... , 9} + {'eot'}
eos = null

eor = null

eors = null

eows = null

word = *(alphabet)

title = *({'word'} x word)

titleseq = *( word ⊕ eos)

wordseq = *(word ⊕ eows)

rtoken = word ⊕ eor

rstoken = word ⊕ eor ⊕ eors

rotseq = *((rtoken)

rotationseq = *(rstoken)
```

Figure 6: Concrete representation of domains for kwic

(Note: The specification functions generally define the required
behaviour when applied to an empty input sequence. However there can
be no primitive operation in the implementation language to test
whether a stream contains the empty sequence. Such a test would
be tantamount to asking whether any more data items will be transmitted by the stream. Nevertheless it is possible to adopt a
convention within the program for signalling the end of a sequence
to be transmitted by a stream by agreeing that termination is
indicated by the transmission of some distinguished type i.e. an
EOS marker).

We can identify functions R(representation) and A(abstraction)
defined on the abstract and concrete domains corresponding to
each syntactic class. They show (R) how an abstract object is to be
given a concrete representation and (A) the abstract object that a

sequence from a concrete domain denotes.

For example, for a word sequence:

R_{WS} : words $\rightarrow$ words^C

w : word; s : words

<u>cases</u>

R_{WS} (λ) = eows

R_{WS}(w::s) = R_w(w)::R_{WS}(s)

<u>end</u>

A_{WS} : words^C $\rightarrow$ words

w : word^C; s : words^C

<u>cases</u>

A_{WS}(eows) = λ

A_{WS}(w::s) = A_w(w)::A_{WS}(s)

<u>end</u>

4.3.2   <u>Realisations</u>

Suppose we consider a function f : $D_1 \rightarrow D_2$ from our abstract specification and suppose we can supply representation and abstraction functions R_1, R_2, A_1, A_2 for concrete domains D^C_1, D^C_2. If we now supply a realisation f' : $D^C_1 \rightarrow D^C_2$ of the function f it is a simple matter to formulate the required property that f' is consistent with f under the chosen representation i.e.

$$f'(x) = R_2(f(A_1(x))) \qquad\qquad \forall\ x\ \epsilon\ D^C_1$$

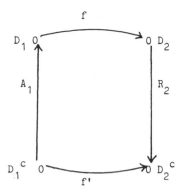

Figure 7: Diagram illustrating consistency of a realisation

If the chosen representation models the implementation
sufficiently closely we can use the representation and abstraction
functions in formulating the assertions required to prove the
consistency of the final imperative program. However, the proof of
consistency is usually sufficiently tedious without constantly
mapping to and from the abstract functions and it is more straightforward to supply a function definition for the realisation. In
general a design may be developed through several stages of
functional realisation to ensure that the problems considered at
each stage are kept manageable.

4.4   Specifying Processes

In practice it is convenient to use the representation implicitly
to produce assertions for a process in terms of the abstract
functions it implements. In addition we generally require a process
to perform a computation on an <u>initial</u> <u>subsequence</u> of the data items
transmitted by each input stream. More precisely we wish to
identify the <u>longest</u> <u>initial</u> <u>subsequence</u> of data items that can be
identified as belonging to the set of allowable inputs to the process.

To facilitate this we extend predicates and relations to apply to sequences and introduce a high-order function to identify the largest initial subsequence of a sequence satisfying some predicate.

4.4.1 Predicates and Relations on Sequences

For a given set of data items D, we may define predicates which map from D, D x D, ... into the boolean values.

It is a simple matter to extend a predicate P defined on a set of data items D, P : D → boolean, to apply to the sequences of data items taken from D, i.e. P : *(D) → boolean

function P : *(D) → boolean

  i : D ; s : *(D)

cases

  P(λ)   = true

  P(i::s) = if P(i) then P(s)

                   else false

end

For a sequence s ε *(D), P(s) iff the predicate P is true for all data items in s.

We may similarly extend a binary relation R defined on D x D to apply to sequences of items taken from D

function R : *(D) → boolean

  i, j : D ; s *(D)

cases

R(λ)   = true

R(i)   = true

R(i::j::s) = if R(i, j) then R(j::s)

                 else false

end

The predicate R is defined to be true when applied to the empty sequence or a single item from D. For any other sequence s ∈ *D, R(s) implies that R holds between all pairs of consecutive data items in s.

In our subsequent discussions we find it convenient to assume that these schema are used implicitly to extend all predicates and relations to apply to sequences.

4.4.2   Longest Initial Subsequence Operator

We introduce a scheme for a high-order function μ which takes a sequence predicate P and sequence s as arguments and identifies the longest initial subsequence of s that satisfies P. The function μ is defined by the following scheme; where 'sequence predicate' denotes

*(D) → boolean

function : sequence predicate X *(D) → *(D)

r : D ; s *(D); P : sequence predicate

cases

μ(P, λ)   = λ

μ(P, s::r) = if (Ps::r) then s::r

                        else μ(P, s)

end

Examples:

If s is a sequence from *(intval) then

(i)   μ(<, s) identifies the longest initial subsequence of s in which the (integer) values of the data items are strictly ascending.

(ii)   μ(less than 100, μ(<, s)) identifies the longest initial subsequence of a satisfying < in which the value of every item satisfies the predicate "lessthan100".

The operator ν maps a sequence predicate P, and a sequence s, into the sequence obtained by removing from s the longest initial sequence of s that satisfies P.

<u>function</u> ν: sequence predicate X *(D) → *(D)

r : D ; s *(D) ; P : sequence predicate

<u>cases</u>

   ν(P, λ)   = λ

   ν(P, s::r) = <u>if</u> P(s::r) <u>then</u> λ

                     <u>else</u> ν(P, s)::r

<u>end</u>

     Operators μ, ν are introduced to facilitate the description of processes.

4.4.3   <u>Example</u>

     Suppose we wish to specify a process 'filter' described by the abstract function asc:*(intval) → *(intval) of section 3.2.4.

We use μ,ν to define functions describing how filter affects its output stream and input stream respectively, assuming that the predicate 'isint' is true iff its argument is composed entirely of intval items and false otherwise:

<u>function</u> out: *(D) → *(intval)

s : *(D)

<u>cases</u>

   out(s) = asc(μ(isint, s))

<u>end</u>

<u>function</u> in : *(D) → *(D)

s : *(D)

<u>cases</u>

   in(s) = ν(isint, s)

<u>end</u>

(Note: D denotes the universe of data items).

Functions in, out can be used in the pre- and post-assertions for the
imperative process. Typical of such assertions are

Pre.filter:input = i and kind(head(ν(isint, i))) = eos and output = 0

Post.filter:output = 0::out(i)::eos and input = tail(in(i))

4.5   Implementation

The final development step is to construct an imperative
program and prove its consistency with the functional specification. This
problem is discussed in [4] which introduces the kernel of a language
for distributed programs and supplies a proof system for partial correctness.

The program proofs are concerned only with simple consistency arguments. The function definitions can be used (i) in the construction of
assertions and (ii) as a 'theory' to be used in proving that the
assertions are satisfied by the program. Proving that the implementation
is faithful to the design need not consider the more general questions
concerning the global correctness of the program. Such properties will
already have been verified in terms of the design.

It is possible that the implementation may result in an inefficient
program and the application of program optimisation may be desirable.
The optimisations may be applied as transformations on the program
statements and standard correctness preserving transformations may be
available. Another possibility is that alternative definitions may
be constructed for functions in the specification. Examples of the
former include techniques for recursion removal while alternative
function definitions might indicate greater degrees of concurrency in
imperative implementations.

5. MECHANISING THE PROOFS

It is generally easier to prove theorems about functions than about imperative programs. In addition mechanical aids are available for proving and checking proofs of theorems about functions. The Boyer and Moore theorem prover can, with human assistance, prove theorems about Lisp programs. It uses sophisticated heuristics to produce proofs using induction in the computational logic described in [2]. Edinburgh LCF [13] is similarly a computer system for doing formal proofs interactively It is based on the "Logic for Computable Functions" due to Dana Scott in which facts about recursively defined functions can be formulated and proved.

We have successfully formulated earlier versions of the functions to generate all rotations of a title, in the kwic example, and machine-checked that they possess the desired properties using the Boyer-Moore theorem prover. The main lesson learned from this experience is the value of being forced to adopt a rigorous approach and a formal notation (in this case Lisp). The extra effort this involves is offset by being able to delegate the often tedious task of proof checking to a machine and the resulting increased confidence that the proving process is reliable. Using functions to specify imperative programs appears to be a major step towards the use of mechanical proof techniques at all stages of program development.

6. CONCLUSIONS

We have shown how to develop programs by refinement using complementary implicit and functional specifications. The functional abstraction is sufficiently powerful to describe a major class of distributed programs. Section 3 introduced a typed functional notation developed for that purpose.

Proof techniques can be employed at each stage of program development and the resulting separation of the different aspects of the correctness of a program simplifies each step of the task. A similar approach can be found in [5], in which algebraic specifications of the Fisher-Galler algorithm are used to demonstrate the proof of a design. A top-down, rigorous design method is also described in [10].

Several levels of realisation may be employed before arriving at a detailed specification. The consistency of each new realisation of a function can be proved as it is introduced. The correctness of the final implementation is purely a matter of consistency with its specification. The use of functional specifications may make feasible the mechanisation of large parts of a program's proof.

Acknowledgement

We are pleased to acknowledge the generous help and patient guidance given by Robert S. Boyer and J. Strother Moore in the use of their theorem prover, at SRI International, Menlow Park, California.

References

1. APT, K. R. FRANCEZ, N. and de ROEVER, W.   A Proof System for
   Communicating Sequential Processes,
   ACM Transactions on Programming Languages and Systems,
   vol 2, No 3, July 1980, Page 359-385.

2. BOYER, R. S. and MOORE, J. S.   A Computational Logic,
   Academic Press, Inc. (London) Ltd., 1979.

3. BURSTALL, R. M.   Proving Properties of Programs by Structural
   Induction
   Computer Journal, 12(1) 41 - 48, February 1969.

4. COLEMAN, D and GALLIMORE, R.   Partial Correctness of Distributed
   Programs,
   these Proceedings.

5. CORRELL, C. H.   Proving Programs Correct through Refinement,
   Acta Informatica, 9, 121-139 (1978).

6. de BAKKER, J.   Mathematical Theory of Program Correctness,
   Prentice-Hall International, Inc., London 1981.

7. FLOYD, R. W.   Assigning Meanings to Programs.
   AMS 19, 19-32 (1967).

8. HOARE, C. A. R.   An Axiomatic Basis for Computer Programming,
   Communications of the ACM 12, 576-580 (1969).

9. HOARE, C. A. R.   Communicating Sequential Processes,
   Communications of the ACM 21, 8, 666-677 (1978).

10. JONES, C. B.   Software Development: A Rigorous Approach,
    Prentice Hall International, Inc., London 1980.

11. KAHN, G. and MacQUEEN, D. B.   Coroutines and Networks of Parallel
    Processes,
    Proc. IFIP Congress, 1977, North-Holland, Amsterdam 1977,
    pp 993-998.

12. LEVIN, G. M. and GRIES, D.   A Proof Technique for Communicating
    Sequential Processes,
    Acta Informatica 15, 281-302 (1981).

13. GORDON, M. J., MILNER, A. J. and WADSWORTH, C. P.   Edinburgh LCF,
    Lecture Notes in Computer Science 78,
    Springer-Verlag, Berlin 1979.

14. OWICKI, S. S., and GRIES, D.   Verifying Properties of Parallel
    Programs: An Axiomatic Approach,
    Communications of the ACM 19, 5 (May 1976), 279-285.

15. SCOTT, D. S. and STRACHEY, C.   Towards a Mathematical Semantic
    for Computer Languages,
    in Proc. Symp. Computers and Automata (J. Fox ed)
    pp 19-46, Polytechnic Institute of Brooklyn Press 1971.

16. GALLIMORE, R.M. and COLEMAN, D.   Specification of a KWIC
    Index Generator,
    These proceedings.

ROBUST DATA TYPES

Flaviu CRISTIAN

Computing Laboratory
University of Newcastle upon Tyne
Newcastle upon Tyne NE1 7RU
England

ABSTRACT

The concept of a data type with total operations and exceptions is proposed as a basic structuring tool for the design of verifiable robust software. A notation for the specification of such data types is presented and the issues underlying their implementation in a programming language supporting data abstraction and exception handling are discussed and illustrated by examples. Existing proof methods are extended to permit verification of the total correctness of programs which implement or make use of data types with total operations and exceptions.

Key-words and phrases: Data Abstraction, Partial Operations, Exception Handling, Total Operations, Program Verification, Software Engineering.

1. Introduction

It is customary in current approaches to data abstraction to leave the result of an operation invocation unspecified if certain preconditions do not hold. For example the result of invoking the top operation on a stack may be specified to be the top element of the stack if the stack is not empty. Troubles arise when the stack is empty since then there does not exist a top-element. This situation is referred to as an exception occurrence.

The need for taking into account exceptions is not even explicitly recognised in certain academic spheres. Software engineers on the other hand know that substantial parts of the programs they usually write are devoted to detecting and handling exceptions. The argument most often advanced for not specifying what happens if exceptions occur is that static verification methods can be used to guarantee that such situations never arise, provided the environments in which the programs run satisfy certain hypotheses. In reality strong assumptions about the behaviour of these environments can rarely be made, especially if their correctness is not verified or verifiable (e.g. human users). It is then essential to specify what should happen if exceptions occur.

One possibility is to specify that an exception occurrence leads to program abortion. This (somewhat radical) solution is simple and has been modelled mathematically by several authors (e.g. [6,8]). While it may be satisfactory for certain kinds of programs (e.g. student programs) it is certainly not satisfactory for other kinds of programs (e.g. operating systems, data base systems, process control systems).

In this paper we show how exceptions may be used to structure the specification, implementation and verification of programs which are robust, i.e. can continue to work in spite of exception occurrences. The goal is to demonstrate that the construction of robust programs can be made subject to rigorous design methods similar to those (e.g. [11,6,20,3,14]) proposed for the development of programs without any provision for exception handling.

As we consider the concept of a data type to be one of the most important software structuring tools, the focus will be on the design of robust data types. These may be used as building blocks for larger robust systems. The concept of an exception is rigorously defined, a notation for specifying data types with total operations and exceptions is proposed and it is shown how such data types may be implemented in a programming language supporting encapsulation and exception mechanisms. The elaboration of these issues sheds new light on some basic aspects of exception handling, such as the identification and specification of exceptions for operations, the precise detection of exception occurrences, the recovery of consistent states after exception detections and the propagation of exceptions. A method for proving the correctness of implementations with respect to specifications is also proposed. By this method the verification of a program which may signal $k \geq 0$ exceptions is factored into $k+1$ independent proofs: one (classical) proof of correct standard behaviour and k proofs of correct exceptional behaviour. This separation of concerns can be taken as an indication that the effort required for producing robust programs is not much greater than that required for producing programs which deliver their specified result only if they do not have some other unpredictable behaviour.

The paper is composed of two main parts. In the first we introduce the concept of a robust data type together with a simple example and sketch criteria for verifying the total correctness of data type implementations with specifications. By total correctness it is meant that the implemented operations terminate cleanly (without unanticipated exception detections). In the second part we use the simple example to construct a more elaborate hierarchically structured example. This allows a natural generalisation of the earlier correctness criteria and presents some important (but not much explored) aspects of exception handling in hierarchies of data abstractions.

2. Robust Data Types

For a definition of an exception to be precise, it is first necessary to have a clear idea about what is meant by a data type with partial operations. Thus, although our interest is in data types with total operations and exceptions, we devote the sections 2.1, 2.2, 2.3 of this first part of the paper to discuss issues underlying the specification, implementation and total correctness of data types with partial operations. The concept of an exception is defined in section 2.4 and section 2.5 describes the exception mechanism we use. The last three sections take up the issues discussed in the first three sections (i.e. specification, implementation, total correctness) for data types with total operations and exceptions.

2.1. Data Types with Partial Operations

Data abstraction has emerged from recent research in programming as a means of extending the data definition and manipulation facilities of a programming language with new (abstract) data types. In an imperative language, like that considered in this paper, one can view a data type as being a (finite) set of values plus a (finite) set of operations specified in terms of some underlying logical data space. By a data space we mean a mathematical structure consisting of several sorts of sets and operators among those sets [9]. The semantics of the operations of the type is expressed by formulae in the language of this structure and a distinguished ´sort of interest´ can be used to specify the set of values of the type [10].

A data space can be defined implicitly by axioms [9,21,10,7,17] or can be constructed explicitly in terms of some well-understood fixed mathematical language [11,20,3,14,1]. This second definition method (to be used in this paper) leads to shorter presentations since it relies on the reader´s familiarity with the concepts used when defining new data spaces. However, as our solution to exception handling is entirely at the programming language level, it can acommodate within any particular technique which may be adopted for defining the underlying data spaces.

We assume a programming language with variables: an instance of a data type T is declared in a program as a variable of type T. A mapping from program variables to values (of their type) is a program state. When we speak about the state (or value) of a variable we mean the result of applying a state function to it.

Let A be a set of program states. The abstract meaning of an operation OP of a data type T can be defined to be a state transition relation [20,14,7]. A pair of states $(a´,a) \in A \times A$ is in this relation if the final state $a \in A$ is an intended outcome of invoking OP in the initial state $a´ \in A$ (as in [20,7] states prior to operation invocations are primed). In practice, such a relation is not defined by enumerating its component pairs, but by giving its characteristic (binary) predicate:

$$post \in A \times A \rightarrow \{true, false\}$$

called (for reasons to become clear later) the abstract standard postcondition of OP. In general post is a partial relation: there exist initial states which do not have successors in post. A total unary predicate, the abstract standard precondition of OP:

$$pre \in A \rightarrow \{true, false\}$$

will be used in what follows to characterise the domain of post, i.e. the set of those initial states which have successors in post:

$$pre(a´) = true \equiv a´ \in dom(post)$$

where

$$dom(post) \equiv \{a´ \in A | \exists a \in A: post(a´, a) = true\}$$

An operation is called partial if its meaning is a partial state transition relation. We wait until section 2.6 to see how exceptions can be used to build total operations.

In order to make the notions discussed so far more tangible we specify a simple data type RESOURCES, often used in operating systems to manage an arbitrary number $n > 0$ of resources. The positive (machine representable) integer n is a generic parameter of the type. The resources are identified by the set of integer constants $\{1,2,...,n\}$ denoted [n]. The data space underlying RESOURCES contains three sorts of sets (booleans, machine representable integers and the set of subsets of [n] denoted P[n]) together with a collection of operators among these sets. Some of the operators are total and others partial. Among the first we mention: "$\in$" (membership), "$\sqcup$" (set union), "$-$" (set difference), "$||$" (cardinality), etc. Among the second there is the partial (nondeterministic) choice operator "oneof" which for a subset r of [n] yields an element of r if r is not empty, i.e. $\forall r \in P[n]: |r| > 0 \Rightarrow oneof(r) \in r$. With partial operators we associate total predicates "def" indicating whether they are applied to elements of their domain or not (e.g. $def(oneof(r)) \equiv |r| > 0$). For machine representable data types with finite underlying data spaces, such total predicates always exist. The properties of our data space may be inferred from its definition, e.g. if $|r| < n$ then $r \sqcup \{oneof([n]-r)\} \in P[n]$, $|r \sqcup \{oneof([n]-r)\}| = |r| + 1$, etc.

A notation close to that of [20] is used in Figure 1 to specify the RESOURCES type. Some conventions are used to shorten the notation. In order to avoid explicit mention of state functions, we write variable identifiers in capital letters and variable values in lower case letters (e.g. if V is a program variable v stands for a value of V). Also, if an operation does not change the state of a variable we omit explicit mention of this fact (e.g. the term $i = i´$ indicating that RELEASE does not alter the value parameter I is omitted in line 10 and in line 9 we have written i∈r´ instead of i´∈r´).

```
1     specification of type RESOURCES(generic N:INTEGER>0)
2     values  r∈P[n]
3     initial value r={}
4     operations
5        function GET returns I:INTEGER
6        pre   |r´|<n
7        post  i=oneof([n]-r´) & r=r´⊔{i}
8        procedure RELEASE(I:INTEGER)
9        pre   i∈r´
10       post  i∈r´ & r=r´-{i}
```

Figure 1. Specification of a data type with partial operations

Line 2 defines a value of an arbitrary variable R of type
RESOURCES(N) to be a subset of [n]. The predicate in line 3 specifies
the value assumed by such a variable after its declaration to be the
empty subset. The intention is to make the value of R be the subset of
those resources which are allocated. Lines 5 and 8 define the syntax
for invoking the operations GET and RELEASE. Following [11] this syntax
will be I:=R.GET and R.RELEASE(I). Line 7 states that the standard
result of GET is to return an integer value i identifying a resource
which was previously free, i.e. i=oneof([n]-r´), and which after the
invocation becomes allocated, i.e. r=r´⊔{i}. The standard result of
invoking RELEASE with a parameter I (line 10) is to deallocate the
resource i, i.e. r=r´-{i}, if it was previously allocated, i.e. i∈r´.
The preconditions in lines 6,9 characterise the domains of the postconditions in lines 7,10. As these abstract standard domains are strictly
included in the set of (abstract) states which can exist for the couple
of variables R,I, the two operations GET and RELEASE are partial.

2.2. Implementation

We assume a PASCAL-like (deterministic) programming language providing a SIMULA class like construct [11] for the implementation of
abstract data types. An implementation of a data type T defines a concrete internal representation for the set of values specified for T, the
bodies B(OP) of the routines implementing the operations OP and an
internal state initialisation algorithm INIT, which we assume to be
automatically invoked at instance creation.

Let C be the set of internal states associated with the variables
of an implementation. The intended meaning of a routine B(OP) can be
specified by a concrete standard postcondition

cpost ∈ CxC → {true,false}

A pair of states (c´,c) is in cpost if c is an intended outcome of an
invocation of B(OP) in the initial state c´. On the other hand, each
routine is a sequence of commands available in the programming language
being used, and as such has an actual meaning which is imposed by the
semantic definition of this language.

The actual standard meaning of B(OP) can be defined to be another
(partial) relation

reachable(B(OP)) ∈ CxC → {true,false}

with the understanding that a pair (c´,c) is in this relation if when invoked in the state c´ B(OP) terminates cleanly in c [2]. However for program proofs, one is interested to know not only if a program terminates, but if it terminates in a state satisfying a given postcondition [6]. For this purpose, the use of the backward predicate transformer semantics given in [2] is more suitable. This semantics is similar to that of [6]. One difference is that the predicates we consider are binary, i.e. primed states may occur in them. A more important difference is that in predicates we use noncommutative logical connectives & (conditional and) and V (conditional or) and that we take special care in dealing with data types (e.g. bounded integers, finite arrays) with partial operations. For example let T be a language defined type with a partial unary operator f in its underlying data space. If the standard effect of invoking an operation OP on a variable V of type T is the assignment of a new value f(v) to V, then the standard meaning of OP is given in [2] as

$$wp("V.OP",Q) \equiv def(f(v)) \ \& \ Q[f(v)/v]$$

where Q is an arbitrary predicate and Q[f(v)/v] stands for the result of substituting all free occurrences of v in Q by f(v), after all the usual precautionary measures for avoiding name clashes. The guard def(f(v)) at the left of the noncommutative "&" is essential for ensuring that the term f(v) to be substituted is well defined, i.e. is obtained by applying f to an element of its domain. A detailed discussion of the technical issues related to the use of such a noncommutative logic is beyond the scope of this paper. We limit ourselves to state that its use seems to be necessary whenever one wishes to avoid the occurrence of undefined terms in the verification conditions generated during program proofs.

Returning now to our discussion about the actual standard meaning of a routine we define it to be its backward predicate transformer (derivable as the composition of the predicate transformers associated with its component commands). In particular, we define the concrete standard precondition cpre of a routine to be the weakest precondition associated with its body and its concrete standard postcondition:

$$cpre \equiv wp("B(OP)",cpost)$$

where

$$wp("B(OP)",cpost)(c´) \equiv \exists c \in C: reachable(B(OP))(c´,c) \ \& \ cpost(c´,c)$$

Thus, cpre characterises the set of initial states c´ for which B(OP) terminates cleanly in a final state c satisfying cpost(c´,c).

An implementation of the RESOURCES data type is given in Figure 2. We assume that the positivity of the generic parameter N is checked by the compiler. The AND, OR operations of the BOOLEAN language defined type are noncommutative as their corresponding logical connectives & and V (e.g. if the loop guard in line 9 is evaluated in a state j=n+1 then the well defined result false is obtained even though ¬def(t(n+1)=used)). The concrete standard postconditions stated as comments (between % symbols) in lines 12, 16 specify the intended meaning of the GET and RELEASE routines. The concrete standard preconditions in lines 7, 14 have been derived using the semantics given in [2].

```
1      type RESOURCES =
2      class(generic N:INTEGER>0);

3          type RESOURCE-STATE = (FREE,USED);
4          var T:ARRAY (1..N) of RESOURCE-STATE;

5          function GET returns I:INTEGER;
6          var J:INTEGER;
7          begin % cpre = ∃j: 1≤j≤n & t´(j)=free %
8              J:=1;
9              while (J≤N)AND(T(J)=USED) do J:=J+1;
10             T(J):=USED;
11             I:=J;
12         end; % cpost≡ 1≤i≤n & t´(i)=free & t(i)=used  %

13         procedure RELEASE(I:INTEGER);
14         begin % cpre= 1≤i≤n & t´(i)=used %
15             T(I):=FREE;
16         end; % cpost≡ 1≤i≤n & t´(i)=used & t(i)=free  %

17     begin for I:=1 to N do T(I):=FREE %INIT%
18     end RESOURCES.
```

Figure 2.   Implementation of a data type with partial operations

2.3. Correctness

In order to prove the correctness of a data type implementation
with a specification, it is first necessary to establish a correspondence between internal and abstract states. Following [11] this
correspondence will be defined by an abstraction (or representation)
function denoted rep.

In our example, the rep function is defined[1] on any value t that
the variable T declared in Figure 2 may reach:

$$rep(t) \equiv \{j|(1\le j\le n)\&t(j)=used\}$$

Clearly, for every reachable t, rep(t)∈P[n] holds.

Criteria for establishing the consistency of a data type implementation with a specification within a partial correctness semantic framework are discussed in [11]. Such a proof of correctness guarantees that
whenever an operation is invoked in an initial state satisfying its
precondition, either it terminates in a state satisfying the postcondition or it does not terminate properly, i.e. loops indefinitely or
leads to an (unanticipated) exception detection. Our interest is in
clean termination. We therefore will strengthen the criteria given in
[11] as follows.

---

[1] As all the routines of this paper have parameters or return values of
language defined types and the abstraction functions for them are identity functions we omit their explicit mention.

Let C be the set of internal states reachable by an instance of a data type T, INIT be the initialisation algorithm and rep be the representation function. First, it is necessary to verify that the constraints on the generic parameters of T guarantee that INIT yields a state c for which rep(c) satisfies the ´initial value´ predicate of T:

(VC0) constraints on generic parameters $\Rightarrow$ wp(INIT,initial-value(rep(c)))

Furthermore, for each operation OP of T it is necessary to show that its concrete meaning is consistent with its abstract meaning. Let post be the specification of the abstract standard meaning of OP and pre characterise the domain of post. At the implementation level, let cpost be the specification of the concrete standard meaning of B(OP) and cpre = wp("B(OP)",cpost) characterise the initial states c´ for which B(OP) yields final states c such that cpost(c´,c). The first verification condition ensures that, whenever OP is invoked in a state c´ for which rep(c´) has a successor in post, then for c´ there exists a reachable successor in cpost:

(VC1) pre(rep(c´)) $\Rightarrow$ cpre(c´)

The second verification condition ensures that the successor c reached after the (clean) termination of B(OP) corresponds through rep to a specified abstract successor of rep(c´):

(VC2) cpost(c´,c) $\Rightarrow$ post(rep(c´),rep(c))

As an example, we state bellow (without proof) the verification conditions which ensure that the implementation of ´RESOURCES is totally correct with the specification of Figure 1.

1) Correct initialisation

(I)   n>0 $\Rightarrow$ wp("INIT", rep(t)={})

2) Correctness of the standard effect of GET

(G1) |rep(t´)|<n $\Rightarrow$ cpre(GET)(t´)

(G2) cpost(GET)(t´,t) $\Rightarrow$ i=oneof([n]-rep(t´)) & rep(t)=rep(t´)$\sqcup${i}

3) Correctness of the standard effect of RELEASE:

(R1) i∈rep(t´) $\Rightarrow$ cpre(RELEASE)(t´)

(R2) cpost(RELEASE)(t´,t) $\Rightarrow$ i∈rep(t´) & rep(t)=rep(t´)-{i}

In deriving the above verification conditions we have used the predicate transformer semantics [2] of a language supporting the predefined types BOOLEAN, INTEGER, ARRAY. Now that we have extended this language with the RESOURCES type it would be interesting to express the semantics of its operations in terms of predicate transformers also. That would allow programs using RESOURCES to be verified in the same manner as if only predefined types were used (a main idea in data abstraction is to place abstract and predefined types on an equal footing). The last part of this section investigates this point briefly.

We assume in what follows that whenever an operation OP of an abstract type T is invoked on a variable V in a state outside the standard domain, i.e. ¬pre(v´), then OP does not terminate normally (a systematic method for enforcing this behaviour is given later). Our second assumption is that the abstract postcondition of OP describes explicitly how the new state v is obtained by applying a (generally partial) operator f of the underlying data space to v´, i.e. post≡v=f(v´) where pre(v´)⟹def(f(v´))². Under the above assumptions, the truth of the (VC0,VC1,VC2) verification conditions ensures that pre(v´) is the necessary and sufficient condition for the standard termination of V.OP in a state satisfying v=f(v´). Another way of saying this is the following: the necessary and sufficient condition for the standard termination of V.OP in a state satisfying an arbitrary predicate Q is the truth of pre(v)&Q[f(v)/v] before the invocation of V.OP:

$$wp("V.OP",Q) \equiv pre(v) \ \& \ Q[f(v)/v]$$

Thus, under the assumption that the operations specified for RESOURCES do not terminate normally outside their standard domains, we can give their predicate transformer semantics as follows:

(1) $wp("I:=R.GET",Q) \equiv |r|<n \ \& \ Q[x/i,r\sqcup\{x\}/r]$ <u>where</u> x=oneof([n]-r)

(2) $wp("R.RELEASE(I)",Q) \equiv (i \in r) \ \& \ Q[r-\{i\}/r]$

The expression Q[a/b,c/d] stands for the result of simultaneously substituting in Q all free occurrences of b by a and all free occurrences of d by c.

As an example, let us use (1) to derive the necessary and sufficient condition for the algorithm

C1 I:=R.GET;
C2 J:=R.GET;

to terminate normally. This condition is $wp("C1;C2",true)$ and by expanding it we obtain successively:

$wp("C1",wp("C2",true))$ (by 1 with Q=true)

$=wp("C1",|r|<n)$ (by 1 with Q=|r|<n)

$=|r|<n \ \& \ |r\sqcup\{oneof([n]-r)\}|<n$ (properties of underlying data space)

$=|r|\leq n-2$

Thus, C1;C2 terminates normally iff initially there are at least two free resources.

2.4. Exceptions

Let A be an integer array with domain 1..N and I,R be variables of type INTEGER and RESOURCES(N) respectively. Suppose that in order to achieve some desired state transition we compose the following two commands into a program:

---

² The case when OP has parameters or returns some value can be dealt with similarly.

```
C1    I:=R.GET;
C2    A(I):=1;
```

Such sequential compositions are based on the (most often implicitly made) assumption that when the ´next´ command C2 is invoked, the
standard state transition of C1 has been accomplished. Here the invocation of C2 makes sense only if the state s2 after C1 is such that
s2(I)=i is a newly allocated resource name and thus is a valid index for
accessing A. If the state s1 prior to the invocation of C1 was such
that r=[n] ,where r=s1(R), then a state s2 such that post(GET)(s1,s2)
cannot be reached (it is impossible to assign to I the name of a free
resource since such a resource does not exist). In such circumstances,
the initial assumption that the execution of C1 should be followed by
that of the ´next´ command C2 has to be revised.

Problems do not arise only in the programs which use data types but
also in those which implement them. For example if the GET routine of
Figure 2 is invoked in an initial state in which all the entries of T
are used, the loop in line 9 terminates with j=n+1 and the invocation of
the ´next´ command in line 10 results in an array bounds violation. The
implementation of Figure 2 is nevertheless consistent with the specification of Figure 1, since this specification does not say what should
happen in such circumstances and therefore any behaviour of GET would be
´consistent´ with that specification.

A possible solution to the above difficulties is to abort a program
whenever one of its component operations is invoked outside its standard
domain. Conceptually that can be modelled by specifying that such an
invocation does not produce a successor state (the operation "fails to
terminate" [6]) or that some error value – and hence error state – is
produced and the program remains for ever in it (the following operations produce error values from error values [8]). This paper is
devoted to the discussion of another possible solution (widely used in
practice but for some reason not rigorously treated until now).

Let us define an invocation of an operation outside its abstract
standard domain to be an exception occurrence. By the definition of
this domain it follows that once the goal of an operation invocation is
specified to be some (partial) state transition relation post, the set
of initial states which lead to exception occurrences is uniquely determined as A-dom(post), where A is the set of possible initial states.
The set A-dom(post) will be called the abstract exceptional domain of
the operation.

The solution to exception handling we want to explore is based on
the following simple idea: an exception occurrence should cause an
(exceptional) alteration of the (standard) sequential composition rule
for operation invocations. A programming language control mechanism
allowing to express how the standard continuation of an operation invocation is to be replaced by an exceptional continuation when the
occurrence of an exception is detected will be called an exception
mechanism. In what follows we assume that the exception mechanism
introduced in [4] (similar to some extent to those of [15,13]) is available in our programming language. Because of space limitations, we
present here only those features of the mechanism which are needed for
the understanding of this paper.

2.5. Exception Mechanism

Exceptional continuations for exception occurrences are defined by using exception labels. The designer of a routine OP can declare that whenever OP is invoked in its exceptional domain an E exception label is signalled:

procedure OP;signals E

and an invoker of OP can define the exceptional continuation, if E is signalled, to be some exception handler K:

OP[E⟹K]

In order to detect and handle the occurrence of the (by now labelled) E exception, the implementor of OP can insert in B(OP) one of the following syntactic constructs:

(b) [B⟹H]

(c) C[F⟹H]

In the first, B stands for a boolean expression without side effects. In (c), F stands for an exception label which may be signalled by the command C. H stands for an exception handler. All the handlers to be used in this paper follow the syntax:

H ≡ H1;signal E

where H1 is a (possibly empty) command[3]. Exceptional continuations can be associated with operation invocations and exception labels only by using (c) constructs (e.g. OP[E⟹K] is an instance of such a construct).

The concept of a continuation function used in denotational semantics [19] can be used to express formally the meaning of the signal command used in the (b,c) constructs. However, in what follows we choose (for simplicity reasons) to remain within the traditional data abstraction approach to programming in which to abstract from such ´control´ issues (in order to better concentrate on data representation issues) is an integral part of the ´divide and conquer´ underlying philosophy. We therefore limit ourselves to give a predicate transformer semantic characterisation of the (b,c) constructs. This characterisation captures that part of their meaning which can be described in terms of program states and is sufficient for proving the correctness of programs which implement or make use of data types with exceptions.

Let us first present informally that aspect of the (b,c) constructs which will not be described in terms of predicate transformers: the ´signal´ command. Some context-sensitive syntactic rules have to be obeyed when using such a command in a routine: it can occur only in an exceptional construct surrounded by square brackets and the signalled label E must be declared in the header of the routine (so that invokers

---

[3] Issues related to standard handler terminations (corresponding to exception propagations being stopped - or masked) are discussed in [4,5] and will not be considered in this presentation.

may define exceptional continuations for occurrences of E). These constraints can be checked by a compiler without difficulty. If we adopt
the convention of denoting by

$$C[P \Longrightarrow H]$$

either a (b) or a (c) construct (if C is empty then P stands for a
boolean expression B and otherwise it stands for a label F which may be
signalled by C) then the pattern of syntactically legal use is:

```
         procedure OP;signals E;
         begin C1;
(u)              C[P⟹H1;signal E];
                 C2;
         end;
```

where C1 or C2 are (possibly empty) commands. The effect of executing
the "signal E" command is the following: the standard continuation of
the C[P⟹H] construct (the ´next´ C2) is ignored and OP terminates
exceptionally with E being signalled, i.e. an exception handler K associated (by using a (c) syntactic construct) with E in the invocation
context of OP is activated. An exception mechanism must be designed so
as to guarantee that such an exceptional continuation always exists and
is uniquely defined. For a detailed discussion of these exception
mechanism design issues the interested reader is referred to [4].

We now come to those aspects of the (b,c) constructs which can be
described in terms of predicate transformers (under the assumption that
the above constraints relative to ´signal´ commands and exceptional continuations are enforced). Assume that a (b) construct is inserted in a
routine according to the (u) pattern and that B has always a well-
defined value. The local effect of inserting the construct in B(OP) can
be defined as follows. If the preceding command (C1) terminates in a
state s in which the value b=s(B) of B is false, then the following command (C2) is invoked in the (same) state s in a standard manner
(independently of what the meaning of H might be):

(bs) $wp("[B \Longrightarrow H]",Q) \equiv \neg b \& Q$

Otherwise, i.e. if the preceding command (C1) terminates in a state e in
which e(B)=b is true, the exception handler following the "[B⟹" syntactic fragment is invoked in the (same) state e:

(be) $wp("[B \Longrightarrow ",Q) \equiv b \& Q$

Thus, a (b) construct acts as a switching point. By using it one
can write in a linear notation two sequentially composed programs which
share their entry points but have distinct exit points and perform different state transitions: C1;[B⟹H];C2 behaves like C1;C2 in the standard case (bs) and like C1;H in the exceptional case (be). One could
remark that the program C1;if B then H else C2 can do the same job. We
prefere the (b) syntax for several reasons. First, it leads to a clear
separation between what is standard and what is exceptional in programs.
Second, it provides a means for forbiding signal commands to occur ´hid-
den´ within standard constructs (like the previous "if B then H else
C2"). If the signal command could occur within them, then the semantic
definition of every standard construct would have to be modified to

reflect this possibility. Our opinion is that the need to define an exceptional semantics for programming constructs should not interfere with, but rather be a completion of, their standard semantics which should remain unchanged. This point is further elaborated when the predicate transformer characterisation of the (c) construct is given. We also show that the restriction to use signals only in exceptional constructs enables one to prove separately properties relative to the standard or exceptional behaviour of programs.

As a first example of such a proof, let us use the (bs,be) clauses to derive the conditions for standard and exceptional termination of a (slightly modified) version of the GET routine of Figure 2 in which

$$[J>N \Rightarrow \underline{signal} \ OV]$$

is inserted as shown in Figure 4 of section 2.7. Let C1 and C2 be the sequential compositions of the commands preceding (lines 7,9) and following (lines 10,11) this exceptional construct:

C1≡ J:=1; $\underline{while}$(J≤N)AND(T(J)=USED)$\underline{do}$J:=J+1

C2≡ T(J):=USED; I:=J

The condition for exceptional termination in a state $t=t'$ with the OV(erflow) exception being signalled is:

wp("C1;[J>N⇒",$t=t'$)=   (by the be clause)

=wp("C1",(j>n)&($t=t'$))

⇒∀j: (1≤j≤n)⇒(t'(j)=used)

The condition for standard termination with the internal state being changed as specified by cpost(GET) is

wp("C1;[J>N⇒$\underline{signal}$ OV];C2",cpost(GET))=

=wp("C1;[J>N⇒$\underline{signal}$ OV]",(1≤j≤n)&(t'(j)=free))   (by the bs clause)

=wp("C1",(1≤j≤n)&(t'(j)=free))

⇒∃j:(1≤j≤n)&(t'(j)=free)

Thus, the insertion of the exceptional construct for OV in GET does not alter the standard properties of this routine. However, if the routine is now invoked in an initial state for which cpre(GET) does not hold, then the invocation of C2 is replaced by that of the handler of the OV exception, in this example a simple signal OV command. This causes the exceptional termination of GET and the invocation of a handler K associated with the label OV in the invocation context of GET:

I:=R.GET[OV⇒K]

K may in its turn handle the occurrence of another exception specified for the program which invoked GET. We postpone a discussion of the issues related to exception propagations until section 3.5 and content ourselves for the moment to emphasize that the phrases ´handler of E´ and ´handler associated with E´ are used to designate distinct handlers.

Predicate transformer characterisations similar to (bs,be) can be given also for (c) constructs. Assume that such a construct is inserted in a routine by following the (u) pattern. The necessary and sufficient condition for the command (C2) following the C[F⟹H] construct to be invoked in a state satisfying a predicate Q is the standard termination of C in such a state (independently of what the meaning of H might be):

(cs) $wp("C[F⟹H]",Q) \equiv wp("C",Q)$

Thus, by adjoining in a program a [F⟹H] exceptional construct to a command C, one does not change the standard behaviour of that program. For example if C is I:=R.GET then the standard meaning of I:=R.GET[OV⟹K] is the same as that of I:=R.GET for any K:

(1´) $wp("I:=R.GET[OV⟹K]",Q) \equiv |r|<n \& Q[x/i,r \sqcup \{x\}/r]$ <u>where</u> x=oneof([n]-r)

However, if an invocation of C is an F exception occurrence, the presence of [F⟹H] triggers the invocation of H. Assume that the (exceptional) state transition produced by C in such circumstances is specified to be the identity relation over states. Then the necessary and sufficient condition for H to be invoked in a state satisfying some predicate Q is the exceptional termination of C when invoked in such a state:

(ce) $wp("C[F⟹",Q) \equiv \neg wp("C",true) \& Q$

For example we want an OV exception occurrence to let the state of the program variables unchanged and just trigger the invocation of a handler associated with the OV label:

(1e) $wp("I:=R.GET[OV⟹",Q) \equiv |r|=n \& Q$

The next sections will discuss how such operations can be specified and correctly implemented. Before embarking on this we give a property of the (b,c) constructs which is of use when H1 is not the empty command:

(h) $wp("C[P⟹H1",Q) = wp("C[P⟹",wp("H1",Q))$

This can be interpreted as follows: the state when E is signalled is the result of invoking H1 in the state which existed when the occurrence of E was detected by the evaluation of P.

2.6. Data Types with Total Operations and Exceptions

A specification method should allow the description of not just the standard effect of operations, but also of possible exceptional effects. The specification of exceptional effects should state when exceptions occur and what the result should be in such cases.

Let A be a set af abstract states for some data type T and let OP be an operation of T with abstract standard postcondition post and standard domain pre. Let E be an exception label to be signalled if OP is invoked in the exceptional domain $pre(E) \equiv \neg pre$ and let post(E) be a (possibly partial) state transition relation over A such that every initial state satisfying pre(E) is in the domain of post(E). The construct

$$E: \text{pre}(E) \rightarrow \text{post}(E), \text{pre} \rightarrow \text{post}$$

will be used to specify the meaning of the operation OP as a pair of (exceptional and standard) state transition relations. If at the invocation of OP the initial state $a´\in A$ satisfies pre(E), the exceptional state transition labelled by E occurs: the relation between $a´$ and the successor state $a\in A$ is post(E) and the continuation in the invocation context of OP is exceptional, i.e. a handler associated with E is invoked instead of the ´next´ statement in that context. If at the invocation of OP the initial state $a´$ satisfies pre, the standard state transition occurs: the relation between $a´$ and a is post and the continuation in the invocation context is standard, i.e. sequential.

Because by definition pre(E)$\lor$pre=true, it follows that an operation specified as indicated above is <u>total</u> (every possible initial state has a successor either in post(E) or in post).

If all the operations specified for a data type are total then the data type will be termed <u>robust</u> (since its operations have a well defined behaviour for any possible initial state and that exception occurrences do not cause program abortion or a subsequent cascade of error notifications).

Total operations for which the abstract exceptional postconditions are identity state transition relations, i.e. post(E)$\equiv$(a=a´), will be called <u>atomic</u> (in the sense that their invocation has for an external observer an ´all or nothing´ effect: either the standard state transition takes place or the state remains unchanged).

As far as the robustness of programs is concerned, the fundamental concept is that of a total operation. However, in what follows we choose (for simplicity reasons) to give only examples of atomic operations. When specifying such operations we omit to write their exceptional postconditions and their standard preconditions (which can be immediately retrieved by negating the written exceptional preconditions).

```
1    specification of type RESOURCES(generic N:INTEGER>0)
2    values  r∈P[n]
3    initial value r={}
4    operations
5       function GET returns I:INTEGER; signals OV
6       OV: |r´|=n,
7       i=oneof([n]-r´) & r=r´⊔{i}
8       procedure RELEASE(I:INTEGER);signals ILL
9       ILL: i∉r´,
10      i∈r´ & r=r´-{i}
```

Figure 3. Specification of a data type with atomic operations

Figure 3 presents a robust version of the RESOURCES data type. The data space underlying the new specification is the same as that presented in section 2.1. The standard behaviour of the operations is also specified to be the same, but now the operations are atomic. When invoked outside their standard domains the exceptions OV(erflow) and ILL(egal) are signalled.

2.7. Implementation

Assume that in order to implement an operation OP, which may signal an exception E, an exceptional construct is inserted in B(OP) according to the (u) syntactic pattern. This has the effect of extending the standard meaning of B(OP) wp("B(OP)",Q) with an exceptional meaning wp("C1;C[P⇒H1",Q), where Q stands for an arbitrary predicate. Thus, the actual meaning of B(OP) becomes a pair of (standard and exceptional) predicate transformers. If cpost is the concrete standard postcondition specified for B(OP), then the concrete standard precondition cpre is defined (as in section 2.3)

$$cpre \equiv wp("B(OP)",cpost)$$

A concrete exceptional postcondition cpost(E) can be used to specify the internal state transition intended to be produced when E occurs. The concrete exceptional precondition will be defined to be

$$cpre(E) \equiv wp("C1;C[P⇒H1",cpost(E)).$$

Thus, while cpre still characterises the initial states for which the termination of B(OP) in a state satisfying cpost is standard, cpre(E) becomes the characteristic predicate of the initial states for which B(OP) terminates exceptionally by signalling E in a state satisfying cpost(E). In both cases the termination will be called <u>clean</u>, since infinite looping or unanticipated (i.e. unspecified) exception detections are excluded.

```
1    type RESOURCES =
2    class(generic N:INTEGER >0);

3        type RESOURCE-STATE=(FREE,USED);
4        var T:ARRAY(1..N) of RESOURCE-STATE;

5        function GET returns I:INTEGER; signals OV;
6        var J:INTEGER;
7        begin J:=1;
8            while (J<N)AND(T(J)=USED) do J:=J+1;
9            [J>N ⇒ signal OV];
10           T(J):=USED;
11           I:=J
12       end;

13       procedure RELEASE(I:INTEGER);signals ILL;
14       begin [(I<1)OR(I>N)OR(R(I)=FREE) ⇒ signal ILL];
15           T(I):=FREE
16       end;

17   begin for I:=1 to N do T(I):=FREE
18   end RESOURCES
```

Figure 4.   Implementation of a data type with atomic operations

An implementation of the robust version of RESOURCES specified in Figure 3 is given in Figure 4. The only additions we have made to that given in Figure 2 are the exception label declarations in lines 5,13 and the exceptional constructs in lines 9,14. The standard algorithms obtainable by removing the text between square brackets are the same.

Each of the exceptional constructs of Figure 4 contains a boolean expression (a run-time check) and a corresponding signal command. We want such checks to be _precise_ in the sense that they become true whenever the initial state is in the exceptional domain and they remain false if the initial state is in the standard domain. A second property should be _efficiency_. The place for inserting checks should be chosen so as to minimise their evaluation cost. For example the insertion of a check for OV at the entry of GET (by using a loop similar to that of line 8) would not be optimal since its evaluation would be redundant with the following search for a free entry in T. The placement of the check after the loop is better. Intuitively one might say that if there is a choice between testing a predicate with quantifiers and a predicate without quantifiers, the later is to be preferred. Issues related to the derivation and placement of precise checks in programs which are written in a language having both a backward and forward predicate transformer semantics are discussed in [2].

2.8. Correctness Criteria

In order to prove that a data type with total operations and exceptions is correctly implemented, two new verification conditions (for correct exceptional behaviour) have to be added to those of section 2.3. The first verification condition concerning the correct internal state initialisation is the same as that given in Section 2.3.:

(VC0) constraints on generic parameters $\Rightarrow$wp(INIT,initial-value(rep(c)))

Let now OP be an arbitrary total operation specified by

E: pre(E) $\rightarrow$ post(E), pre $\rightarrow$ post

where pre=dom(post)=$\neg$pre(E). Assume that the implementor of OP has decided that the best place for inserting an exceptional construct in the body B(OP) of OP is as shown below:

B(OP)=C1;[B$\Rightarrow$H];C2

where B is the check for, and H=H1;signalE is the handler of, E. H1 may be empty as in the examples of Figure 4. Also C1 or C2 may be empty, i.e. a check may be placed at the entry or at the exit of a routine. Let cpost be the standard concrete postcondition of OP and cpost(E) be the concrete exceptional postcondition to hold just before E is signalled. Let furthermore cpre, cpre(E) be the concrete standard and exceptional preconditions as defined previously. The verification conditions for correct standard behaviour are the same as those of section 2.3:

(VC1)   pre(rep(c´)) $\Rightarrow$ cpre(c´)

(VC2)   cpost(c´,c) $\Rightarrow$ post(rep(c´),rep(c))

The verification conditions for correct exceptional behaviour ensure that whenever OP is invoked outside its abstract standard domain, the occurrence of the specified E exception is detected and the resulting exceptional concrete state transition is consistent with that specified:

(VCE1) pre(E)(rep(c´)) $\Rightarrow$ cpre(E)(c´)

(VCE2) cpost(E)(c´,c) $\Rightarrow$ post(E)(rep(c´),rep(c))

The derivation of cpre and cpre(E), as well as the proofs of correct standard and exceptional behaviour can be carried out completely separately. If OP has been specified to be atomic, then the proof of (VCE2) is often trivial. This is the case in our RESOURCES example.

The verification conditions (VC1) and (VCE1) ensure in particular that B is a precise run-time check for the occurrence of E, since (VCE1) states that the handler H of E is activated if the initial state is exceptional and (VC1) states that H is not activated if the initial state is in the standard domain. In fact, whenever these two verification conditions hold, the concrete exceptional and standard preconditions determine a (strict) partition over the set of initial internal states which may exist when the routine OP is invoked. Indeed, from pre(E)$\lor$pre=true, (VC1) and (VCE1) it follows that cpre(E)$\lor$cpre=true, and from cpre(E) $\Rightarrow$ wp("C1",b) and cpre $\Rightarrow$ wp("C1",$\neg$b) it follows that cpre(E)&cpre $\Rightarrow$ wp("C1",b&$\neg$b)=false, i.e. cpre(E)&cpre=false.

Conversely, assume that classical proof methods have been used to show that the standard algorithm C1;C2 of OP is correct. If the preciseness of the check B is established directly by

$\neg$cpre=wp("C1;[B$\Rightarrow$",true)

then by virtue of the (bs,be) clauses it follows that the robust algorithm B(OP) has the same standard behaviour as C1;C2. Thus, the proof of correct standard behaviour can be retained for the extended B(OP) unchanged. This is a significant point since it shows that exceptional constructs can be inserted for robustness purposes in non-robust programs without altering the correctness of their standard behaviour.

Returning now to the implementation of Figure 4, we can apply the semantic clause (be) to show that the run-time check for ILL is precise:

$\neg$cpre(RELEASE)=wp("[(I<1)OR(I>N)OR(T(I)=FREE)$\Rightarrow$",t=t´)

The preciseness of the check for OV has been already discussed in section 2.5. It is not difficult to show that the verification conditions (VCE1,VCE2) hold for GET and RELEASE:

(GE1) |rep(t´)|=n $\Rightarrow$ $\neg$cpre(GET)(t´)

(GE2) t=t´ $\Rightarrow$ rep(t)=rep(t´)

(RE1) i$\notin$rep(t´) $\Rightarrow$ $\neg$cpre(RELEASE)(t´)

(RE2) t=t´ $\Rightarrow$ rep(t)=rep(t´)

The above conditions together with the conditions (I,G1,G2,R1,R2) of section 2.3 establish the total correctness of the implementation of Figure 4 with the specification of Figure 3. In particular the conditions (GE1,RE1) for the GET and RELEASE operations ensure that the assumption of section 2.3 concerning their exceptional termination holds. Thus, the standard predicate transformer semantics of the operations of Figure 3 is that given by the formulae (1,2) of section 2.3.

Their meaning in exceptional circumstances is:

(1e) $wp("I:=R.GET[OV\Rightarrow]",Q)\equiv |r|=n \ \& \ Q$

(2e) $wp("R.RELEASE(I)[ILL\Rightarrow]",Q)\equiv i\notin r \ \& \ Q$

Before ending this introduction to robust data types we would like to discuss on their use in the design of robust algorithms. More specifically, we will show on a simple example how the (cs,ce) clauses of section 2.5 can be used to derive the conditions for exceptional termination of such algorithms. Aspects related to exception occurrences in loops will also be briefly discussed.

Assume we want to design a robust version of the two-resources allocation algorithm given in section 2.3:

C1   I:=R.GET[OV$\Rightarrow$H1];
C2   J:=R.GET[OV$\Rightarrow$H2];

We are interested to know under which condition the above algorithm terminates exceptionally. The condition for OV to be signalled by C1 is:

$wp("I:=R.GET[OV\Rightarrow]",true)= |r|=n$ (by 1e)

The condition for OV to be signalled by C2 is:

$wp("C1;J:=R.GET[OV\Rightarrow]",true)$ (by 1e)

$=wp("C1",|r|=n)$ (by 1´)

$=|r|<n \ \& \ |r\sqcup\{oneof([n]-r)\}|=n$ (properties of underlying data space)

$=|r|=n-1$

It follows that C1;C2 terminates exceptionally whenever initially there exists at most one free resource.

In general if a command C which may signal an exception E has to be iteratively invoked, the syntactic construct

(L)   <u>while</u> B <u>do</u> C[E$\Rightarrow$H]

can be used [4] to define the scope of the association of H with E to be the whole loop, i.e. if E is detected during some iteration the exceptional continuation is H. The insertion of [E$\Rightarrow$H] does not change the standard behaviour of the loop: the condition for standard termination in a state satisfying some predicate Q (if B is always well-defined) is that defined in [6]

(Ls) $wp("\underline{while}\ B\ \underline{do}\ C[E\Rightarrow H]",Q) \equiv wp("\underline{while}\ B\ \underline{do}\ C",Q)= \exists i\geq 0:\ S_i$

      $S_0 = \neg b \ \& \ Q,\quad S_{i+1} = b \ \& \ wp("C",S_i)$

where S_i is the condition for standard termination after exactly i iterations. The necessary and sufficient condition for exceptional termination can be defined similarly:

(Le) $wp("\underline{while}\ B\ \underline{do}\ C[E\Rightarrow]",Q) \equiv \exists j\geq 1:\ E_j$

$$E_1 = b \ \& \ wp("C[E\Rightarrow",Q), \qquad E_{j+1} = b \ \& \ wp("C",E_j)$$

where E_j is the condition for exceptional termination with E being signalled during the jth iteration. If for every integer n both S_n and E_n are false then the loop will never terminate.

Using the (Le,1,le) clauses one can show for example that the loop

$$\underline{while} \ TRUE \ \underline{do} \ I:=R.GET[OV\Rightarrow H]$$

always terminates exceptionally, since

$$wp("\underline{while} \ TRUE \ \underline{do} \ I:=R.GET[OV\Rightarrow", true) = \exists k\geq 0: \ |r|+k=n$$

holds for any initial state $r\in P[n]$. The two-resources example can be similarly generalised to the case when $k\geq 1$ resources need to be allocated and recorded in some integer array A with index domain 1..P, $k\leq p$:

$$wp("\underline{for} \ I:=1 \ \underline{to} \ K \ \underline{do} \ A(I):=R.GET[OV\Rightarrow H]", true) = \ |r|+k\leq n$$

$$wp("\underline{for} \ I:=1 \ \underline{to} \ K \ \underline{do} \ A(I):=R.GET[OV\Rightarrow", true) = \ |r|+k>n$$

These examples will (it is hoped) convince the reader that the derivation of conditions for the exceptional termination of programs bears a great similarity to, and is not more complicated than, the derivation of conditions for standard termination [6]. Other examples are to be found in the Appendix.

3. Exception Handling in Hierarchies of Data Abstractions

Programming with abstract data types leads to hierarchically structured programs. Rather than give an abstract general presentation of the problems encountered when handling exceptions in such programs, we prefer to introduce them through an example. We therefore devote the first sections of this second part of the paper to present a top-down hierarchically constructed program which provides the abstraction of a pool of SEGMENTS in terms of the RESOURCES data type and some other language provided types such as ARRAY, RECORD, etc. This example allows to introduce in section 3.5 general total correctness criteria for the implementation of robust data types with partitioned exceptional domains and representation invariants. The example is further used in the remaining sections to discuss some basic aspects of exception handling in hierarchies of data abstractions, such as exception propagation and recovery of consistent states after exception occurrences.

3.1. An Example

The data space underlying the SEGMENTS type contains all the sorts of mathematical objects mentioned in section 2.1, as well as a new sort of objects: functions. It also contains all the operators mentioned in section 2.1 together with some new operators on functions. The notation which will be used to denote this new objects and operators is briefly introduced in what follows.

Let A,B be finite sets. A partial function f from A to B is a subset $f\subseteq A\times B$ such that if (a,b1)$\in$f and (a,b2)$\in$f then b1=b2. f(a) stands for the unique b which corresponds to a. The domain of f is dom(f)={a∈A|∃b∈B:f(a)=b} and its range is ran(f)={f(a)|a∈dom(f)}. If dom(f)=A then f is total. If |dom(f)|=|ran(f)| then f is injective. The set of partial functions from A to B is denoted A→B, the set of total functions from A to B is denoted A→B and the set of total and injective functions from A to B is denoted A↦B. If f∈A→B then we write f=oneof(A→B). B can itself be a set of functions B=C→D. In such a case, if x∈dom(f) then f(x) is a function. If y∈dom(f(x)) then f(x)(y) denotes the application of f(x) to y and rran(f) denotes the union of the ranges of the f(x) functions:

$$rran(f) \equiv \bigcup_{x \in dom(f)} ran(f(x))$$

Two operators (function extension "⊔" and function restriction "\") will be used to construct new functions from old functions. If x∉dom(f) and y∈B then f⊔x,y is the extension of f to the domain dom(f)⊔{x} defined by (f⊔x,y)(a)= if a∈dom(f) then f(a) else if a=x then y. If x∈dom(f) then f\x is the restriction of f to the domain dom(f)-{x} defined by (f\x)(a)= if a∈dom(f)-{x} then f(a).

The SEGMENTS data type is often used in operating systems to create contiguous (virtual) memory spaces composed of pages from a set of available (real) memory blocks. In its specification (Figure 5) we consider three generic parameters that may vary from one system to another: xs - the maximum number of segments, xp - the maximum number of pages that a segment can have and xb - the maximum number of available physical blocks.

If 0≤z≤xp is a segment size, then a segment of this size is a function f∈[z]↦[xb] (recall [n] is used to denote {1,2,...,n}). The set of pages of f is dom(f)=[z] and its blocks are ran(f)∈P[xb]. If a segment has a domain [0] then it is empty. Consider now the set of all non-empty segments:

$$nes = \bigcup_{z \in [xp]} [z] \leftrightarrow [xb]$$

We want our abstract data type to record a correspondence between segment names in [xs] and non-empty segments in nes, so that these can be retrieved if their name is known. Thus an abstract value of this type is defined (line 2) to be an element s of [xs]→nes.

3.2. Partitioned Exceptional Domains

As for the RESOURCES example of Figure 3, the operations specified for SEGMENTS are atomic. What is new is that two of them can signal more than one exception. Let us look at NEW. Its standard effect (line 9) is to extend the previous state s´ with a new segment name and a new segment of the required z size. The returned result is the new segment name. The standard domain is

pre(NEW) = ¬pre(NOV)&¬pre(BSZ)&¬pre(BOV)

Indeed, a successor state satisfying the abstract postcondition of NEW exists if the following conditions are satisfied. First, ¬pre(NOV)=|dom(s´)|<xs should hold, so that a new segment name from [xs]-dom(s´) can be chosen. Otherwise, the exception names overflow (NOV) may be signalled. Second, ¬pre(BSZ)=z∈[xp] should hold, so that

```
1    specification of type SEGMENTS(generic XS,XP,XB:INTEGER:>0)

2    values  s ∈ [xs] -> ⊔  [z]↦>[xb]
                         z∈[xp]

3    initial value dom(s)={}

4    operations

5        function NEW(Z:INTEGER) returns N:INTEGER;signals NOV,BSZ,BOV
6        NOV: |dom(s´)|=xs,
7        BSZ: z∉[xp],
8        BOV: |rran(s´)|+z > xb,
9        n=oneof([xs]-dom(s´)) & s=s´⊔n,oneof([z]↦>([xb]-rran(s´)))

10       procedure DESTROY(N:INTEGER);signals BN
11       BN: n∉dom(s´),
12       n∈dom(s´)& s=s´\n

13       function READ(N,P:INTEGER) returns B:INTEGER;signals BN,BP
14       BN: n∉dom(s´),
15       BP: n∈dom(s´) & p∉dom(s´(n))
16       b=s(n)(p)
```

Figure 5. The specification of SEGMENTS.

the required size is a legal one. Otherwise the exception bad size
(BSZ) is signalled. Third, ¬pre(BOV)=|rran(s´)|+z≤xb should also hold,
so that a segment in [z]↦>([xb]-rran(s´)) with z distinct new blocks can
be chosen. Otherwise we have the exception blocks overflow (BOV).

Such partitionings of the exceptional domains are frequently
encountered in practice, whenever the intention is to convey (through
distinct exception labels) more information about the particular circumstances of an exception occurrence. This can be useful for diagnos-
tic purposes, or for allowing the association of distinct handlers with
different exception labels so that different recovery actions may be
taken [4,15,13,2].

Often, the different exception preconditions do not determine a
strict partition of the exceptional domain (e.g. NEW can be invoked with
a bad size in a state dom(s´)=[xs]). To impose at the specification
level some a priori order on the actual evaluation of the concrete
exception preconditions would severely restrain the freedom of an implementor to choose the best places for inserting exceptional constructs.
Thus, a specification should allow for some non-determinism on the order
in which exception preconditions are evaluated, similar to that of the
guarded commands [6].

We define the meaning of a total operation specification

$$E_1 :pre(E_1) \rightarrow post(E_1), \ldots ,E_k :pre(E_k) \rightarrow post(E_k), pre \rightarrow post$$

where ¬pre(E_1)&...&¬pre(E_k) = pre = dom(post) as follows. If the operation is invoked in an initial state a´ outside the standard domain, then
some exception E_i, for which pre(E_i)(a´) was true initially, is sig-

nalled and the relation between a´ and the successor state a is post(E_i). Otherwise the standard effect is provided.

For example if NEW is invoked in some initial state satisfying pre(NOV)&pre(BSZ), then according to the specification of Figure 5 either the NOV or BSZ exceptions may be signalled.

3.3. Implementation

Let us focus now on providing an implementation for SEGMENTS. First, we need to decide on some internal state representation. The abstract integer intervals [xs], [xp], [xb] can be represented by using language provided scalar types

    type S-NAME=1..XS; P-NAME=1..XP; B-NAME=1..XB;

and the set of functions [xp]→[xb] can be represented by an array

    type FUNC=ARRAY(P-NAME) of B-NAME;

A segment is a restriction of such a function to an interval [sz] where sz is a value of type SIZE=0..XP. Such a restriction can be described by its domain and the corresponding ´pages – blocks´ mapping, i.e. by an element of the Cartesian product ´sizes´ x ´mappings´. Abstract Cartesian products can be conveniently represented by records

    type S-DESCRIPTOR = RECORD SZ:SIZE; B:FUNC end;

The set of allocated segment names dom(s) is a subset of [xs]. Thus we have a good opportunity to use our RESOURCES data type to represent dom(s)∈P[xs] as a possible state of

    var NAMES: RESOURCES(XS);

We can represent the set of allocated blocks rran(s)∈P[xb] in a similar manner by using another state variable of type RESOURCES

    var BLOCKS: RESOURCES(XB);

Finally, by using another array, we can represent an arbitrary function from segment names to segments as a possible state of

    var SG: ARRAY(S-NAME) of S-DESCRIPTOR;

A complete implementation of SEGMENTS in terms of the above internal state representation is given in Figure 6.

Concretely, the routines work as follows. When a segment of size z has to be created, NEW requests a new segment name m (line 11), allocates z unused blocks, updates the descriptor SG(m) (lines 12,13) and returns m (line 14). DESTROY first checks that the name n of the segment to be deleted corresponds to some previously created segment. If so, the blocks of n are released (line 18), the size of the corresponding descriptor is set to 0 and n is also released. Otherwise the exception bad name BN is signalled. READ just returns the pth block of the segment with name n if possible, otherwise signals BN or BP (bad page).

237

```
1    type SEGMENTS=
2    class(generic XS,XP,XB:INTEGER>0);

3       type S-NAME=1.XS; P-NAME=1..XP; B-NAME=1..XB; SIZE=0..XP;
4          FUNC=ARRAY(P-NAME) of B-NAME;
5          S-DESCRIPTOR=RECORD SZ:SIZE; B:FUNC end;
6       var NAMES:RESOURCES(XS);BLOCKS:RESOURCES(XB);
7          SG:ARRAY(S-NAME) of S-DESCRIPTOR;

8       function NEW(Z:INTEGER) returns N:INTEGER signals NOV,BSZ,BOV;
9       var M:INTEGER;
10      begin [(Z<1)OR(Z>XP)⟹signal BSZ];
11         M:=NAMES.GET[NAMES.OV⟹signal NOV];
12         SG(M).SZ:=Z;
13         for I:=1 to Z do SG(M).B(I):=BLOCKS.GET[BLOCKS.OV⟹HBOV];
14         N:=M
15      end;

16      procedure DESTROY(N:INTEGER);signals BN;
17      begin [(N<1)OR(N>XS)OR(SG(N).SZ=0)⟹signal BN];
18         for I:=1 to SG(N).SZ do BLOCKS.RELEASE(SG(N).B(I));
19         SG(N).SZ:=0;
20         NAMES.RELEASE(N)
21      end;

22      function READ(N,P:INTEGER) returns B:INTEGER signals BN,BP;
23      begin [(N<1)OR(N>XS)OR(SG(N).SZ=0)⟹signal BN];
24         [(P<1)OR(P>SG(N).SZ)⟹signal BP];
25         B:=SG(N).B(P)
26      end;

27   begin % NAMES and BLOCKS do not need to be explicitly initialised %
28      for I:=1 to XS do SG(I).SZ:=0
29   end SEGMENTS
```

Figure 6. An implementation of SEGMENTS

3.4. Representation invariant

The data definition facilities of the PASCAL like language
(extended with the RESOURCES type) used to represent the internal states
of SEGMENTS do not allow for a direct expression of all our intentions:
the set of states which may be assummed by the variables NAMES, BLOCKS
and SG is much bigger than the set of internal states we really want.
When chosing the internal state representation for SEGMENTS the intention has been in fact to make every reachable internal state satisfy the
following properties:

1) Only segments whose names are recorded in the NAMES state variable
are non-empty:

$$I_{sn} \equiv \forall n \in [xs]: n \in names \Leftrightarrow sg(n).sz > 0$$

2) Every non-empty segment n is a total function from its set of pages
[sg(n).sz] to the set of allocated blocks:

$$I_{st} \equiv \forall n \in names \; : \; B(n) \subseteq blocks$$

where by

$$B(n) = \{sg(n).b(p) \mid 1 \leq p \leq sg(n).sz\}$$

we denote the set of blocks of the segment with name n.

3) Every non empty segment is injective:

$$I_{si} \equiv \forall n \in names: \; |B(n)| = sg(n).sz$$

4) Only those physical blocks which are actually allocated to non-empty segments are recorded in the BLOCKS state variable:

$$I_{ba} \equiv blocks \subseteq \bigsqcup_{n \in names} B(n)$$

5) Two distinct segments have disjoint sets of blocks:

$$I_{sd} \equiv \forall n, m \in names: \; n \neq m \Rightarrow B(n) \bigcap B(m) = \{\}$$

Let I_c be the conjunction of all the above constraints:

$$I_c \equiv I_{sn} \& I_{st} \& I_{si} \& I_{ba} \& I_{sd}$$

A proof that the initial internal state of SEGMENTS satisfies I_c and that every possible operation invocation preserves I_c is given in the Appendix. It follows by induction on the length of invocation sequences that I_c is a concrete (or representation) invariant [20] of the implementation of Figure 6.

The rep function for SEGMENTS will be defined only on those internal states $c \in C$ which satisfy these constraints (this partiality of rep is however not inconvenient since all the reachable internal states satisfy I_c).

Let c be such a reachable internal state. The truth of I_c ensures that for every $n \in names$ the relation

$$f(n) \subseteq [sg(n).sz] \; x \; \{sg(n).b(p) \mid 1 \leq p \leq sg(n).sz\}$$

defined by

$$\forall p \in [sg(n).sz]: \; (p, sg(n).b(p)) \in f(n)$$

is in fact a total and injective function $f(n) \in nes$. We therefore can define the result of applying rep to c to be that element of $[xs] \rightarrow nes$ which has the domain c(NAMES)=names and mapps every $n \in names$ to $f(n)$:

$$\forall c \in C: \; I_c(c) \Rightarrow dom(rep(c)) \equiv names \; \&$$
$$\forall n \in names: \; dom(rep(c)(n)) \equiv [sg(n).sz] \; \&$$
$$\forall p \in dom(rep(c)(n)): \; rep(c)(n)(p) \equiv sg(n).b(p)$$

Thus, all the internal states satisfying I_c correspond trough rep to possible abstract states of SEGMENTS:

239

$\forall c \in C: I_c(c) \Rightarrow rep(c) \in [1, xs] \rightarrow nes$

We call such internal states <u>consistent</u> (with the abstraction we want them to represent).

3.5. General Correctness Criteria

In order to prove that the implementation of Figure 6 is consistent with the specification of Figure 5, we cannot apply directly the criteria given in section 2.8, since at that stage we did not take into account the possible existence of representation invariants or partitioned exceptional domains. The verification conditions given there will now be generalised to cover also this case.

Let A be the set of abstract states specified for some data type T and C be the set of internal states of an implementation of T. If rep is the representation function, then it is first necessary to ensure that every state satisfying the concrete invariant I_c is a valid [20] representation of some possible abstract state:

$\forall c \in C: I_c(c) \Rightarrow rep(c) \in A$

After initialisation, the internal state must be consistent with that specified:

(VC0) constraints on generic parameters$\Rightarrow$wp(INIT,I_c(c)&initial-value(rep(c))

Let OP be an arbitrary operation of T specified by

$$E_1: pre(E_1) \rightarrow post(E_1), \ldots, E_k: pre(E_k) \rightarrow post(E_k), \quad pre \rightarrow post$$

where dom(post)=pre=$\neg$pre(E_1)&...&$\neg$pre(E_k). Let B(OP) be the body of the routine implementing OP, cpost be its concrete standard postcondition and cpre=wp("B(OP)",cpost) be the standard concrete precondition of OP. The verification conditions for correct standard behaviour ensure that whenever OP is invoked in its standard domain then a concrete state transition which is consistent with that specified takes place:

(VC1) $\quad I_c(c')\&pre(rep(c'))\Rightarrow cpre(c')$

(VC2) $\quad I_c(c')\&cpost(c',c)\Rightarrow I_c(c)\&post(rep(c'),rep(c))$

Assume that for each specified exception E_i an exceptional construct is inserted in B(OP) according to the (u) pattern of section 2.5:

$$B(OP)=C1;C[P\Rightarrow H_i;\underline{signalE_i}];C2$$

Let cpost(E_i) be the concrete postcondition to hold before E_i is signalled and

$$cpre(E_i) \equiv wp(C1;C[P\Rightarrow H_i",cpost(E_i))$$

be the corresponding concrete exceptional precondition. By the definition of cpre(E_i) it follows that any invocation of OP in an internal state c' satisfying cpre(E_i) leads to the exceptional termination of OP in a state satifying cpost(E_i). In order to prove the correct implementation of the exceptional effects, it is necessary to ensure that whenever OP is invoked outside its standard domain some specified exception is detected:

(VCE1) $I_c(c')\&\neg pre(rep(c'))\Rightarrow(cpre(E_1)\lor \ldots \lor cpre(E_k))(c')$

We also have to make sure that only an exception whose abstract precondition was true at the invocation of OP can be signalled:

(VCE1') $I_c(c')\&cpre(E_i)(c')\Rightarrow pre(E_i)(rep(c'))$

(Remark: when the exceptional domain is not partitioned this condition is always satisfied). Finally, it is necessary to ensure that the internal (exceptional) state transition which will be produced is consistent with that specified:

(VCE2) $I_c(c')\&cpost(E_i)(c',c)\Rightarrow I_c(c)\&post(E_i)(rep(c'),rep(c))$

A proof that the implementation of SEGMENTS is consistent with the specification of Figure 5 is given in the Appendix.

The above verification conditions ensure in particular that any reachable internal state is consistent. Indeed, (VC0) ensures that the initial state is consistent, (VC1,VCE1) ensure that if an operation is invoked in a consistent state then the only possible state transitions are those specified by cpost or $cpost(E_i)$ and (VC2,VCE2) ensure that all these state transitions preserve I_c. The invariance of I_c over any sequence of operation invocations – even if some are exception occurrences – is essential for an implementation to behave in a predictable manner (an example in the next section shows that if an inconsistent state is reached after an exception occurrence not appropriately handeld, then unpredictable behaviour – usually revealed by later exception detections – follws). Thus a correct implementation of a data type with total operations and exceptions is robust because its internal state consistency no longer depends on the assumption that its users always invoke the operations within their standard domains, as was the case in most previous approaches to data abstraction [11,20,3,10,14,7,1].

In order to achieve robustness it is however not required that exceptional constructs should be inserted in programs whenever possible. The existence of invariant properties can be used to avoid unnecessary insertions. For example in Figure 6 we have not associated any handlers with the ILL exception of RELEASE since the truth of I_c whenever DESTROY is invoked guarantees that this exception cannot occur (for more details see the Appendix). If the RELEASE operation on the NAMES and BLOCKS variables cannot be invoked from other programs than that of Figure 6, then one can also remove the exceptional construct for ILL from the body of the RELEASE routine of these instances. The approach to exception handling presented here is of use when the known invariants are too weak to rule out possible exception occurrences. We therefore consider it to be complementary to those oriented towards proving the absence of exception occurrences.

3.6. Exception Detection

For an exception occurrence to be detected it is necessary in principle that some (precise) run-time check evaluates to true. For example an occurrence of the BSZ exception (Figure 6) is detected if the boolean expression in line 10 evaluates to true. The value of this expression depends only on the state of the Z actual parameter and this state can be directly accessed in the context of the NEW routine. However, the use of an encapsulation mechanism for data abstraction purposes may sometimes forbid direct access to the state of a variable belonging to an abstract type. For example the evaluation of the concrete precondition |names´|=xs of NOV cannot be performed in the context of NEW since direct access to the internal state of NAMES is prohibited in accordance with the "information hiding principle". However, by the semantic definition of GET we have

$$wp("M:=NAMES.GET[NAMES.OV \Rightarrow ", true) = |names´|=xs$$

Thus, at the level of SEGMENTS, an occurrence of NOV is actually detected if the lower level exception NAMES.OV is propagated in the NEW routine, i.e. if the handler associated with this exception label is invoked (Figure 6, line 11). Similarly, the exception BLOCKS.OV is signalled if the concrete precondition |blocks´|+z>xb corresponding to pre(BOV) holds at the invocation of NEW. Thus an occurrence of BOV is also detected as a result of the propagation of a lower level exception. A proof that the detection of the BSZ,NOV and BOV exceptions by the above means is precise is given in the Appendix.

Exception propagation is a general technique which can be used to detect the occurrence of (higher level) exceptions in hierarchically structured systems. The general pattern is as follows:

<u>procedure</u> OP1;<u>signals</u> E1
<u>begin</u>
    .
    .
    .
    OP[E⇒HE1]
    .
    .
<u>end</u>

An invocation of OP1 in its exceptional domain pre(E1) causes a lower level operation OP to be invoked in its exceptional domain pre(E). Thus, the propagation of E in OP1 <u>coincides</u> with the detection of the higher level exception E1 in OP1. Although the handler HE1 of E1 is syntactically associated with the E exception label by using a (c) construct, it is essential to understand that its semantics (the exceptional state transition it performs) is determined by the specification of the E1 exceptional effect of OP1. Thus the phrase ´handler associated with´ reflects a syntactic fact while the phrase ´handler of´ reflects a semantic knowledge.

When an exception occurrence is detected (either by the evaluation of a run-time check or as a result of a lower level exception propagation) an intermediate internal state, not satisfying a representation invariant, may exist. For example when the occurrence of the BOV exception is detected by the exceptional termination of the "for" loop in line 13 Figure 6, the internal state is

$$m \in names$$
$$sg(m).sz=z$$
$$sg(m).b(1) \in blocks$$

$$\cdot$$
$$\cdot$$

$$sg(m).b(i-1) \in blocks$$
$$sg(m).b(i)=?$$

$$\cdot$$
$$\cdot$$

$$sg(m).b(z)=?$$

where $i=xb-|blocks'|$ is the value of the loop counter when the HBOV handler of BOV is invoked (see for more details section A3.2 of the Appendix). Clearly, such an internal state does not satisfy the I_{st} invariant defined in section 3.4 and hence is <u>inconsistent</u>.

If an instance of a data type is left in an inconsistent internal state (because an exception occurrence is not appropriately handled) then further operation invocations can lead to unpredictable (i.e. unspecified) results and to later unanticipated exception detections. For example if an instance of SEGMENTS were left in the above state, then during a next invocation of READ or DESTROY with an actual parameter m, there would be a possibility of detecting either a language defined exception UNINITIALISED (when some variable $SG(m).B(j)$, $i \leq j \leq z$, is accessed) or an ILL exception (if the RELEASE operation on BLOCKS is invoked with such a parameter). An other possible outcome is that no exception is immediately detected and incorrect state transitions continue to take place until the state of the system using SEGMENTS becomes seriously corrupted.

In order to avoid the occurrence of such dangerous situations, it is essential for the designer of a handler to know if an inconsistent state may exist when the handler is invoked. If that is the case, he should provide for the recovery of a consistent state (so that the VCE2 condition is satisfied). The need for such recovery actions is recognised in recent exception mechanism proposals (e.g. in [15] such actions are called "clean-up" actions and in [13] these are said to be "the last wishes of a procedure before disappearing"). However, no precise guidelines for programming them are given. The next section is an attempt at clarifying this issue.

3.7. Recovery of internal consistent states

Assume that an operation OP specified for a data type T may signal an exception E and that a handler of E is inserted in the body of OP according to the (u) pattern of section 2.5:

$$B(OP)=C1;C[P \Rightarrow H;\underline{signal}\ E];C2$$

Assume also that, when OP is invoked, the internal state c' is consistent and when the occurrence of E is detected (i.e. H is invoked) the intermediate state c_i is inconsistent. The task of H is to change c_i into a consistent state c. The unit of internal state change will be considered to be the change of a simple variable, i.e. a variable whose type is not an ARRAY or RECORD structured type. Variables belonging to

243

such types will be considered to be aggregates of simple variables accessible through the selector functions specified for these types.

A set of simple variables R(E) will be called a <u>recovery set</u> of E if by changing the state of each V∈R(E) to some value v, an internal state c such that $I_c(c)$&post(E)(rep(c´),rep(c)) can be reached. For example the set of variables {NAMES, BLOCKS, SG(m).SZ, SG(m).B(1), ..., SG(m).B(xp)} is a recovery set of the BOV exception, since if the values {names´, blocks´, 0, 0, ..., 0} are assigned to them, a state c such that $I_c(c)$&(rep(c)=rep(c´)) can be obtained. This is possible because the values of the I_c and rep functions defined in section 3.4 do not depend on the values of SG(m).B(j), $1 \leq j \leq xp$, when sg(m).sz=0. However, a decision that the handler HBOV of BOV (Figure 6, line 13) should recover this R(BOV) would not be the best, since too much work would be done. From a performance point of view, the most interesting recovery sets are those with the fewest elements. And because the representation functions are rarely injective and there may exist many recovery sets for an exception, the choice of a good recovery set is important.

A recovery set IS(E) such that for any other recovery set R(E): |IS(E)|≤|R(E)| will be called an <u>inconsistency set</u> of E. Because of this minimality property, one can think of an inconsistency set as containing that set of simple state variables which are ´really´ inconsistent with respect to the I_c and rep functions of T (inconsistency sets have been called "errors" in [18]) In our example we have IS(BOV)={NAMES,BLOCKS,SG(m).SZ}.

```
13.1   % HBOV≡ % for J:=1 to I-1 do BLOCKS.RELEASE(SG(M).B(J));
13.2            SG(M).SZ:=0; NAMES.RELEASE(M);
13.3            signal BOV
```

Figure 7. The handler of the BOV exception

A proof that the final state c reached after the execution of the handler HBOV in Figure 7 satisfies I_c&(rep(c)=rep(c´)) is given in the Appendix. This handler recovers for the variables of IS(BOV) the values {names´,blocks´,0} before signalling the occurrence of BOV. It is easily shown that no other ´smaller´ recovery set exists.

If the decision is taken by the system designers that all the data types used to structure a system should have atomic operations, then two other kinds of recovery sets may be of interest. Let us define the <u>inconsistency closure</u> IC(E) of an exception E to be the set of simple state variables modified by C1 up to the moment when the occurrence of E is detected. For the BOV exception, the inconsistency closure is IC(BOV) ={NAMES, BLOCKS, SG(m).S, SG(m).B(1), ..., SG(m).B(i-1)}. As the NEW operation has been specified to be atomic, clearly IC(BOV) is a recovery set, since if all the modified variables recover their previous values a state c identical to the initial c´ is obtained and, hence the $I_c(c)$&(rep(c)=rep(c´)) property is trivially satisfied. The second kind of recovery set we want to mention is the crudest approximation one can imagine for an inconsistency set (an inconsistency closure is a better one). This approximation is obtained by taking the whole set of state variables with their respective previous values to form a <u>check-point</u> CP of the internal state.

After the above discussion, one can state with precision what a handler H of an exception E has to do if E is detected in an inconsistent state: H must recover some R(E). If post(E) is not the identity state transition relation, i.e. OP is not atomic, then <u>forward recovery</u>[18] has to be used. From an implementation point of view, the recovery of an R(E) is ´forward´ if $\exists V \in R(E)$ for which the value v after recovery is different from v´. The determination of an R(E) (preferably IS(E)) for forward recovery requires knowledge of post(E), I_c, rep. Thus, handlers for forward recovery have to be <u>explicitly</u> inserted by humans. However, if the operations are intended to have an atomic behaviour, then the determination of either the IC(E) or CP recovery sets can be performed independently of such knowledge and can be automatised. Check-pointing techniques have long been used for that. More recently, the idea of leaving the task of continuously updating the inconsistency closures associated with all potential exception occurrences to a recovery cache device has been proposed [12]. Automatic recovery of inconsistency closures or check-points is known as <u>backward recovery</u>[18]. From an implementation point of view, a recovery action can be termed ´backward´ if every variable V of the recoverd R(E) is restored to its previous value v´ (e.g. the recovery action performed by HBOV is backward). Automatic backward recovery does more work than strictly necessary (since in general $|IS(E)| < |IC(E)| < |CP|$) but this is the price to be paid if the intention is to provide <u>default</u> exception handling for fault tolerance purposes.

Default exception handling attempts at providing a solution to the following problem: if the exceptional domain of some operation OP is not accurately identified or the checks for detecting exceptions are not precise, then for some exception occurrences (if they are detected because of lower level propagated exceptions) there will be no explicitly provided exception handlers in B(OP). The idea is then to force the invocation of a default handler able to recover an inconsistency closure or checkpoint [4]. If subsequent masking attempts (e.g. invocation of alternate algorithms [12]) are not successful, then the produced ´unanticipated´ exceptional state transition is identified for the invoker of OP by some FAILURE or ERROR predefined exception label. The aim of introducing such a label in a programming language is, on one hand, to guarantee the existence of a (default) exceptional continuation for every possible exception occurrence [4,15], and, on the other hand, to try and make non-total operations ´total´ in the following sense:

$$..,E_i:pre(E_i)\rightarrow post(E_i),...,FAILURE:\neg(\bigvee pre(E_i)\bigvee pre)\rightarrow c=c´, \quad pre\rightarrow post$$

A general model for explicit [15,13] and default [12] exception handling in hierarchies of data abstractions is presented in [5]. The concepts presented formally in this paper are used there to show the unity which exists between these complementary exception handling techniques, developed independently for the same purpose: the production of robust systems.

4. Conclusion

A continuing problem with work on data abstraction has been the difficulty of specifying and handling exceptions in a satisfactory way. And the situation was the more worrying as exceptions are essential and intrinsic features of data types.

An attempt to tackle this problem at the level of an algebraic specification language, in terms of which the semantics of the data types of a conventional programming language can be expressed, is presented in [9] and is further developed in [8].

In this paper we have investigated an other possible solution, based upon the introduction of an exception mechanism [4,15,13] in a programming language supporting data abstraction. As such, one can consider the approach presented here to be merely a formalisation of what is common software engineering practice. Our goal was to specify the operations of the data types of an (extensible) programming language in such a way as to ensure that the following conditions are satisfied. First, exception occurrences should not mean program abortion. Second, the semantics of the operations of a type should be well-defined when exceptions occur. Third, this semantics should be defined so as to ensure that, in the verification conditions obtainable in program proofs, the operators of the specification language are always aplied to elements of their domains (i.e. the "error terms" studied in [8] are never generated). Another goal has been the achievement of a proper separation between standard and exceptional aspects of program behaviour. In that sense, we consider the concept of an exception to be a useful software structuring tool, which should take its place alongside such established structuring concepts like procedures, parameters, processes, etc.

An approach similar to that presented in this paper, but using a partial correctness semantic framework is presented in [16]. The use of such a framework ensures that, if an operation invocation does not lead to an infinite loop or to an unanticipated exception detection, then the specified standard and exceptional effects are correctly provided. Our interest was in robustness properties. We therefore have used the stronger predicate transformer semantic framework introduced in [2]. Present verification systems use a weak programming logic, and the ability to use them in proving the partial correctness of the standard and exceptional algorithms of operations may well counterbalance the fact that such verification tools do not provide any guarantee of robustness. The question of how to construct verification systems able to guarantee the robustness of the verified programs is a matter of future research. The ever increasing reliance which is placed on computer systems may well make the availability of such tools become necessary.

Acknowledgements

The author would like to thank E. Best, P. Cousot, S. Gerhart, J. Horning, C. Jones, S. Krakowiak, J. Mitchell, B. Randell, J. Rushby and J. Thatcher for discussions valuable in clarifying the ideas presented in this paper. The reported research has been successively sponsored by the French National Center for Scientific Research and by the U.K. Science Research Council.

APPENDIX: Correctness of the implementation of SEGMENTS

The notations introduced in the paper are used to outline the main steps of a proof that the implementation of SEGMENTS (Figures 6,7) is consistent with the specification of Figure 5.

A1. Validity of the internal state representation

A justification that the choosen internal state representation of SEGMENTS satisfies the validity constraint

$$\forall c \in C : I_c(c) \implies rep(c) \in [xs] \rightarrow \bigsqcup_{z \in [xp]} [z] \mapsto [xb]$$

has been given in § 3.3.

A2. The internal state initialisation is correct

The positivity constraints on the generic parameters XS,XP,XB ensure that after initialisation the internal state satisfies:

$$cpost(INIT) \equiv (names=\{\}) \ \& \ (blocks=\{\}) \ \& \ (\forall n \in [xs]:sg(n).sz=0)$$

The concrete invariant I_c is thus (trivially) satisfied and by the definition of rep we have:

(VC0) $cpost(INIT)(c) \implies I_c(c) \ \& \ (dom(rep(c))=\{\})$

A3. Correctness of the NEW operation

The concrete postcondition $cpost(NEW)=N1\&N2\&N3$ where

$N1 \equiv \{n\}=names-names'$, $N2 \equiv sg(n).sz=z$

$N3 \equiv (B(n)=blocks-blocks') \& (|B(n)|=z) \& (z \geq 1)$

specifies the intended standard meaning of the NEW routine. The concrete exceptional postconditions we want to hold (just before the BSZ, NOV and BOV exceptions are signalled) are $cpost(BSZ)=cpost(NOV)=(c=c')$ and $cpost(BOV)=N4\&N5\&N6$ where

$N4 \equiv (m \in [xs]-names') \& (names=names')$ $N5 \equiv blocks=blocks'$ $N6 \equiv sg(m).sz=0$

A3.1 Correctness of the standard behaviour

From the semantic definition of GET given in § 2.3 we obtain

$wp("M:=NAMES.GET",\{m\}=names-names')= |names'|<xs$

$wp("FB(Z);N:=M",N3)= (1 \leq m \leq xs) \ \& \ (1 \leq z \leq xp) \ \& \ (|blocks'|+z \leq xb)$

where $FB(Z) \equiv \underline{for} \ I:=1 \ \underline{to} \ Z \ \underline{do} \ SG(M).B(I):=BLOCKS.GET.$

Using the above intermediate derivation steps and the (bs,cs) semantic clauses of § 2.5 we obtain

$cpre(NEW)=wp("B(NEW)",cpost(NEW)) = P1\&P2\&P3$

where

$P1 = |names'|<xs$, $P2 = 1 \leq z \leq xp$ and $P3 = |blocks'|+z \leq xb$

In order to show that the (VC1) verification condition holds for NEW we can proceed as follows:

$I_c(c')\&\neg pre(NOV)(rep(c'))\Rightarrow P1$ (because of the definition of rep)

$I_c(c')\&\neg pre(BSZ)(rep(c'))\Rightarrow P2$ (because $a\&b\Rightarrow b$)

If $I_c(c')$ holds then

$$|rran(rep(c'))|\equiv|\bigcup_{n\in names'} ran(rep(c')(n))|=$$

$$=\sum_{n\in names'}|ran(rep(c')(n))| \quad\quad (by\ I_{sd})$$

$$=\sum_{n\in names'} sg(n).sz'=|blocks'| \quad (by\ I_{si}\&I_{st}\&I_{ba}\&I_{sd})$$

Thus, we also have:

$I_c(c')\&\neg pre(BOV)(rep(c'))\Rightarrow P3.$

From the above implications it follows that:

(VC1) $I_c(c')\&pre(NEW)(rep(c')) \Rightarrow cpre(NEW)(c')$

In order to prove (VC2) we will show first that the standard concrete state transitions preserve the concrete invariant. We have:

$(I_{sn}\&I_{si})(c')\&(N1\&N2\&N3)(c',c)\Rightarrow(I_{sn}\&I_{si})(c)$

$(I_{sn}\&I_{st}\&I_{ba}\&I_{sd})(c')\&(N1\&N3)(c',c)\Rightarrow(I_{sn}\&I_{st}\&I_{ba}\&I_{sd})(c)$

Thus:

$$I_c(c')\&cpost(NEW)(c',c)\Rightarrow I_c(c) \tag{1}$$

In order to show that the concrete – by (1) consistent – successor c corresponds through rep to a legal abstract successor, we use the definition of rep, known properties of the data spaces underlying the data types used to represent the internal states of SEGMENTS and the "no state variable change – no mention" convention for writing postconditions to show that:

$I_c(c')\&N1(c',c)\&I_c(c)\Rightarrow n=oneof([xs]-dom(rep(c')))$

$I_c(c')\&(N1\&N2\&N3)(c',c)\&I_c(c)\Rightarrow$

       $rep(c)=rep(c')\sqcup n,oneof([z]\mapsto([xb]-rran(rep(c'))))$

From the above implications it follows that:

$$I_c(c')\&cpost(NEW)(c',c)\&I_c(c)\Rightarrow post(NEW)(rep(c'),rep(c)) \tag{2}$$

By the logical tautology $(a\Rightarrow b)\&(a\&b\Rightarrow c)\Rightarrow(a\Rightarrow b\&c)$ from (1,2) it follows that the second verification condition for correct standard behaviour also holds:

(VC2) $I_c(c')\&cpost(NEW)(c',c)\Rightarrow I_c(c)\&post(NEW)(rep(c'),rep(c))$

A3.2 Correctness of the exceptional effects

By applying the semantic clauses (be,bs,ce) of § 2.5 we obtain:

$$cpre(BSZ)=wp("[(Z<1)OR(Z>XP)\Rightarrow", cpost(BSZ))= (z<1) \lor (z>xp)$$

$$cpre(NOV)=wp("B1[NAMES.OV\Rightarrow", cpost(NOV))=\neg cpre(BSZ)\&|names'|=xs$$

where B1 denotes the fragment of B(NEW) preceding the exceptional construct for NOV (line 11) :

$$B1\equiv[(Z<1)OR(Z>XP)\Rightarrow\underline{signal}\ BSZ];M:=NAMES.GET$$

The derivation of cpre(BOV) requires more work. By the definition of the exception mechanism [4] the set of program variables which are visible to a handler H associated with some exception label E signalled by a command C is the set of variables which were visible at the invocation of C. Thus the scope of the I loop counter of line 13 is extended to the exceptional construct [BLOCKS.OV$\Rightarrow$HBOV1;$\underline{signal}$ BOV] associated with the loop, where

$$HBOV1\equiv \underline{for}\ J:=1\ \underline{to}\ I-1\ \underline{do}\ BLOCKS.RELEASE(SG(M).B(I));$$
$$\overline{SG(M)}.SZ:=0;\ NA\overline{MES}.RELEASE(M)$$

is the fragment of HBOV (Figure 7) preceding the signal command. Moreover, if the command C is atomic the state of the variables visible to H is the same as that which existed just before the invocation of C which signalled E. Thus, if during some i_0+1 iteration the BLOCKS.OV exception is signalled, the value of I at the invocation of HBOV is i_0+1. The precise formulation of the above phrases is:

$$wp("B2(Z)[BLOCKS.OV\Rightarrow", Q)=$$

$$\exists i_0:(0\leq i_0<z)\&(|blocks'|+i_0=xb)\ \&\ wp("B2(i_0)", Q[i_0+1/i]) \qquad (3)$$

where Q is some predicate (possibly) containing i free and B2 is the fragment of B(NEW) textually preceding HBOV:

$$B2(Z)\equiv B1;SG(M).SZ:=0;FB(Z);$$

In addition to the condition H for the loop FB(Z) defined in § A3.1 to terminate exceptionally (see also section 2.8):

$$H \equiv \exists i_0:(0\leq i_0<z)\&(|blocks'|+i_0=xb) \Leftrightarrow (|blocks'|+z>xb) \qquad (4)$$

formula (3) also states that the state when HBOV is invoked is that reached after the first i_0 standard terminating iterations which caused pre(OV)(blocks) to become true.

By applying the semantic definition of RELEASE, we can derive without difficulty that:

$$wp("HBOV1", cpost(BOV)) = N7\&N8(i-1) \qquad (5)$$

where $N7\equiv(m\in names)\&(names'=names-\{m\})$ and

$$N8(i-1)\equiv(0\leq i-1\leq xp)\&(B(m,i-1)\subseteq blocks)\&(|B(m,i-1)|=i-1)\&(blocks'=blocks-B(m,i-1))$$

where $B(m,i-1)=\{sg(m).b(j)|\ 1\leq j\leq i-1\}$

Let us now define $B3 \equiv B2(Z)[BLOCKS.OV\Rightarrow HBOV]$ to be the set of all statements invoked before the BOV exception is signalled. By formula (h) of § 2.5 and (3,4,5) it follows that

$$wp("B3",cpost(BOV))= H\ \&\ wp("B2(i_0)",N7\&N8(i_0)) \qquad (6)$$

The second term of the right hand side of (6), in which i_0 is bound by the existential quantifier in H, can be expanded (in a way analogous to that used to derive cpre(NEW) in § A3.1) to

$$wp("B2(i_0)",N7\&N8(i_0)) = (1\leq z\leq xp)\&(|names^-|<xs)$$

If this result is replaced in (6) one obtains

$$cpre(BOV)=wp("B3",cpost(BOV))= H\ \&\ (1\leq z\leq xp)(|names^-|<xs)$$

Thus by (4) it follows that:

$$cpre(BOV)=\neg cpre(BSZ)\&\neg cpre(NOV)\&(|blocks^-|+z>xb)$$

By making use of the definition of rep it is now possible to show that whenever NEW is invoked outside its abstract standard domain one of its specified exceptions is detected:

(VCE1) $I_c(c^-)\&\neg pre(NEW)(rep(c^-))\Rightarrow(cpre(BSZ)\lor cpre(NOV)\lor cpre(BOV))(c^-)$

A3.2.1 The BSZ exception

Clearly

(VCE1$^-$) $I_c(c^-)\&cpre(BSZ)(c^-)\Rightarrow pre(BSZ)(rep(c^-))$

and

(VCE2) $I_c(c^-)\&cpost(BSZ)(c^-,c)\Rightarrow I_c(c)\&(rep(c)=rep(c^-))$

Thus if NEW is invoked outside its abstract standard domain and BSZ is signalled, the initial state satisfied pre(BSZ) and the concrete successor state satisfies (trivially) the atomicity requirement.

A3.2.2 The NOV exception

By the definition of rep and I_c :

(VCE1$^-$) $I_c(c^-)\&cpre(NOV)(c^-)\Rightarrow(\neg pre(BSZ)\&pre(NOV))(rep(c^-))$

$$\Rightarrow pre(NOV)(rep(c^-))$$

Thus, because we know how the NOV exceptional effect is implemented, we know that the nondeterministic choice between signalling either BSZ or NOV (if NEW is invoked in a state pre(BSZ)&pre(NOV)) is systematically resolved by giving priority to the BSZ exception signal. This implementation choice has been made because the evaluation of the precondition of BSZ is faster than that of NOV. As for BSZ, the atomicity requirement is (trivially) satisfied:

(VCE2) $I_c(c')\&cpost(NOV)(c',c)\Rightarrow I_c(c)\&(rep(c)=rep(c'))$

A3.2.3 The BOV exception

By the definition of rep and I_c:

(VCE1') $I_c(c')\&cpre(BOV)(c')\Rightarrow(\neg pre(BSZ)\&\neg pre(NOV)\&pre(BOV))(rep(c'))$

$$\Rightarrow pre(BOV)(rep(c'))$$

Thus, at the implementation level, we know that the evaluation of the concrete precondition of the BOV exception has the lowest priority. This design decision has been taken in order to avoid the recovery of the inconsistency set IS(BOV), see § 3.7, whenever possible. By applying the definitions of rep and I_c (more precisely the fact that their value does not depend on $sg(m).b(1),\ldots,sg(m).b(xp)$ if $sg(m).sz=0$) the following implication can be proved without difficulty

(VCE2) $I_c(c')\&cpost(BOV)(c',c)\Rightarrow I_c(c)\&(rep(c)=rep(c'))$

A4 Correctness of the DESTROY operation

We take as standard concrete postcondition the assertion $cpost(DESTROY) = D1 \& D2 \& D3$ where

$D1\equiv(n\in names')\&(names=names'-\{n\})$ $D2\equiv sg(n).sz=0$ $D3\equiv blocks=blocks'-B(n)$

The concrete exceptional postcondition is $cpost(BN)\equiv(c=c')$.

A4.1 Correctness of the standard effect

By the standard semantic definition of RELEASE we have

$wp("NAMES.RELEASE(N)",D1)=$ $n\in names'$

$wp("\underline{for}\ I:=1\ \underline{to}\ SG(N).SZ\ \underline{do}\ BLOCKS.RELEASE(SG(N).B(I))",D3)$

$=(1\leq n\leq xs)\&(B(n)\subseteq blocks')\&(|B(n)|=sg(n).sz')$

By the semantic clause (bs) of § 2.5 we have further

$cpre(DESTROY)=wp("B(DESTROY)",cpost(DESTROY))=$
$=(n\in names')\&(B(n)\subseteq blocks')\&(|B(n)|=sg(n).sz')$

The proof of the first verification condition for DESTROY strongly relies on the truth of the $I_{sn}\&I_{st}\&I_{si}\&I_{sd}$ invariant:

(VC1) $I_c(c')\&pre(DESTROY)(rep(c'))\Rightarrow cpre(DESTROY)(c')$

The standard state transitions preserve the representation invariant, since from

$(I_{sn}\&I_{st}\&I_{si}\&I_{sd})(c')\&(D1\&D2)(c',c)\Rightarrow(I_{sn}\&I_{st}\&I_{si}\&I_{sd})(c)$
$(I_{sn}\&I_{ba})(c')\&(D1\&D3)(c',c)\Rightarrow(I_{sn}\&I_{ba})(c)$
one can infer:

$I_c(c')\&cpost(DESTROY)(c',c)\Rightarrow I_c(c)$ (7)

By the definition of the restriction operator "\" we have also

$$I_c(c')\&cpost(DESTROY)(c',c)\&I_c(c)\Rightarrow post(DESTROY)(rep(c'),rep(c)) \qquad (8)$$

From (7) and (8) we conclude that the second verification condition for correct standard behaviour also holds:

(VC2) $I_c(c')\&cpost(DESTROY)(c',c)\Rightarrow I_c(c)\&post(DESTROY)(rep(c'),rep(c))$

A4.2 Correctness of the exceptional effect

By the semantic clause (be) of § 2.5 we have

$$cpre(BN)=wp("[(N<1)OR(N>XS)OR(SG(N).SZ=0)\Rightarrow",cpost(BN))=$$

$$= (n<1)\lor(n>xs)\lor(sg(n).sz'=0)$$

It is not difficult to show that, because of I_{sn}, the following verification conditions (see § 2.8) hold:

(VCE1) $I_c(c')\&pre(BN)(rep(c'))\Rightarrow cpre(BN)(c')$

(VCE2) $I_c(c')\&cpost(BN)(c',c)\Rightarrow I_c(c)\&(rep(c)=rep(c'))$

<u>Remark</u>. At first glance the predicate cpre(BN) does not look like ¬cpre(DESTROY). Therefore one may think that the disjunction of the concrete exceptional and standard preconditions of DESTROY does not cover all the possible initial states. At this point of our proof we can however affirm that DESTROY is always invoked in a consistent internal state, since the verification conditions (VC0) and (VC1,VC2,VCE1,VCE2) for DESTROY and RELEASE –the only internal state modifying routines– have been shown to hold.

Thus, when DESTROY is invoked in some state c', I_c holds and under this assumption one can show that cpre(BN)$\lor$cpre(DESTROY) is true since

$$I_c \Rightarrow (cpre(BN) \Leftrightarrow \neg cpre(DESTROY))$$

The term $\neg(B(n)\subseteq blocks') \lor (|B(n)|\neq sg(n).sz') \lor (n\notin names')$
of ¬cpre(DESTROY) can never be true, once the entry check in B(DESTROY) is passed over. Thus, the exception preconditions pre(ILL)(names) and pre(ILL)(blocks) are invariantly false during an execution of DESTROY. We therefore have omitted to associate handlers with ILL in Figure 6.

A4 Correctness of READ

The proofs of the verification conditions for correct exceptional and standard behaviour for this routine are straightforward applications of the definition of rep and are therefore omitted.

REFERENCES

1. J.R. Abrial, "The Specification Language Z - Syntax and Semantics", Programming Research Group, Oxford University (1980).

2. E. Best and F. Cristian, "Systematic Detection of Exception Occurrences", Science of Computer Programming Vol. 1(1), North Holland Pub. Co. (1981).

3. D. Bjorner, "Formalisation of Data Base Models", pp. 144-215 in Abstract Software Specification, ed. D. Bjorner, Springer Verlag Lecture Notes in Comp. Sc. (1979).

4. F. Cristian, "Le Traitement des Exceptions dans les Programmes Modulaires", Doctoral Thesis, Univ. of Grenoble (1979).

5. F. Cristian, "Exception Handling and Software-Fault Tolerance", Proc. of the 10th Int. Symp. on Fault Tolerant Computing, Kyoto, pp.97-103 (1980).

6. E.W. Dijkstra, A Discipline of Programming, Prentice-Hall (1976).

7. S.L. Gerhart et al., "An Overview of AFFIRM - a Specification and Verification System", Proc. of the IFIP80 Congress, Tokyo (1980).

8. J.A. Goguen, "Abstract Errors for Abstract Data Types", pp. 492-525 in Formal Description of Programming Concepts, ed. E.J. Neuhold, North-Holland (1978).

9. J.A. Goguen, J.W. Thatcher, and E.G. Wagner, "An Initial Algebra Approach to the Specification, Correctness and Implementation of Abstract Data Types", pp. 80-149 in Current Trends in Progr. Methodology, ed. R.T. Yeh, Prentice-Hall (1978).

10. J. Guttag and J.J. Horning, "Formal Specification As a Design Tool", Proc. of the 7th ACM Symp. on Principles of Progr. Languages, Las Vegas (1980).

11. C.A.R. Hoare, "Proof of Correctness of Data Representations", Acta Informatica Vol. 1(4), pp.271-281 (1972).

12. J.J. Horning, H.C. Lauer, P.M. Melliar-Smith, and B. Randell, "A Program Structure for Error Detection and Recovery", in Lecture Notes in Comp. Sc., Springer Verlag (1974).

13. J. Ichbiah et al., "Rationale for the Design of the ADA Programming Language", SIGPLAN Notices Vol. 14(6) (1979).

14. C.B. Jones, Software Development : A Rigorous Aproach, Prentice-Hall (1980).

15. B.H. Liskov and A. Snyder, "Exception Handling in CLU", IEEE Trans. on Softw. Eng. Vol. SE-5(6), pp.546-558 (1979).

16. D.C. Luckham and W. Polak, "ADA Exception Handling : An Axiomatic Approach", ACM Trans. on Progr. Lang. and Systems Vol. **2**(2), pp.225-233 (1980).

17. R. Nakajima, M. Honda, and H. Nakahara, "Hierarchical Program Specification and Verification - A Many-Sorted Approach", Acta Informatica Vol. **14**, pp.135-155 (1980).

18. R. Randell, P.A. Lee, and P.C. Treleaven, "Reliability Issues in Computing Systems Design", Computing Surveys Vol. **10**(2), pp.123-165 (1978).

19. J.E. Stoy, Denotational Semantics : the Scott-Strachey Approach to Programming Language Theory, MIT Press, Cambridge (1977).

20. W.A. Wulf, R.L. London, and M. Shaw, "Abstraction and Verification in ALPHARD : Introduction to language and Methodology", Comp. Sc. Dept, Carnegie-Mellon Univ. (1976).

21. S.N. Zilles, "An Introduction to Data Algebras", pp. 248-272 in Abstract Software Specifications, ed. D. Bjorner, Springer Verlag, Lect. Notes in Comp. Sc. (1979).

A Reduction Specification for DTL

J.W. Hughes
M.S. Powell

Department of Computation
U.M.I.S.T.
PO Box 88, Manchester M60 1QD

July 1981

Abstract

This paper describes techniques which are being used to specify the behaviour of programs written in DTL. The intended Semantics of DTL are similar in many respects to those of Hoare's CSP. However, DTL forces a hierarchical structure on a network of communicating processes and the language specification described capitalises on this to simplify the definition.

The principle technique employed in the DTL Semantic specification involves the generation of a set of reduction rules. Each rule specifies a class of behaviours for some DTL construct. An important aspect of these reduction rules is that they can be viewed as defining the behaviour of a reduction machine which would execute the specification of a particular DTL program. Such a reduction machine could be implemented by software on conventional machines or with much greater efficiency on the kind of recursive architecture made possible by VLSI technology.

1   Introduction

An earlier paper (6) has described the use of DTL as a language for the specification of programs. The reasons claimed for using such artificial languages rather than English or Danish for specifying programs are that specifications in natural languages may be imprecise or ambiguous whereas specifications in an artificial "programming" or "specification" language are unambiguous, because the language itself is unambiguous, and can be checked for consistency and completeness. Furthermore, these properties of specification and programming languages permit proof of properties of the systems specified and their implementations. However, the use of such artificial languages merely transfers the problem of the meaning of a verbal specification of a system to the meaning of constructs in the artificial language. In order to reason about or implement a specification written in any language, a formal definition of the meaning of constructs in that language is needed. Thus in order for a specification language to be useful it must have two properties.

1   It must be capable of specifying the required systems for which it is to be used.

2   It must be capable of a readily understood formal definition of its meaning.

The capabilities of DTL for specifying programs have been demonstrated in (6). We describe here work which is currently in progress in defining formally the meaning of DTL itself.

The semantic formalisation of programming languages falls broadly into three categories, in order of increasing abstractness.

(i)   Operational - meaning is described in terms of the execution of programs by an abstract machine.

(ii)   Denotational - meaning is described in terms of abstract mathematical objects, particularly functions of appropriate types.

(iii)   Axiomatic - meaning is described solely in terms of logical formulae which describe the effect of executing programs.

The formalisation of the semantics of DTL described here lies somewhere in the first and second categories, in that although the meaning of constructs in DTL is described in terms of functions, which may be viewed as denotational, it is easy to visualise an abstract machine which evaluates these functions thus giving an operational interpretation of the definitions. Whether or not the functions could be used to yield an axiomatic definition remains to be seen.

2 The Apply Function

The functions defining the meaning of DTL owe their origins to the notion that a sequential translation defines a function which when applied to its input stream(s) yields the output stream(s) as its result, so we can define a function Apply which given an input sequence and a sequential translation yields an output sequence.

$$A \, (aab) \, (\langle T_1 \rangle :: = \, *(a \, [c \,]) \, b) = cc$$
$$A \, (aab) \, (\langle T_2 \rangle :: = a \, [c] \langle T_2 \rangle \, b) = cc$$
$$A \, (aabc) \, (\langle T_3 \rangle :: = \, * (a \, [d] | b \, [e]) \, c \, [f]) = ddef$$

Figure 1 shows some intuitively understandable examples of application of the Apply function. Using this notion the pipeline operator is represented suitably by functional composition so

$$A \, (i \, , \, T_1 \, (i | x) \gg T_2 \, (x | y)) = A \, (A \, (i \, , T_1 \,), \, T_2)$$

A fair amount of progress was made in defining the apply function for each syntactic category of DTL translations. Its main drawback was that it seemed incapable of expressing the synchronisation of the stream communications between translations, but rather gave a meaning consistent with unbounded buffering on streams similar to the semantics of Kahn's simple language for parallel programming (7) and Wadge's Lucid (1). We particularly wanted a semantic specification which defined full synchronisation since buffering can be explicitly specified in fully synchronised DTL whereas full synchronisation cannot be specified in a language allowing unbounded buffering and furthermore, a distributed implementation of the language is likely to be more easily realisable using full synchronisation.

3 A Reduction Language View

It soon became clear that any language specification in which stream values occur explicitly is likely to give problems when it comes to expressing fully synchronised communication. What is required is a specification which abstracts from stream values in much the same way that denotational definitions of conventional languages abstract from program states. Combining these ideas with Turner's work on the use of Combinators (8) and Backus' Turing Award Paper (2) suggested the approach that a DTL system together with it inputs and outputs be regarded as an expression which is reducible according to a set of semantic reduction rules.

We take as a starting point an abstract syntax of DTL which is assumed to be generated from the concrete syntax by a compiler and therefore assume that the semantic specification will never be used for the analysis or evaluation of syntactically invalid DTL programs. The problem of generating the abstract syntax from the concrete is the subject of a separate (parallel) investigation. It is hoped that this compilation process can be expressed by a similar set of reduction rules.

4   Abstract Syntax

DTL translation network expressions compile directly into prefix expressions with operators **>>** (pipeline) and , (parallel). The bodies of sequential translations compile into expressions representing alternative translation sequences. The primitive components of sequences are either input data items, output data items or assignment between an attribute and an expression. Figure 2 shows the compiled form of the three forms of sequence.

Concrete	Abstract
s.d(a) **<T>**	IN s d a **<T>**
$\left[\,s.d(a)\,\right]$ **<T>**	OUT s d a **<T>**
$\left\{\,v := e\,\right\}$ **<T>**	:= (REF v) e **<T>**

Figure 2

Thus the abstract form of a sequence whose first item is an input data item compiles into a primitive (IN or OUT) with four arguments - a stream identifier, data item identifier, attribute list and the compiled form of the rest of the sequence. The attribute list is either empty or it has the form

:: firstattribute attribute-list

The empty translation sequence compiles into empty and alternative sequences of the form (a b)c are transformed into

|(compiled form of ac)(compiled form of bc)

Assignments can be written explicitly in sequential translations and are also generated as a result of the assignment of output attribute values to input attribute variables when communication occurs. The effect of a sequential translation translating an input sequence depends on attribute values of input data items because they determine the succeeding behaviour of the translation. Each translation is therefore evaluated in a local environment which associates values with attributes, representing its "local store" in abstract machine terms.

The meaning of a DTL translation translating a set of possibly parallel input sequences is given by evaluating in an empty environment, the expressions given by pipelining its compiled form between a translation which outputs the input sequences and a primitive operator which builds a list in its environment of all communications output to it. Thus the effect of a translation T when presented with an input sequence ab is given by

A empty (≫(OUT s a empty (OUT s b empty empty))
    (≫T (GEN empty))

. The Apply Reductions

The evaluation of the Apply function depends on the form of its arguments and the result is an environment. Figure 3 shows the reductions which can be used in evaluating Apply.

A e (≫ s t) = ≫ (A e s)(A e t)
A e (, s t) = ,(A e s)(A e t)
A e (│ s t) = │(A e s)(A e t)
A e (: = x y t) = A (↑e (→(V e x)(V e y))) t
A fail t = fail
A e empty = empty

Figure 3

The first three rules show that A simply distributes an environment over pipeline, parallel and alternative operators. Application of the assignment operator has the effect of applying its successor (t) in an environment updated by the assignment.

The Apply function with a failed environment argument results in a failed environment and with an empty translation argument results in an empty environment. A e (IN s d a t) and A e (OUT s d a t) are not reducible alone (see section 7).

6 Updating and Using Environments

↑ is the function which updates an environment and V extracts a value from an environment. → associates an attribute with a value and the environment consists of a list of such associations concatenated by the operator ::. Updating is achieved by the reductions shown in fig 4.

$$↑ x \text{ empty} = x$$
$$↑ \text{empty } x = :: x \text{ empty}$$
$$↑ (:: (→ x \text{ } y) \text{ } f)(→ x \text{ } z) = ::(→x \text{ } z)f$$
$$↑ (:: (→x \text{ } y) \text{ } f) (→w \text{ } z) = :: (→x \text{ } y)(↑f (→ w \text{ } z))$$

figure 4

Evaluation of an expression in an environment, represented by V (environment) (expression) is achieved by the reductions shown in fig 5.

$$V(:: (→ x y) e) x = y$$
$$V \text{ a (REF } x) = x$$
$$V(:: (→x \text{ } y) e) z = V \text{ } e \text{ } z$$
$$V \text{ empty } C = C$$
$$V \text{ e (OP } x \text{ } y) = OP \text{ } (V \text{ } e \text{ } x) (V \text{ } e \text{ } y)$$

Figure 5

Figure 5 shows that if the first item in the environment list is an association for the attribute represented by the second argument of V, the result is the associated value, otherwise the result is obtained by applying V to the remainder of the environment list. If the second argument of V is a REF expression, the result is the argument of REF. REF is used to distinguish between variables on the left and right hand side of assignments. It also allows the use of, for example, subscripted variables so that x [e]: = y   T , compiles into :=([(REF x) e) y T. Evaluation of an expression in an empty environment results in the expression itself and V distributes its environment argument over operands within an expression.

7   Synchronised Communication

As described in section 5, A e (IN s d a t) and A e (OUT s d a t) are not in themselves reducible but when they occur as operands of $\gg$ in an expression, the expression as a whole may be reducible. Figure 6 shows the reductions which may be applied to pipelines.

$\gg$ (A e (OUT s d y t)) (A f (IN s d x u))
 = SYNC (A e t)(A f (:= x (V e y) u))

$\gg$(A e (OUT s d y t))($\gg$ (A f (IN s d x u)) v)
 = SYNC (A e t)($\gg$ (A f (:= x (V e y u)))v)

$\gg$ (A e (OUT s d y t))(A f (IN v w x u))
 = fail

$\gg$ (A e (OUT s d y t))($\gg$(A f (IN w z x u)) v)
 = fail

$\gg$ (A e (OUT s d y t)) empty
 = fail

$\gg$ empty (A e (IN s d y t))
 = fail

$\gg$ empty empty = empty

$\gg$ ($\gg$s t) u =$\gg$s ($\gg$ t u)

$\gg$ (| s t) u = block ($\gg$ s u)($\gg$ t u)

$\gg$ s (| t u) = block ($\gg$s t)($\gg$s u)
   <u>Figure 6</u>

The first two reductions show that when adjacent translations in a pipeline are in a state where communication can take place they synchronise and the first translation proceeds in an unchanged environment while the second performs an attribute assignment with the left hand side evaluated in its own environment and the right hand side evaluated in the environment of the sending translation. Communication can only take place if the stream and data item arguments of the OUT and the IN are identical, otherwise the communication fails. Similarly, communication with empty fails and empty pipelined to empty reduces to empty. The next reduction right associates nested pipelines. The final two reductions introduce the block primitive when $\gg$ distributes over alternatives. Its purpose is described in section 9.

8 Structured Assignment

The := introduced by the first two reductions in figure 6 has a first operand which is a (possibly empty) list of attributes and a second operand which is a list of expressions. The intended meaning is that the assignments take place in the order of the elements in the list. Figure 7 gives the necessary reduction rules

: = (:: x y)(:: z w) t = : = x z (: = y w t)

: = empty empty t = t

Figure 7

9 Failed, Empty and Nondeterministic Alternatives

Figure 8 shows some forms of productions which can occur in sequential translations. They are used to explain the purpose of reductions involving BLOCK and SYNC primitives by considering the desired effect of pipelining each of the

(i)   S1. a $<$A$>$| S1. b $<$B$>$

(ii)   [S1. a]

(iii)   [S1. c]$<$C $>$

(iv)   [S1. a]$<$D$>$ | [S1. b]$<$E $>$

Figure 8

expressions (ii) to (iv) with expressions (i). Using reductions given in previous sections (ii) pipelined with (i) reduces to

BLOCK (SYNC empty $<$ A$>$) fail

The intention is that if an a is communicated on S1 the translation updates its environment and continues to behave like $<$A $>$. We therefore require that the expression above should select the non failed blocked alternative and reduce to

SYNC empty $<$A$>$

If expression (iii) is pipelined to (i), the expression

BLOCK fail fail

results. It is the intended meaning that the complete pipeline should fail in this case. We therefore require it to reduce to fail.

When expression (iv) is pipelined to (i) the resulting expression reduces to

BLOCK (BLOCK (SYNC <D> <A>) fail)(BLOCK fail (SYNC <E> <B>))

In this case because either of two communications are successfully matched the result is nondeterministic. The successive behaviour of the translation is either like $\gg$ <D> <A> or like $\gg$ <E> <B>. The primitive OR is used to denote nondeterministic results.

The reductions shown in figure 9 therefore reflect the desired meaning of expressions involving BLOCK and SYNC.

BLOCK fail fail = fail

BLOCK (SYNC s t) fail = SYNC s t

BLOCK fail (SYNC s t) = SYNC s t

BLOCK (SYNC s t)(SYNC u v) = OR ($\gg$ s t)($\gg$ u v)

$\gg$ (SYNC s t) u = $\gg$ s ($\gg$ t u)

$\gg$ s (SYNC t u) = $\gg$ s ($\gg$ t u)

$\gg$ s (OR t u) = OR ($\gg$ s t)($\gg$ s u)

$\gg$ (OR s t) u = OR ($\gg$ s u)($\gg$ t u)

OR s s = s

<u>Figure 9</u>

The first four rules in figure 9 express the desired behaviour in that succesful communication takes precedence over failure and alternative successful communication represents nondeterministic behaviour. When the appropriate reductions have been performed on blocked alternatives, the translations can continue. The following four reductions in figure 9 show how this is achieved. When all BLOCKS have been evaluated, a pipeline with a SYNC operand reduces to a nested pipeline and the pipeline operand distributes over OR. The final reduction rule in figure 9 allows identical nondeterministic behaviours to be reduced.

From the implementation point of view, OR a b could nondeterministically reduce to either a or b so that OR's are removed from expressions. From the specification point of view they are not removed unless both arguments are identical.

The purpose of introducing the SYNC and BLOCK primitives is to enforce fully synchronised communication and non-backtracking over the selection of alternatives by blocking them when $\gg$ distributes over $|$. This prevents both the distribution of $\gg$ over a blocked alternative and the premature selection of a blocked alternative until both operands have been evaluated.

10 Disjoint Parallel Translations

So far we have omitted rules for pipelining to a disjoint parallel translation. The disjoint parallel composition of sequential translations is defined as in Hoare's CSP (4) as the alternative of all possible sequentialisations, given by the reduction rules in figure 10. Where, for brevity α and β each stand for IN or OUT.

, empty t = t

, t empty = t

, (A e (αa b c d))(A f(β g h i j))

= | (A e (αa b c (PAR   d (A f (βg h i j)))))

  (A f (βg h i (PAR j (A e (αa b c d)))))

A e (PAR b(A f c)) = , (A e b)(A f c)

figure 10

When a pipeline is in disjoint parallel composition with a translation, it is reformulated as a pipeline of disjoint parallel compositions as shown in figure 11.

, ($\gg$ a b)($\gg$ c d) = $\gg$(, a c)(, b d)

, ($\gg$ a b) c = $\gg$(, a c)(, b I)

, a ($\gg$ b c) = $\gg$ (, a b)(, c I)

figure 11

11 The Result Generator, Termination, Failure and Deadlock

Figure 12 shows the reductions involving the result generator. Whenever a translation pipelined to GEN is in a state to output, the first three arguments of the OUT are appended to GEN's result list argument. When all translations have terminated its argument is a time ordered list of items output from the DTL translation.

$\gg$ (A e (OUT s d y t))(GEN f)

  = $\gg$(A e t)(GEN (APPEND f (s d y)))

APPEND empty (s d y) = :: (s d y) empty

APPEND (:: f g) (s d y) = :: f (APPEND g (s d y))

figure 12

264

For any finite input sequence of data items, the translation components of a system progress until each translation terminates by either becoming empty or failing. With the reductions given in figure 13, all terminating systems therefore reduce to one of the three final forms given in figure 14 where t_1 and t_2 have, recursively, one of the three final forms.

$\gg$ empty empty = empty

$\gg$ fail empty = fail

$\gg$ empty fail = fail

$\gg$ fail fail = fail

$\gg$ (A e (OUT s d x t)) empty = fail

$\gg$ (A e (OUT s d x t))fail = fail

$\gg$ empty (A e (IN s d x t)) = fail

$\gg$ fail (A e (IN s d x t)) = fail

figure 13

$\gg$ empty (GEN result)

$\gg$ fail (GEN partresult)

OR t_1 t_2

figure 14

2 Discussion

The DTL language fulfills the dual roles of being both a program design and specification notation and a program implementation language. In many cases the program specification should be directly implementable in an efficient manner on a wide range of computer architectures. In a similar manner the reduction semantic definition of the language can be used as both a language specification and an implementation definition. In the latter role the implementation defined may be especially suitable for use with the recursive non-von Neumann architectures made possible by VSLI technology.

The use of the SYNC and BLOCK primitives to indicate a commitment to some particular behaviour, enables fully synchronised communication and non-backtraking behaviour to be specified in a straightforward manner.

The major difference between the interpretation of the reductions as a language specification and an implementation specification involves the non-deterministic primitive OR. In implementation terms it represents the opportunity to reduce the

complexity of a computation as soon as possible by choosing between two equal
valid alternatives. In specification terms occurrences of OR which remain i
the final irreducible expression denote truly nondeterministic behaviour of t
program concerned.

Fail is used to denote the behaviour of a pipeline expression in which transl
tions are unable to match input and output communications or the behaviour of
sequential translation in which the evaluation of an expression which forms
part of an assignment fails (eg by dividing by zero). This is comparable to
use of undefined in the semantics of Pascal (5), but unlike undefined it is
terminating computation. Thus run time failure is moved into the sphere of p
tial correctness as is undefined in (3). Furthermore the reductions as speci
result in deadlocked translations reducing to fail, so both the specification
the implementation can detect deadlock. In the earlier attempts at specifica
where streams had explicit values, no way was found of expressing deadlock.
finite input sequences the only form of translation which can give rise to a
terminating computation (or set of reductions) are *(x:=y) and left recursi
expressions. Providing these can be detected as erroneous by the compiler,
compiled DTL translations will reduce to one of the final irreducible forms
figure 14.

Not all of the abstract syntax and its meaning has been described here.   So
parts such as input and output guards, the association of formal and   actual
streams in expressions and nonterminal attributes are merely more of the same

The remaining problems are the specification of reduction rules for the cycl
operator and order dependencies in the evaluation of reduction rules. A furt
area of investigation, prompted by the observation that groups of the reducti
rules have similar forms (eg distribution of operators), is the possibility
reducing the number of rules by the use of combinators.

Acknowledgement

The work described here has been supported by SERC grant No. GRB35062.

References

1   Ashcroft E.A. and Wadge W.W.
    "Lucid: a formal system for writing and proving programs"
    SIAM J. Computing 5, 3 pp 336 - 354 (Sept 1976)

2   Backus J.
    "Can programming be liberated from the von-Neumann Style?"
    A Functional Style and its Algebra of Programs"
    CACM 21, 8 pp 613 - 641 (August 1978)

3   Coleman D. and Hughes J.W.
    "The Clean Determination of Pascal Programs"
    Acta Informatica 11, pp 195 - 210 (1979)

4   Hoare C.A.R.
    "Communicating Sequential Processes"
    CACM 21, 8 pp 666 - 677 (August 1978)

5   Hoare C.A.R. and Wirth N.
    "An Axiomatic Definition of the Programming Language PASCAL"
    Acta Informatica 2, pp 335 - 353 (1973)

6   Hughes J.W. and Powell M.S.
    "Program Specifications using DTL"
    Workshop on Program Specification, Aarhus (August 1981)

7   Kahn G.
    "The Semantics of a Simple Language for Parallel Programming"
    Information Processing 74 - North Holland Publishing Co (1974)

8   Turner D.A.
    "A New Implementaion Technique for Applicative Languages"
    Software P and E 9, pp 31 - 49 (1979)

RECURSIVE DEFINITIONS OF OPERATIONS IN UNIVERSAL ALGEBRAS

H.A. Klaeren

Lehrstuhl für Informatik II, RWTH Aachen

Büchel 29-31, D-5100 Aachen

West Germany

Introduction

In principle, every abstract software specification will be of the form $<S,\Sigma,\Delta>$ where S is a set of <u>sorts</u> or <u>types</u>, Σ a set of <u>operation symbols</u> typed over S and Δ a set of <u>definitions</u> for Σ. Apart from different syntactic sugar, the various approaches to abstract software specification differ essentially only in the nature of Δ. Objects like $<S,\Sigma>$ happen to be familiar to mathematicians: they are many-sorted <u>signatures</u> determining categories $\underline{Alg}_{<S,\Sigma>}$ of S-sorted universal Σ-algebras. It is therefore legitimate to consider abstract software specifications as presentations for algebras and to apply well-known results of universal algebra to software specification problems.

From the algebraic point of view the most obvious approach is to take for Δ a set of universally quantified equations between Σ-terms. SPEC $= <S,\Sigma,E>$ determines a category $\underline{Alg}_{SPEC}$ which is also called an <u>algebraic variety</u> and which has always an initial algebra T_{SPEC}, the abstract data type identified by SPEC. This is the initial algebra approach to software specification, mainly attributed to the so-called ADJ group (J.A. Goguer, J.W. Thatcher, E.G. Wagner, J.B. Wright).

There are two fundamental questions to be asked about all specification methods: the question of <u>adequacy</u> and the question of <u>reliability</u>. It was first pointed out by M. Majster that the adequacy of equational specifications can be doubted, since certain simple data types are not finitely specifiable. Subsequent work of Bergstra and Tucker showed, that with a limited use of so-called "hidden functions" every computable data type (software module) can be finitely specified. (For exact bibliographic data see for instance [1,3].)

Somewhat more connected to the practice of specifying abstract data types is the question of reliability: can we feel confident that a careful specification really expresses what we had in mind? It must be admitted that here the axiomatic specification method shows some deficiencies. The semantics of operations Σ in a specification $\langle S, \Sigma, E \rangle$ is defined using a factorization of the Σ-word algebra by the congruence generated by E. This is a natural procedure for a mathematician, but for a programmer it has some rather unnatural consequences. If an algebraic specification is developed step by step in a systematic way then it seems very likely that one wants to add a new operation ("enrich"), possibly together with a new sort ("extend"), to an already existing specification SPEC. Of course the new operation is defined by further axioms, but the factorization induced by these new axioms can have unpleasant consequences on previously defined operations or the set of possible data. At worst, T_{SPEC} breaks down to a one-element algebra.

The question of adequacy that was quoted above in a purely semantic context can also be asked with a pragmatic aspect: does the algebraic technique allow to specify abstract data types such as they are, without artificial additions, unrealistic constraints or other peculiarities? Some cautious doubts seem to be well suited. It occurs, for instance, rather frequently that elements of data types have an observable structure, which is reflected by structural operations such as constructors which generate new elements (possibly using old ones), selectors which give access to components of structured objects and indicators which identify the constructor which has last contributed to the generation of a specific data object. It's a rule that data types which do have constructors are inductively generated by these; all other operations can then be defined by their effect on terms build up with constructors. However with the axiomatic approach all operations have equal rights; it is not possible to distinguish a priori generating and defined operations. In fact, this is one reason for the problems with enrichments or extensions mentioned before. It has quite some merits to insist on a generation principle for data types as described above: first, we can prove theorems by induction and then we can define operations by a recursion on constructor terms.

Of course, phenomena which look like constructor-selector relationships and recursive definitions can frequently be discovered in an axiomatic specification SPEC. But the point is that for the construction of T_{SPEC} the axioms are not interpreted that way. T_{SPEC} is (except for $E = \emptyset$) not inductively generated either. The usefulness of an induction principle was also realized by the advocates of the initial algebra approach when they introduced the canonical Σ-term algebra isomorphic to T_{PSEC}, which is nothing else but an attempt to mark out constructors for SPEC a posteriori.

This author thinks that this is a bit like putting the cart before the horse. If there are constructors, then let it be constructors a priori; if there are recursive definitions, then let it be recursive definitions and not equations. Equations can be used for expressing properties of the constructors such as commutativity, accociativity, absorptive laws and so on. Hence our specifications are of the form $<S,\Sigma,E;O>$ where Σ is now the set of constructors, E (if non-empty) describes their properties and O is a set of certain recursion schemata for the definition of operations. These schemata are constructive definitions insofar as they suggest a method for actually computing the application of the operations to some arguments, which is not true of equations. J. Loeckx [6] and F. Nourani also vigorously argue for constructive operation definitions. Our specifications have a lot in common with Loeckx's specifications; in particular, they can be decomposed into a structural component describing the underlying data and a functional component defining the admissible operations of the specified data type or software module. We need not care about consistency and completeness of the operation definitions; in particular, the enrichment/extension problem does not exist in either of these two approaches. Considering the fundamental importance of extensions and enrichments of specifications with respect to a methodic ("structured") development of specifications, this is particularly significant. The main point is that the recursion schemata used for operation definition have no effect or influence whatsowever on each other nor on the constructors.

The main difference between the present approach and Loeckx's work (which was developed independently) lies in the treatment of the structural component: Loeckx has no equations for the description of the properties of constructors, so he has only to do with term algebras. Equivalent constructor terms are characterized by an equality predicate and non-normalized constructor terms are filtered out by an acceptor function. Both acceptor function and equality predicate are recursive schemata operating on the term algebra. In contrast with this procedure, we allow equations over constructor terms, thus leaving the term algebra. The useful properties of term algebras – structural induction and recursion – are then recovered by certain well-founded decomposition mappings which indicate how an element of an algebra can be generated by the constructors. Decomposition mappings can be considered as a combination of the indicator and selectors mentioned before.

Note that we do not completely question the usefulness of equational or axiomatic specifications: they are quite valuable in the early stages of a specification development process when we only have some ideas about operation properties but are yet unable to describe them constructively. However, when a specification is more and more refined and developed, we must keep in mind that we probably aim at an implementation where we must of course eventually give algorithms. So axiomatic definitions have to be replaced step by step, as our insight into the problem grows, by constructive specifications. The present paper briefly sketches the theory of constructive specifications and gives some hints on a formal environment for proving that a constructive specification implements an axiomatic one.

1. Structural recursive definitions

For this section we must assume some familarity with standard algebraic concepts.

It $<S,\Sigma>$ is a signature, then an S-sorted set A , together with operations F_A for each $F \in \Sigma$, is called a Σ-algebra.

We write A^s for the set of elements of A of sort $s \in S$ and define $A^w := A^{w_1} \times \ldots \times A^{w_n}$ for $w = w_1 \ldots w_n \in S^*$. We write $\Sigma^{(w,s)}$ for the set of operation symbols in Σ with arity w and coarity s and, similarly, $Ops^{(w,s)}(A) := \{f : A^w \to A^s \mid w \in S^*, s \in S\}$. Let $\Sigma^{(s)} := \bigcup_{w \in S^*} \Sigma^{(w,s)}$. The free Σ-algebra generated by X is denoted by $T_\Sigma(X)$; instead of $T_\Sigma(\emptyset)$ we write T_Σ . We think of $T_\Sigma(X)$ as consisting of variables $x \in X$ and Σ-X-terms $Ft_1 \ldots t_n$. If E is a set of Σ-equations, $T_{\Sigma,E}$ denotes the initial algebra in the category of all Σ algebras satisfying E . $T_{\Sigma,E}$ can be thought of as consisting of congruence classes of Σ-terms $t \in T_\Sigma$ where the congruence is generated by E . It is well-known that in $T_\Sigma(X)$ we can prove assertions by induction on the structure of terms; furthermore, the freeness property guarantees the unique existence of certain recursively defined operations on $T_\Sigma(X)$. Both results are based mainly on the unique decomposition of terms in $T_\Sigma(X)$; in $T_{\Sigma,E}$ however, and all the more in other Σ-algebras, they are not true.

For the rest of this paper, we restrict attention to Σ-algebras by $\emptyset$. These are the most natural candidates for models of Σ-specifications, since the unique homomor phisms $h_A : T_\Sigma \to A$ is surjective in this case, which means that each element of A can be referred to by at least one "abstract name" $t \in T_\Sigma$. So this excludes non-standard elements in models.

1.1 Definition: Let A be a Σ-algebra generated by $\emptyset$ and let $W(A)$ denote the set of all finite words over A , with empty word ϵ .

Then a mapping $d : A \to (\Sigma \times W(A))$ is called a decomposition of A iff for all $a \in A$

$$d(a) = (F,b_1 \ldots b_k) \implies F_A(b_1,\ldots,b_k) = a \text{ and}$$
$$d(a) = (F,\epsilon) \qquad \implies F_A = a \quad .$$

Define $a \sqsubseteq_d b$ iff $d(b) = (F,c_1 \ldots c_k)$ and $a = c_i$ for some i . Then d is called a well-founded decomposition iff there is no infinite descending chain $a_0 \sqsupseteq_d a_1 \sqsupseteq_d a_2 \sqsupseteq_d \ldots$

Let $<_d$ denote the transitive closure of $\sqsubseteq_d$.

1.2 Definition: A Σ-decomposition algebra (Σ-d algebra, for short) is a Σ-algebra A generated by $\emptyset$ together with a well-founded decomposition d_A

Σ-d algebras are very closely related to the canonical term algebras (CTA's) introduced by the ADJ group; see [1] for some comments on this subject. The important point is that in Σ-d algebras the principle of structural induction, i.e. induction on $<_d$, and a generalized principle of primitive recursion are valid.

1.3 Theorem (Structural Recursion): Let A be a Σ-decomposition algebra, $v \in S^*$, $s,t \in S$. Let $\Sigma^{(s)} := \bigcup_{w \in S^*} \Sigma^{(w,s)}$.

Then for every $\Sigma^{(s)}$-indexed family g of operations on A such that

$$F \in \Sigma^{(w,s)} \implies g_F \in Ops^{(vwt^k,t)}(A) \quad , \text{ where } k \text{ is the number of}$$
occurrences of s in w ,

there is a unique $h : A^v \times A^s \to A^t$ with

$$h(\underline{x},y) = g_F(\underline{x},y_1,\ldots,y_r,h(\underline{x},y_{i_1}),\ldots,h(\underline{x},y_{i_k}))$$

for $d(y) = (F,y_1\ldots y_r)$ and y_{i_j} of sort s .

In applications, Σ will always be finite. We can therefore define the operation h schematically by

$$h(\underline{x},y) = \text{case} \ y \ \text{of}$$
$$F_1(y_1,\ldots,y_{r_1}) : \tau_1 \ ;$$
$$\vdots$$
$$F_n(y_1;\ldots;y_{r_n}) : \tau_n$$

$$\text{esac}$$

where $\tau_j = g_{F_j}(\underline{x},y_1,\ldots,y_{r_j},h(\underline{x},y_{i_1}),\ldots,h(\underline{x},y_{i_{k_j}}))$.

Note that this is only a syntactically sugared variant of 1.3. Simplifying a little, we will call this a structural recursive schema and the operation h uniquely defined by this schema a structural recursive operation. (Formally, the class of structural recursive schemata over a signature Σ is defined by introducing a derived operation alphabet $D(\Sigma)$ which contains the basic operation symbols Σ as constants, special constant symbol for projections, and combinator symbols for substitution and structural recursion of any type. (See [3] for details). Then a structural recursive schema is an element of the initial algebra $T_{D(\Sigma)}$. By also defining a derived algebra $D(A)$ with carrier $Ops(A)$ for every Σ-d algebra A , we can use initiality to define the semantics of structural recursive schemata, which gives structural recursive operations.)

1.4 Definition: An abstract software specification is given by $D = \langle S,\Sigma,E;0 \rangle$

where $\langle S,\Sigma,E \rangle$ is a finite equational specification [1, 3] and
0 is a finite set of structural recursive Σ-schemata.

The elements of Σ are called formal constructors.

A model of D is a Σ-decomposition algebra A which satisfies E . A model
A induces a set $O \subseteq Ops(A)$ of admissible operations given by the semantics
of O .

A model is called a free model iff it is a canonical term algebra isomorphic
to $T_{\Sigma,E}$ with decomposition inherited from T_Σ .

The essential point in this definition is that we make a distinction between constructing operations which generate all data elements and defined operations which
only work on data elements described by the constructing operations. Constructors may
have some properties such as associativity, distributivity etc; these are expressed
by the equations E . In most cases, however, E will be empty.

1.5. Example: A fragment of finite set of integers
     For the example, we use our language SRDL [2] , since the present paper
     contains no formal treatment of structural recursive Σ-schemata.

```
module sets =
sorts   nat, set;
constructors nat = (zero, suc(nat));
             set = (empty, insert(set,nat));
variables   s:set ; i,j : nat;
equations   insert(insert(s,i),i) = insert(s,i);
            insert(insert(s,i),j) = insert(insert(s,j),i);
operations union(s,t : set) : set = case t of
                                    empty : s;
                                    insert(t1,i) : insert(union(s,t1),i)
                          esac;
           card(s : set): nat = case s of
                                empty : zero;
                                insert(s1,i) : suc(card(s1))
                          esac
end
```

At first glance, the definition of card seems to be problematic ; for instance, a simple-minded application of card seems to yield card(insert(insert(create,zero),zero)) = suc(suc(zero)) while of course the proper result is suc(zero) using the first equation. Here it is essential to remark that the structural recursion representec by case ... esac involves the well-founded decomposition mechanism which makes the result of the case test unique. For an operational interpretation of the schemata over $T_{\Sigma,E}$ this means that each term must be brought into a certain normal from before evaluating the test.

The following "Mezei-Wrignt like" result is essential for the definition of <u>abstract software modules</u>:

1.6 <u>Theorem</u>: Let D = <S,Σ,E;$\mathcal{O}$> be a specification, A a model thereof. Then there is a free model C of D and a D(Σ)-homomorphism p : D(C) → D(A) . (See the remarks after 1.3)

<u>Remark</u>: Note that this implies commutativity of diagram

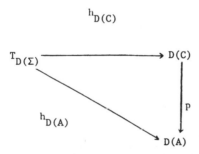

where $h_{D(C)}$, $h_{D(A)}$ arc the unique D(Σ)-homomorphisms. The semantics $[s]^A$, $[s]^C$ of a structural recursive schema $s \in T_{D(\Sigma)}$ in A and C , resp. is defined by $[s]^A = h_{D(A)}(s)$ and $[s]^C = h_{D(C)}(s)$. Thus, theorem 1.6 implies $[s]^A = p \circ [s]^C$.

1.7 <u>Definition</u>: The abstract software module specified by D = <S,Σ,E;$\mathcal{O}$> is the Σ-isomorphism class of free models of D .

2. Correctness of abstract software specifications

For considering correctness concerns of any kind of object, we always need some
reference with which this object should be compared. In the case of abstract
software specification, there can be three kinds of references :

(i)   a special algebra,

(ii)   a second abstract specification and

(iii)   a purely equational specification (see the comments in the introduction).

It is one of the characteristics of our approach that specifications $D = <S,\Sigma,E;O>$
are split into a structural component $<S,\Sigma,E>$ describing the data (i.e. the carrier
of an algebra) and a functional component O describing the applicable operations
in terms of data elements. This motivates the following two definitions :

2.1 Definition :

Let $D = <S,\Sigma,E;O>$ be a specification, A a model of D . From A we can
derive an O-algebra by associating with the name of each structural recursive
Σ-schema its semantics in A (cf. 1.6):

$$s_A := [\![s]\!]^A \quad .$$

This gives a new algebra A^O which we call the operational algebra of A .

We will not further distinguish between a schema and its name, hoping that this
will not cause confusion.

2.2 Definition : (Correctness w.r.t. a special algebra) Let $D = <S,\Sigma,E;O>$ be a

specification, B an $<S',\Sigma'>$-algebra. Then D is called correct w.r.t. B iff
$S' \subseteq S$, $\Sigma' \subseteq O$ and there is a free model C of D such that the $<S'\Sigma'>$ - reduct
the operational algebra C^O is Σ'-isomorphic to B .

This means that for every b$\in$B there is exactly one corresponding abstract object
in the data structure described by $<S,\Sigma,E>$ and that for every operation σ of B
there is a corresponding schema in O which has the same properties. The specification may involve more sorts and more operations, as sometimes auxiliary construction
(hidden sorts / operations) are necessary. However it will rarely occur that we want
an abstract specification for a concrete algebra. It is much more likely that we war
to compare two abstract specifications which arise in a program development process
and where one of them is in a certain sense more refined or closer to actual implementation. These concepts are of course hardly measurable, but at least we can

formalize correctness of one specification w.r.t. the other. In the present paper, we restrict attention to case (iii) since this is more interesting.

2.3 <u>Definition</u> : (<u>Correctness w.r.t. an equational specification</u>) Let
$D = <S,\Sigma,E;O>$ be a specification, SPEC = $<S1,\Sigma1,E1>$ an equational specification. D is called correct w.r.t. SPEC iff $S1 \subseteq S$, $\Sigma1 \subseteq O$ and there is a free model C of D such that the $<S1,\Sigma1>-$ reduct of the operational algebra C^O is $\Sigma1$-isomorphic to T_{SPEC}.

There exist quite a lot of methods for proving the isomorphism required in 2.3 ; one of them is summarized by the following lemma :

2.4 <u>Lemma</u> : Under the premises of 2.3, the $<S1,\Sigma1>$-reduct C' of C^O is $\Sigma1$-isomorphic to T_{SPEC} iff
(i)   C' satisfies the equations E1,
(ii)   for every $c \in C'$ there is a $\Sigma1$-term t such that $[\![t]\!]^C = c$ and
(iii) there is a surjective mapping $a:C' \to T_{SPEC}$ ("abstraction mapping")

<u>Proof</u> : If C' satisfies the equations E1, then C' $\in$ <u>Alg</u> $_{SPEC}$ which implies that there is a (unique) homomorphism $i:T_{SPEC} \to C'$. If (ii) holds, then C' is generated by $\emptyset$ (as a $\Sigma1$-algebra) which implies that i is surjective. If the abstraction mapping exists, then i must be injective too.
For correctness proofs of specifications, it is therefore essential to prove equations between terms over structural recursive schemata.

2.5 <u>Definition:</u> Let D = $<S,\Sigma,E;O>$, X an S-sorted variable alphabet. The equation $t_1 = t_2$ for $t_1,t_2 \in T_O(X)$ is called <u>valid</u> iff for all models A of 1 and all assignments $\theta : X \to A$ and the induced O-homomorphisms $\hat{\theta} : T_O(X) \to A^O$ we have $\hat{\theta}(t_1) = \hat{\theta}(t_2)$.

It is a standard technique in universal algebra to consider a term $t \in T_O(X)$ as a <u>polynomial schema</u> and to associate with it a polynominal $[\![t]\!]^A_p$ on every O-algebra A . So we can reformulate 2.5 as follows, using additionally theorem 1.6:

2.6 <u>Lemma:</u> Let $D = \langle S, \Sigma, E; 0 \rangle$, X an S-sorted variable alphabet,

$w = s_1 \ldots s_n \in S^*$, $X_w \subseteq X$ such that X_w contains exactly length(w) variables

of sorts $s_1, \ldots, s_n$, respectively.

Then $t_1 = t_2$ for $t_1, t_2 \in T_0(X_w)$ is valid iff for all <u>free models</u> C of D

all $t \in C^w$ we have

$$(*) \quad [\![t_1]\!]_p^C \, (\underline{t}) \;=\; [\![t_2]\!]_p^C \, (\underline{t}) \quad .$$

(Please note that there is an obvious injection $T_0(X_w) \to T_0(X_{w'})$ for

every $w' \in S^*$ which somehow contains w ; so this is no restriction on

equations.)

It seems natural to prove (*) by structural induction (either on a single component

of $\underline{t}$ or simultaneously on several components). Note that structural induction is

valid in Σ-d algebras. For the evaluation of either side of (*), we can use the

following equalities:

(A)   For all $s \in 0$, $s t_1 \ldots t_n \in T_0(X_w)$

$$[\![s t_1 \ldots t_n]\!]_p^C \;=\; [\![s]\!]^C \, ([\![t_1]\!]_p^C \,, \ldots, [\![t_n]\!]_p^C \,)$$

Here, $[\![s]\!]^C$ is the semantics of the schema s in C (cf. 1.6).

(This equation is equivalent to the homomorphism property of $\hat{\theta}$ in 2.5) .

(B)   Since free models are canonical term algebras which come equipped with decom-

position inherited from T_Σ , it is easy to compute $[\![s]\!]^C$:

Let s be given by

$$s(x_1 : s_1 ; \ldots x_n : s_n) : s_{n+1} = \underline{\text{case}} \; x_i \; \underline{\text{of}}$$

$$F_1(y_1, \ldots, y_{m_1}) \; : \; t_1;$$

$$\vdots$$

$$F_k(y_1, \ldots, y_{m_k}) \; : \; t_k$$

$$\underline{\text{esac}} \qquad\qquad ;$$

then $[\![s]\!]^C (c_1,\ldots,c_{i-1},F_j b_1 \ldots b_r, c_{i+1},\ldots,c_n) = t'_j$ where t'_j is obtained from t_j by replacing each x_m by c_m and each y_m by b_m .

It seems appropriate to call step (B) a $\underline{\text{symbolic evaluation of } s}$. For practial proofs we omit the semantic brackets $[\![\ ]\!]$ and $[\![\ ]\!]_p$ and we write $t \vdash t'$ if t' can be derived from t by a single application of (B) and possibly several applications of (A) .

A proof that the operation union in example 1.5 satisfies the associative law would than proceed as follows :

2.7 Example : To show : union(s, union (t,u)) = union (union(s,t),u).

    Case 1 : u = empty

           Left hand side : union(s,union(t,empty)) $\vdash$ union(s,t)

           Right hand side: union(union(s,t),empty) $\vdash$ union(s,t)

    Case 2 : u = insert(m,i)

           Induction hypothesis : For all $y < u$ (with the decomposition ordering $<$ (see 1.1) of the unique term decomposition inherited from T_Σ) we have

$$\text{union}(s,\text{union}(t,y)) = \text{union}(\text{union}(s,t,),y).$$

           Left hand side : union(s,union(t,insert(m,i))

                    $\vdash$ union(s,insert(union(t,m),i))

                    $\vdash$ insert(union(s,union(t,m)),i)

        hyp.

               $=$ insert(union(union(s,t),m),i)

           Right hand side: union(union(s,t),insert(m,i))

                    $\vdash$ insert(union(union(s,t),m),i)

The case distinction is justified by the fact that we have to prove this equation for a free model of the specification 1.5 ; this is an algebra whose carrier is a canonical term algebra isomorphic to T_{SPEC} (where SPEC is the $\underline{\text{sorts}}$ - $\underline{\text{constructors}}$ - $\underline{\text{equations}}$ of 1.5.)

3. Conclusions

The constructive definition of operations by structural recursive schemata offers some advantages over axiomatic specifications as far as reliability and maintainability are concerned. Every addition of a new operation is a safe, harmless process because it has no side effects on the data structure or the other operations. The consequences of a change in a definition can be easier localized than in an axiom system. The algorithmic nature of primitive recursive definitions is very convenient for automatic implementation [2]. All this is not true of axiomatic specifications, especially if we think of the specification of large systems involving several hundreds of equations : even the slightest modification of a single equation or the smallest addition can have unwanted secondary effects and possibly cause the breakdown of the whole system. Automatic implementation of axiomatic specifications is by no means straightforward ; equations can only be handled interpretively and it is difficult to keep the interpreter from running into endless loops. Nevertheless, equational specifications seem appropriate for the first steps in a specification development process, but then they should soon be replaced by constructive specifications which are correct relatively to them. The method has been applied successfully to the description of programming language semantics and compilers ; see [4,5].

References

[1]   H.A. Klaeren

A simple class of algorithmic specifications for abstract software modules

9th MFCS (1980), Springer Lect. Not. Comp. Sc. 88, 362-374

[2]   H.A. Klaeren

The SRDL specification experiment

--- This volume ---

[3]   H.A. Klaeren

A constructive method for abstract algebraic software specification

To appear 1981

[4]   H.A. Klaeren, H. Petzsch

The development of an interpreter by means of abstract algebraic software specifications

Int. Coll. on Formalization of Prog. Concepts, Peniscola 1981

Springer Lect. Not. Comp. Sc. 107, 335-346

[5]   H.A. Klaeren, H. Petzsch

Algebraic software specification and compiler generation - a case study

RWTH Aachen, Schriften zur Informatik & Ang. Math. Nr. 68, 1981

[6]   J. Loeckx

Algorithmic specifications of abstract data types

8th ICALP (1981)

The SRDL specification experiment

H.A. Klaeren

Lehrstuhl für Informatik II, RWTH Aachen

Büchel 29-31, D-5100 Aachen

West Germany

Abstract

In [1] a constructive software specification technique based on structural recursion
is proposed. Here we describe a specification language SRDL which was developed
according to these ideas and its implementation. SRDL was implemented by H. Petzsch
with occasional assistance of U. Goltz.

Introduction

In [1,2] a constructive method for abstract software specification based on so-called
structural recursion is developed. The main ideas of this technique are sketched in [
In [2], recursive operations over algebras with a well-founded decomposition are intr
duced using a derived operation alphabet with special operators for projections and
recursive definitions. By defining also a derived algebra, the semantics of such
"structural recursive schemata" can be given in a simple and mathematically elegant
way using initiality. Nevertheless, the semantics of the structural recursion combin
is rather complex and it takes quite some time to discover the meaning even of simpl
schemata. For instance, taking the signature of linear lists, with

$$\text{sorts} \quad S = \{item, list\} \quad \text{and}$$
$$\text{operations} \quad \Sigma = \{empty^{(\varepsilon, list)}, add^{(list\ item, list)}\},$$

the definition of the operation <u>first</u> which gives the first item in the list would

$$\underline{first} = srs^{(list, item)}(error_{item}, srs^{(item^2\ list, item)}(\pi_1^{item^2}, \pi_2^{item^2\ list\ item^2})\ \circ$$
$$[\pi_2^{list\ item^2}; \pi_3^{list\ item^2}; \pi_1^{list\ item^2}])$$

where the π's are projection symbols and srs is the recursion combinator .
Of course, this notation is unintelligible. Therefore [1] proposes a language SRDL
where structural recursive definitions are presented in a more convenient form using
syntactic constructs known from programming languages.
For instance, the above schema would be represented by the following text:

```
first(s:list): item = case s of
                        empty: error;
                        add(s1,i): case s1 of
                                    empty: i;
                                    add(s2,j): first(s1)
                                   esac
                 esac
```

The SRDL language has now been implemented (INTAS system, [3]), mainly for the following reasons:

1.) The correctness of a specification can only be checked by matching it with another formal specification [1] or some other formalized environment. The very first formal specification must be compared with informal, intuitive ideas. Therefore it seems useful to have a capability of applying a formal specification to some test data and see whether the results agree with the informal concept.

2.) The algorithmic nature of structural recursive definitions suggests the conjecture that it should be easy to generate an automatic implementation for SRDL specifications. Of course, this implementation may be inefficient ; for instance, the head of a queue could be searched by beginning with the tail. But we can imagine cases where efficiency is not the most important property of an implementation ; then it is convenient to have the INTAS system providing us very quickly with at least an inefficient implementation.

In the present paper, we briefly summarize the language SRDL, explain the main characteristics of the INTAS system, give some examples for dialogues with the system and an outlook on future plans with the system.

1. The language SRDL

The main construct of SRDL is the module which corresponds to an abstract software specification as defined in [1]. A specification in SRDL is a sequence of modules separated by semicolons where a module limits the scope of identifiers. A module contains declarations of four kinds of objects : sorts, constructors, variables and operations. Additionally it is possible to specify equations relating to terms over constructors. The equations have only the purpose of specifying certain properties of the constructors and dependencies between them ; they are not meant for the recursive definition of operations. In most cases, it is possible to do without any equations ; this can be achieved by an appropriate definition of the operations. Since we don't want to comment on all details of SRDL syntax, it seems best to explain the syntax using examples.

Example 1 : (A fragment of integers)
```
    MODULE INTEGER1 =
    SORTS INT;
    CONSTRUCTORS INT = (ZER, SUC(INT),PRE(INT));
    VARIABLES N:INT;
    EQUATIONS SUC(PRE(N)) = N;
              PRE(SUC(N)) = N;
    OPERATIONS
                INC(N: INT): INT = SUC(N);
                DEC(N:INT):INT = PRE(N);
                PLUS(N,M: INT):INT = CASE M OF
                        ZER: N;
                        SUC(M1): SUC(PLUS(N,M1));
                        PRE(M1): PRE(PLUS(N,M1))
                      ESAC;
                MINUS(N,M:INT):INT = CASE M OF
                        ZER: N;
                        SUC(M1): PRE(MINUS(N,M1));
                        PRE(M1): SUC(MINUS(N,M1))

                      ESAC;
                INVERT(N: INT): INT = CASE N OF
                        ZER: ZER;
                        SUC(N1): PRE(INVERT(N1));
                        PRE(N1): SUC(INVERT(N1))
                      ESAC
    END
```

Explanation : A module begins with module and ends with end.Within a module, t
order of the key words sorts, constructors, variables, equations and operations
is obligatory although some of them may be omitted. The constructors statement lis
for every sort name all constructors which generate objects of this sort ; if the co
tructors have arguments, then the respective sorts of these are specified in the sam
order as they appear when using this constructor. The variables statement has the
only purpose to declare variables which can be used in the equations statement.

The declaration of an operation begins with the name of the operation followed by a
parameter list which assigns names and sorts to the arguments of the operation. The
parameterlist is followed by the specification of the result sort and the definition
of the operation. This can be either a simple expression containing only constructor
or previously defined operations or a recursive definition involving the case...esa
clause, which contains a list of label-expression pairs. Admissible labels are all
the constructors belonging to the sort of the expression being tested. To the argume
of the constructors (if any) are assigned new names for use in the expression follow
the corresponding label. For the semantics of case...esac see [1]. case - express
can be nested as in the following example 2. Any kind of declared object can be impo
from other modules in the same specification by the include statement which specif
one or more module names followed by a list of sorts, constructors and operatio
All objects of the specified module which are not contained in this list will not be
known to the current module.

Example 2 :

```
MODULE BOOLEAN =
SORTS BOOL;
CONSTRUCTORS BOOL = (TRUE, FALSE);
OPERATIONS AND(X,Y: BOOL): BOOL = CASE Y OF
                                       TRUE: X;
                                       FALSE: FALSE
                                   ESAC;
            OR (X,Y: BOOL): BOOL = CASE Y OF
                                       TRUE: TRUE;
                                       FALSE: X
                                   ESAC;
            NOT (X: BOOL): BOOL = CASE X OF
                                       TRUE: FALSE;
                                       FALSE: TRUE
                                   ESAC
END
MODULE INTEGER1 =
INCLUDE BOOLEAN (BOOL,TRUE,FALSE);
SORTS INT;
CONSTRUCTORS INT = (ZER, SUC(INT),PRE(INT));
VARIABLES N:INT;
EQUATIONS SUC(PRE(N)) = N;
          PRE(SUC(N)) = N;
OPERATIONS EQ(N,M: INT): BOOL = CASE M OF
                                   ZER: CASE N OF
                                           ZER: TRUE;
                                           SUC(N1),PRE(N2): FALSE
                                        ESAC;
                                   SUC(N1): CASE N OF
                                               SUC(N2): EQ(N1,N2);
                                               ZER,PRE(N2): FALSE
                                            ESAC;
                                   PRE(N1): CASE N OF
                                               PRE(N2): EQ(N1,N2);
                                               ZER,SUC(N2): FALSE
                                            ESAC
                                ESAC
END
```

The module INTEGER1 knows only the sort name BOOL and its constructors TRUE and FALSE.
The names and definitions of the operations AND,OR and NOT are not known to INTEGER1
since they are not contained in the include list. Note that it is dangerous to intro
duce new constructors or equations for a sort which has been included from another
module ; this may completely change the properties of this sort.   In fact, this is
forbidden in SRDL although our present implementation does'nt check it.
SRDL has also parameterized modules ; however, since we are reporting here mainly on
the implementation and since the parameterization mechanism is not yet implemented, we
will not comment on this. For details about parameterizations please refer to [2,4].

2. The INTAS system

The INTAS system consists of two main parts: a compiler and a run time system. The

compiler reads an SRDL specification, checks it for syntactic correctness and gene
rates the following objects which are to be handed over to the run time system :

1.) A symbol table of all declared objects of the specification.
2.) An internal representation of the specified equations. Equations are interpreted
    as reduction rules from left to right. The run time system will try to "normaliz
    every term occuring in a computation by reducing it according to the equations
    until no further reduction is applicable.
3.) One PASCAL procedure for every operation definition. This procedure will evaluat
    calls of the corresponding operation under the assumption that the argument tern
    are normalized. The run time system will make sure that this is always the case
    before an operation procedure is called.

Output from the compiler is an incomplete PASCAL program containing the information
described above and some flags for the insertion of the run time system procedures.
After compiling an SRDL specification using the INTAS compiler, the result of th
compilation process can be passed to the PASCAL compiler which inserts the appropr
run time routines from a special library. Afterwards, the run time system can be. sta
and operations can be evaluated interactively.
The compiler is a standard recursive descent compiler ; so there is no need to comme
on it here. The run time system has one main loop where terms can be input and are
then simplified by the system. This is done in leftmost-innermost order. Terms begir
with an operation symbol are handed over for evaluation to the corresponding procedu
generated by the INTAS compiler whereas terms beginning with a constructor symbol
are passed to an equational interpreter which is supposed to normalize this term acc
ding to the equations. The interpreter is relatively poor compared with other exis
equational interpreters. We can put up with that readily because of the limited use
equations in SRDL . Since equations are not used for recursive definitions we can d
without them in most cases ; for the rest we can restrict ourselves to confluent and
noetherian sets of equations. These are handled properly by our present interpreter.
For easier localization of specifications errors, the system can be instructed to re
every normalization up to a specified level of term nesting.
Further details about dialogues with the system are reported in section **3**. Both th
INTAS compiler and the run time system were implemented on the CYBER 175 of the
RWTH Aachen in PASCAL 6000 Rel. 3.

3. Example dialogues

The numbers in the following example refer to the comments below. User input is lowe
case , system responses upper case.

```
    /algcomp,int1
    MODULE INTEGER1 =
    SORTS INT;
    CONSTRUCTORS INT = (ZER, SUC(INT),PRE(INT));
    VARIABLES N:INT;
    EQUATIONS SUC(PRE(N)) = N;
              PRE(SUC(N)) = N;
    OPERATIONS
                INC(N: INT): INT = SUC(N);
                DEC(N:INT):INT = PRE(N);
                PLUS(N,M: INT):INT = CASE M OF
                                         ZER: N;
                                         SUC(M1): SUC(PLUS(N,M1));
                                         PRE(M1): PRE(PLUS(N,M1))
                                     ESAC;
                MINUS(N,M:INT):INT = CASE M OF
                                         ZER: N;
                                         SUC(M1): PRE(MINUS(N,M1));
                                         PRE(M1): SUC(MINUS(N,M1))

                                     ESAC;
                INVERT(N: INT): INT = CASE N OF
                                         ZER: ZER;
                                         SUC(N1): PRE(INVERT(N1));
                                         PRE(N1): SUC(INVERT(N1))
                                     ESAC
    END

        0.097 CP SECS,  14226B CM USED.
```
② /pascal,compile/l-,g+
③ BITTE SORTE EINGEBEN
④ ? _int
⑤ SORTE:
   INT
⑥ ? _6
⑦ ? plus(inc(inc(inc(inc(dec(zer)))))),inc(inc(zer)))
   EINGEGEBENER TERM:
   PLUS(INC(INC(INC(INC(DEC(ZER))))),INC(INC(ZER)))
   *DEC(ZER)
   =PRE(ZER)
   *INC(PRE(ZER))
   =ZER
   *INC(ZER)
   =SUC(ZER)
   *INC(SUC(ZER))
   =SUC(SUC(ZER))
   *INC(SUC(SUC(ZER)))
   =SUC(SUC(SUC(ZER)))
   *ZER
   =ZER
   *INC(ZER)
   =SUC(ZER)
   *INC(SUC(ZER))
   =SUC(SUC(ZER))
   *PLUS(SUC(SUC(SUC(ZER))),SUC(SUC(ZER)))
   =SUC(SUC(SUC(SUC(SUC(ZER)))))
   ERGEBNIS:
   SUC(SUC(SUC(SUC(SUC(ZER)))))

```
? _9
? invert(inc(inc(dec(inc(inc(dec(dec(zer)))))))))
 EINGEGEBENER TERM:
 INVERT(INC(INC(DEC(INC(INC(DEC(DEC(ZER)))))))))
 *ZER
 =ZER
 *DEC(ZER)
 =PRE(ZER)
 *DEC(PRE(ZER))
 =PRE(PRE(ZER))
 *INC(PRE(PRE(ZER)))
 =PRE(ZER)
 *INC(PRE(ZER))
 =ZER
 *DEC(ZER)
 =PRE(ZER)
 *INC(PRE(ZER))
 =ZER
 *INC(ZER)
 =SUC(ZER)
 *INVERT(SUC(ZER))
 =PRE(ZER)
 ERGEBNIS:
 PRE(ZER)
? invert(inc(inc(dec(inc(inc(dec(inc(zer)))))))))
 EINGEGEBENER TERM:
 INVERT(INC(INC(DEC(INC(INC(DEC(INC(ZER)))))))))
 *ZER
 =ZER
 *INC(ZER)
 =SUC(ZER)
 *DEC(SUC(ZER))
 =ZER
 *INC(ZER)
 =SUC(ZER)
 *INC(SUC(ZER))
 =SUC(SUC(ZER))
 *DEC(SUC(SUC(ZER)))
 =SUC(ZER)
? 
      0.080 CP SECS,  13560B CM USED.
```

Comments :

1.) The INTAS compiler ("ALGCOMP") is instructed to compile a specification loca
in file "INT1". The following lines are output from the compiler. The result o
the compilation is written to a file "COMPILE".

2.) The PASCAL compiler is instructed to compile this file without writing a lis
and to execute it immediately.

3.) The INTAS run time system requests the input of a sort name. After the users
response "INT" (4.) preceded by an escape character "_" the system is ready to
evaluate terms of the specified sort.

5.) The system confirms the input sort "INT".

6.) This instructs the system to report all normalizations up to nesting level 6.

7.) A term is input and, since it is syntactically correct and belongs to the specified sort "INT", it is confirmed by the system. In the following lines, every
pair of lines beginning with an asterisk is the report of a single function evaluation. It can be seen from the output that the system normalizes the arguments
of "PLUS" in a leftmost-innermost fashion.

8.) The dialogue is terminated by an empty answer.

At any time it is possible to change the current sort of interest by simply typing
in the name of another sort after the escape character "_". This is used in the following example specification for strings of integers. Note that these are precisely the
PL/I strings with the "built-in functions" belonging to them. The only difference is
the use of the prefix operation "concat" instead of the infix operation "I".

```
/alocomp,strings
MODULE BOOLEAN =
SORTS BOOl ;
CONSTRUCTORS BOOL = (TRUE, FALSE);
OPERATIONS ANO(X,Y: BOOL): BOOL = CASE Y OF
                                      TRUE: X;
                                      FALSE: FALSE
                                  ESAC;
            OR (X,Y: BOOL): BOOL = CASE Y OF
                                      TRUE: TRUE;
                                      FALSE: X
                                  ESAC;
            NOT (X: BOOL): BOOL = CASE X OF
                                      TRUE: FALSE;
                                      FALSE: TRUE
                                  ESAC
END
MODULE INTEGER =
INCLUDE BOOLEAN (BOOL,TRUE,FALSE,AND,OR,NOT);
SORTS INT;
CONSTRUCTORS INT = (0, S(INT),P(INT));
VARIABLES N:INT;
EQUATIONS S(P(N)) = N;
          P(S(N)) = N;
OPERATIONS
            INC(N: INT): INT = S(N);
            DEC(N:INT):INT = P(N);
            +(N,M: INT):INT = CASE M OF
                                  0: N;
                                  S(M1): S(+(N,M1));
                                  P(M1): P(+(N,M1))
                              ESAC;
            -(N,M:INT):INT = CASE M OF
                                  0: N;
                                  S(M1): P(-(N,M1));
                                  P(M1): S(-(N,M1))

                              ESAC;
            +\-(N: INT): INT = CASE N OF
                                  0: 0;
                                  S(N1): P(+\-(N1));
                                  P(N1): S(+\-(N1))
                              ESAC;
```

```
                EQ(N,M: INT): BOOL = CASE M OF
                                0: CASE N OF
                                        0: TRUE;
                                        S(N1),P(N2): FALSE
                                     ESAC;
                                S(N1): CASE N OF
                                        S(N2): EQ(N1,N2);
                                        0,P(N2): FALSE
                                     ESAC;
                                P(N1): CASE N OF
                                        P(N2): EQ(N1,N2);
                                        0,S(N2): FALSE
                                     ESAC
                        ESAC
END

        MODULE STRING =
        INCLUDE BOOLEAN(BOOL,TRUE,FALSE,AND,OR,NOT);
                INTEGER(INT,0,S,-,EQ);
        SORTS STR;

        CONSTRUCTORS STR = (EMPTY, ADD(STR,INT));
        OPERATIONS
                CONCAT (S1,T: STR): STR = CASE T OF
                                        EMPTY: S1;
                                        ADD(T1,X): ADD(CONCAT(S1,T1),X)

                                ESAC;
                LENGTH (T:STR): INT = CASE T OF
                                        EMPTY: 0;
                                        ADD(S1,X): S(LENGTH(S1))
                                ESAC;

                INDEX (Y:INT; T:STR): INT =
                        CASE T OF
                            EMPTY: 0;
                            ADD(S1,X): CASE EQ(X,Y) OF
                                    TRUE: S(LENGTH(S1));
                                    FALSE: INDEX(X,S1)
                                ESAC
                        ESAC;
                SUBSTR (T:STR; I,J:INT): STR =

                CASE T OF
                    EMPTY: EMPTY;
                    ADD(S1,X): CASE J OF
                            0: EMPTY;
                            S(J1): CASE EQ(I,S(S(-(LENGTH(S1),J)))) OF
                                    TRUE: ADD(SUBSTR(S1,I,J1),X);
                                    FALSE: SUBSTR(S1,I,J)
                                ESAC
                        ESAC
                ESAC
        END

        0.318 CP SECS,  14362B CM USED.
/pascal,compile/l-,g+
 BITTE SORTE EINGEBEN
? _bool
 SORTE:
 BOOL
? _5
? and(and(or(true,false),not(false)),false)
 EINGEGEBENER TERM:
 AND(AND(OR(TRUE,FALSE),NOT(FALSE)),FALSE)
 *TRUE
 =TRUE
 *FALSE
 =FALSE
 *OR(TRUE,FALSE)
 =TRUE
 *FALSE
 =FALSE
 *NOT(FALSE)
 =TRUE
 *AND(TRUE,TRUE)
 =TRUE
 *FALSE
 =FALSE
 *AND(TRUE,FALSE)
 =FALSE
 ERGEBNIS:
 FALSE
```

```
_0
_string
FALSCHE EINGABE:
STRING
***KEIN SORT NAME
_str
SORTE:
STR
 concat(add(add(add(empty,0),0),s(0)),add(add(empty,p(0)),s(0)))
EINGEGEBENER TERM:
CONCAT(ADD(ADD(ADD(EMPTY,0),0),S(0)),ADD(ADD(EMPTY,P(0)),S(0)))
 ERGEBNIS:
ADD(ADD(ADD(ADD(ADD(EMPTY,0),0),S(0)),P(0)),S(0))
 length(add(add(add(empty,0),0),0))
 FALSCHE EINGABE:
LENGTH(
***NAME NICHT IN SYMBOLTABELLE UNTER ENTSPRECHENDER SORTE
_int
SORTE:
INT
 length(add(add(add(empty,0),0),0))
EINGEGEBENER TERM:
LENGTH(ADD(ADD(ADD(EMPTY,0),0),0))
ERGEBNIS:
S(S(S(0)))
 index(0,add(add(add(empty,s(0)),p(0)),0))
EINGEGEBENER TERM:
INDEX(0,ADD(ADD(ADD(EMPTY,S(0)),P(0)),0))
ERGEBNIS:
S(S(S(0)))
 index(p(0),add(add(add(empty,s(0)),p(0)),0))
EINGEGEBENER TERM:
INDEX(P(0),ADD(ADD(ADD(EMPTY,S(0)),P(0)),0))
ERGEBNIS:
S(S(0))
 index(0,add(add(add(empty,s(0)),s(0)),p(0)))
EINGEGEBENER TERM:
INDEX(0,ADD(ADD(ADD(EMPTY,S(0)),S(0)),P(0)))
ERGEBNIS:
0
 substr(add(add(add(empty,0),p(0)),s(0)),s(0),s(s(0)))
FALSCHE EINGABE:
SUBSTR(
***NAME NICHT IN SYMBOLTABELLE UNTER ENTSPRECHENDER SORTE
_str
SORTE:
STR
 substr(add(add(add(empty,0),p(0)),s(0)),s(0),s(s(0)))
EINGEGEBENER TERM:
SUBSTR(ADD(ADD(ADD(EMPTY,0),P(0)),S(0)),S(0),S(S(0)))
ERGEBNIS:
ADD(ADD(EMPTY,0),P(0))
 concat(substr(add(add(add(empty,0),p(0)),s(0)),s(0),s(s(0))),add(empty,0))
EINGEGEBENER TERM:
CONCAT(SUBSTR(ADD(ADD(ADD(EMPTY,0),P(0)),S(0)),S(0),S(S(0))),ADD(EMPTY,0))
ERGEBNIS:
ADD(ADD(ADD(EMPTY,0),P(0)),0)
_int
SORTE:
INT
_6
 length(concat(add(add(empty,0),p(0)),add(add(add(empty,0),s(0)),p(0))))
EINGEGEBENER TERM:
LENGTH(CONCAT(ADD(ADD(EMPTY,0),P(0)),ADD(ADD(ADD(EMPTY,0),S(0)),P(0))))
*EMPTY
=EMPTY
*0
=0
*ADD(EMPTY,0)
=ADD(EMPTY,0)
*0
=0
*P(0)
=P(0)
*ADD(ADD(EMPTY,0),P(0))
=ADD(ADD(EMPTY,0),P(0))
*EMPTY
=EMPTY
*0
=0
```

```
*ADD(EMPTY,0)
=ADD(EMPTY,0
*0
=0
*S(0)
=S(0)
*ADD(ADD(EMPTY,0),S(0))
=ADD(ADD(EMPTY,0),S(0))
*0
=0
*P(0)
=P(0)
*ADD(ADD(ADD(EMPTY,0),S(0)),P(0))
=ADD(ADD(ADD(EMPTY,0),S(0)),P(0))
*CONCAT(ADD(ADD(EMPTY,0),P(0)),ADD(ADD(ADD(EMPTY,0),S(0)),P(0)))
=ADD(ADD(ADD(ADD(EMPTY,0),P(0)),0),S(0)),P(0))
*LENGTH(ADD(ADD(ADD(ADD(ADD(EMPTY,0),P(0)),0),S(0)),P(0)))
=S(S(S(S(S(0)))))
ERGEBNIS:
S(S(S(S(S(0))))))
? _str
 SORTE:
 STR
? _7
? add(add(empty,+\-(s(0))),+(s(0),s(0)))
 EINGEGEBENER TERM:
 ADD(ADD(EMPTY,+\-(S(0))),+(S(0),S(0)))
 *EMPTY
 =EMPTY
 *0
 =0
 *S(0)
 =S(0)
 *+\-(S(0))
 =P(0)
 *ADD(EMPTY,P(0))
 =ADD(EMPTY,P(0))
 *0
 =0
 *S(0)
 =S(0)
 *0
 =0
 *S(0)
 =S(0)
 *+(S(0),S(0))
 =S(S(0))
 *ADD(ADD(EMPTY,P(0)),S(S(0)))
 =ADD(ADD(EMPTY,P(0)),S(S(0)))
 ERGEBNIS:
 ADD(ADD(EMPTY,P(0)),S(S(0)))
?
      0.030 CP SECS,  20652B CM USED.
```

4. Future plans

The first thing we must of course do is the implementation of the parameterization mechanism as reported in [2,4]. In a second step, it would be desirable to let the user have his own module library from where he can include frequently needed objects. This should even be supported by a systems module library containing certain standard (mostly parameterized) modules. At the time being, every specification must contain all modules from which informations are to be included, and the INTAS compiler must process these completely.

Furthermore, it is by now not possible to process numbers, characters or strings in their familiar form ; instead they must always be explicitly specified. This has some nasty consequences ; first, the notation is relatively complex since, for instance, the string "INPUT" would appear as "$I(N(P(U(T(\epsilon)))))$" and the number 231150 would be a rather long expression with SUC and ZER . Furthermore, the arithmetic operations of the abstract specification INTEGER are very expensive w.r.t. computing time. It is therefore planned to have at least numbers, boolean values and characters (strings) as predefined modules with an efficient implementation. From the human engeneering point of view, it would furthermore be an advantage to have the capability of specifying infix operators like STRING 1 ‖ STRING 2 or IF p THEN q ELSE r. A long-range goal is it to have the system supporting inductive proofs like in [1], Example 2.7 under the interactive guidance of the user.

5. References

[1]   H.A. Klaeren
       Recursive definitions of operations in universal algebras
       --- This volume ---

[2]   H.A. Klaeren
       A constructive method for abstract algebraic software specification
       To appear 1981

[3]   H. Petzsch
       INTAS - Ein System zur Interpretation algebraischer Spezifikationen
       Berichte des Lehrstuhls für Informatik II, RWTH Aachen, Nr. 5, 1981

[4]   H.A. Klaeren
       On parameterized abstract software modules using inductively specified
       operations
       RWTH Aachen, Schriften zur Informatik & Ang. Math., Nr. 66, 1980

PROGRAM SPECIFICATION BY MODULE TREES.

J. Steensgaard-Madsen
University of Copenhagen
Sigurdsgade 42
DK-2200 Copenhagen

Introduction

A brief presentation of tools used for program specification
is given as background for an example specification of a KWIC-
index generation program. The example has been presented to
the Workshop on Program Specification in Aarhus, Aug. 4. - 7.,
1981.

A program structure is described by means of a *module
tree*. This leads to an identification of *modules* to be used
in a program. The program task is expressed by combined use
of modules in an expression that will be the main program
when the semantics of the modules has been successfully specified.

A module consists of an interface and a body. The semantics of a module is given by the body in a specification language or in ordinary programming language. If an ordinary programming language is used the module is said to be implemented,
and when all modules are implemented the program is developed.
For module implementation a Pascal-like ordinary programming
language has been chosen. This has influenced the design of a
formal specification language. The formal specification language is the implementation language with its type definition
facilities replaced by more idealised ones.

The more powerful type-definition facilities are restricted

algebraic typespecifications. The restrictions are imposed with an intent to avoid errors easily committed by simple minded users (as the author). However, the restrictions also allow an intuitively appealing concept of equality, and this again provides for simpler specifications in some cases.

Although based on algebraic typespecification, an unusual syntax has been chosen for type definitions. In itself the departure from conventions is hardly justified; but considering the facilities as part of a whole, conventional notation is inattractive. Also, considered in isolation, the facilities may be thought too simple; since, for instance, no parametrization of a type definition is allowed apart from context assumptions. However, it is my belief that the entire set of concepts is adequate; the parametrization of type definitions, for example, is possible by use of the module interface; and it is not just possible but deliberately left as the only way to obtain this kind of parametrization.

The remaining part of the paper is divided into sections with headings: Module Trees, A model for Module Trees, Notation, Encapsulation, Types, Paramter Types, Program Development, and An Example.

Module Trees

It is possible to achieve what is commonly known as information hiding in a block structured language as, say, Pascal. The technique is based on extensive use of procedures and functions as arguments, and it is implicitly explained in a later section.

Module trees reflect the essentials of the resulting program structure, when the technique mentioned is used. This postulate will have to do as justification for the properties ascribed to a module tree, which otherwise appears as a magician white rabbit.

A module tree is drawn as an ordinary tree with two kinds of nodes as in Figure 1. The edges in the tree must connect nodes of different kinds. Each node in a module tree has a name and represents a subroutine. Seen from either kinds of nodes, the nodes of the other kind re-presents statements that may be used according to specific rules, as defined later.

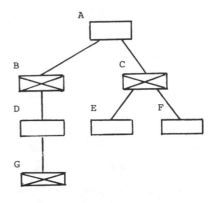

Figure 1

The edges of a module tree are implicitly considered directed "downwards". An edge represents the right to use the statement represented by the node to which the edge points. This right is *introduced in* and *belongs to* the node from which the edge originates. Thus, in Figure 1, the right to use statements B and C belongs to A, and the right to use G is introduced in D. Similarly, C considers E and F as statements belonging to it.

When B is applied in A, say, D must be *defined* for that application of B. Syntactically A's use of B is expressed as B(...), where the elipsis must be replaced by the definition of D. A definition of D is the exercising of rights *obtained for* D, and since these include the rights introduced in D the simplest example of using B in A is B(G); but we should also like nested use of B as in B(B(G)), and similarly C(B(C(G,B(G)))).

Such nested applications of statements illustrate the need for rights that are *inherited from* a surrounding *context*. A context is the set of rights obtained for the definition of a statementpart. It consists of rights inherited from the textually surrounding context, supplemented with rights that are introduced in a given part.

An example closer to ordinary statements is obtained from Figure 2. Assuming that usual assignment statements, variables, and relations are available we may write a PROGRAM (i.e. a definition of that part of the tree) as

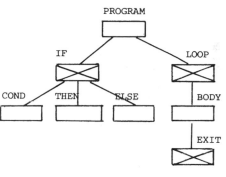

Figure 2

```
LOOP
  (IF  (x < y,  y := y - x,
        IF  (x = y,  EXIT,  x := x - y)))
```

The dual view of the blank nodes as statements from the point of view of the other kind of nodes is used in explanations of the semantics of LOOP and IF. Thus LOOP is supposed to iterate the statement BODY until BODY uses EXIT. At a lower level of abstraction one may express this as LOOP being defined by a routine like

```
label1:  BODY(goto label2);  goto label1;  label2: return
```

Here goto label 2 is consequently the definition of EXIT.

Notice how restrictions in rights may be reflected by a module tree. Thus EXIT may not be used in the definition of a THEN-part unless the right to use EXIT is inherited from a surrounding BODY-part.

Notice also the implied difference from trees reflecting the static nesting of blocks in block structured languages. With reference to such trees ordinary scope rules correspond to the inheritance of rights from father to son. The rules given for statements described by module trees correspond to the inheritance of rights from grandfather to grandson.

It is a little artificial not to distinguish the value returning property of nodes like a COND-part of an IF-statement. In the following, circles will be used for nodes with this property instead of boxes.

By the use of module trees specialized statements may be described. As an example Figure 3 describes statements tuned to the handling of sequential files, including a SORT statement for the sorting of sequences.

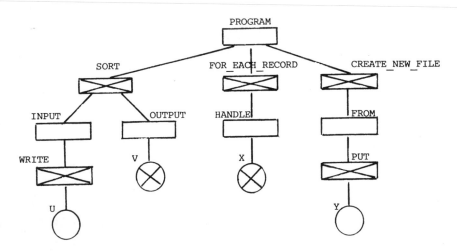

Figure 3

The term *module* will be used for an identified collection of nodes in a module tree. The collection shall consist of all the nodes of one kind in a subtree, and it shall include the root node of the subtree. The collection shall be identified by the node identifier of the root of the subtree; thus the SORT-module in Figure 3 consists of the nodes SORT, WRITE, and V.

In Figure 3 the FOR_EACH_RECORD-module is intended for the inspection of an existing file. Any application must provide a definition of HANDLE, which expresses the handling of an arbitrary file record identified by X. The semantics of FOR_EACH_RECORD must then express that HANDLE is applied repeatedly such that every record is handled once.

Similarly the CREATE_NEW_FILE-module is intended for the creation of a sequential file. The definition of FROM, which is provided in an application of CREATE_NEW_FILE, will be activated once; and during the activation PUT must be used to add records to the initially empty new file. A program that copies records from an old to a new file might then be

    CREATE_NEW_FILE
        (FOR_EACH_RECORD (PUT (X)))

Finally, the SORT_module is intended for the reordering of sequences. An original sequence is characterized by the definition of INPUT just as FROM characterizes a sequence of records in a new file. The reordered sequence is obtained through activations of OUTPUT in analogy with HANDLE. Consequently, a new file may be created such that it contains the records from an old file in a particular order by the following program.

```
CREATE_NEW_FILE
   (SORT
      (FOR_EACH_RECORD(WRITE(X))        -- INPUT-part
      , PUT(V)                          -- OUTPUT-part
      )

   )
```

More details are required in practice; for example a file identification and an ordering relation. An example of substantial size and complexity is given in the proceedings of the
workshop.

A Model for Module Trees

In order to justify the consistency of the concepts used in
connection with module trees a correspondence is established
between certain module trees and ordinary λ-calculus based
function definition. The restriction to pure functions is of
no consequence for the general claim of consistency, but simplifies the presentation.

The term "offspring subtrees of a node" will be used to
denote the subtrees whose roots are the sons of the node. Consequently we may indicate how a (subtree of a) module tree can
be described by a formula: the formula consists of the identifier of the root, possibly followed by a parenthesis with
a list of formulas describing the offspring subtrees of the
root, if such offsprings exist.

Two concepts are associated with subtrees of a module
tree: *definition* and *application*. A definition of a subtree is
a formula in which the offspring subtrees of the root may be
applied in addition to other subtrees to which licence of use
has been granted. An application of a subtree is a formula
that consists of the root identifier, possibly followed by a
parenthesis containing a list of definitions of the offspring
subtrees of the root.

Definitions and applications may be transformed into ordinary function definitions and expressions. The only thing
needed is to explicitly bind some identifiers in a definition.
The identifiers to be bound are those of the sons of the root
of the subtree being defined. We shall use the common λ-notation
to express the binding, and may thus illustrate the transforma-

tion with reference to the tree in Figure 4.

First of all we notice, that the restriction to pure functions means that all nodes in the module tree are circular; furthermore, that "constants" appear as leaves in the tree. Thus prepared, let us consider the following definition of expr:

insert(cons(cons(∅,one),one),add(x,y),zero)

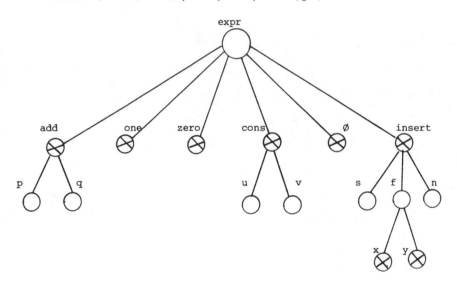

Figure 4

In order to transform the definition we express all bindings explicitly. In so doing we should remember that the subformula add(x,y) is a definition of the subtree f, and that binding of x and y is needed. We then obtain

λadd,one,zero,cons,∅,insert.
insert(cons(cons(∅,one),one),λx,y.add(x,y),zero)

as a conventional definition of expr.

An application of expr must provide definitions for add,
one, ..., insert; for example

   expr(p + q, 1, 0, u & v, ε, "definition of insert")

which we transform into

   expr (λp,q.p + q, 1, 0, λu,v. u & v, ε,

       λs,f,n. "definition of insert")

This is also quite conventional if we disregard the possibility
of a conventional recursive definition of insert. To cater for
that a more elaborate notation is needed:

   expr (λp,q.add(p,q) <u>where</u> add(p,q) = p + q

       1, 0,

       λu,v.cons(u,v) <u>where</u> cons(u,v) = u & v,

       ε,

       λs,f,n.insert(s,f,n)

               <u>where</u> insert(s,f,n) =

                   (s = ε → n,

                   s = t & a → f(insert(t,λx,y.f(x,y),n),a)))

Here, the more elaborate notation is not needed in the first
two cases. It is shown just to point out the possibility of a
blindfolded version of the transformation.

   The expression above corresponds to the following application of the tree expr:

   expr (p + q, 1, 0, u & v, ε,

       (s = ε → n,

       s = t & a → f(insert(t,f(x,y),n),a)))

The rule for the definition of a subtree given so far does not allow for unbounded recursion as required in this definition of insert. On the other hand we have seen that the transformation rules as given will support unbounded recursion. Thus, if we trust the consistency of the conventional concepts used for function definitions, we should also trust the consistency of the corresponding concept for module trees: In a definition of a subtree, the subtree being defined may itself be applied.

So far we have established that module trees that are restricted to functions, and the associated concepts of definition and application, are as consistent as conventional concepts used for function definitions. The following consideration of notation should justify the conclusion that module trees without restrictions, and corresponding concepts of definition and application, are as consistent as the conventional concepts used for subroutine definitions in block structured languages.

Notation

In the previous section, the only way a definition could formally be associated with a subtree was through an application. Below we shall see a notation that explicitly associates a definition with a formula describing a (sub)tree. Details relate once more to function definition, but it should be no problem to follow the informal generalization to subroutine definitions given afterwards.

A function definition has the form

left_hand_side → expression.

For the left_hand_side we shall use a formula that describes

a module tree, e.g. insert(s, f(x,y), n) . For the expression
we may use an application of either a module tree for which a
definition is given explicitly or one of the offspring subtrees
of the root of the tree being defined. Furthermore we may use
the McCarthy conditional: $(c_1 \to e_1, c_2 \to e_2, \ldots, c_n \to e_n)$, where
c_i denotes a condition and e_i an expression for $i = 1, 2, \ldots, n$.
The value of this conditional is the value of the unique e_j
such that c_k = false for $0 < k < j$ and c_j = true.

      Example:

      insert(x,f(x,y),n) $\Rightarrow$ (s = $\varepsilon \to$ n, s = t & a $\to$ f(insert(t,f(x,y),n),a))

Except for the complete specification of the functional properties of "parameters", and the use of identifiers x and y in
the recursive application of insert, this is quite conventional.
We notice that this definition must appear in a context where
ε and & are meaningful. We may assume also that the following
is a meaningful application of insert:

      insert(ε & 1 & 2 & 3, x * y, 1)

(intended to give the result (1 * 2) * 3) . The meaning is given
as

      (s = $\varepsilon \to$ n, s = t & a $\to$ f(insert(t,f(x,y)n),a))

      <u>where</u>

          s $\Rightarrow \varepsilon$ & 1 & 2 & 3,

          f(x,y) $\Rightarrow$ x * y,

          n $\Rightarrow$ 1

which consequently leads to

  (1)   insert(ε & 1 & 2, x * y, 1) * 3

(2) $(s = \varepsilon \rightarrow n, \ s = t \ \& \ a \rightarrow f(insert(t,f(x,y),n),a)) * 3$

where

    $s \Rightarrow \varepsilon \ \& \ 1 \ \& \ 2,$

    $f(x,y) \Rightarrow x * y,$

    $n \Rightarrow 1$

(3) $insert(\varepsilon \ \& \ 1, x * y, 1) * 2 * 3$

(4) $(s = \varepsilon \rightarrow n, \ s = t \ \& \ a \rightarrow f(insert(t,f(x,y),n),a)) * 2 * 3$

where

    $s \rightarrow \varepsilon \ \& \ 1,$

    $f(x,y) \Rightarrow x * y,$

    $n \Rightarrow 1$

(5) $insert(\varepsilon, \ x * y, \ n) * 1 * 2 * 3$

(6) $(s = \varepsilon \rightarrow n, \ s = t \ \& \ a \rightarrow f(insert(t,f(x,y),n),a)) * 1 * 2 * 3$

where

    $s \Rightarrow \varepsilon$

    $f(x,y) \Rightarrow x * y$

    $n \Rightarrow 1$

(7) $1 * 1 * 2 * 3$

Compared to conventional notation, this one varies in two respects only

(a)   the left_hand_side of a definition contains a complete specification of parameters.

(b)   in applications we use, instead of function identifiers, expressions that are implicitly parametrized according to the specification of the corresponding parameter.

Generalizing to block structured languages we obtain:

(A)   the heading of a subroutine declaration should contain
      a complete specification of parameters (as in the pro-
      posed standard for Pascal for instance).

(B)   in subroutine calls arguments corresponding to parameter
      functions must be expressions, and arguments correspond-
      ing to parameter procedures must be blocks; both kinds
      of arguments must be implicitly parametrized according
      to the specification of the corresponding parameter.

This generalization should justify, that module trees without
the restrictions relate to ordinary block structured languages,
as the restricted module trees relate to conventional function
definitions. Consequently, any module tree structure may be represented by use of a block structured programming language.
This is done most easily in a block structured language that
adopts the rules (A) and (B) above.

Encapsulation

Module trees are capable of describing program structures that
involve "information hiding", because the nodes belonging to
a particular *module* M do not have direct access to data associated with nodes in the *subtree* M not belonging to the module
M. Consider for instance the module tree in Figure 5.

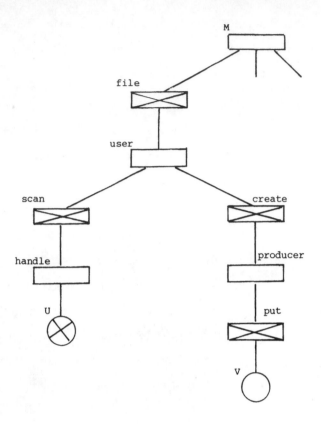

Figure 5

The module M consists of all blank nodes in the tree, and they have no access to data associated with the others. According to the previous section a corresponding program structure must exist. Figure 6 exhibits a program text for the definition of the file module. Obviously no caller of the procedure file has access to data local to file. These data are consequently accessible only through calls of scan and create according to the rules for application of file.

```
procedure file
    (procedure user
        (procedure scan (procedure handle (U : T));
        procedure create
            (procedure producer ( procedure put (V : T)))
        )
    );

    var f: array [1.. max] of T;
        pos: integer;
    status: (undefined, defined, scanning);
begin
    status := undefined;
    user
        (-- the block that defines scan:
            begin
                if status = defined then begin
                    status := scanning;
                    for k := 1 to pos do handle (f[k]);
                    status := defined
                end  -- else ...
            end,

        -- the block that defines create

            begin
                if status ≠ scanning then begin
                    status := undefined; pos := 0;
                    producer
                        (-- the block that defines put (V)
                            begin
                                if pos < max then begin
                                    pos := pos + 1; f[pos] := V
                                end  -- else ...
                            end
                        );
                    status := defined
                end  -- else ...
            end
        )
end
```

Figure 6

Types

The example given in the previous section shows an implementation of a module. The programming language used is Pascal, except for the adoption of rules (A) and (B) given previously. The example can ben seen as one possible implementation of the module, or as a specification of the module. For more complicated modules and in order to stress the specification point of view, it may be advantageous to use an idealized type definition system instead of Pascal's. Since definitions local to a module are not directly accessible from outside, any type definition system – or even different systems in different modules – may be used. In this section one possible type definition system is presented.

A type definition consists of three parts: (1) a syntax for a language whose strings are *distinct values*; (2) a syntax for a language of *reducible expressions*; and (3) a set of *reduction rules and tabus* for reducible expressions. Values of the type may be compared for equality and inequality. A reducible expression is meaningless if it fulfills the condition of a tabu; otherwise a reduction rule must exist which prescribes an equivalent value or an equivalent, simpler reducible expression. It must be possible in a finite number of steps either to assert that a reducible expression is equivalent to a value or to a reducible expression that is meaningless.

Figure 7 gives as an example the definition of a type MAP, which informally can be characterized as a finitely tabulated function of DOMAIN-values to RANGE-values. The three parts mentioned above follow the symbols type, with, and for respectively.

The metalanguage used for syntax is similar to BNF, with the following deviations: (a) non-terminals are written as a sequence of capital letters; (b) the symbol = is used instead of ::=; (c) a dot terminates a rule of the grammar. Eventually, non-terminals will be recognized by context, so that rule (a) should be considered as a temporary rule. As the example indicates we shall identify the concepts non-terminal and type-identifier.

type

    -- the syntax for the language of MAP-values:

        MAP = void | MAP<DOMAIN, RANGE>.

with

    -- the syntax of reducible expressions depending on MAP-values:

        RANGE = MAP[DOMAIN].

        BOOLEAN = defined (MAP, DOMAIN).

        MAP = drop (MAP, DOMAIN).

for   d,d1: DOMAIN; f: MAP; r: RANGE let

        f<d,r>[d1] ⇒ if(d=d1) then r else f[d1],

        tabu f[d1] if not defined (f,d1),

        defined (f<d,r>,d1) ⇒ if (d=d1) then true else defined (f,d1),

        defined (void,d1) ⇒ false,

        drop (f<d,r>,d1) ⇒ if (d=d1) then f else drop (f,d1)<d,r>,

        drop (void,d1) ⇒ void

end

Figure 7

The reduction rules and tabus depend on the application of variables denoting parts of reducible expressions. The first reduction rule following the symbol _let_ applies to expressions of the form MAP[DOMAIN]. The DOMAIN part is denoted d1, such that it may be used as part of an equivalent expression. Furthermore, the rule applies only if the MAP part has the structure MAP<DOMAIN,RANGE>, and identifiers are used to denote the parts.

Values may be compared for equality. This is convenient, but we could have required an explicit definition of reducible identity expressions. For MAP we could have had a syntax like:

BOOLEAN = MAP ≡ MAP.

and reduction rules:

void ≡ void ⇒ true,

f<d,r> ≡ f1<d1,r1> ⇒ f ≡ f1 ∧ d ≡ d1 ∧ r ≡ r1,

void ≡ f<d,r> ⇒ false,

f<d,r> ≡ void ⇒ false

The general pattern of such reduction rules should be obvious, and consequently there is no need to require explicit definition of neither syntax nor reduction rules for identity expressions. Of course one should be aware of the cases where another equivalence relation is more appropriate.

In addition to comparisons for equality, an if-then-else reducible expression may be used without explicit definition. The general pattern of the excluded detailed definitions should be obvious from the following example

```
MAP = if BOOLEAN then MAP else MAP.    -- syntax
```

if true then f_1 else $f_2 \Rightarrow f_1$,   -- reduction rule

if false then f_1 else $f_2 \Rightarrow f_2$ -- reduction rule

where true and false are values of type BOOLEAN.

A conventional algebraic specification of a type is easily obtained from a type definition as described. Basically we just have to state, in reverse order, the essentials of a production rule (i.e. the non-terminals), and associate a function with it. The non-terminals should then be considered as set identifiers (or sorts in common algebra terminology), and the reversed rules as statements of functionality. Thus, corresponding to Figure 7 we would get

```
void    :                        →  MAP
extend  :  DOMAIN x RANGE    →  MAP

value   :  MAP x DOMAIN      →  RANGE
defined :  MAP x DOMAIN      →  BOOLEAN
drop    :  MAP x DOMAIN      →  MAP
```

Ordinary practice is <u>not</u> to distinguish formally between two groups of functions. Furthermore, a function corresponding to equality would have to be described explicitly along with the required reduction rules. Then the reduction rules would have to be modified such that tests for equality were replaced by the corresponding function, and the reduction rules themselves should be expressed as equalities (simply by replacing ⇒ with =). Finally, tabus will have to be replaced by so called "error--axioms", the form of which is not agreed upon.

Relative to algebraic type specifications the described

system differs essentially with respect to which expressions may be described as equivalent. The distinction between reducible expressions and values, and the restriction of reduction rules to apply to reducible expressions only, has no counterparts in algebraic type specification. The convenience obtained by allowing infix notation for functions is of no theoretical consequence, and thus we find that the present system is a restricted form for algebraic specification.

Parameter Types

It has been shown that encapsulation can be described by module trees, and that a corresponding program structure can be build with a block-structured programming language. The parameter mechanism is heavily used for what is commonly known as import and export of rights. Parameter types are usually not allowed, however. In order to use the parameter mechanism also for import and export of types we shall allow parameter types, as described in this section.

A function is expected to return a result of some type. It will be assumed that the type must be indicated by an identifier, and that results cannot be identical if their types are indicated by different identifiers. In a purely functional system we must then expect the type of parameters to be specified by such type identifiers. Thus we see that it is through type identifiers that the dependencies among results and operations are expressed. In other words: no other programming language construct is needed to express such dependencies, which theoretically are expressed in algebras.

Sometimes a uniform definition seems to be valid for a

family of functions. An example is

$$min(x : T, y : T) : T \Rightarrow (x < y \to x, \text{ true} \to y)$$

for the computation of the least value of x and y of any type
T. Since we expect the type of parameters to be specified by
an identifier, we need to indicate that, in this case, the
identifier is used merely to reflect interrelations between
type requirements. For such indications we adopt a syntax as
exemplified with

$$min \underline{of} \ T \ (x : T, y : T) : T \Rightarrow (x < y \to x, \text{ true} \to y)$$

i.e. the types of parameters are indicated as in Pascal, and
a list of parameter type identifiers may preceed the usual
list of parameters. The list of parameter type identifiers
follows the symbol of.

Next we must consider the operation x < y, which cannot be
expected to be defined for every type. The operation may be required as an additional parameter of min, as expressed in

$$min \underline{of} \ T \ (x : T, y : T, lt \ (a : T, b : T) : BOOLEAN) : T$$
$$(lt \ (x,y) \to x, \text{ true} \to y)$$

In an automatic computing system, the last definition will be
adequate for the function eventually used, even if a user is
not required to give the last argument explicitly. Since the
question of anticipating the cleverness of such systems is of
no concern here, every parameter shall be matched by a corresponding argument, even parameter types. Thus, an application
of min may be

$$min \underline{of} \ integer \ (u, 5, a < b)$$

(which of course is inattractive for such a simple computation).

The only operations common to all the types that may be defined by the means described in the previous section are test for equality and the if-then-else function. These functions are not supplied as arguments.

Passing again from a purely functional system to a block structured programming language we must consider other uses of type identifiers. First we shall allow any type identifier, including parameter type identifiers, to be used for variable declaration. Assignment of a value of type T to a variable of type T is unconditionally allowed. Finally, we allow any type identifier to be used as non-terminal in a type definition. As a consequence we need no parametrization of type definitions themselves.

Program Development

Program development is considered as consisting of three phases. First a phrase structure for the formulation of the overall program structure is devised and described by module trees. The semantics of the phrases will be understood informally by the designer; that is, module trees for the phrases are not specifications in themselves. To keep a record of his informal understanding, a designer may use whatever means he finds fit. It may be a natural language description, or expressions similar to path-expressions to keep track of the application pattern of different parts. Although only understood informally, the phrases are tested for adequacy through attempts to express the main program.

In the second phase the semantics of the designed phrases

are formally defined. One set of tools has been emphasized here. It may be replaced by another; but it is important that the formal specification of semantics is encapsulated, seen from the point of view of a phrase user. Actually, the ease of specifying the semantics of module tree structures could be used as evaluation criterion for specification languages.

The final phase consists of program implementation. Although any programming language might be used, it will be advantageous if the major components of the design can be mapped onto corresponding components of the final program. This means that phrase applications and phrase definitions are easily recognized and well separated from irrelevant parts.

In the next section an example is given which condense the major aspects of part of the KWIC-index generation program.

An Example

The module tree shown in Figure 8 describes a phrase structure by which a list of lists of items may be generated. Different lists of items contain the same items but in different sequences. The phrase shiftlists provides means by which the items must be introduced initially. Furthermore, the lists of items are treated as objects having an internal structure, but whose structure is accessible only through a primitive means for iterating over components. The producer part must introduce the items that shall enter the lists. When all items have been introduced, the consumer part will be activated repeatedly for different values of lists y. These lists will contain the items in cyclic shifted sequences, including the sequence in which

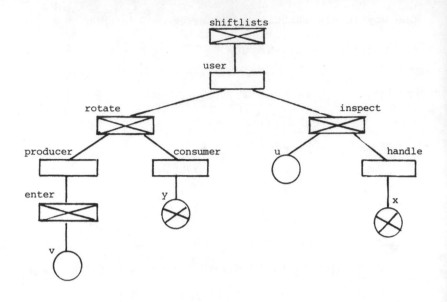

Figure 8

the items have been dynamically entered. The inspect subphrase
may be used to iterate over the items x in the list u.

The pattern of application of parts may be stated by expressions as follows

```
shiftlists = user    -- the user part will be activated once
user = {(rotate | inspect)}   -- user may apply the two at will
rotate = producer {consumer}
producer = {enter}
enter = v
consumer = y
inspect = u {handle}
handle  = x
```

One way to use shiftlists would be

```
shiftlists of char       -- the items are characters
    (begin
        rotate
            (begin       -- producer
                enter('a'); enter('b'); enter('c')
            end,
            begin        -- consumer
                writeln(output);
                inspect(y, begin write(x) end)
            end)
    end)
```

with the intended result:

```
        a b c
        b c a
        c a b
```

So far we have illustrated the first phase of the development of (part of) a program. In the second phase we must formally specify the properties of shiftlists. This is done as shown in Figure 9.

```
procedure shiftlists of T
    (procedure user of lists
        (procedure rotate
            (procedure producer (procedure enter(v : T));
             procedure consumer(y : lists)
            );
        procedure inspect(u : lists; procedure handle(x : T))
        )
    );

type
    SEQUENCE = Ø | SEQUENCE & T.
with
    SEQUENCE = cut(SEQUENCE).
    T        = first(SEQUENCE).
for s : SEQUENCE; t : T let
    cut(s & t) ⇒ if s = Ø then Ø else cut(s) & t,
    tabu cut(s) if s = Ø
    first(s & t) ⇒ if s = Ø then t else first(s)
    tabu first(s) if s = Ø
end;

begin
    user of SEQUENCE
        (-- the block that defines rotate:
            var s1, s2 : SEQUENCE;
        begin
            s1 := Ø;
            producer (begin s1 := s1 & v end);
            s2 := s1;
            while s2 <> Ø do begin
                consumer(s1); s1 := cut(s1) & first(s1); s2 := cut(s2)
            end;
        end,
        -- the block that defines inspect
            var s : SEQUENCE;
        begin
            s := u;
            while s <> Ø do begin handle(first(s)); s := cut(s) end
        end
        )
end
```

Figure 9

The important points to notice are: (1) the use of parameter types for both import and export (T and lists respectively); (2) that the definition of type SEQUENCE is in fact parametrized by T; (3) that SEQUENCE is used as argument corresponding to the parameter type lists; and (4) that in the block that defines inspect, u denotes a SEQUENCE value, since the definition is part of an application of user in which SEQUENCE corresponds to lists.

The third phase will not be illustrated, since it should be rather obvious what has to be done: the type SEQUENCE must be defined in the implementation language; and the operations Ø, &, cut and first must be defined, either as proper functions or as in-line code wherever they are used.

PARAMETER PASSING IN
ALGEBRAIC SPECIFICATION LANGUAGES

June 1981

Hartmut Ehrig and Hans-Jörg Kreowski

Technische Universität Berlin
Fachbereich Informatik (20)
Institut für Software und Theoretische Informatik
Otto-Suhr-Allee 18/20
D-1000 Berlin 10, Germany

James Thatcher, Eric Wagner and Jesse Wright

IBM Research Center
Mathematical Sciences Department
P.O. Box 218, Yorktown Heights 10598
New York, USA

ABSTRACT

In this paper we study the semantics of the parameter passing mechanism in
algebraic specification languages. More precisely, this problem is studied
for parameterized data types and parameterized specifications. The given
results include the extension of the model functor (which is useful for
correctness proofs) and the semantic properties of the result of inserting
actual parameters into paramterized specifications. In particular, actual
parameters can be parameterized and the result is nested parameterized specification. Correctness of an applied (matrix(int)) or a nested
(bintree(string())) parameterized specification is shown given correctness
of the parts. The formal theory in this paper is restricted to the basic
algebraic case where only equations are allowed in the parameter declaration
and parameter passing is given by specification morphisms. But we also give
the main ideas of a corresponding theory with requirements where we allow
different kinds of restrictions in the parameter declaration.

CONTENTS:

ACKNOWLEDGEMENTS

A short and slightly different version of this paper has appeared as /ADJ 80/
in the proceedings of 7th ICALP (Nordwijkerhout 1980). The present paper is
a restriction of our March 1980 draft version to the basic algebraic case.
However, it is also the basis for a theory of parameterized specifications
with requirements (see /Ehr 81/) which avoids the concept of generalized parameter passing in /ADJ 80/.

This paper is part of a common project of the ADJ-group at IBM Yorktown Heights
and the ACT-group at TU Berlin. Thanks to all of them especially to W. Fey
and P. Padawitz and in addition to R. Burstall, H.-D. Ehrich and J.A. Goguen
and to the organizer and participants of the Aarhus Workshop on Program Specification for several fruitful discussions on the subject of this paper, and to
H. Barnewitz for excellent typing.

syntax, semantics, semantical requirements and correctness of parameter passing are carefully distinguished, motivated and studied in detail within Section 2.

In Section 3 the parameterized types string(param) and matrix(ring) and bintree(data) are specified as typical examples for the basic algebraic case studied in this paper. For examples like set(data) using non equational requirements in the parameter declaration we refer to /Ehr 81/.

In Section 4 we start with the simplest case of "standard parameter passing" where actual specifications like int are inserted for formal parameters like param in string(param) leading to actual value specifications like string(int). Corresponding correctness results are given in Section 5. The key for the proofs is the Extension Lemma 5.1 which was motivated by corresponding constructions in /ADJ 78/, /Ehr 78/ and /EL 79/. In addition to the construction of pushouts in the category of specifications, which is also considered in /Ehr 78/, /EL 79/, /BG 79/ and /BG 80/, we also have an explicit and a universal construction for the semantics of the value specification, which for a special case was considered in /ADJ 78/. This Extension Lemma 5.1 is sufficient to show correctness of standard parameter passing in Theorem 5.2 and induced correctness of value specifications in Theorem 5.4.

In Section 6 we study "parameterized parameter passing" where the actual parameter to be inserted is again a parameterized specification. Hence the value specification becomes a parameterized specification like bintree(string(param)). This parameterized value specification can also be considered as the composition of the parameterized specifications bintree(data) and string(param). The theory of parameterized parameter passing is not much different from that of standard parameter passing. A slight modification of results and proofs shows that also parameterized parameter passing is correct (Theorem 6.3) and that we have induced correctness of composite parameterized specifications (Theorem 6.4).

Iterated compositions and different evaluation strategies built up by standard parameter passing and parameterized parameter passing steps are studied in Section 7. Associativity of the composition (Theorem 7.1) and compatibility of composition and actualization (Theorem 7.2) shows that the result of iterated parameter passing is independent of the choice of the evaluation strategy (Corollary 7.4).

1. INTRODUCTION

Procedural abstraction has been with us a long time both in practice and in theory, although the semantic theory for procedures taking procedures as parameters is relatively recent, c.f. Scott /Sco 62/. A practical analog of procedural abstraction for data definition is relatively new (for example see /GT 77/, /Gut 75/, /LSAS 77/, /LZ 77/, and /WLS 76/). The semantic theory for parameterized types is the subject of this paper. There has been little work on the mathematics of parameter passing with the exception that Burstall and Goguen have tackled it for the mathematical semantics of CLEAR because procedures in CLEAR correspond to parameterized types /BG 77/, /BG 79/, /BG 80/. Also Ehrich /Ehr 78/ and /EL 79/ studies parameterization on a syntactic level, as a relationship between specifications. Although ADJ /ADJ 78/ provides us with an algebraic formulation for parameterized types, they barely touch the question of parameter passing.

The problem of parameter passing for data abstractions is, we believe, an important one. Hierarchical design of large programming systems depends on the use of parameterized data abstractions (even familiar string( ), array( ) or structure( )) and an understanding of the semantics of parameter passing is a prerequisite to the understanding of the mathematical semantics of the hierarchical design.

In this paper we do several things. First of all, we give a precise mathematical definition of what it means to insert a parameter into a parameterized type (e.g., inserting int into string( )). Our approach is sufficiently general that it provides the necessary apparatus for approaching many related problems, e.g., the inserting of non-parameterized specifications into parameterized specifications, the composition of parameterized types or specifications, the compatibility of different "call by name" strategies, compatibility of "call by name", and "call by value", proofs of correctness (e.g. that if we have a correct specification for int and string( ), then this implies the correctness of the specification string(int)), etc. We will treat all of these in detail within the present paper while a short and slightly different version including only part of the results is given in our proceedings version /ADJ 80/.

Following the general frame of our paper on algebraic implementations /EKP 80/

In contrast to our short version in /ADJ 80/ this paper is restricted to the basic algebraic case where instead of universal Horn sentences we only use equations in all our specifications including the parameter declaration. Moreover parameter passing is defined using specification morphisms which automatically imply passing consistency in the sense of /ADJ 80/. Due to these restrictions a number of interesting parameterized specifications like set(data), stack(attr) and queue(items) are excluded if non equational requirements are used to define an equality predicate in the parameter declaration. On the other hand the mathematical theory in the basic algebraic case is much simpler than that in /ADJ 80/ and can be fully extended to an algebraic theory of parameterized specifications with requirements (see /Ehr 81/). Requirements in our sense were motivated and include those of Burstall-Goguen and Hupbach-Reichel which are called Σ-constraints in /BG 80/ and initial restrictions in /Rei 80/. Some basic results and examples of our theory with requirements are given in /Ehr 81/ and /EF 81/ but the complete theory is still in development. A summary of the present paper, the main ideas of our theory with requirements and a comparative discussion of other approaches are given in our conclusion (Section 8).

2. PARAMETERIZED TYPES AND SPECIFICATIONS

We shall assume the algebraic background of /ADJ 76-78/, /EKP 78/ or /Kre 78/
which is based on universal algebra (see /Coh 65/, /Gra 68/) and category
theory (see /AM 75/, /HS 73/, /ML 71/). But we will review the most important
notions in connection with this paper. We shall introduce the basic algebraic
case of parameterized data types and specifications as given in /ADJ 78/.

An abstract data type is regarded as (the isomorphism class of) a many-sorted
(heterogeneous) algebra which is minimal, meaning that all data elements are
"accessible" using constants and operations of the algebra. A many-sorted
algebra consists of an indexed family of sets (called carriers) with an indexed
family of operations between those carriers. The indexing system is called a
signature and consists of a set S of sorts which indexes the carriers and a
family $\langle \Sigma_{w,s} /w \in S^{*}$ and $s \in S \rangle$ of operation names (Σ is called the operator domain);
a symbol $\delta \in \Sigma_{w,s}$ with $w = s_1 \ldots s_n$ names an operation $\delta_A : A_{s_1} \times \ldots \times A_{s_n} \longrightarrow A_s$ in an
algebra A with signature Σ. The pair $\langle S, \Sigma \rangle$ determines the category $\underline{Alg}_{\langle S, \Sigma \rangle}$
of all S-sorted Σ-algebras with Σ-homomorphisms between them.

A specification, SPEC$=\langle S, \Sigma, E \rangle$, is a triple where $\langle S, \Sigma \rangle$ is a signature and E is
a set of equations. $\underline{Alg}_{SPEC}$ is the category of all SPEC-algebras, i.e., all
S-sorted Σ-algebras satisfying the equations E. When we write the combination
SPEC'=SPEC+$\langle S', \Sigma', E' \rangle$ we mean that S and S' are disjoint, that Σ' is an
operator domain over S+S' which is disjoint from Σ, and that E' is a set of
axioms over the signature $\langle S+S', \Sigma+\Sigma' \rangle$.

Although some authors see the equations as "semantics" (see /Gut 75+76/), we
follow /ADJ 76-78/ in saying that the semantics of a specification SPEC is the
(isomorphism class of the) algebra T_{SPEC} which is initial in $\underline{Alg}_{SPEC}$. T_{SPEC}
can be constructed as a quotient $T_{SPEC} = T_{\langle S, \Sigma \rangle}/\equiv_E$ of the term algebra $T_{\langle S, \Sigma \rangle}$
(corresponding to the signature $\langle S, \Sigma \rangle$) by the congruence generated from the
equations E.

A specification SPEC$=\langle S, \Sigma, E \rangle$ is called correct with respect to a model algebra
A in $\underline{Alg}_{MSPEC}$ if the model specification MSPEC$=\langle MS, M\Sigma, ME \rangle$ is included in SPEC,
i.e. MS $\subseteq$ S, M$\Sigma \subseteq \Sigma$ and ME $\subseteq$ E, and the MSPEC-reduct of T_{SPEC} is isomorphic to A.
(The MSPEC-reduct of T_{SPEC} consists of those carriers and operations belonging
to sorts of MS and operation symbols of MΣ respectively.) Note that this
definition allows to use "hidden functions" which are included in the specification but not in the model specification. Moreover in most cases ME will

be the empty set of equations.

Now let us consider parameterized data types and specifications:

2.1 DEFINITION

A <u>parameterized data type</u> PDAT=$\langle$SPEC,SPEC1,T$\rangle$ consists of the following data:

    PARAMETER DECLARATION   SPEC=$\langle S,\Sigma,E\rangle$

    TARGET SPECIFICATION   SPEC1=SPEC+$\langle$S1,Σ1,E1$\rangle$

and a functor $T:\underline{Alg}_{SPEC} \longrightarrow \underline{Alg}_{SPEC1}$. PDAT is called <u>persistent</u> (<u>strongly</u>
<u>persistent</u>) if T is, i.e. for every SPEC-algebra A, we have $V(T(A))\cong A$ (resp.
$V(T(A))=A$) where V is the forgetful functor from SPEC1 to SPEC-algebras (see
4.2).

Remark: If T is equipped with a (natural) family of homomorphisms
$\langle I_A:A \longrightarrow V(T(A))\rangle$ such that for each SPEC-algebra A, the set $\{I_A(a)\,|\,a\in A\}$
generates T(A) then PDAT is called <u>abstract parameterized data type</u>. (This
generalizes the condition that an algebra has to be minimal to be considered
as abstract data type.) As discussed in /ADJ 78/, the family I tells how to
find each parameter algebra A in the result of the construction T(A). Each
abstract parameterized data type must be equipped with such a natural transformation but not the model data types. The motivation for persistence is
given in /ADJ 78/; the idea is that the parameter algebra "persists" (up to
isomorphism) in the result of the construction T. In contrast to /ADJ 78/ and
/ADJ 80/ we only allow equations in   specifications.   Negative conditiona
and universal Horn axioms may be included in requirements (see Section 8).

To illustrate our definitions we will construct the model functor SETO corresponding to a simplified version <u>setO</u>(<u>dataO</u>) of a set specification where only
the operations CREATE and INSERT are considered. In this simplified version
we do not need the equality predicate and hence also not <u>bool</u> in the parameter
declaration.

2.2 EXAMPLE

      PARAMETER DECLARATION (SPEC=$\langle S,\emptyset,\emptyset\rangle$):<u>dataO</u> =

          sorts(S): <u>data</u>

      TARGET SPECIFICATION (MSPEC1=SPEC+$\langle$S1,Σ1,$\emptyset\rangle$):<u>MsetO</u> =

          <u>dataO</u> +

sorts(S1): $\underline{set}$

opns(Σ1): CREATE: $\longrightarrow$ $\underline{set}$

INSERT: $\underline{data}$ $\underline{set}$ $\longrightarrow$ $\underline{set}$

The model functor SETO:$\underline{\underline{Alg}}_{dataO} \longrightarrow \underline{\underline{Alg}}_{MsetO}$ takes each $\underline{\underline{dataO}}$-algebra E=$\langle E_{data}\rangle$, which is simply a set of parameter elements, to the $\underline{\underline{MsetO}}$-algebra A=$\langle A_{data}, A_{set}$, CREATE$_A$,INSERT$_A\rangle$ with $A_{data}=E_{data}$, $A_{set}=\mathcal{P}_{fin}(E_{data})$ the set of all finite subsets of E_{data}, CREATE$_A=\emptyset$ and INSERT$_A$(e,s)=$\{e\}\cup$ s for all e$\in E_{data}$ and s$\in\mathcal{P}_{fin}(E_{data})$. The model functor is strongly persistent because we have V(SETO(E))=V(A)=A_{data}=E. In the following we shall show that the simplified version $\underline{\underline{setO}}(\underline{\underline{dataO}})$ of our set specification is correct with respect to the parameterized model data type PMDAT=$\langle\underline{\underline{dataO}},\underline{\underline{MsetO}},\underline{\underline{SETO}}\rangle$ defined above.

.3   DEFINITION

1. A parameterized specification PSPEC=$\langle$SPEC,SPEC1$\rangle$ consists of the following data:

PARAMETER DECLARATION	SPEC=$\langle$S,Σ,E$\rangle$
TARGET SPECIFICATION	SPEC1=SPEC+$\langle$S1,Σ1,E1$\rangle$

The semantics of the specification is the free construction (see /ADJ 78/), F:$\underline{\underline{Alg}}_{SPEC} \longrightarrow \underline{\underline{Alg}}_{SPEC1}$, i.e., the (abstract) parameterized type PDAT=$\langle$SPEC,SPEC1,F$\rangle$.

Remark: We will talk about the "parameterized type$\langle$SPEC,SPEC1$\rangle$" and mean the type whose (model) functor is the free construction from SPEC-algebras to SPEC1-algebras.

2. Let PDAT=$\langle$MSPEC,MSPEC1,T$\rangle$ be a parameterized data type and PSPEC=$\langle$SPEC, SPEC1$\rangle$ a parameterized specification. Then PSPEC is called correct with respect to PDAT if we have MSPEC$\subseteq$ SPEC, MSPEC1$\subseteq$ SPEC1 and (up to isomorphism) T•U=U1•F with surjective forgetful functor U:$\underline{\underline{Alg}}_{SPEC} \longrightarrow \underline{\underline{Alg}}_{MSPEC}$, forgetful functor U1:$\underline{\underline{Alg}}_{SPEC1} \longrightarrow \underline{\underline{Alg}}_{MSPEC1}$ and F:$\underline{\underline{Alg}}_{SPEC} \longrightarrow \underline{\underline{Alg}}_{SPEC1}$ the semantics (free construction) of PSPEC.

Remark: If U and U1 are identiy functors correctness means that the free construction F is equal to the given model functor T. Otherwise they have to be equal up to renaming and forgetting of those sorts and operations which are in SPEC1 but not in MSPEC1. Surjectivity of U (which is not assumed in /ADJ 78/ and /ADJ 80/

makes sure that for each model parameter algebra in $\underline{Alg}_{MSPEC}$ there is also a corresponding parameter algebra in $\underline{Alg}_{SPEC}$.

2.4 FACT

The parameterized specification $\underline{\underline{set0}}(\underline{\underline{data0}})$ - given by $\underline{\underline{data0}}$ and $\underline{\underline{set0}}=\underline{\underline{Mset0}}+E1$ as in Example 2.2 with E1 consisting of the equations INSERT(d,INSERT(d,s))= =INSERT(d,s) and INSERT(d,INSERT(d',s))=INSERT(d',INSERT(d,s)) - is correct with respect to the parameterized type PMDAT=$\langle\underline{\underline{data0}},\underline{\underline{Mset0}},SET0\rangle$ (see 2.2).

Proof: In our case U and U1 are identity functors and it remains to show that the functor SET0 considered as functor from $\underline{Alg}_{\underline{\underline{data0}}}$ to $\underline{Alg}_{\underline{\underline{set0}}}$ is the free construction with respect to the forgetful functor $V:\underline{Alg}_{\underline{\underline{set0}}} \longrightarrow \underline{Alg}_{\underline{\underline{data0}}}$. This means that we have to show for each $B\in\underline{Alg}_{\underline{\underline{set0}}}$ and each homomorphism $\overline{f}:E \longrightarrow V(B)$ that there is a unique $\underline{\underline{set0}}$-morphism $g:SET0(E) \longrightarrow B$ with $g_{data}=f_{data}$. Since g must be a $\underline{\underline{set0}}$-morphism we have for the $\underline{\underline{set}}$-component of $g:g(\emptyset)=g(CREATE_A)=$ $=CREATE_B$ and $g(\{e\}\cup s)=g(INSERT_A(e,s))=INSERT_B(f(e),g(s))$. Using the INSERT-equations for $INSERT_B$ it is easy to show that the equations above define a well defined $\underline{\underline{set0}}$-morphism $g:SET0(E) \longrightarrow B$ with $g_{data}=f_{data}$.

$\square$

Now we want to consider a more complete version $\underline{\underline{set}}(\underline{\underline{data}})$ of a set specification which also includes the operations DELETE,MEMBER and EMPTY. In /ADJ 78/ it is shown that this also implies that we need an equality predicate EQ on $\underline{\underline{data}}$. To express that EQ is really an equality predicate needs a negative conditional axiom like

$$X \neq Y \implies EQ(X,Y) = FALSE$$

which is not allowed in the basic algebraic case. Hence we only consider the equation EQ(X,X) = TRUE at the moment while the general case with requirements is discussed in Section 8.

2.5 EXAMPLE ($\underline{\underline{set}}(\underline{\underline{data}})$ without requirements)

PARAMETER DECLARATION: $\underline{\underline{data}}$ =

    $\underline{\underline{bool}}$ +

    sorts: $\underline{data}$

    opns: EQ: $\underline{data}$ $\underline{data}$ $\longrightarrow$ $\underline{\underline{bool}}$

    eqns: EQ(X,X) = TRUE

```
TARGET SPECIFICATION: set(data) =

    data +
    sorts:  set
    opns:   CREATE:⟶ set
            INSERT: data set ⟶ set
            DELETE: data set ⟶ set
            MEMBER: data set ⟶ bool
            EMPTY: set ⟶ bool
            IF-THEN-ELSE: bool set set ⟶ set
    eqns:   INSERT(d,INSERT(d',s))=IF EQ(d,d') THEN
                        INSERT(d,s)ELSE INSERT(d',INSERT(d,s))
            DELETE(d,CREATE)=CREATE
            DELETE(d,INSERT(d',s))=IF EQ(d,d')THEN
                        DELETE(d,s)ELSE INSERT(d',DELETE(d,s))
            MEMBER(d,CREATE)=FALSE
            MEMBER(d,INSERT(d',s))=IF EQ(d,d')THEN TRUE
                                    ELSE MEMBER(d,s)
            EMPTY(CREATE)=TRUE
            EMPTY(INSERT(d,s))=FALSE
            IF TRUE THEN s1 ELSE s2=s1
            IF FALSE THEN s2 ELSE s2=s2
```

where bool is some correct specification of boolean values including TRUE,
FALSE, AND,OR,NON and IF-THEN-ELSE operations.

In the semantics of this specification, however, we can also use parameter
algebras A where A_{bool} has more than two elements. In this case the free
construction F(A) generates via the IF-THEN-ELSE-operations new data of sort
set which cannot be generated by CREATE or INSERT. This implies that also
new data of sort bool are generated via the operations MEMBER and EMPTY which
means $F(A)_{bool} \neq A_{bool}$ such that F is not persistent and is not correct with
respect to SETO in Example 2.2. This is a common error in parameterized set
specifications (see /ADJ 78/, /ADJ 80/) which can be avoided using initial
restrictions (see /Ehr 81/ and Section 8).

3. THE PARAMETERIZED TYPES string, matrix and bintree

In this section we give some more examples of parameterized types which can be handled within the basic algebraic approach where in the formal parameter part only equations are allowed. In Example 2.5 we have seen that the parameterized type set(data) cannot be handled nicely in the basic algebraic approach because we need an equality predicate and initiality of the bool-part for all formal parameters. This can only be achieved in the case of parameterized specifications with requirements which will be sketched in Section 8. In this more general setting we can also handle parameterized types like stack(attr), queue(par) and array(item) which also use an equality predicate with initial bool-part and, in addition, error handling.

For some specifications, however, like string(param), it is possible to avoid the requirement that the bool-part is initial and that EQ:data data ⟶ bool is really an equality predicate. This specification makes also sense in the case that EQ is only a reflexive relation as well as when the bool- and nat-parts are not initial; these more general cases do not violate the persistency of the semantics of the specification.

In the following we give the parameterized specifications for string(param), matrix(ring), bintree(data) and bintreetraversal(data) and a few remarks concerning the semantics. For complete semantical models and corresponding correctness proofs in the sense of 2.3.2 we refer to /Fey 81/.

3.1 EXAMPLE (string(param)

PARAMETER DECLARATION: param =

    nat + bool +
    sorts: data
    opns: EQ: data data ⟶ bool
    eqns: EQ(X,X)=TRUE
    Comment: We only require reflexivity and not
             equality or an equivalence relation

TARGET SPECIFICATION: string(param) =

    param +
    sorts: string
    opns: EMPTY: ⟶ string

```
              LETTER: data ⟶ string

              CONCAT: string string ⟶ string

              LADD: data string ⟶ string

              RADD: string data ⟶ string

              ROTATE: string ⟶ string

              REVERSE: string ⟶ string

              SHUFFLE: string string ⟶ string

              LENGTH: string ⟶ nat

              IS-EMPTY: string ⟶ bool

              IS-IN: data string ⟶ bool

eqns:    CONCAT(S,EMPTY)=CONCAT(EMPTY,S)=S

         CONCAT(CONCAT(S,S'),S")=CONCAT(S,CONCAT(S',S"))

         LADD(D,S)=CONCAT(LETTER(D),S)

         RADD(S,D)=CONCAT(S,LETTER(D))

         ROTATE(EMPTY)=EMPTY

         ROTATE(LADD(D,S))=RADD(S,D)

         REVERSE(EMPTY)=EMPTY

         REVERSE(LADD(D,S))=RADD(REVERSE(S),D)

         SHUFFLE(EMPTY,S)=SHUFFLE(S,EMPTY)=S

         SHUFFLE(LADD(D,S),LADD(D',S'))=LADD(D,LADD(D',SHUFFLE(S,S')))

         LENGTH(EMPTY)=O

         LENGTH(LADD(D,S))=SUCC(LENGTH(S))

         IS-EMPTY(EMPTY)=TRUE

         IS-EMPTY(LADD(D,S))=FALSE

         IS-IN(D,EMPTY)=FALSE

         IS-IN(D,LADD(D',S))=EQ(D,D') OR IS-IN(D,S)
```

The parameter declaration param consists of a specification nat for natural
numbers with zero (O) and successor (SUCC), bool with boolean operations AND
and OR, a sort data and a reflexive relation EQ on data. Hence param-algebras
are 3-sorted where the nat- and bool-parts are (not necessary initial) nat-
resp. bool-algebras and the data-part is a set with a reflexive relation. Even
if the bool-part is not two-valued the relation can be defined as preimage
of TRUE. The semantics of string(param) is the free construction F which
is persistent and assigns to each param-algebra A the free algebra F(A) where
$F(A)_{string}$ is the free monoid A^{*}_{data} containing all strings over the

alphabet $A_{\underline{data}}$. EMPTY creates the empty string, LETTER creates for each data a the corresponding string of length 1, CONCAT is concatenation of strings, LADD (resp. RADD) is left (resp. right) addition of a data to a string, ROTATE is rotation of the string by one position to the left where the first letter becomes the last, REVERSE reverses the string, SHUFFLE of two strings construc the shuffle product, LENGTH measures the length of each string which, however, counts modulo m if $A_{\underline{nat}}$ is isomorphic to $I\!\!N$ (mod m), IS-EMPTY and IS-IN are predicates assigning the value TRUE if the string is empty resp. the string contains an element EQ-related (or equal if EQ is the equality on data) to the given one.

3.2   EXAMPLE (<u>matrix</u>(<u>ring</u>))

For simplicity we only consider 2x2-matrices:

PARAMETER DECLARATION: <u>ring</u> =

    sorts: <u>ring</u>

    opns: 0,1: $\longrightarrow$ <u>ring</u>

           +,*: <u>ring</u> <u>ring</u> $\longrightarrow$ <u>ring</u>

           -: <u>ring</u> $\longrightarrow$ <u>ring</u>

    eqns: $(X+Y)+Z = X+(Y+Z)$

           $X+Y=Y+X$

           $X+(-X)=0$

           $X+0=X$

           $(X*Y)*Z=X*(Y*Z)$

           $X*Y=Y*X$

           $X*1=X$

           $X*(Y+Z)=X*Y+X*Z$

TARGET SPECIFICATION: <u>matrix</u>(<u>ring</u>) =

    <u>ring</u> +

    sorts: <u>matrix</u>

    opns: ZERO,UNIT: $\longrightarrow$ <u>matrix</u>

           MATRIX: <u>ring</u> <u>ring</u> <u>ring</u> <u>ring</u> $\longrightarrow$ <u>matrix</u>

           ADD,SUB,MUL: <u>matrix</u> <u>matrix</u> $\longrightarrow$ <u>matrix</u>

           DET: <u>matrix</u> $\longrightarrow$ <u>ring</u>

    eqns: ZERO=MATRIX(0,0,0,0)

           UNIT=MATRIX(1,0,0,1)

           ADD(MATRIX(A1,A2,A3,A4),MATRIX(B1,B2,B3,B4))

```
                  =MATRIX(A1+B1,A2+B2,A3+B3,A4+B4)
        SUB(MATRIX(A1,A2,A3,A4),MATRIX(B1,B2,B3,B4))
           =MATRIX(A1+(-B1),A2+(-B2),A3+(-B3),A4+(-B4))
        MUL(MATRIX(A1,A2,A3,A4),MATRIX(B1,B2,B3,B4))
           =MATRIX(A1*B1+A2*B3,A1*B2+A2*B4,
                   A3*B1+A4*B3,A3*B2+A4*B4)
        DET(MATRIX(A1,A2,A3,A4))=A1*A4+(-A2*A3)
```

The parameter declaration <u>ring</u> corresponds to the usual axiomatic definition
of commutative rings with unit. Hence a <u>ring</u>-algebra is an arbitrary commutative ring with unit while the initial <u>ring</u>-algebra is isomorphic to the ring
of integers. The semantics of <u>matrix</u>(<u>ring</u>) is the free construction F which
is persistent and assigns to each ring R the <u>matrix</u>(<u>ring</u>)-algebra F(R) where
$F(R)_{matrix}$ is the set of all 2x2-matrices over R with zero matrix ZERO, unit
matrix UNIT, additon ADD, substraction SUB and multiplication MUL of matrices
while DET calculates the determinant of a matrix. This example could be ex-
tended by an operation IS-SING:<u>matrix</u> $\longrightarrow$ <u>bool</u> testing singularity of matrices
provided that the parameter declaration is extended by <u>bool</u> and an equivalence
relation EQ on <u>ring</u> which corresponds to the equality for a given ring R.
If we want to make sure that EQ is the equality on <u>ring</u> we need similar requirements as for EQ on <u>data</u> in <u>set</u>(<u>data</u>) (see Section 8).

.3 <u>EXAMPLE</u> (<u>bintree</u>(<u>data</u>) and <u>bintreetraversal</u>(<u>data</u>))

1. We first give a parameterized specification for binary trees
    PARAMETER DECLARATION: <u>data</u> =
        sorts: <u>data</u>
    TARGET SPECIFICATION: <u>bintree</u>(<u>data</u>) =
        <u>data</u> +
        sorts: <u>bintree</u>
        opns: LEAF: <u>data</u> $\longrightarrow$ <u>bintree</u>
               LEFT,RIGHT: <u>data</u> <u>bintree</u> $\longrightarrow$ <u>bintree</u>
               BOTH: <u>data</u> <u>bintree</u> <u>bintree</u> $\longrightarrow$ <u>bintree</u>

This skeleton specification of binary trees which has no equations can be enriched by typical tree operations like HEIGHT, BREADTH, NODES, EDGES, BAL and
DEG measuring the height, the number of leaves, nodes and edges of the tree

and testing whether it is balanced resp. degenerated (i.e. without branching).
However, such an enrichment in the target specification needs an extension of
the parameter declaration by a nat- and a bool-part. But unlike set(data) in
2.5 initiality of nat and bool is not necessary to show persistency and
correctness (see /Fey 81/).

2. A parameterized specification corresponding to the different tree traversal
algorithms is the following:

> PARAMETER DECLARATION: data =
>> sorts: data
>
> TARGET SPECIFICATION: bintreetraversal(data) =
>> bintree(data) +
>> sorts: string
>> opns: PRE,IN,END: bintree ⟶ string
>>> EMPTY,LETTER,CONCAT,LADD,RADD (see 3.1)
>> eqns: PRE(LEAF(D))=LETTER(D)
>>> PRE(LEFT(D,T)=PRE(RIGHT(D,T))=LADD(D,PRE(T))
>>> PRE(BOTH(D,T,T'))=LADD(D,CONCAT(PRE(T),PRE(T')))
>>
>>> IN(LEAF(D))=LETTER(D)
>>> IN(LEFT(D,T))=RADD(IN(T),D)
>>> IN(RIGHT(D,T))=LADD(D,IN(T))
>>> IN(BOTH(D,T,T'))=CONCAT(IN(T),LADD(D,IN(T')))
>>
>>> END(LEAF(D))=LETTER(D)
>>> END(LEFT(D,T))=END(RIGHT(D,T))=RADD(END(T),D)
>>> END(BOTH(D,T,T'))=CONCAT(END(T),RADD(END(T'),D))

> eqns for CONCAT,LADD,RADD (see 3.1)

In bintreetraversal(data) we have specified three well-known tree traversal
algorithms given by the operations PRE(preorder), IN(inorder) and END(endorder)
The result of these algorithms is in each case a string of data. This requires
part of the string(param) specification must be included in the target specification of bintreetraversal(data).

STANDARD PARAMETER PASSING

We come now to the problem of parameter passing. We need a mechanism which allows us to replace the formal parameters, given by the parameter declaration of a parameterized specification, by actual parameters, given by actual specifications. This mechanism will be called "standard parameter passing". The problem of "parameterized parameter passing" where the actual parameters are parameterized specifications will be studied in Section 6.

The main problem for parameter passing is to develop suitable assignments, called "parameter passing morphisms", from the formal to the actual parameters taking into account possible renamings and/or identifications of sorts and operations and also consistency of the actual parameter with respect to the parameter declaration.

Recall the parameterized specification set0(data0) of 2.4 and consider nat as actual parameter. There is an "obvious" morphism h:data0 $\longrightarrow$ nat which identifies the sort data with the sort nat in nat. It is not hard to see (intuitively) that this morphism h "tells us" how we want to modify the parameterized type set0(data0) to get the desired data type set0(nat) with sorts nat and set, operations 0, SUCC, CREATE and INSERT, and with the intended two-sorted algebra A with A_{nat} = the natural numbers, and A_{set} =all finite sets of natural numbers, together with the desired operations on these carriers.

Now let's look at the same process but in a more abstract setting: let para=$\langle$SPEC,SPEC1,T$\rangle$ be a strongly persistent parameterized data type with SPEC=$\langle S,\Sigma,E \rangle$ and SPEC1=SPEC+$\langle$S1,Σ1,E1$\rangle$, and let item=$\langle$SPEC',A'$\rangle$ be a (non-parameterized) data type, where SPEC'=$\langle$S',Σ',E'$\rangle$. Then intuitively what we want for para(item) is some appropriate SPEC1'-algebra B' where SPEC1'=SPEC'+$\langle$S1',Σ1',E1'$\rangle$, S1'=S1 and Σ1', E1' are suitable reformulations of Σ1,E1 respectively. The algebra B' depends, of course, on how we "insert" A' in for the parameter of para. Again what we need is a means for assigning a sort in SPEC' for each sort in SPEC as well as an operation in SPEC' for each operation in SPEC. This process must be done carefully; it must extract from the SPEC'-algebra A', a SPEC-algebra A to which the functor T of para can be applied. This is accomplished by a pair of mappings $\langle$ h$_S$:S $\longrightarrow$ S', h$_\Sigma$:$\Sigma \longrightarrow \Sigma'\rangle$ such that the resulting forgetful functor V_h:Alg$_{SPEC'}$ $\longrightarrow$ Alg$_{SPEC}$ takes A' to SPEC-algebra A. Using the morphism h we are able to define the reformulations $\Sigma1',E1'$ of $\Sigma1,E1$ mentioned above:

$\Sigma1'=h'(\Sigma1)$ and $E1'=h'(E1)$ where $h'=(h_S',h_\Sigma')$ is defined by

$h_S'(s)=$ if $s\in S1$ then s else $h_S(s)$, and

$h_\Sigma'(\sigma)=$ if $\sigma\in\Sigma1$ then σ else $h_\Sigma(\sigma)$.

The desired SPEC1'-algebra B' is then constructed by putting together the appropriate pieces of A' and B=T(A). That is, for each $s\in S'$, $B_S'=A_S'$, and for each $s\in S1$, $B_S'=B_S$.

Note that the strong persistency of T together with the definition of A as $V_h(A')$ ensures that if $s\in S$, then $B_s=A_s=A_{h(s)}'$ so B_s' is well-defined. In a similar manner we define the operations of B' from those of A' and B. However, there is another, rather neat, way to describe B' abstractly. Speaking informally (for now), the morphism h (given above) together with the "inclusion" s:SPEC→SPEC1 and s':SPEC'→SPEC1' induce a similar morphism h' from SPEC1 to SPEC1' yielding a "commuting diagram"

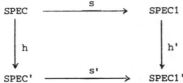

(we make this precise below). The morphisms s' and h' again induce forgetful functors $V_{s'}$ and $V_{h'}$ respectively. The algebra B' is characterized by the fact that $V_{s'}(B')=A'$ and $V_{h'}(B')=B=T(A)=T(V_h(A'))$.

To pull this together we must make it more precise. First we have to introduce the necessary morphism in a precise manner. This will allow us to give a precise statement of the parameter passing mechanism suggested by the above discussion.

4.1   DEFINITION

A specification morphism h:$\langle S,\Sigma,E\rangle\rightarrow\langle S',\Sigma',E'\rangle$ consists of a mapping $h_S:S\rightarrow S'$ and an $(S^*\times S)$-indexed family of mappings, $h_\Sigma:\Sigma\rightarrow\Sigma'$ (where $h_{\Sigma(w,s)}:\Sigma_{w,s}\rightarrow\Sigma_{h_S^*(w),h_S(s)}'$). This data is subject to the condition that every axiom of E, when translated by h, belongs to E', short $h(E)\subseteq E'$. The morphism h is called simple if $S\subseteq S'$, $\Sigma\subseteq\Sigma'$, $E\subseteq E'$ and h_S, h_Σ are the inclusions.

Remark: In /ADJ 80/ we have used signature morphisms instead of specification morphisms as parameter passing morphisms. That means we now assume, in addition, that the translated equations of the parameter part belong to equations of the actual parameter. This is a simplification due to the basic algebraic case which is studied in this paper. Looking at our examples in Section 3, on

one hand we have equations in the parameter declaration for fixed types like
nat and bool which are intended to occur also in the actual parameter. On
the other hand - and this is a drawback of the simplification - we also may
have equations for operations like EQ in the parameter declaration such
that EQ becomes an equivalence relation. Such equations must be expected to
be present in all our actual parameters although EQ may be specified as
equality on the actual parameter using different equations. This difficulty
was avoided in /ADJ 80/ using signature morphisms and the concept of "passing
consistency". But it can also be avoided for parameter declarations with
requirements (see Section 8) where we will only translate the equations and
not the requirements. See also /BG 80/ where theory morphisms are used.

4.2   PROPOSITION

If $h:SPEC \rightarrow SPEC'$ is a specification morphism, then there is a forgetful
functor $V_h : \underline{Alg}_{SPEC'} \rightarrow \underline{Alg}_{SPEC}$.

Proof: For $A' \in \underline{Alg}_{SPEC'}$, $V_h(A')=A$ is given by

$A_s = A'_{h(s)}$ for all $s \in S$ and

$\delta_A = h(\delta)_{A'}$ for all $\delta \in \Sigma$

where $\delta_A : A'_{h(s1)} \times \ldots \times A'_{h(sn)} \rightarrow A'_{h(s)}$ for $\delta : s1 \ldots sn \rightarrow s$.

A becomes a SPEC-algebra because we have $h(E) \subseteq E'$. $V_h(f')$ is defined by
$V_h(f')_s = f'_{h(s)}$ for all $s \in S$. Since V_h preserves identities and composition
it is a functor.

$\sqcup$

Remarks:

1) For each $\langle S', \Sigma' \rangle$-algebra A' we have that A' satisfies the translated
    axioms $h(E)$ iff $V_h(A')$ satisfies E.

2) For all $A',B' \in \underline{Alg}_{SPEC'}$ and each family $f'=(f'_s : A'_s \rightarrow B'_s)_{s \in S}$, we have that
    f' is a $h(\Sigma)$-morphism iff $V_h(f')$ is a Σ-morphism.

4.3   DEFINITION

Given a parameterized specification $PSPEC = \langle SPEC, SPEC1 \rangle$ with
$SPEC1 = SPEC + \langle S1, \Sigma1, E1 \rangle$, a specification $SPEC' = \langle S', \Sigma', E' \rangle$ called actual parameter specification, and a specification morphism $h: SPEC \rightarrow SPEC'$, called
parameter passing morphism   , the mechanism of standard parameter passing is given by the following syntax, semantics, and semantical
conditions:

SYNTAX:

The syntax of standard parameter passing is given by the following diagram,
called parameter passing diagram,

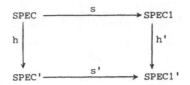

where h is given as above, s and s' are simple specification morphisms and
SPEC1', called value specification, is definded by

$$SPEC1'=SPEC'+\langle S1',\Sigma1',E1'\rangle$$

with $S1'=S1, \Sigma1'=h'(\Sigma1)$, and $E1'=h'(E1)$ where

$$h':SPEC1 \longrightarrow SPEC1'$$

is a specification morphism defined by

$$h'_S(x)= \text{ if } x \in S1 \text{ then } x \text{ else } h_S(x) \text{ and}$$

$$h'_\Sigma(\sigma)= \text{ if } (\sigma:w \longrightarrow s) \in \Sigma1 \text{ then } \sigma:h_S^*(w) \longrightarrow h_S(s) \text{ else } h_\Sigma(\sigma)$$

Notation: Instead of SPEC1 and SPEC1' we will often use the more intuitive
notation SPEC1(SPEC), e.g. setO(dataO), and SPEC1(SPEC')$_h$ or simply SPEC1(SPEC')
e.g. setO(nat), respectively.

SEMANTICS:

The semantics of standard parameter passing is given by

$$(F,T_{SPEC'},T_{SPEC1'}) \text{ or } T_{SPEC1'} \text{ for short}$$

where $F:\underline{Alg}_{SPEC} \longrightarrow \underline{Alg}_{SPEC1}$ is the semantics of PSPEC (see 2.3), $T_{SPEC'}$ and
$T_{SPEC1'}$ are the initial algebras in $\underline{Alg}_{SPEC'}$ and $\underline{Alg}_{SPEC1'}$, respectively.

SEMANTICAL CONDITIONS:

The semantical conditions for standard parameter passing are the following:

1. actual parameter protection, i.e. $V_{s'}(T_{SPEC1'})=T_{SPEC'}$
2. passing compatibility, i.e. $F(V_h(T_{SPEC'}))=V_{h'}(T_{SPEC1'})$

Interpretation: The value specification SPEC1'=SPEC1(SPEC') is the result of
replacing the formal parameter SPEC in SPEC1=SPEC1(SPEC) by the actual parameter SPEC'. We use the notation SPEC1'=SPEC1(SPEC') to point out this replace-
ment. But we have to keep in mind that $\Sigma1$ and E1 are slightly changed to

340

$\Sigma 1'=h'(\Sigma 1)$ and $E1'=h'(E1)$ respectively. This depends on the specific choice
of the parameter passing morphism $h:SPEC \longrightarrow SPEC'$ which uniquely defines h'.
Note that we don't have the semantical condition "passing consistency" i.e.
$V_h(T_{SPEC'}) \in Alg_{SPEC}$ which was assumed in /ADJ 80/. Since our parameter passing
morphism - unlike /ADJ 80/ - are specification morphisms this condition is
always satisfied, as stated in Remark 1 of 4.2. But we still need a similar nontrivial"passing consistency" condition for h in the case of parameterized specifications with requirements (see Section 8):$V_h(T_{SPEC'})$ must satisfy the requirements of the parameter declaration.

The semantical condition "actual parameter protection" means that the actual
parameter SPEC' is protected in the value specification SPEC1'. In other words
SPEC1' is assumed to be an extension of SPEC'. Certainly this requirement meets
an intuitive understanding of parameterized data types in software engineering.
On the other hand also slightly weaker requirements, like $V_{s'}(T_{SPEC1'}) \subseteq T_{SPEC''}$
may also meet the intuitive understanding. An interesting example might be
adding of error elements for suitable sorts (see Remark 5.3). This is an
example where the free construction F is not persistent. We cannot handle this
case in general,at this point,because we also need the persistency of F to show
(see Theorem 5.2) our second semantical condition: "passing compatibility".
Passing compatibility means that the semantics of parameter passing, especially
the transformation from $T_{SPEC'}$ to $T_{SPEC1'}$ is compatible with the semantics F
of the given parameterized specification PSPEC.

We are convinced that passing compatibility in our sense - or in a slightly
modified version - is an important requirement which pulls together the semantics of the formal and the actual parameter part. Unfortunately this or a
similar condition is not considered for the procedure concept in
CLEAR (see /BG 77/ and /BG 79/) because the parameterized specifications are
not assumed to be persistent. In /BG 80/, however, a similar feature is part of
their concept of F-freeness. We will show (see Theorem 5.2) that persistency of
the parameterized specification is necessary and sufficient
for correctness of parameter passing. Moreover passing compatibility is the
key to showing induced correctness of the value specification in Theorem 5.4.
Finally let us point out that the syntax diagram for standard parameter passing
becomes a pushout diagram in the category of specifications and specification
morphisms which corresponds to the syntactical construction given by Ehrich in
/Ehr 78/. Moreover the semantical construction can be extended to a free

functor $F':\underline{\underline{Alg}}_{SPEC'} \longrightarrow \underline{\underline{Alg}}_{SPEC1}$, which is persistent and satisfies V_h, $F'=F\ V_h$ (see Extension Lemma 5.1).

4.4 EXAMPLES

1. Given the parameterized specification $\underline{\underline{string}}(\underline{\underline{param}})$ (see Example 3.1) and the following actual parameter

$\underline{\underline{actual}}$ =

$\underline{\underline{nat}}$ + $\underline{\underline{bool}}$ +

opns: EQUAL: $\underline{nat}$ $\underline{nat}$ $\longrightarrow$ $\underline{bool}$

eqns: EQUAL(x,x)=TRUE

EQUAL$(O,SUCC(x))$=EQUAL$(SUCC(x),O)$=FALSE

EQUAL$(SUCC(x),SUCC(y))$=EQUAL(x,y)

which is $\underline{\underline{nat}}$ + $\underline{\underline{bool}}$ enriched by an equality predicate on $\underline{\underline{nat}}$. Since we are interested in strings of natural numbers and natural numbers are already presen in $\underline{\underline{param}}$ (necessary for the operation LENGTH) we do not have to put another cop of $\underline{\underline{nat}}$ into the actual parameter because our parameter passing morphisms are allowed to be noninjective (see below). If instead we are interested in string of integers our actual parameter has to include $\underline{\underline{nat}}$, $\underline{\underline{bool}}$ and $\underline{\underline{int}}$ together with the equality, some equivalence or at least a reflexive relation EQR on $\underline{\underline{int}}$. In the latter case the parameter passing morphism h:$\underline{\underline{param}}\longrightarrow$ $\underline{\underline{actual}}$ would be in- jective mapping $\underline{data}$ to $\underline{int}$ and EQ to EQR. In our example above for strings of natural numbers the parameter passing morphism h:$\underline{\underline{param}}\longrightarrow$ $\underline{\underline{actual}}$ is defined by h$(\underline{\underline{nat}})$=$\underline{\underline{nat}}$, h$(\underline{\underline{bool}})$=$\underline{\underline{bool}}$, $h_S(\underline{data})$=$\underline{nat}$ and $h_\Sigma(EQ)$=EQIV. Especially we have $h_S(\underline{nat})$=$h_S(\underline{data})$=$\underline{nat}$ such that h_S is noninjective. Since h preserves the equations it is a specification morphism. (This would have not been the case we would have replaced the first equation by EQUAL(O,O)=TRUE although this would be sufficient to specify the equality on $\underline{\underline{nat}}$). Due to the construction in 4.3 the value specification is the following

$\underline{\underline{string}}(\underline{\underline{actual}})$=$\underline{\underline{actual}}$ +

sorts: $\underline{string}$

opns: EMPTY: $\longrightarrow$ $\underline{string}$

LETTER: $\underline{nat}$ $\longrightarrow$ $\underline{string}$

CONCAT: $\underline{string}$ $\underline{string}$ $\longrightarrow$ $\underline{string}$

LADD, RADD, ROTATE, REVERSE, SHUFFLE, LENGTH

IS-EMPTY, IS-IN (like 3.1 with $\underline{data}$ replaced by $\underline{nat}$)

eqns: (like 3.1 with EQ replaced by EQUIV and variables D,D' of sort $\underline{data}$ replaced by variables N,M of sort $\underline{nat}$)

2. The value specification $\underline{\underline{string}}(\underline{\underline{actual}})$ can be used as actual parameter for the parameterized specification $\underline{\underline{bintree}}(\underline{\underline{data}})$ given in 3.3. There are, howeve

several choices for the parameter passing morphism $h:\underline{data}\longrightarrow\underline{string}(\underline{actual})$. The obvious one would be to define $h1_S(\underline{data})=\underline{string}$ such that the value specification $\underline{bintree}(\underline{string}(\underline{actual}))_{h1}$ defines binary trees with integer strings as labels in the nodes. But we can also define $h2_S(\underline{data})=\underline{nat}$ such that the value specification $\underline{bintree}(\underline{string}(\underline{actual}))_{h2}$ defines binary trees with natural numbers as labels in sort $\underline{bintree}$ and strings of natural numbers in sort $\underline{string}$. Another possibility would be to define $h3_S(\underline{data})=\underline{bool}$ which would lead to binary trees with boolean values as labels in the nodes. This example demonstrates that the value specification highly depends on the parameter passing morphism h which is reflected in the notation $SPEC1(SPEC')_h$ but not in the usual notation without subscript h.

5. CORRECTNESS OF STANDARD PARAMETER PASSING

In this section we will show that standard parameter passing is correct, i.e. the semantical conditions are satisfied, provided that the parameterized speci fication is persistent. Moreover persistency turns out to be necessary for actual parameter protection and hence for correctness. In the main result of this section we show that –roughly speaking - correctness of parameter passing implies correctness of the value specification. More precisely correctness of parameter passing, and correctness of the parameterized specification PSPEC=$\langle$SPEC,SPEC1$\rangle$ with respect to a parameterized persistent model data type PDAT=$\langle$MSPEC,MSPEC1,T$\rangle$, and correctness of the actual specification SPEC' with respect to an MSPEC'-algebra A implies correctness of the value specification SPEC1' with respect to the "T-extension of A", provided that the model speci-fications MSPEC and MSPEC' are "compatible" with the parameter passing morphism h:SPEC$\longrightarrow$ SPEC', i.e. h(MSPEC)$\subseteq$MSPEC'. This induced correctness of the value specification is most important for correct design of software systems because once some basic specifications (e.g. nat,int,bool) and some basic parameterized specifications (e.g. setO(dataO),string(param),matrix(ring)) are proven to be correct we have induced correctness for all possible value specifications (e.g. setO(nat),matrix(int),string(matrix(int)),setO(string(matrix(int))) etc.

The main tool to prove these correctness results is the following Extension Lemma which provides extensions of specifications and functors. A special case will be the Persistency Lemma which is stated separately for future reference.

5.1 EXTENSION LEMMA

1. Given a parameterized specification PSPEC=$\langle$SPEC,SPEC1$\rangle$ as in 2.3 and a specification morphism h:SPEC$\longrightarrow$ SPEC' then there is a well-defined parameter passing diagram

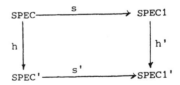

as defined in 5.3 which is a pushout in the category of specifications and
specification morphisms, i.e. we have

(i) $s' \bullet h = h' \bullet s$, and

(ii) for all specifications SPEC" and all specification morphisms
s":SPEC' $\longrightarrow$ SPEC" and h":SPEC1 $\longrightarrow$ SPEC" satisfying s"$\bullet$h=h"$\bullet$s there is
a unique specification morphism f:SPEC1' $\longrightarrow$ SPEC" such that
$$f \bullet s' = s" \quad \text{and} \quad f \bullet h' = h"$$

2. Given a (strongly) persistent parameterized data type PDAT=$\langle$PSPEC,F$\rangle$
with PSPEC and a specification morphism h as above then there is a
(strongly) persistent functor F':$\underline{Alg}_{SPEC'} \longrightarrow \underline{Alg}_{SPEC1'}$, called
extension of F via (h,s), satisfying for all A'$\in\underline{Alg}_{SPEC'}$
$$V_{h'}(F'(A')) = F(V_h(A')).$$
Moreover F'(A') is uniquely determined by A' and B=F(V_h(A')) in the
following sense:

For all B'$\in\underline{Alg}_{SPEC1'}$ satisfying $V_{s'}$(B')=A' and $V_{h'}$(B')=B we have already
B'=F'(A').

3. If in addition F is free (left adjoint to V_s) then F' is also free
(left ajoint to $V_{s'}$).

COROLLARY (PERSISTENCY LEMMA)

Let SPEC1=SPEC+$\langle$S1,Σ1,E1$\rangle$ and SPEC'=SPEC+$\langle$S',Σ',E'$\rangle$ where S1 and S' as
well as Σ1 and Σ' are pairwise disjoint. Moreover let
$$SPEC1'=SPEC1+\langle S',\Sigma',E'\rangle = SPEC'+\langle S1,\Sigma1,E1\rangle$$
and assume that the free construction F:$\underline{Alg}_{SPEC} \rightarrow \underline{Alg}_{SPEC1}$ is (strongly)
persistent. Then also the free construction F':$\underline{Alg}_{SPEC'} \rightarrow \underline{Alg}_{SPEC1'}$ is
(strongly) persistent.

$\square$

Proof of the Extension Lemma:

1. Defining SPEC1', s' and h' as in 5.3, where h' becomes a specification morphism $h':SPEC1 \to SPEC1'$, we have $s' \circ h = h' \circ s$. Note that s and s' are inclusions for sorts, operations and equations. Given specification morphisms s" and h" with $s" \circ h = h" \circ s$ we define $f:SPEC1' \to SPEC"$ as follows:

$$f_S(x) = \text{if } x \in S1' \text{ then } h"_S(x) \text{ else } s"_S(x)$$
$$f_{\Sigma}(y) = \text{if } y \in \Sigma1' \text{ then } h"_{\Sigma}(y) \text{ else } s"_{\Sigma}(y).$$

This implies $f \cdot s' = s"$ and $f \cdot h' = h"$ where the only nontrivial cases to consider are $x \in S$ where $f_S(h'_S(x)) = f_S(h_S(x)) = s"_S(h_S(x)) = h"_S(s_S(x)) = h"_S(x)$ and similarly for $y \in \Sigma$. The uniqueness of f follows from the fact that s' and h' are jointly surjective, i.e. each item in SPEC1' has a preimage under s' or h'. It remains to show $f(E' + E1') \subseteq E"$. This follows from $s"(E') \subseteq E"$ and $f(E1') = f(h'(E1)) = h"(E1) \subseteq E"$ using the fact that s" and h" are specification morphisms.

2. Given $A' \in Alg_{SPEC'}$, let $A = V_h(A') \in Alg_{SPEC}$ and $B = F(A) \in Alg_{SPEC1}$. We will construct a SPEC1'-algebra B' such that $V_{s'}(B') = A'$ and $V_{h'}(B') = B$. Then we will define $F'(A') = B'$ and we will define F' on SPEC'-morphisms such that F' becomes a strongly persistent functor $F':Alg_{SPEC'} \to Alg_{SPEC1'}$ satisfying the desired property by construction of B'.

The following construction of B' needs essentially the (strong) persistence of F (i.e. $V_s(B) = A$) to be well-defined:

$$B'_s = \text{if } s \in S' \text{ then } A'_s \text{ else } B_s \quad \text{for all } s \in S' + S1'$$
$$\delta_{B'} = \text{if } \delta \in \Sigma' \text{ then } \delta_{A'} \text{ else } \delta_B \quad \text{for all } \delta \in \Sigma' + \Sigma1'.$$

This construction implies $V_{s'}(B') = A'$ and $V_{h'}(B') = B$ (see below) once we have shown that B' is a well-defined SPEC1'-algebra. For $\delta:s1...sn \to sn+1$ we will show that $\delta_{B'}$ is a function $\delta_{B'}:B'_{s1} \times ... \times B'_{sn} \to B'_{sn+1}$. For $\delta \in \Sigma'$ we have $\delta_{B'} = \delta_{A'}$ and $B'_{si} = A'_{si}$ for $i=1,...,n+1$ such that we are done. In the following we omit the subscripts S and Σ for h and h':

For $\delta \in \Sigma1' = h'(\Sigma1)$ we have $\delta \in \Sigma1$ with $\delta:t1...tn \to tn+1$ for some $ti \in S + S1$ with $h'(ti) = si$ for $i=1,...,n+1$. Since $\delta_B:B_{t1} \times ... \times B_{tn} \to B_{tn+1}$ we have to show $B'_{si} = B_{ti}$. For each $i=1,...,n+1$ we have to consider the case $ti \in S$ and $ti \in S1$. For $ti \in S$ we have $si = h'(ti) = h(ti) \in S'$ such that

$$B'_{si} = A'_{si} = A'_{h(ti)} = V_h(A')_{ti} = A_{ti} = B_{ti}$$

because $V_s(B) = A$ by strong persistency of F. For $ti \in S1$ we have $si = h'(ti) = ti \in S1 = S1'$ such that

$$B'_{si} = B_{si} = B_{ti}.$$

This completes well-definedness of B'.

Next we will show $V_{h'}(B')=B$. By construction of B' this is clear for sorts S1 and operations $\Sigma 1$. It remains to be shown for S and Σ which means $V_s(V_{h'}(B'))=V_s(B)$. Using again the persistency $V_s(B)=A$ and $V_{s'}(B')=A'$ we have

$$V_s(V_{h'}(B'))=V_h(V_{s'}(B'))=V_h(A')=A=V_s(B).$$

It remains to show that B' satisfies the equations E' and E1'. This follows from $V_{s'}(B')=A'$ and $V_{h'}(B')=B$ because A' satisfies E' with s'(E')=E' and B satisfies E1 with h'(E1)=E1' respectively (see remark 1 in 5.2). Up to now we have shown that F'(A'):=B' is a SPEC1'-algebra satisfying the desired properties. To complete part 2 of the proof it remains to define F' on SPEC'-morphisms $f:A'\rightarrow A''$ such that $F'(f):F'(A')\rightarrow F'(A'')$ becomes a SPEC1'-morphism. Let

$$F'(f)_s = \text{ if } s\in S' \text{ then } f_s \text{ else } F(V_h(f))_s.$$

It is left to the reader to show that F'(f) is well-defined and, using remark 2 in 5.2, to show that F'(f) preserves $\Sigma'+\Sigma 1$-operations. Immediately from the definition it follows that F' preserves identities and composition of morphisms such that F' becomes a functor $F':\underline{Alg}_{SPEC'}\rightarrow \underline{Alg}_{SPEC1'}$.

Finally to show the uniqueness property of F'(A') let $B1'\in\underline{Alg}_{SPEC1'}$ with $V_{s'}(B1')=A'$ and $V_{h'}(B1')=B$. Then we have B1'=B'=F'(A') by construction of B'=F'(A').

3. We have to show that for each SPEC1'-algebra B' and each SPEC'-morphism $f':A'\rightarrow V_{s'}(B')$ there is a unique SPEC1'-morphism $g':F'(A')\rightarrow B'$ such that the following diagram commutes:

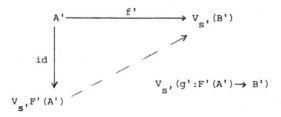

Let $A:=V_h(A')$, $B:=V_{h'}(B')$ and $f:=V_h(f')$. Since F is left adjoint to V_s there is a unique SPEC1-morphism $g:F(A)\rightarrow B$ such that $V_s(g)=f$. The morphisms f' and g are combined to define $g':F'(A')\rightarrow B'$ by

$$g'_s = \text{if } s \in S' \text{ then } f'_s \text{ else } g_s$$

Using $V_{h'}(F'(A'))=F(A)$ and $V_{s'}(F'(A'))=A'$ (see step 2), $V_{s'}(B')_s=B'_s$
for $s \in S'$ and $B_s=B'_s$ for $s \in S1=S1'$ we conclude that g'_s is in fact a
mapping from $F'(A')_s$ to B'_s for all $s \in S'+S1$. By construction we have
$V_{s'}(g')=f'$. In order to show uniqueness of g' let also g'' satisfy
$V_{s'}(g'')=f'$. Then we have

$$V_s \cdot V_{h'}(g'') = V_h \cdot V_{s'}(g'') = V_h(f') = f$$

which implies $V_{h'}(g'')=g$ by uniqness of g. Together with $V_{s'}(g'')=f'$
this implies $g'=g''$ by construction of g'.

It remains to show that g' is a $\Sigma'+\Sigma1'$-morphism. Since $V_{s'}(g')=f'$ it
is clear that g' is a Σ'-morphism because f' is one. Using $g''=g'$ we
have $V_s \cdot V_{h'}(g')=f$ which together with $V_s(g)=f$ implies $V_{h'}(g')=g$. Hence
$V_{h'}(g')$ is a $\Sigma+\Sigma1$-morphism which implies by remark in 5.2 that g' is
a $h'(\Sigma1)$-morphism. By definition of $\Sigma1'$ we have $\Sigma1'=h'(\Sigma1)$ such that
g' is also a $\Sigma1'$-morphism.

$\square$

5.2   THEOREM (CORRECTNESS OF STANDARD PARAMETER PASSING)

Given a parameterized specification PSPEC=⟨SPEC,SPEC1⟩ then standard parameter passing is correct, i.e. for all actual parameters SPEC' and all parameter
passing morphisms h:SPEC⟶ SPEC' we have actual parameter protection and
passing compatibility, iff PSPEC is persistent.

Proof: First let us assume that PSPEC is persistent. We have to show actual
parameter protection (4.3.1) and passing compatibility (4.3.2). The Extension
Lemma 5.1 can be used to apply the extended functor F' to the initial algebra
T_{SPEC}. 5.1.3 implies that $F'(T_{SPEC'})$ is free and hence initial in $\underline{Alg}_{SPEC1'}$,
i.e. $T_{SPEC1'}=F'(T_{SPEC'})$. Strong persistency and extension property of
F' (5.1.2) means

$$V_{s'}(F'(T_{SPEC'}))=T_{SPEC'} \text{ and } V_{h'}(F'(T_{SPEC'}))=F(V_h(T_{SPEC'}))$$

which together with $T_{SPEC1'}=F'(T_{SPEC'})$ implies actual parameter protection and
passing compatibility respectively.

Conversely assume that the semantical conditions 4.3.1 and 4.3.2 are satisfied
for all actual parameters SPEC' and all parameter passing morphisms
h:SPEC⟶ SPEC'. Further let A an arbitrary SPEC-algebra. Now

let SPEC'=SPEC+$\langle\emptyset, \Sigma A, EA\rangle$ where ΣA contains a 0-ary operation symbol x for each $x \in A_s$ and $s \in S$ and EA consists of all those equations t=t' with $t, t' \in T_{\Sigma + \Sigma A}$ which are true in A. This construction implies that $V_h(T_{SPEC'}) = A \in \underline{Alg}_{SPEC}$ and actual parameter protection implies:

$$V_s(F(A)) = V_s(F(V_h(T_{SPEC'}))) = V_s(V_{h'}(T_{SPEC1'}))$$
$$= V_h(V_{s'}(T_{SPEC1'})) = V_h(T_{SPEC'}) = A$$

Hence we have strong persistency of F and PSPEC. Note that SPEC' becomes an "infinite specification" in general.

$\square$

3

REMARK (PASSING COMPATIBILITY)

We have shown that persistency of PSPEC is necessary for correctness of parameter passing as defined in 4.3. It remains open how far persistency or a similar weaker condition is necessary for passing compatibility if actual parameter protection in the strong version of 4.3.1 is not required. The following example shows that the nonpersistent parameterized specification PSPEC=$\langle$SPEC,SPEC1$\rangle$ "insertion of an error element" with SPEC= $\langle\{s\}, \emptyset, \emptyset\rangle$ and SPEC1=SPEC+$\langle\emptyset, \{e\}, \emptyset\rangle$ is not passing compatible in general. Taking SPEC'=<u>nat</u>+$\{SUCC(SUCC(x))=SUCC(x)\}$ and h(s)=<u>nat</u> we have:

$$T_{SPEC'} \cong \{0,1\}, \quad F(V_h(T_{SPEC'})) \cong \{0,1,e\}, \quad \text{and} \quad T_{SPEC1'} \cong \{0,1,e,f\}$$

Hence we have no passing compatibility nor actual parameter protection because $F(V_h(T_{SPEC'}))$ and $V_{h'}(T_{SPEC1'})$ as well as $T_{SPEC'}$ and $T_{SPEC1'}$ have different cardinality.

4

THEOREM (INDUCED CORRECTNESS OF VALUE SPECIFICATIONS)

Given

(1) a persistent parameterized specification PSPEC=$\langle$SPEC,SPEC1$\rangle$ which is correct with respect to a parameterized persistent model data type PDAT=$\langle$MSPEC,MSPEC1,T$\rangle$, and

(2) an actual specification SPEC' which is correct with respect to an MSPEC'-algebra A', and

(3) a parameter passing morphism h:SPEC⟶ SPEC'

and

(4) compatibility of the parameter passing morphism h with the model specifications MSPEC and MSPEC', i.e.

$$h(MSPEC) \leq MSPEC'$$

then we have:

(5) the value specification SPEC1' is correct with respect to the MSPEC1'
algebra T'(A'), called <u>T-extension of A'</u>, which is uniquely defined by

$$V_m,(T'(A'))=A' \quad \text{and} \quad V_k,(T'(A'))=T(V_k(A'))$$

where k:MSPEC⟶ MSPEC' is the restriction of h (see (4)) and MSPEC1' the
model value specification in the model parameter passing diagram

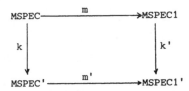

Remark: The compatibility in (4) means that the actual parameter has to be
correct at least with respect to those parts of the actual parameter which
are image under the assignment of the correct components of the formal parameter. This excludes for example MSPEC'=∅ if MSPEC is nonempty.

Proof: From assumptions (1)-(4) we are able to construct the following
3-cube of specifications and specification resp. parameter passing morphisms
where th⌐ back square is defined as in (5), i' is the unique supplement in
the left square which exists by (4), and j' is the unique supplement in the
right and bottom square which exists by the pushout properties of MSPEC1'
(see 5.1.1 (ii)).

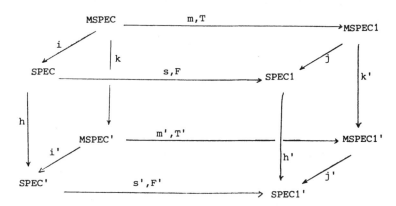

All morphisms are specification morphisms such that the Extension Lemma can be
applied to yield a unique specification morphism $j':MSPEC1' \longrightarrow SPEC1'$.
The existence and uniqueness of the T-extension $T'(A')$ of A' follows from part
2 of the Extension Lemma applied to the algebra A'.

We want to show correctness of SPEC1' with respect to $T'(A')$ which means
$V_j \cdot (T_{SPEC1'}) = T'(A')$ provided that we have $V_i \cdot (T_{SPEC'}) = A'$ (assumption 2)
By the uniqueness property of $T'(A')$ (see 5.1.2) it sufficies to show
$$V_m \cdot (V_j \cdot (T_{SPEC1'})) = A' \text{ and } V_k \cdot (V_j \cdot (T_{SPEC1'})) = T(V_k(A')).$$
Since SPEC' is correct with respect to A' we have $V_i \cdot (T_{SPEC'}) = A'$ and
$V_s \cdot (T_{SPEC1'}) = T_{SPEC'}$ by actual parameter protection (see 5.2) such that
$$V_m \cdot (V_j \cdot (T_{SPEC1'})) = V_i \cdot (V_s \cdot (T_{SPEC1'})) = V_i \cdot (T_{SPEC'}) = A'.$$
On the other hand passing compatibility, i.e. $V_h \cdot (T_{SPEC1'}) = F(V_h(T_{SPEC'}))$,
and correctness of PSPEC, i.e. $V_j \cdot F = T \cdot V_i$, implies
$$V_k \cdot (V_j \cdot (T_{SPEC1'})) = V_j(V_h \cdot (T_{SPEC1'})) = V_j(F(V_h(T_{SPEC'})))$$
$$= T(V_i(V_h(T_{SPEC'}))) = T(V_k(V_i \cdot (T_{SPEC'}))) = T(V_k(A'))$$
This completes the correctness proof.

$\square$

.5   EXAMPLE

We have the correctness of the parameterized specification set0(data0) with
respect to the parameterized data type $\langle$ data0,Mset0,SET0$\rangle$ shown in Theorem
2.4 and the correctness of nat with respect to the natural numbers $\mathbb{N}$. This
implies by Theorem 5.4 the correctness of the value specification set0(nat) in
the Introduction of Section 4 with respect to the set0(nat)-algebra A=SET0'($\mathbb{N}$)
with $A_{nat} = \mathbb{N}$, $A_{set} = \mathcal{P}_{fin}(\mathbb{N})$, 0_A and $SUCC_A$ zero and successor in $\mathbb{N}$, and CREATE$_A$
and INSERT$_A$ defined as in 2.2 for E=$\mathbb{N}$.

6.   PARAMETERIZED PARAMETER PASSING

In this section we consider the parameter passing problem for parameterized
actual parameters. In other words we want to insert a parameterized specification, e.g. matrix(ring), into another parameterized specification, e.g.
string(param), leading to a parameterized value specification, e.g.
string * matrix(ring). The parameterized value specification can be regarded
as the composition of the given parameterized specifications. This composition, however, depends on the choice of the parameter passing morphism.
The mechanism of parameterized parameter passing will be defined strictly
analogous to that of standard parameter passing in Section 4. Actually the
standard mechanism turns out to be a special case of the parameterized
mechanism. In analogy to the correctness results for standard parameter
passing in Section 5 we will show correctness of parameterized parameter
passing and induced correctness of composite parameterized specifications.

6.1   DEFINITION

Given parameterized specifications PSPEC=⟨SPEC,SPEC1⟩ and PSPEC'=⟨SPEC',SPEC
with SPEC1=SPEC+⟨S1,Σ1,E1⟩ and SPEC1'=SPEC'+⟨S1',Σ1',E1'⟩ respectively, wher
PSPEC' is called parameterized actual specification, and a specification
morphism h:SPEC ——→SPEC1', called parameter passing morphism
the mechanism of parameterized parameter passing is given by the following
syntax, semantics, and semantical conditions:

SYNTAX:

The syntax of parameterized parameter passing is given by the following
diagram, called parameterized parameter passing diagram,

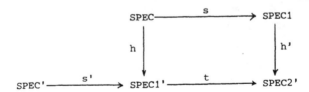

where h is given as above, s, s' and t are simple specification morphisms
and PSPEC*_h PSPEC'=⟨SPEC',SPEC2'⟩, called parameterized value specification
or composite parameterized specification, is defined by

$$\text{SPEC2'}=\text{SPEC1'}+\langle S2',\Sigma2',E2'\rangle$$

with $S2'=S1$, $\Sigma2'=h'(\Sigma1)$, and $E2'=h'(E1)$ where

$$h':\text{SPEC1} \longrightarrow \text{SPEC2'}$$

is a specification morphism defined by

$$h'_S(x)= \text{if } x\in S1 \text{ then } x \text{ else } h_S(x) \text{ and}$$
$$h'_\Sigma(\delta)= \text{if } (\delta:w\longrightarrow s)\in\Sigma1 \text{ then } \delta:h^*_S(w)\longrightarrow h(s) \text{ else } h_\Sigma(\delta)$$

Notation: Instead of SPEC1, SPEC1' and SPEC2' we will often use the more
intuitive notation SPEC1(SPEC), e.g. $\underline{\underline{\text{string}}}(\underline{\underline{\text{param}}})$, SPEC1'(SPEC'), e.g. $\underline{\underline{\text{matrix}}}(\underline{\underline{\text{ring}}})$,
and SPEC2'(SPEC') or SPEC1$*_h$SPEC1'(SPEC'), e.g. $\underline{\underline{\text{string}}}*_h$ $\underline{\underline{\text{matrix}}}(\underline{\underline{\text{ring}}})$, resp.
We also use $*$ instead of $*_h$ if the parameter passing morphism is clear from
the context.

SEMANTICS:

The semantics of parameterized parameter passing is given by

$$(F,F',F*_hF') \text{ or } \qquad F*_hF' \text{ for short,}$$

where F,F', and $F*_hF'$ are the semantics of PSPEC, PSPEC', and PSPEC$*_h$PSPEC'
respectively (see 2.3).

SEMANTICAL CONDITIONS:

The semantical conditions of parameterized parameter passing are the
following

1. parameterized parameter protection, i.e. for all $A'\in\text{Alg}_{\text{SPEC'}}$
$$V_t(F*_hF'(A'))-F'(A')$$
2. parameterized passing compatibility, i.e. for all $A'\in\text{Alg}_{\text{SPEC'}}$
$$V_{h'}\circ(F*_hF')(A')=F\cdot V_h\cdot F'(A')$$

Interpretation:

Considering SPEC1' as an actual parameter of PSPEC in the sense of standard
parameter passing (see 4.3) SPEC2' is exactly the corresponding value specification. For parameterized parameter passing, however, it makes no sense to
consider SPEC2' as a value specification because it still includes the formal
parameter SPEC' of PSPEC'. Hence we consider the pair $\langle$SPEC',SPEC2'$\rangle$ to be
the value of the parameterized parameter passing mechanism which motivates the
name "parameterized value specification". On the other hand this pair

corresponds to some sort of composition $PSPEC*_h PSPEC'$ of the given parameterized specifications PSPEC and PSPEC' motivating the name "composite parameterized specification". Although the composition $*$ is actually a parameterized composition $*_h$, because it depends on the choice of the parameter passing morphism h, it makes sense to speak of a composition. Actually the composition $*$ behaves like the usual composition of functions where we have associativity, i.e. $f\cdot(g\cdot h)=(f\cdot g)\cdot h$, and compatibility with evaluation, i.e. $(f\cdot g)(x)=f(g(x))$. The corresponding properties for $*$ will be shown in Section 7, e.g. we will have

$$\underline{string} * \underline{matrix}(\underline{int}) = \underline{string}(\underline{matrix}(\underline{int})).$$

The semantics $F*_h F'$ is also a parameterized composition. Note, that the usual composition $F\cdot F'$ is not defined because the range of F' is $\underline{Alg}_{SPEC1'}$ but the domain of F is $\underline{Alg}_{SPEC}$. Hence we can only define the following composition $F\cdot V_h \cdot F'$ corresponding to the semantics of PSPEC and PSPEC'. This semantics, however, should be compatible with the semantics $F*_h F'$ of $PSPEC*_h PSPEC'$. This compatibility is exactly the second semantical condition: parameterized passing compatibility.

Parameterized parameter protection means that the parameterized actual parameter F'(A') is protected. If F and F' are persistent then also $F*_h F'$ is persistent such that all actual parameters A' are protected by $F*_h F'$.

Finally let us point out that standard parameter passing is a strict special case of parameterized parameter passing (including syntax, semantics and semantical conditions) which will be shown in the following lemma:

6.2   **LEMMA**

If the parameterized actual specification $PSPEC'=\langle SPEC',SPEC1'\rangle$ is an actual specification, i.e. $SPEC'=\emptyset$, then parameterized parameter passing coincides with standard parameter passing. Moreover we have for $SPEC'=\emptyset$ and $h:SPEC\rightarrow SPEC1'$

(1) $SPEC1'(\emptyset)=SPEC1'$, and

(2) $SPEC1*_h SPEC1'(\emptyset)=SPEC1(SPEC1'(\emptyset))_h=SPEC1(SPEC1')_h$.

Proof:

Replacing SPEC' in 4.3 by SPEC1' in 6.1 the syntactical construction of
SPEC1' in 4.3 is equal to that of SPEC2' in 6.1. For SPEC'=$\emptyset$ the free construction $F*_h F'$ in 6.1 is given by $F*_h F'(T_\emptyset)=T_{SPEC2}$, corresponding to the
semantics of standard parameter passing. Moreover F' is given by
$F'(T_\emptyset)= T_{SPEC1}$, such that the semantical requirements in the parameterized
case are equivalent to those in the standard case. The formulas in (1) and
(2) are well-defined because SPEC'=$\emptyset$ implies that there is a unique parameter passing morphism $h:\emptyset \to \emptyset$. Moreover SPEC=SPEC'=$\emptyset$ in 4.3 implies
SPEC1'=SPEC1, i.e. the value specification applied to $\emptyset$ coincides with the
given specification. This implies (1).

To show (2) we apply PSPEC*PSPEC' with SPEC'=$\emptyset$ to $\emptyset$ with
$h":\emptyset \to \emptyset$ which yields SPEC1$*_h$SPEC1'($\emptyset$)=SPEC2'. On the other hand we have by
(1) and coincidence of the syntactical constructions in 4.1 and 6.1 (shown
above) SPEC1(SPEC1'($\emptyset$))$_h$=SPEC1(SPEC1')$_h$=SPEC2'. This proves (2).

□

THEOREM (CORRECTNESS OF PARAMETERIZED PARAMETER PASSING)

Parameterized parameter passing is correct for persistent parameterized specifications. In more detail:

Given (strongly) persistent parameterized specifications PSPEC=⟨SPEC,SPEC1⟩
and PSPEC'=⟨SPEC',SPEC1'⟩ and a parameter passing morphism h:SPEC→ SPEC'
then we have

(1)   parameterized parameter protection

(2)   parameterized passing compatibility

(3)   (strong) persistency of the composition PSPEC$*_h$PSPEC'.

Proof:

Similar to the proof of Theorem 5.2 (correctness of standard parameter
passing) Extension Lemma 5.1 can be applied to all algebras
$F'(A') \in Alg_{SPEC1}$, for $A' \in Alg_{SPEC'}$ instead of $T_{SPEC'}$ showing properties (1)
and (2) above. Note, that the property $F'(T_{SPEC'})=T_{SPEC1}$, in the proof of
5.2 can be replaced by $G(F'(A'))=F*_h F'(A')$ where G is the free construction
$G:Alg_{SPEC1} \to Alg_{SPEC2}$. This follows from the well-known fact that the
composition of free functors is free, i.e. $G\cdot F'=F*_h F'$. It remains to show
persistency of $F*_h F'$. But this is clear because F' is persistent by assumption and G is persistent by 5.1.2.

□

THEOREM (INDUCED CORRECTNESS OF COMPOSITE PARAMETERIZED SPECIFICATIONS)

Given

(1)   a persistent parameterized specification PSPEC=⟨SPEC,SPEC1⟩ which is correct with respect to a parameterized persistent model data type PDAT=⟨MSPEC,MSPEC1,T⟩, and

(2)   a persistent parameterized actual specification PSPEC'=⟨SPEC',SPEC1'⟩ which is correct with respect to a parameterized model data type PDAT'=⟨MSPEC',MSPEC1',T'⟩ such that the forgetful functor $V_1:\underline{Alg}_{SPEC'} \to \underline{Alg}_{MSPEC'}$ is surjective, and

(3)   a parameter passing morphism h:SPEC→ SPEC1' satisfying parameterized passing consistency, and

(4)   compatibility with the model specifications MSPEC and MSPEC1', i.e. h(MSPEC)≦ MSPEC1' ,

then we have

(5)   the composition PSPEC$*_h$PSPEC' is correct with respect to the <u>composite parameterized model data type</u>

$$PDAT*_k PDAT':=⟨MSPEC',MSPEC2',T*_k T'⟩$$

where k:MSPEC→ MSPEC1' is the restriction of h (see (4)), MSPEC2' the model value specification in the model parameter passing diagram

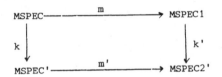

and the functor $T*_k T':\underline{Alg}_{MSPEC'} \to \underline{Alg}_{MSPEC2'}$ is uniquely defined on objects $B'\in\underline{Alg}_{MSPEC'}$ by

$$V_m,(T*_k T'(B'))=T'(B') \text{ and } V_{k'}(T*_k T'(B'))=T(V_k(T'(B')))$$

(6)   If in addition also PDAT' is persistent then also the composition PDAT$*_k$PDAT' is persistent.

Proof:

The proof of Theorem 5.4 can be extended using similar modifications as in the proof of Theorem 6.3 such that we obtain for all $A'\in\underline{Alg}_{SPEC'}$

(*) $V_j,(F*_h F'(A'))=G'(V_i,(F'(A')))$.

where $G':\underline{Alg}_{MSPEC1'} \to \underline{Alg}_{MSPEC2'}$ is the extension of T via (k,m') .

Surjectivity of V_1 implies that $T*_k T'$ becomes a functor with
$T*_k T'(B')=G'(T'(B'))$ for all $B' \in \underline{Alg}_{MSPEC'}$.
Correctness of PSPEC' means
$$V_i, (F'(A'))=T'(V_1(A'))$$
such that together with (*) we obtain the desired correctness for all
$A' \in \underline{Alg}_{SPEC'}$
$$V_j, (F*_k F'(A'))=T*_k T'(V_1(A')).$$
The uniqueness of $T*_k T'(B')$ in (5) follows from the uniqueness of $T'(A')$ in
6.4 (5)

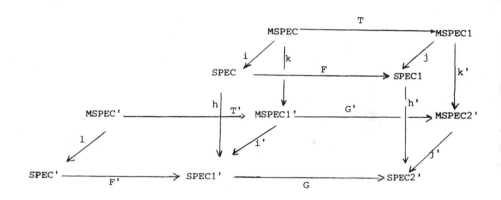

Finally   persistency of G' implies persistency of $T*_k T'$ if T' is
persistent.

$\square$

7. ITERATED TYPES AND SPECIFICATIONS

In this section we want to study the compatibility of standard and parameterized parameter passing. The aim is to build up large specifications like bintree(string(matrix(int))) from small basic specifications like int, matrix(ring), string(param) and bintree(data). Using the techniques of Sections 4.6 we are already able to build these specifications and we know that they are correct with respect to a canonical induced model. But we have not considered the problem of the extend to which the value specification is independent of the special construction we have chosen.

Perhaps the most obvious way to construct bintree(string(matrix(int))) is the following "call by value" strategy where the actual specification int is inserted in matrix(ring), the value specification matrix(int) is inserted in string(param) leading to string(matrix(int)), which finally is inserted into bintree(data). This strategy uses only standard parameter passing. On the other hand there is a "call by name" strategy construction first (bintree * string)(param), then ((bintree * string) * matrix)(ring) by parameterized parameter passing, and finally ((bintree * string)*matrix)(int) by standard parameter passing. Moreover there is another "call by name" strategy constructing first (string * matrix)(ring) then (bintree*(string*matrix))(ring) and finally (bintree*(string*matrix))(int). Last but not least,there are two "mixed strategies" leading to (bintree*string)(matrix(int)) and bintree((string*matrix)(int)) respectively.

We will show that all these strategies are leading to the same value specification. This corresponds to a Church-Rosser-property of standard and parameterized parameter passing.

The key to show this result is to show that the composition of parameterized specifications is associative like the composition of functions, e.g. (f∙g)∙h=f∙(g∙h), and that composition of parameterized specifications is compatible with standard actualization like composition and evaluation of functions, e.g. (f∙g)(x)=f(g(x)). Hence we can apply the usual rules known for the evaluation of composite functions. This is remarkable because composition and standard actualization of parameterized data types depend on the choice of the parameter passing morphisms. Actually in the composition and the compatibility results it is shown that there are always canonical induced parameter passing morphisms such that

all the parameter passing mechanisms are correct provided that all parameterized specifications are persistent.

7.1   THEOREM (ASSOCIATIVITY OF COMPOSITION)

The composition of persistent parameterized specifications is associative.
In more detail we have:
Given persistent parameterized specifications
    PSPECi=$\langle$SPEC(i-1),SPECi$\rangle$ for i=1,3,5
and parameter passing morphisms
    h0:SPEC0$\longrightarrow$ SPEC3 and h2:SPEC2$\longrightarrow$ SPEC5

Then there is a canonical parameter passing morphism h2*h0:SPEC0$\longrightarrow$ SPEC7
such that we have
    (PSPEC1*$_{h0}$PSPEC3)*$_{h2}$PSPEC5=PSPEC1*$_{h2*h0}$(PSPEC3*$_{h2}$PSPEC5)
where all compositions are well-defined and SPEC7 is the value specification
of PSPEC3*$_{h2}$PSPEC5.

Remark: Using the notation SPEC1(SPEC0) for PSPEC1, SPEC1*SPEC3(SPEC2) for
PSPEC1*PSPEC3,and similarly for the other parameterized specifications we obtain
the following equivalent formulation:
    ((SPEC1*$_{h0}$SPEC3)*$_{h2}$SPEC5)(SPEC4)=(SPEC1*$_{h2*h0}$(SPEC3*$_{h2}$SPEC5))(SPEC4)
where both specifications are equal to SPEC8,and SPEC6 is the value specification of PSPEC1*$_{h0}$PSPEC 3 in the following parameter passing diagrams
(1)-(3).

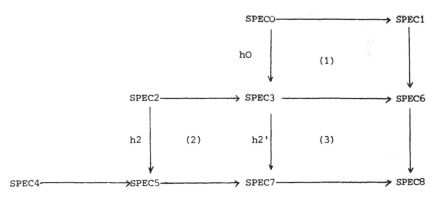

The canonical parameter passing morphism h2✱h0 is defined by

$$h2✱h0:=h2' \circ h0: SPEC0 \longrightarrow SPEC7$$

where h2' is induced from h2 (see Definition 6.1).

Proof: The main idea of the proof is that diagrams (1)-(3) above are push-outs in the category of specifications and specification morphisms (see 5.1) which can be combined in different ways:

It is well-known from category theory (see /AM 75/, /HS 73/, /ML 71/ that the composition of pushouts is again a pushout, i.e. with diagrams (1) and (3) is also (1)+(3) and with (2) and (3) is also (2)+(3) pushout. Combining one way we have

$$SPEC6=SPEC1✱_{h0}SPEC3(SPEC2) \qquad\qquad (1) \text{ is pushout}$$
$$SPEC8=SPEC6✱_{h2}SPEC5(SPEC4) \qquad\qquad (2)+(3) \text{ is pushout}$$

and combining the other way we have

$$SPEC7=(SPEC3✱_{h2}SPEC5)(SPEC4) \qquad\qquad (2) \text{ is pushout}$$
$$SPEC8=(SPEC1✱_{h2'\circ h0}SPEC7)(SPEC4) \qquad\qquad (1)+(3) \text{ is pushout}$$

Hence we obtain by substitution

$$((SPEC1✱_{h0}SPEC3)✱_{h2}SPEC5)(SPEC4)=(SPEC1✱_{h2✱h0}(SPEC3✱_{h2}SPEC5))(SPEC4)$$

which is (see remark) the desired result.   □

7.2   COROLLARY (COMPATIBILITY OF COMPOSITION AND ACTUALIZATION)

Standard actualization of composite parameterized specifications is equal to iterated standard actualization of parameterized specifications. In more detail we have:

Given persistent parameterized specifications

$$PSPEC1=\langle SPEC0,SPEC1\rangle \quad \text{and} \quad PSPEC3=\langle SPEC2,SPEC3\rangle$$

an actual specification SPEC5 and parameter passing morphisms

$$h0:SPEC0 \longrightarrow SPEC3 \quad \text{and} \quad h2:SPEC2 \longrightarrow SPEC5.$$

Then there is a canonical parameter passing morphism $h2✱h0:SPEC0 \longrightarrow SPEC7$ such that we have

$$(SPEC1✱_{h0}SPEC3)(SPEC5)_{h2}=SPEC1(SPEC3(SPEC5)_{h2})_{h2✱h0}$$

where h2✱h0 is defined as in 7.1.

Proof: Take SPEC4=∅ in Theorem 7.1 and use Lemma 6.2

$$(SPEC1✱_{h0}SPEC3)(SPEC5)_{h2}=((SPEC1✱_{h0}SPEC3)✱_{h2}SPEC5)(∅) \qquad\qquad \text{(by 6.2)}$$

$$=SPEC1*_{h2*h0}(SPEC3*_{h2}SPEC5))(\emptyset) \qquad \text{(by 7.1)}$$

$$=SPEC1(SPEC3*_{h2}SPEC5(\emptyset))_{h2*h0} \qquad \text{(by 6.1)}$$

$$=SPEC1(SPEC3(SPEC5)_{h2})_{h2*h0} \qquad \text{(by 6.1)}$$

$\square$

7.3 REMARK (ITERATED PARAMETER PASSING)

The associativity of the composition of parameterized specifications (Thm. 7.1) and the compatibility of composition and standard actualization (Thm. 7.2) are the basic results to show that the result of iterated parameter passing is independent of the "evaluation strategy" in which parameterized and standard parameter passing are applied. Instead of a formal treatment of this phenomenon let us consider the following example:

Assume that we have given the parameterized specifications bintree(data) string(param), matrix(ring) the actual specification int and parameter passing morphisms h1,h2, and h3 which are passing consistent, i.e. we have given an "iterated parameter passing situation" defined by the slim arrows in the following diagram. An evaluation strategy consists of an arbitrary

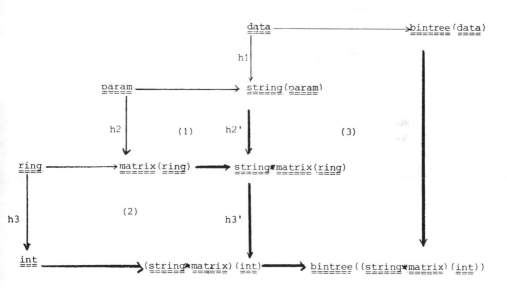

sequence of the following two steps until no more step can be applied

PARAMETERIZED STEP: Apply parameterized parameter passing to one triangle (except the left) and consider the new iterated parameter passing situation resp. value specification.

STANDARD STEP: Apply standard parameter passing to the left most triangle and consider the new iterated parameter passing situation resp. value specification.

The result of iterated parameter passing with respect to a given evaluation strategy is the resulting value specification.

In our example we first have applied a parameterized step (1) and then two standard steps (2) and (3). Note that the parameter passing morphism for (3) is h3'·h2'·h1 where h2' and h3' are the induced from h2 and h3 respectively. This is a "mixed strategy". The "call by value" strategy consists of standard steps only applied from left to right leading to the value speci fication bintree(string(matrix(int))).The "call by name" strategy consists of parameterized steps applied from right to left followed by one standard step such that we obtain the value specification ((bintree*string)*matrix)(int).

7.4   COROLLARY (INDEPENDENCE OF STRATEGIES)

The result of iterated parameter passing is independent of the choice of the evaluation strategy applied to a given iterated parameter passing situation.

Proof: Iterated application of Theorem 7.1 and 7.2.

☐

CONCLUSION

Let us start with a short summary of the main constructions and results in this paper.

A parameterized specification PSPEC=⟨SPEC,SPEC1⟩ consists of a pair of specifications where the parameter declaration SPEC is included in the target specification SPEC1. Parameter passing from the formal parameter SPEC to an actual parameter SPEC' is given by a "specification morphism" $f:SPEC \longrightarrow SPEC'$. The value specification SPEC1' is more or less a "renaming" of the target specification SPEC1 where the SPEC-parts of SPEC1 are renamed by the corresponding SPEC'-parts of the actual parameter. Mathematically SPEC1' is the pushout object of SPEC1 and SPEC' via f in the category CATSPEC of algebraic specifications and specification morphisms. Moreover, we can also pass parameterized specifications as actual parameters leading to parameterized value specifications. The first important result is correctness of parameter passing (see Theorems 5.2 and 6.3) meaning that the semantical conditions "parameter protection" and "passing compatibility" (see 4.3 and 6.1) are satisfied if the parameterized specifications are persistent. The benefit of correct parameter passing is not only economy in presentation but we also have automatically induced correctness of all the value specifications provided that the parameterized specification and all the actual specifications are correct (see Theorems 5.3 and 6.4). This is a most important property in order to build up larger data types and software systems from small pieces in a correct way. Similar to procedures in programming languages parameterized specifications promise to become one of the most important structuring principle for the design of software systems. The third important result is based on the associativity of the composition of parameterized specifications (see Theorem 7.1): We are able to show that all different evaluation strategies - including "call by name" and "call by value" - for iterated parameter passing situations lead to the same result (see 7.4). Technically all the results are based on the EXTENSION LEMMA in 5.1 which allows to extend specifications and also functors.

The theory in this paper is called "the basic algebraic case" because it is the common basis for several other approaches like those in /ADJ 80/, /Ehr 81/, /Gan 80a+b/, /HR 81/ and /Kla 80/.

It is also closely related to the concept of parameterized specifications in /Rei 80/ and /Hup 81/ and to the procedures in CLEAR (see /BG 80/) where, however, the semantics is not functorial. It seems possible to study semantical conditions like "actual parameter protection" and "passing compatibility" in these more general frameworks allowing in addition to algebraic equations "initial restrictions" and "constraints" respectively (see below).

Although our theory in the basic algebraic case seems to be very smooth it turns out that the applicability to common data types in software practice is somewhat limited. In several applications we need an equality predicate on the formal parameter, like EQ:data data $\longrightarrow$ bool in the parameterized specification set(data). In order to show correctness of such specifications we need requirements for the operation EQ making sure that EQ is really an equality predicate on all admissable parameter algebras A, i.e. $EQ_A(d,d')=\underline{if}$ d=d' $\underline{then}$ TRUE $\underline{else}$ FALSE for all d,d'$\in A_{data}$. Unfortunately there seem to be no equations but only negative conditional axioms to assure this property, e.g. EQ(X,X)=TRUE and $X\neq Y\Longrightarrow EQ(X,Y)$=FALSE (see /ADJ 78/). Moreover we have to make sure that the bool-part of A consists exactly of two distinct elements TRUE and FALSE. The most convenient way to obtain these properties is the requirement "initial(bool)" which makes sure that the bool-part of A is isomorphic to the initial boolean algebra T_{bool}.

Such requirements are called "initial restrictions" in /Rei 80/ and "constraints" in /BG 80/ which become special cases of our more general notion of requirements. In /Ehr 81/ a set R is called "set of requirements" on a specification SPEC if for all r$\in$R there is a well-defined subclass VALID(r) of all SPEC-algebras. This very general definition is easy to handle and allows also to state all kinds of predicate formulas as requirements, especially the negative conditional axioms for EQ as given above. Hence a parameterized specification of set(data) with requirements can be given as in Example 2.5 where, however, the equation EQ(X,X)=TRUE in the parameter declaration is replaced by the following

REQUIREMENTS:

    initial(bool)

    EQ(X,X)=TRUE

    $X\neq Y\Longrightarrow$ EQ(X,Y)=FALSE

This parameterized specification set(data) with requirements is similar to that in /ADJ 78/ except of different requirement handling which has significant consequences for the semantics.

Another important feature of parameterized specifications with requirements is the possibility to specify bounded data types such as arrays of fixed bounded length B. The bound B, however, is supposed to be a parameter which may take different values in different actual parameters. In most cases it seems to be convenient to construct the specification of bounded types as an extension of bounded natural numbers $\underline{\underline{nat}}$ ($\underline{\underline{bound}}$) where $\underline{\underline{nat}}$ is some correct specification of natural numbers with operations O, SUCC and ADD.

8.1   EXAMPLE ($\underline{\underline{nat}}$($\underline{\underline{bound}}$))

PARAMETER DECLARATION: $\underline{\underline{bound}}$ =

    $\underline{\underline{nat}}$ +

        opns: BOUND: $\longrightarrow$ $\underline{nat}$

REQUIREMENTS:

    initial($\underline{\underline{nat}}$)

TARGET SPECIFICATION: $\underline{\underline{nat}}$ ($\underline{\underline{bound}}$)

    $\underline{\underline{bound}}$ +

        sorts: $\underline{bnat}$

        opns: MOD: $\underline{nat}$ $\longrightarrow$ $\underline{bnat}$

                  MODO: $\longrightarrow$ $\underline{bnat}$

                  MODSUCC: $\underline{bnat}$ $\longrightarrow$ $\underline{bnat}$

                  MODADD: $\underline{bnat}$ $\underline{bnat}$ $\longrightarrow$ $\underline{bnat}$

        eqns: MOD(ADD(BOUND,n))=MOD(n)

                  MODO=MOD(O)

                  MODSUCC(MOD(n))=MOD(SUCC(n))

                  MODADD(MOD(n1),MOD(n2))=MOD(ADD(n1,n2))

Remark: Note that the requirement initial($\underline{\underline{nat}}$) implies that BOUND picks out some well-defined natural number B. Without the initiality requirement BOUND may define a new value which does not correspond to any natural number. The semantics of our specification is $I\!N$ mod B (natural numbers modulo B).

In /Ehr 81/ it is shown that all the results of this paper can be extended to the case with requirements. The main idea is to prove an R-EXTENSION LEMMA which generalizes the EXTENSION LEMMA 5.1 of this paper to the case of para-meterized specifications with requirements R and "passing consistent" morphisms. Up to now we have only considered the initial algebra approach where the semantics of parameterized types is given by free constructions. In /Kla 80/ it is shown how to make use of inductively specified operations and in /Gan 80a+b/ how to extend the basic algebraic case from initial to final algebra semantics: The main idea in /Gan 80a+b/ is to replace the free construction

$F: \underline{Alg}_{SPEC} \longrightarrow \underline{Alg}_{SPEC1}$ by a quotient functor $CF: \underline{Alg}_{SPEC} \longrightarrow \underline{Alg}_{SPEC1}$ of F such that persistency of F is equivalent to persistency of CF. Theorem 1 in /Gan 80b/ shows that if CF is persistent, then it is the right adjoint (cofree functor) of the forgetful functor, provided we take the subcategory of SPEC1-algebras B that are generated by their parameter part as the range of CF. Moreover Theorem 5 in /Gan 80b/ shows that the extension CF' of a persistent cofree functor CF along a passing consistent parameter passing morphism is again a persistent cofree functor. This allows to replace in all those definitions, constructions and results of Sections 2 to 7 where persistency is assumed the free construction F by the cofree construction CF. Hence we obtain a final algebraic theory for parameterized specifications. Similar problems are studied in /HR 81/ for inequalities which is a special case of requirements. In /WB 80/ it is suggested to study also other semantics than the initial and final case. This might be extended to parameterized specifications provided that part 3 of the EXTENSION LEMMA remains valid.

Another important issue is the implementation of parameterized data types extending the algebraic implementation concept in /EKP 80/. A first more or less syntactical treatment is given in /Gan 80a/ where, however, a slightly different implementation concept is used. Abstract implementation and parameter substitution based on initially restricting algebraic theories (see /Rei 80/) are studied in /Hup 81/.

An interesting application of parameter passing with requirements is the identification of common subtypes in different specifications.
In CLEAR (see /BG 80/) identification of common subtypes is handled using general colimit constructions. This problem should become a special case of parameter passing such that no additional feature in syntax and semantics is needed.
Finally let us note that the algebraic concept of parameterized specifications is already used in the programming language MODLISP (see /Jen 79/) which is used for the implementation of the algebraic manipulation system NEWSPAD (see /JT 81/). NEWSPAD is an ambitious endeavor to structure a computer algebra system based on categories and functors, with user defined parameterized types (like matrix(ring) as in Example 3.2) playing a central role. Although their current work deals with models only (functions and representations are always given) one would hope that this work would employ specification in a more central way in future development.

9. BIBLIOGRAPHY

/ADJ 75/   (JAG,JWT, EGW, JBW)[+)]: Abstract data types as initial algebras and correctness of data representations; Proc. Conf. on Computer Graphics, Pattern Recognition and Data Structure, May 75, pp. 89-93

/ADJ 76/   (JWT, EGW, JBW)[+)]: Specification of abstract data types using conditional axioms, IBM Research Report RC-6214, Sept. 1976

/ADJ 76-78/   (JAG, JWT, EGW)[+)]: An initial algebra appraoch to the specification, correctness, and implementation of abstract data types, IBM Research Report RC-6487, Oct. 1976. Current Trends in Programming Methodology, IV: Data Structuring (R.T.Yeh,Ed.) Prentice Hall, New Jersey (1978), pp. 80-149

/ADJ 78/   (JWT, EGW, JBW)[+)]: Data Type Specification: parameterization and the power of specification techniques, Proc. SIGACT 10th Annual Symp. on Theory of Computing, May 1978, pp. 119-132

/ADJ 80/   (HE, HJK, JWT, EGW, JBW)[+)]: Parameterized data types in algebraic specification languages (short version), Proc. 7th ICALP Nordwijkerhout, July 1980: Lect. Not. in Comp. Sci.85 (1980), pp. 157-168

/AM 75/   Arbib, M.A., Manes, E.G.: Arrows, Structures and Functors: The categorical imperative, Academic Press, New York, 1975

/BG 77/   Burstall, R.M., Goguen, J.A.: Putting Theories together to make Specifications, Proc. 1977 IJCAI, MIT, Cambridge, MA, Aug. 1977

/BG 79/   --: Semantics of CLEAR, Working Note - Draft Version, Dept. of Artificial Intelligence, Edinburgh University, Jan. 1979

/BG 80/   --: The Semantics of CLEAR, a Specification Language, Proc. 1979 Copenhagen Winter School on Abstract Software Specifications (1980), Lect. Not. in Comp. Sci. (1980)

/Coh 65/   Cohn, P.M.: Universal Algebra, Harper and Row, New York, 1965

/Ehr 78/   Ehrich, H.-D.: On the theory of specification, implementation and parameterization of abstract data types, Research Report Dortmund 1978

/EL 79/   Ehrich, H.-D., Lohberger, V.G.: Constructing Specifications of Abstract Data Types by Replacements, Proc. Int. Workshop Graph Grammars and Appl. Comp. Sci. and Biology, Bad Honnef 1978, Lect. Not. in Comp. Sci. 73 (1979), pp. 180-191

+) ADJ-Authors: J.A. Goguen (JAG), J.W. Thatcher (JWT), E.G. Wagner (EGW), J.B. Wright (JBW)
     co-authors: H. Ehrig (HE), H.-J. Kreowski (HJK)

BIBLIOGRAPHY (cont'd)

/Ehr 81/   Ehrig, H.: Algebraic Theory of Parameterized Specifications
                with Requirements, Proc. 6th CAAP, Genova 81, Lect. Not. in
                Comp. Sci. 112 (1981), pp. 1-24

/EF 81/   Ehrig, H., Fey, W.: Methodology for the specification of
                software systems: From requirement specifications to algebraic
                design specifications, Proc. GI 81, München

/EK 80/   Ehrig, H., Kreowski, H.-J.: Kategorien und Funktoren, LV-
                Skript SS 1980, FB 20, TU Berlin (1980)

/EKP 77/   Ehrig, H., Kreowski, H.-J., Padawitz, P.: Some remarks con-
                cerning correct specification and implementation of abstract
                data types: Technical University of Berlin, Report 77-13,
                August 1977

/EKP 78/   --: Stepwise specification and implementation of abstract
                data types: Technical University of Berlin, Report, Nov. 1977
                Proc. 5th ICALP, Udine, July 1978: Lect. Not. in Comp. Sci.
                62 (1978), pp. 205-226

/EKP 80/   --: Algebraic Implementation of Abstract Data Types: Concept
                Syntax, Semantics, Correctness; Proc. 7th ICALP, Nordwijkerhout
                July 1980, Lect. Notes in Comp. Sci.85 (1980), pp.142-156

/Fey 81/   Fey, W.: Some Examples of Algebraic Specifications and Imple-
                mentations, Part 4, Technical University of Berlin,
                Report No. 81-   , 1981

/Flo 81/   Floyd, Ch.: Proc. 2nd German Chapter of The ACM-Meeting
                "Software Engineering - Entwurf und Spezifikation" (editor),
                Teubner Verlag 1981

/Gan 80a/   Ganzinger, H.: Parameterized Specifications: Parameter
                Passing and Implementation, version Sept. 1980, to appear in
                TOPLAS

/Gan 80b/   --: A final algebra semantics for parameterized specification
                draft version, UC Berkeley, November 1980

/GT 77/   Goguen, J.A., Tardo, J.: OBJ-0 preliminary users manual;
                UCLA, Los Angeles, CA., 1977

/Gra 68/   Graetzer, G.: Universal Algebra, Van Nostrand, Princeton,
                N.J. 1968

/Gut 75/   Guttag, J.V.: The specification and application to programmin
                of abstract data types; Univ. of Toronto, Comp. Systems Re-
                search Group, Technical Report CSRG-59, Sept. 1975

BIBLIOGRAPHY (cont'd)

/Gut 76/   --: Abstract data types and the development of data structures;
                supplement to Proc. Conf. on Data Abstraction, Definition, and
                Structure, SIGPLAN Notices 8, March 1976

/HR 81/   Hornung, G., Raulefs, P.: Initial and Terminal Algebra
                Semantics of Parameterized Abstract Data Type Specification
                with Inequalities, Proc. 6th CAAP, Genova 81, Lect. Not. in
                Comp. Sci. 112 (1981), pp. 224-237

/HS 73/   Herrlich, H., Strecker, G.: Category Theory, Allyn and Bacon,
                Rockleigh 1973

/Hup 81/   Hupbach, U.L.: Abstract Implementation and Parameter Sub-
                stitution, submitted to 3rd Hungarian Comp. Sci. Conf.,
                Budapest 1981

/Jen 79/   Jenks, R.D.: MODLISP: An Introduction, Lect. Not. in Comp.
                Sci. 72 (1979), pp. 466-480, new version in preparation

/JT 81/   Jenks, R.D., Trager, M.B.: A language for computer algebra,
                Proc. 1981 ACM Symp. on Symbolic and Algebraic Computation,
                August, 1981

/Kla 80/   Klaeren, H.A.: On Parameterized Abstract Software Modules
                using Inductively Specified Operations, Research Report TH
                Aachen Nr. 66, (1980)

/Kre 78/   Kreowski, H.-J.: Algebra für Informatiker; LV-Skript WS 78/79,
                FB 20, TU Berlin (1978)

/LSAS 77/   Liskov, B., Snyder, A., Atkonson, R., Schaffert, C.: Abstrac-
                tion Mechanisms in CLU; CACM 20, Nr. 8 (1977), pp. 564-576

/LZ 77/   Liskov, B., Zilles, St.: Programming with abstract data types;
                SIGPLAN Notices 9, Nr. 4 (1977), pp. 50-59

/ML 71/   MacLane, S.: Categories for the Working Mathematician;
                Springer Verlag, New York/Heidelberg/Berlin 1971

/Rei 80/   Reichel, H.: Initially Restricting Algebraic Theories, Proc.
                MFCS'80, Rydzyna, Sept. 1980, Lect. Not. in Comp. Sci. 88
                (1980), pp. 504-514

/Sco 62/   Scott, D.: Mathematical concepts in programming language
                semantics; Proc. AFIPS Spring Joint Comp. Conf., 1962, pp.225-234

/WB 80/   Wirsing, M., Broy, M.: Abstract Data Types as Lattices of
                Finitely Generated Models, Proc. MFCS'80, Rydzyna, Sept. 1980,
                Lect. Not. in Comp. Sci. 88 (1980), pp. 673-685

/WLS 76/   Wulf, W.A., London, R.L., Shaw, M.: An introduction to the
                construction and verification of Alphard programs: IEEE
                Transactions on Software Engineering SE 24 (1976), pp. 253-265

A Few Remarks on Putting Formal Specifications to
Productive Use

John Guttag
Laboratory for Computer Science
Massachusetts Institute of Technology
August, 1981

1. Introduction

Over the last few years specifications in general, and formal specifications in particular, hav
become "hot" topics of research. Most of the published work in this area has been centere
around one or another aspect of the presentation and evaluation of a particular specificatio
language or class of specification languages. In the two short talks given at the Aarhu
workshop on the specification of programs we tried to step back and take a somewhat broa
view of the role of formal specifications in the program development process. This view i
an outgrowth of problems we encountered in trying to apply our earlier work on forma
specifications.

As our understanding of the theoretical and linguistic aspects of formal specification
improved, we began to try to use them in developing interesting software. We ran int
serious problems doing this, and were eventually forced to conclude that the use of form
specifications was not helping us either to produce better software or to produce softwa
more efficiently. The difficulty was not that we encountered things that were intrinsicall
difficult to specify, but that

> a) We found ourselves uncertain about how we should use formal specifications in th
> ongoing process of developing relatively large programs, and

> b) We found ourselves getting bogged down by the clerical details involved i
> managing and maintaining the consistency of large specifications.

In this note we discuss both the various uses to which we believe one can productively p
formal specifications, and also the need for sophisticated tools to assist in the constructio
and use of them. The reader should be warned that what we have to say on these subjects

----

The work reported on here was partially supported by the National Science Foundatio
under grant MCS78-01798 and by an Office of Naval Research Contract with DARP
funding.

ery preliminary. For this we do not apologize. This note, like the talks given at Aarhus, is designed to provide a thought-provoking departure point for future work in the area, not a set of well-formulated results. By the time it appears in print, our views on a number of the issues raised may well have changed. We do apologize for our failure to include any cferences in this rather short and idiosyncratic note. We have certainly profitted from our tudy of the work of many others, e.g., Burstall, Goguen, Jones, Musser, Parnas and Zilles. Finally, we would like to point out that while we take full responsibility for the contents of this note, our thinking in this area has been heavily influenced by extensive conversations vith Jim Horning of Xerox PARC and Jeannette Wing of MIT.

Some vocabulary

symptomatic of our problems, was our use of the same words to mean a number of different things. So we begin this note with some informal (and occasionally circular) definitions:

A *specification language* is a notation for presenting specifications. A *formal specification language* is a precisely defined unambiguous notation. BNF is a suitable specification language for unambiguously specifying (possibly ambiguous) grammars. A programming language is a language for unambiguously specifying programs.

A *specification* is a description of a specificand set. E.g., a grammar is a specification of a formal language; a program is a specification of a set of computations.

A *specificand set* is the set of objects conforming to a specification. The specificand set of the grammar G is the language, i.e., the set of sentences, L(G). The specificand set of a rogram is the set of computations one could get by running it. We will call a member of the specificand set a *specificand.*

Notice that the mapping from a specification to its specificand set is determined by the emantics associated with the specification language. One might, for example, consider the pecificand set of an algebraic specification of an abstract type to be a set of algebras, a set of theorems (a theory), or a set of programs. One might consider the specificand set of a higher vel language program to be a set of functions, a set of computations, or a set of machine nguage programs.

Given a precisely defined specification language the mapping from specification to pecificand set is one to one, while that from specificand set to specification is one to many. specificand set can thus be viewed as an abstraction from all of the members of the nfinite) set of specifications that could be used to describe it. The specificand set can also e viewed as an abstraction from all of its elements.

3. On the uses of formal specifications

3.1. What, when, and who

If we wish to understand better the various uses of formal specifications, we need to try to answer the following questions:

a) What is accomplished by constructing formal specifications of programs?

b) What is accomplished by the existence of a formal specification of a program?

c) When should they be written?

d) By whom should they be written?

e) By whom should they be read?

In trying to answer these questions it became apparent to us that there was not a single set of answers. In particular, it became clear that without explicitly acknowledging it we had been using "specifications" in at least three distinct ways: as local specifications, as system specifications, and as structural specifications. We have been successfully writing local specifications for some time, know quite a bit about them, and will discuss them in some detail. We have almost no experience with the successful application of system or structural specifications, we don't have much to say about them, and what we do have to say is highly speculative.

3.2. Local specifications

A local specification describes the observable behavior of single program module -- either a procedural abstraction or a data abstraction. It is local specifications that appear most often in the literature on formal specifications, e.g., specifications of stacks, sets, factorials, etc. A distinguishing characteristic of these specifications is that they are small.

Typically a local specification is written after the crucial step of software design, the breaking down of the software into relatively small independent modules. They are written either by system designers or by programmers, and are read primarily by programmers. Constructing them serves to focus our attention in a systematic way upon local decisions that remain to be made. Once they are written, local specifications serve to document local decisions and provide the information necessary to perform unit testing (or verification) of individual modules.

We believe that at present there is little research left to be done in the area of local specification. It is time for those of us working in the area of formal specifications to devote our time to promoting the use of local specifications, rather than to making ever less important refinements of our methods and languages.

3.2.1. The form of local specifications

We believe that almost all of the issues raised in this note are specification language independent. Neverthess, we introduce a particular specification language here in order facilitate the discussion of some of these issues.

A local specification of a type abstraction has the form:

> *Type abstraction* ⟨type name⟩ *exports* ⟨list of procedure names⟩
>
> > *Auxiliary specification*
> >
> > > ⟨list of type specifications⟩
> >
> > *end auxiliary*
> >
> > *Exported procedures*
> >
> > > ⟨list of specifications of procedural abstractions⟩
>
> *end* ⟨type name⟩.

ecification of a procedural abstraction has the form:

> *Procedural abstraction* ⟨procedure name⟩
>
> > *Auxiliary specification*
> >
> > > ⟨list of type specifications⟩
> >
> > *end auxiliary*
> >
> > ⟨procedure heading⟩
> >
> > ⟨requires clause⟩
> >
> > ⟨effects clause⟩
>
> *end* ⟨procedure name⟩.

he factorizafion of a specification into two levels is very important. The intent is to achieve separation of concerns. In the specification of the exported procedures we define the iterface to the specified module that is available to other modules in the program. In the uxiliary specifications we define a set of relatively simple abstract concepts. These are efined in order to make the specifications of the exported procedures easier to read and asier to write. One might, for example, first define the real numbers and then use this uxiliary specification to define the arithmetic operations provided by a particular floating oint package.

1 our examples we use algebraic axioms for our auxiliary specifications, and pre/post-ondition specifications for the specification of the exported procedures. The form and eaning of the algebraic specifications are independent of the programming language in

which the module being specified is to be implemented. The form and meaning of the pre/post-condition specifications are not. This difference reflects the separation of concerns referred to earlier. In the algebraic specifications we define a closed system of abstractions. In the pre- and post-condition specifications we describe the effect of calling the procedures from elsewhere in the program in which the module is embedded. We will see analogous dependencies on the external environment in system and structural specifications.

3.2.2. An example local specification

A specification of a data abstraction for a CLU program follows. In it we have used the convention of prefacing all of the functions specified in the auxiliary definition section with a #. We have written the specifications of the exported procedures in a somewhat unconventional notation. We have chosen this notation because we expect programmers to be the most common readers of local specifications. The notation appears informal, but given a formal specification of CLU it can be translated into conventional predicate calculus notation.

Data type BoundedIntSet *exports* create, insert, delete, ismember, choose

Auxiliary definitions

operators:

#empty:	Integer	--> BoundedIntSet
#insert:	BoundedIntSet X Integer	--> BoundedIntSet
#delete:	BoundedIntSet X Integer	--> BoundedIntSet
#ismember:	BoundedIntSet X Integer	--> Boolean
#size:	BoundedIntSet	--> Integer
#maxsize:	BoundedIntSet	--> Integer

axioms:
for all s:#BoundedIntSet, i,i',n:Integer

$\#delete(\#empty(n),i) == \#empty(n)$
$\#delete(\#insert(s,i),i') == $ *if* i=i'
    then #delete(s,i')
    else #insert(#delete(s,i'),i)
$\#ismember(\#empty(n),i) == $ false
$\#ismember(\#insert(s,i),i') == $ *if* i=i'
    then true
    else #ismember(s,i')
$\#size(\#empty(n)) == 0$
$\#size(\#insert(s,i)) == $ *if* #ismember(s,i)
    then #size(s)
    else 1+ #size(s)
$\#maxsize(\#empty(n)) == n$
$\#maxsize(\#insert(s,i)) == \#maxsize(s)$

% For those readers unfamiliar with CLU: CLU has a LISP-like semantics in which objects are allocated from a heap, and a value can be bound to each object. Unlike LISP, a type is also associated with each object. The occurrence of the word "signal" in the specification refers to CLU's mechanism for raising exceptions. %

create = *proc* (i:Integer) *returns* (BoundedIntSet)
    pre i>0
    post returns a new object of type intSet with value #empty(i)

% From this we can deduce that if the procedure create is called with a postive integer argument: 1) It will not modify its argument. 2) It will return an object that did not previously exist. 3) The value to which the returned object will be bound has the properties of the value denoted by #empty(i) in the auxiliary specification.%

insert = *proc* (s:BoundedIntSet, i:Integer) *signals* (BoundedIntSetOverflow)
    post if #size(#insert(s,i)) < #maxsize(s)
          then s <- #insert(s,i)
          else signal BoundedIntSetOverflow

% By convention the occurrence of a formal parameter on the left of "<-" denotes the value bound to the object to which that formal is bound on exit from the procedure, and the occurrence of a formal anywhere else denotes the value bound to the object to which that formal is bound on entry to the procedure. The sub-expression "s <- #insert(s,i)" thus defines a relation between the value bound to the object denoted by s on exit from insert and the values bound to the objects denoted by s and i on entry to insert. This convention avoids the need to introduce large numbers of "fresh" variables in which to "save" the initial values of formal parameters. %

delete = *proc* (s:BoundedIntSet, i:Integer)
    post s <- #delete(s,i)

ismember = *proc* (s:BoundedIntSet, i:Integer) *returns* (Boolean)
    post returns an object of type Boolean with value #ismember(s,i)

choose = *proc* (s:BoundedIntSet) *returns* (Integer) *signals*(isempty)
    post if #size(s) > 0
              then returns an object of type Integer with value i such that
                #ismember(s,i)
            else signals(isempty)

ndedIntSet

3.3. System specifications

A system (or requirements) specification describes the observable behavior of a comple
system. That is to say it describes the interactions of a software system with the environmen
in which it is used. Some portion of it, therefore, must be written in a language depender
upon the user environment, e.g., the language of keystrokes and pixels or the language of
receptors and output lines. In theory, there is no essential difference between a syster
specification and a local specification. Each describes the observable behavior of some pa
of a program. Practically speaking, however, they are enormously different in almost a
respects. Failure to recognize this difference has had a deleterious effect on work in th
area.

Perhaps the most fundamental difference is the ease with which one can talk about th
interactions of the specificand with its environment. In constructing a local specification w
are always dealing with a well understood and easily formalized environment.
constructing a system specification deciding how to specify interactions with the environme
can be an overwhelmingly difficult problem.

A second important difference is one of size. System specifications tend to be much larg
than local specifications, and the obvious analogy is a valid one: The process of constructir
large specifications is related to the process of constructing small specifications, as th
process of constructing large programs is related to the process of constructing sma
programs. We have recognized that specific difficulties of size make the process
constructing large programs qualitatively different from the process of constructing sma
ones. We have recognized that programming languages eminently well suited to th
construction of small programs, e.g., APL, are not necessarily well suited to the constructic
of large programs. There is every reason to believe that the same problems will arise
scaling up techniques and languages used in constructing local specifications to techniqu
and languages for constructing system specifications. The key issues here will be t
development of systematic ways of putting specifications together, of modifyi
specifications, of analyzing partially complete specifications, and of managing large amour
of formal information.

I have not seen any convincing examples of the productive application of a formal syste
specification to the production of useful software. Nevertheless this is an area in which
the long run formal specifications may prove extremely useful. The primary potent
benefit of writing a system specification is to come to an understanding of the problem to
solved before beginning to design software to solve it. In order to realize this benefit we w
have to construct system specifications that can be read both by software designers and
clients who understand the intended application. My expectation is that this will be
extremely difficult job that will probably require highly trained specification specialis

Structural specification ⟨type name⟩ *exports* ⟨list of procedure names⟩

    Auxiliary specification

        ⟨list of structural specifications⟩

    end auxiliary

    Exported procedures

        ⟨list of specifications of procedural abstractions⟩

end ⟨type name⟩.

Here, a structural specification is a rooted directed graph. In a complete specification the exported procedures of the root node would be defined in a language related to the environment in which the system being designed was to be used. The exported procedures of other nodes could be defined using any formal language the specifier found convenient. Our expectation is that most system designers will find it convenient not to specify the exported procedures of the root node.

. On tools

.1. Why we want to build tools

It may indeed be true that "It is a poor workman who blames his tools," but it is also true that "It is a foolish workman who does not appreciate good tools." As we suggested in the introduction, we believe that inadequate tools are a significant bottleneck in the application of formal specifications of programs. Following Jim Horning, we think of tools as belonging to one of two general categories: mental tools or metal tools. Over the last few years we have been concerned exclusively with the development of our mental tools.

The mental tools we have developed to aid in constructing specifications include specification methods (the global strategy we use in constructing specifications), specification techniques (local tactics and tricks), and most importantly, our experience. The value of this last mental tool is brought home strongly to us whenever we attempt to teach someone to write formal specifications. The specification language we use can be taught in a day, but we find that it takes weeks for someone to become competent, and months for them to approach the level of experienced specifiers. The difficulty of teaching people to write good specifications has been one of the most serious bottlenecks in expanding the utility of formal specifications. In recent months we have turned our attention to the development of software (a relatively new kind of metal) tools that we hope will alleviate this problem.

We believe that our work on software tools will support the application of our mental tools in several ways. Firstly, the attempt to construct a tool to improve the efficiency and effectiveness with which one carries out a task often serves to deepen our understanding of the mental processes used in carrying out that task. The design of various programming languages, for example, has contributed to our understanding of programming methodology.

3.4. Structural specifications

A structural (design) specification is a high level description of some aspects of a program. Whereas the specificand sets of local and system specifications are restricted to specificands that obey certain constraints on their externally observable behavior, the specificand set of structural specification is restricted to specificands that obey certain constraints on the externally observable behavior and on their internal structure. The purpose of system and local specifications is to define important aspects of the interactions of a system or a module with its environment. While a system or local specification may contain internal structure that structure is purely expository. A particular internal structure should be chosen entirely on the basis of its effect on the ease with which the specification can be read and maintained. The purpose of a structural specification, on the other hand, is to guide the construction of a system. It therefore must deal with the internals of the system. It should contain information both about the behavior of the parts from which the system is to be built and about the way in which those parts are to be assembled. A particular internal structure must be chosen at least partially on the basis of its effect on the efficiency of specificand.

The most useful time to write a structural specification is as one tackles the often difficult problem of deciding upon the way a large software system is to be modularized. By forcing the designers to be relatively precise in describing the modularization, a structural specification serves both to guide and to document the design. The existence of such documentation can serve the dual purpose of permitting a meaningful pre-implementation design review, and of providing unambiguous guidance to implementors.

3.4.1. The form of structural specifications

In theory, there need be no difference in the surface structure of the specification language used to write system and structural specifications. The only necessary difference is in the interpretation one gives to a specification written in the language -- whether or not one abstracts from the internal structure of the specification to the behavior defined at the outermost level. Practically speaking, however, it is highly likely that one will want to use languages with different surface structures. In fact, since the primary readers of structural specifications will be system designers and implementors, we believe that structural specifications should look more like local specifications than like system specifications.

One form a structural specification might take is:

This happens because we design tools in the knowledge that their use will influence the way in which users approach various tasks. To understand what this effect will be, we must think carefully about how we believe these tasks ought to be approached.

Secondly, if we are successful in constructing software tools that encourage people to approach the tasks of writing and using formal specifications in what we believe to be a productive way, the tools will be a valuable asset in teaching people our mental tools. We hope that it will not only impose some structure on the way people approach these tasks, but that it will also provide a mechanism through which the knowledge we have gained through experience can be passed on to others.

Thirdly, we hope that having a good set of software tools available will allow us to concentrate our energy and ingenuity where it is most necessary. That is to say we hope to save both expert and novice users the trouble of performing the surprisingly large amount of routine work involved in writing and reading specifications.

4.2. The dangers of building and having tools

The are certain dangers inherent both in building and in using software tools. The enshrinement of a method or technique in code gives it a certain permanence. Since the tools we use have a significant effect on the way we go about our work, the construction and subsequent use of bad tools can tend to lock us into unfortunate ways of doing things. That is to say the construction and spread of software tools that encourage people to use inappropriate mental tools can have long-lasting and unfortunate effects.

Considering our lack of experience in using formal specifications, it is inevitable that our tools will incorporate some bad ideas. One of the reasons we are interested in building tools is to provide an environment in which our ideas can be rigorously tested. We hope that we will have the good sense to carefully evaluate the effect our tools have upon the way we work, and modify or even discard them as appropriate.

4.3. The tools we are working on

We have given some thought to tools for writing specifications, reading specifications, and reasoning about the relation of specifications to other formal objects (e.g., to programs). We have decided to concentrate our attention on the first two of these. Furthermore, we have decided to concentrate initially on local specifications. The two main components of the system we plan to build will be a specification library and a specification editor. We do not describe them in detail here. That will wait until they have been implemented and evaluated.

Veteran specifiers tend to begin by searching their memory for similar specification problems, and than trying to decide which aspects of previous specifications can be usefully applied to the current one. One of the great problems for neophyte specifiers is that they don't have an extensive repertoire to build upon. In order to ameliorate this problem, we wish to build a library in which one can efficiently search for specifications that may prove helpful. We are not very far along in the design of this library.

We are quite far along in the development of our specification editor. The first design
complete, and implementation is well under way. The primary functions performed by th
editor are:

Supplying templates -- These are the basic building blocks of specifications,

Generation of redundant information -- Information that will make the specificatio
easier to read,

Consistency checking -- Our goal is to catch mistakes early. Experience indicates th
superficial errors, e.g., type errors, are often indicative of serious underlyir
confusion, and catching them early is a valuable service,

Keeping track of missing information -- Supplying the user with a list of things th
still need to be done, e.g., inconsistencies to be resolved or what information
necessary to complete a specification,

Specification to specification mappings -- A collection of syntactic mechanisms f
doing semantically significant things, e.g., abstracting, renaming an operation, addi
properties, or modifying a signature.

A SPECIFICATON LANGUAGE.

by

Ib Holm Sørensen

Programming Reseach Group, Oxford University

ABSTRACT

This paper gives an informal presentation of the *language* currently used at the Programming Research Group, Oxford University for documenting the specification and the design of computer systems. The language is an extension of conventional set theoretical notation. The extensions are simple syntactical conventions and shorthands, which are introduced in order to improve the writebility and readability of specifications. The main aim in the development of this new language has been to provide a uniform notation and a formal framework for reasoning and proving properties about computer systems. The language (in its current form) has been shown to meet this aim (e.g. [Sufrin,1]).

1. INTRODUCTION.

The tools and methods used in the creation of computerised systems are being intensively studied by many researchers with the aim of improving our capability for constructing 'good' computer systems. The quality of such systems depends to a large extent on the methods used for documention during the development process.

The purpose for documentation

The *documentation* of a system has three functions: firstly, it identifies the *needs* which the system is intended to fulfil; secondly, it specifies the decisions taken by the designers of the system as to *how* those needs are to be fulfilled; and thirdly, it gives a detailed description of how the design decisions are realised. The documentation of the needs must be *precise* in order for it to serve as a basis for a contract between the customer and the supplier. The documentation of the design and the realisation must be precise in order to *test* and *verify* whether a suggested implementation fulfills that contract. Furthermore, since the *needs* will change over time it is important that all parts of the documentation (including the programs which document the realisation) are easy to modify.

The methods used

These concerns have inspired the development of numerous methodologies for the creation of software. Current techniques use *informal languages* or *diagrams* as description tools for documenting the requirements, the design decisions and the structure of the realisation. The disadvantage of such techniques lies in the ambiguity inherent in the notational framework. Among other things, this ambiguity makes it impossible to *formally test* a design against a requirement specification, or a realisation against the design decisions (*program verification*). *Theoretical* or *formal* tools which do not have these drawbacks have been proposed, but system developers are reluctant to use such formal methods because they are claimed to be inadequate for the documentation of *real systems* – a claim which is understandable since their usefulness has yet to be demonstrated on large commercial products. However, it is incontestable that formal methods are necessary, since only the use of unambiguous formal descriptions enables us to *verify* whether decisions taken in the development process are consistent with the original specification of the needs.

A formal approach

For a specification to play a useful role in the *development* of systems, statements in the specification must be expressed in a form which is independent of any subsequent realisation, i.e. the statements should only involve *abstract* concepts. Furthermore, to be of any use at all, the statements must be *unambiguous*, so that all readers of the specification (including the author) reach exactly the same understanding of the problem. These points give rise to the requirement for a language or notation in which abstract concepts can be unambiguously expressed. Since the main concern of mathematics is the precise formulation of abstract concepts, it seems appropriate to look to this discipline for a formal notational framework.

Set Theory

The formal language described here is based on *Set Theory*. This theory has the advantage of being the branch of mathematics which is the most intuitively accessible, while being sufficiently powerful; this is important if specifications are to be used (and read) by other than highly skilled mathematicians. Section 2 gives an informal overveiw of our Set theoretical notation.

Abstract structures

Experience shows, however, that this notation is most unwieldy as a language for specifying practical systems, because of the complexity that comes from the large number of concepts involved. In order to manage this kind of complexity we use abstract structures (called SCHEMAS), which permit the encapsulation (or grouping) of several concepts into a single *named* structure. These structures can be viewed as pieces of text. Using the names of structures, instead of the structures themselves in statements about a system simplifies the

ormal text and increases readability without any loss of detail whatsoever, as the abstracted
detail can be recovered by replacing the names with the structures they denote. In order
to enhance the applicability of such schemas their definitions may be parameterised so that
the same schema may be instantiated in different contexts. The *Schema notation* is introduced
in section 3

Extensibility

An important characteristic of the approach to system specification presented in this paper
is the notion of *Extensibility*. The theoretical framework provided by elementary Set Theory
can be extended with user-defined theories (i.e. new axioms which may introduce new
constants or new operations). Success in formalising a system is often dependent on finding
a sufficiently powerful formal framework (theory) for expressing the statements and rules about
that system. Using an inappropriate theory will often lead to a confused and unreadable
description; the 'right' theory will provide the insight necessary and a sufficiently powerful
notational framework for a description to be clear and readable. Hence a specification exercise
will normally involve two distinct tasks. The first is to find the 'right' theory, the second is
to apply that theory to the given problem. In section 4 examples of extensions to the elementary
Set Theory will be given.

2. THE SET THEORETICAL BASIS.

This section is an overview of the basic notation of the proposed language. No attempt is
made to define the semantics of the constructs formally; this and succeeding subsections
are intended only to provide enough information about the language to permit discussion
about specifications written therein.

Sets and Operations on Sets.

The following expression denotes a particular subset of a set X, namely the set of elements
for which PRED holds,

$$\{ x:X \mid PRED(x) \} \qquad\qquad DEF \ (1)$$

where $PRED(x)$ stands for a predicate in which x appears free. This is a rewriting of the
classical form,

$$\{ x \mid x \in X \wedge PRED(x) \}$$

The set above is *non-empty* if and and only if

$$(\exists\ x\ :\ X\ |\ PRED(x)\ )$$

The construction of a set may take a special form, e.g. let $EXP(i)$, for all i in an index set I, denote an element of type X, then the following

$$\{\ EXP(i)\ |\ i\ :\ I\ \}$$

is a rewriting of

$$\{\ x\ :\ X\ |\ (\exists\ i\ :\ I)(\ x\ =\ EXP(i))\ \}$$

The explicit construction of a finite set is denoted as usual by enumerating its elements, as in

$$\{\ a,\ b,\ c,\ d\ \}$$

The following expressions denote, respectively, the set of all subsets of the set X and the set of all finite subsets of the set X

$$\mathbb{P}(X), \qquad \mathbb{F}(X)$$

The empty set is denoted by

$$\{\}$$

The number of elements in a finite set X is

$$card(X)$$

We shall use the standard set operations of union, intersection and difference as well as the inclusion and membership operators. They are denoted as usual by

$$\cup \qquad \cap \qquad - \qquad \subset \qquad \not\subset \qquad \subseteq \qquad \in \qquad \notin$$

Furthermore

$$\cup \qquad \cap$$

will be used as prefix operators to denote the distributed union and intersection respectively

onstruction of a subset of the Cartesian Product

$$X \times Y$$

ay be written

$$\{ \ x:X; \ y:Y \ | \ PRED(x,y) \ \}$$ DEF (2)

stead of

$$\{ (x,y.) \ | \ (x,y.) \ \in \ X \times Y \ \wedge \ PRED(x,y.) \ \}$$

he *introduction* (or the *type declaration*) of a variable x, which can only be bound to values
om the set X, is written,

$$x \ : \ X$$

ee the examples above)

particular element with the value EXP from

$$\{ \ x:X \ | \ PRED(x) \ \}$$

an be written

$$(\mu \ x:X \ | \ PRED(x) \ ) \ (x = EXP)$$ DEF (3)

ovided, of course, that PRED(EXP) holds.

e designation of an *arbitrary* element from the same set is written

$$(\mu \ x \ : \ X \ | \ PRED(x))$$

ovided that

$$\{ \ x : X \ | \ PRED(x) \ \} \ \neq \ \{\}$$

Relations and Operations on Relations.

The set of all binary relations from a set X to a set Y is denoted by

$$X \leftrightarrow Y$$

which simply is a shorthand for

$$\mathbb{P}(\ X \times Y\ )$$

A finite relation can be constructed explicitly as follows,

$$\{\ x_1 \leftrightarrow y_1\ ,\ x_2 \leftrightarrow y_2\ ,\ x_1 \leftrightarrow y_2\ \}$$

which maps x_1 to y_1 and y_2 etc.

Given a binary relation R from X to Y, then the *image* of a subset SX of X through R i.e.

$$\{\ y : Y\ |\ (\exists\ x : SX)\ (x,y.) \in R\ \}$$

is denoted by

$$R(\ SX\ )$$

The *inverse* of a binary relation R from X to Y is denoted by

$$R^{-1}$$

Given a relation $R : X \leftrightarrow Y$ we have

$$R^{-1} \in Y \leftrightarrow X$$

and

$$dom(R)\ =\ R^{-1}(Y)$$
$$ran(R)\ =\ R(X)$$

which denote the *domain* and the *range* of the relation R.

When expressing the relationship between two elements we use the well-known form

$$x\ R\ y$$

which is syntactically equivalent to

$$y \in R(\{x\})$$

The *composition* of two binary relations

$$R_1 \quad : \quad X \leftrightarrow Y$$
$$R_2 \quad : \quad Y \leftrightarrow Z$$

is denoted by

$$R_2 \circ R_1$$

which is a relation from X to Z for which

$$(\forall\ x:X;\ z:Z\ )$$
$$x\ (R_2 \circ R_1)\ z\ \iff (\exists\ y:Y)(x\ R_1\ y\ \wedge\ y\ R_2\ z)$$

Functions.

The set of *partial* functions from X to Y is a subset of the set of all relations between X and Y, and is denoted by

$$X \nrightarrow Y$$

$$X \nrightarrow Y =$$
$$\{\ r:X{\leftrightarrow}Y\ \mid\ (\forall\ y:Y\ \mid\ y \in ran(r))\ r(r^{-1}(\{y\}))=\{y\}\ \}$$

A finite function can be constructed explicitly as follows.

$$\{\ x_1 \rightarrow y_1\ ,\ x_2 \rightarrow y_2\ ,\ x_5 \rightarrow y_6\ \}$$

which maps x_1 to y_1 etc.

The construction of a partial function 'f' from X to Y, which maps an element in X to an element of Y given by the expression EXP(x), might be written,

$$f = (\lambda\ x\ :\ X\ \mid\ PRED(x)\ )\ (EXP(x)) \qquad\qquad DEF\ (4)$$

Provided that

$$(\forall \; x:X \; | \; PRED(x)) \; (\; EXP(x) \; \epsilon \; Y \;)$$

we have

$$dom(f) \; = \; \{ \; x:X \; | \; PRED(x) \; \}$$

Given two predicates PRE and POST then we may construct a function h of type

$$h \; : \; \{x:X|PRE(x)\} \; \twoheadrightarrow \; Y$$

as follows

$$h \; = \; (\lambda \; x:X \; | \; PRE(x))$$
$$((\mu \; y:Y \; | \; POST(x,y)) \; (y \; = \; EXP(x)) \;) \qquad\qquad DEF \; (5)$$

We have

$$dom(h) \; \subseteq \; \{x:X| \; PRE(x)\}$$
$$ran(h) \; \subseteq \; \{y:Y| \; (\exists \; x:X|POST(x,y)) \; \}$$

The domain of h can determined to be

$$dom(h) \; = \; \{x:X| \; PRE(x)\} \; \cap$$
$$\{x:X \; | \; (\exists \; y:Y|POST(x,y) \;) \; y=EXP(x) \; \}$$

The set of *total functions* from X to Y is a subset of all partial functions over these sets and is denoted by

$$X \; \rightarrow \; Y$$

$$X \; \rightarrow \; Y \; = \; \{ \; f:X \twoheadrightarrow Y \; | \; dom(f) \; = \; X \; \}$$

Consider the definition of h above; if

$$(\forall \; x:X|PRE(x)) \; POST(x,EXP(x))$$

then h is a total function i.e.

$$h \; \epsilon \; \{x:X|PRE(x)\} \; \rightarrow \; Y$$

hence the 'transformations' denoted by

$$y = EXP(x)$$

can be considered as a realisation of the specification

$$\dot{n}_{spec} = (\lambda\ x:X\ \mid\ PRE(x))\ ((\mu\ y:Y)(POST(x,y))\ )$$

Given $f : X \rightarrow Y$, then the single element in the *image* of a single element through a function is written as usual,

$$f(x)$$

where

$$f(x) = (\mu\ y\ :\ Y)(y \in f(\{x\}))$$

We can define a function which maps a *non-empty* set into an *abitrary* element of that set as follows

$$\tau : \mathbb{P}(X) \twoheadrightarrow X;$$
$$\tau = (\lambda\ s:\mathbb{P}(X)\ \mid\ s \neq \{\})\ ((\mu\ x:X)(x \in s)\ )$$

. THE SCHEMA NOTATION.

The previous section provided a uniform notation for the implicit construction of sets, elements, relations and functions (see DEF(1-5))

The *syntactic* schema

$$a:\ A;\ b:\ B\ .\ .\ .\ z:\ Z\ \mid\ predicate(a,b,..,z)$$

appears in the characterisation of sets and of the domain and range of functions.

This schema is also used (as above) in the quantified expressions of the Predicate Calculus. e.g. the expressions.

$$(\exists\ x:X\ \mid\ PRED(x))$$
$$(\forall\ x:X\ \mid\ PRED(x))\ (EXP(x)\ \in\ Y)$$

are rewritings of

$$(\exists \ x) \ (x \ \epsilon \ X \ \wedge \ \text{PRED}(x) \ ),$$

and

$$(\forall \ x) \ ((x \ \epsilon \ X \ \wedge \ \text{PRED}(x)) \ \Rightarrow \ (\text{EXP}(x) \ \epsilon \ Y) \ )$$

The notation introduced in this thesis allows the *definition* and *naming* of such syntactic schemas.

Example of the Usage of Schemas.

Let the Natural Numbers be denoted by

$$\mathbb{N}$$

We can give the name TWONUM to the schema

$$n:\mathbb{N} \ ; \ m:\mathbb{N} \ \mid \ n > m$$

either by writing

$$\text{TWONUM} \ \triangleq \ [\ n:\mathbb{N}; \ m:\mathbb{N} \ \mid \ n > m \ ]$$

or by using a *vertical* presentation,

TWONUM _____

> $n \ : \ \mathbb{N};$
> $m \ : \ \mathbb{N}$
>
> _____
>
> $n > m$

The part above the horizontal line within the box is referred to as the *signature*, the part below as the *axiom* or the *invariant*.

The schema TWONUM can be used as a *textual macro* in

1) The implicit construction of a set.

        twonum = {TWONUM}

i.e.

        twonum = {n:$\mathbb{N}$; m:$\mathbb{N}$ | n $\geqslant$ m}

2) The implicit construction of a function.

        subtract : {TWONUM} $\rightarrow$ $\mathbb{N}$
        subtract = (λ TWONUM) (n-m)

3) The construction of elements.

        pair = (μ TWONUM)(n=3; m=2)

NB, the definition is 'valid', since 3 $\geqslant$ 2

4) In quantified expressions,

        ($\exists$ TWONUM)(n = m+10)
        ($\forall$ TWONUM)(n + 1 $>$ m)

5) The definition of *new* schemas, by *extending* existing schemas

```
┌─ INTERVAL ──────────────────────────────────────────────────
│
│     TWONUM;
│     set : $\mathbb{P}(\mathbb{N})$
│
├──────────────
│
│     ($\forall$ i : s) (m $\leqslant$ i $\wedge$ i $\leqslant$ n)
│
└──────────────────────────────────────────────────────────────
```

which is a shorthand for

```
┌─ INTERVAL ──────────────────────────────────────────────────
│
│     n,m   : $\mathbb{N}$;
│     set   : $\mathbb{P}(\mathbb{N})$
│
├──────────────
│
│     n $\geqslant$ m;
│     ($\forall$ i : s) (m $\leqslant$ i $\wedge$ i $\leqslant$ n)
│
└──────────────────────────────────────────────────────────────
```

6) Definition of *new* schemas by *combining* existing schemas.

Let

```
LIMSET _____
    set : P(N);
    _____

    card(set) < 256
_____
```

then we might define

```
SET2 _____
    TWONUM; LIMSET
    _____

    n = card(set);
    m = card({ j : set | j ≠ 0 })
_____
```

Note that the combination of two schemas may introduce 'duplicated' declarations in the signature of the resulting schema. Such a schema is identical to a schema in which one of the declarions is removed, e.g. the schema

```
    [ INTERVAL; LIMSET ]
```

in which the name set 'occurs' twice is

```
    [ INTERVAL; card(set) < 256 ]
```

7) In *Theorems*, as illustrated below.

The signature part of a schema may be empty, hence we can define,

```
SUM_and_AVG_____
    n = x + y ;
    m = (x + y)/2
_____
```

NB '/' is integer division, i.e.

$/ : \mathbf{N} \times \mathbf{N} \to \mathbf{N}$

$(\forall\ i,j,r\ :\ \mathbf{N})\ (r=i/j \iff 0 \leqslant i - m*j < j)$

Given the schema,

PARAM

      $x\ :\ \mathbf{N};\ y\ :\ \mathbf{Nl}$

NB. **Nl** denotes the *non-zero* natural numbers

we can define a function which gives the *sum* and the *average* of two numbers in the following way,

    sumavg $=\ (\lambda\ \text{PARAM})(\mu\ \text{TWONUM})(\text{SUM\_and\_AVG})$

which defines a total function if we can prove the following theorem,

    $x \epsilon \mathbf{N};\ y \epsilon \mathbf{Nl};\ n = x+y;\ m = (x+y)/2$
    $\vdash$
    $n \epsilon \mathbf{N};\ m \epsilon \mathbf{N};\ n \geqslant m$

which leads to the last important use of the schema notation. The theorem above can be written as follows,

    PARAM; SUM_and_AVG $\vdash$ TWONUM

hema Renaming.

e bound variables of a schema (i.e. the variables which appear in the signature part of schema) may be systematically *renamed*. e.g.

    TWONUM'

notes the text

    $n'\ :\ \mathbf{N};\ m'\ :\ \mathbf{N}\ |\ n' \geqslant m'$

d

$$\text{TWONUM}_{ex}$$

denotes

$$n_{ex} \; : \; \mathbf{N} \; ; \; m_{ex} \; : \; \mathbf{N} \; | \; n_{ex} > m_{ex}$$

The schema notation allows individual renaming of one or several variables of the signature, e.g.

$$\text{TWONUM}[k/n]$$

denotes

$$k \; : \; \mathbf{N}; \; m \; : \; \mathbf{N} \; | \; k > m$$

It is important to understand, however, that

$$\{\text{TWONUM}\} = \{\text{TWONUM'}\} = \{\text{TWONUM}_{ex}\} = \{\text{TWONUM}[k/n]\}$$

i.e. systematic renaming of bound variables of a schema does not affect the set which corresponds to that schema, cf.

$$(\lambda x)(x+2) = (\lambda y.)(y+2)$$

Additionally, the schema notation allows for renaming of the free variables in a schema, i.e. given

$$\text{A\_NUM} \; \hat{=} \; [\; n:\mathbf{N} \; | \; n < \text{Limit} \;]$$

then

$$\text{A\_NUM1} \; \hat{=} \; \text{A\_NUM}[\text{L1}/\text{Limit}]$$

denotes a new schema. Note that, if $\text{L1} \neq \text{Limit}$ then

$$\{\text{A\_NUM}\} \neq \{\text{A\_NUM1}\}$$

The main use of schema renaming is in the definition of state transformations, where, informally speaking, the same state variables appear twice.

Example:

Let us define a simple state as follows,

STATE_____
        counter : **N**
_____

A decrement function,

        decr : {STATE} $\twoheadrightarrow$ {STATE}

can be defined using the renaming facility

        decr = (λ STATE) (μ STATE')(counter'=counter-1)

NB

        dom(decr) = {STATE | counter $>$ 0 }

Generic Schemas.

Informal statements or definitions, such as those in section 1 of this paper, often take a *generic* form. Consider the following definition which is generic with respect to X and Y

" let X and Y be sets. The *partial injections* from X to Y are exactly the partial functions from X to Y whose *inverses* are also partial functions."

In the schema notation this concept is formalised. e.g. the above statement will have the form

par_inj_____ X   Y _____
        f : X $\rightarrowtail$ Y
    _____
        f^{-1} $\in$ Y $\twoheadrightarrow$ X
_____

A schema may have several *instances*, e.g. the set of partial injections over the natural numbers is

```
{ par_inj[N,N] }
```

and the set of partial injections from **N** to the Cartesian Product over **N** is,

```
{ par_inj[N,N×N] }
```

4. EXTENSIBILITY.

The importance of the possibility to extend the formal framework in which one wants to present a specification has already been emphasised in the introduction.

The notation provided for extending a theory allows for the introduction of new objects, which are either constructively or axiomatically defined, and for the introduction of new operations on these objects. Such extensions can be grouped and the groups are given names, which enable the writers of a specification to reference theories developed elsewhere. Such groups are refered to as *chapters* or *theories*.

Operations on Relations and Functions.

The elementary Set Theory which was presented in section 2 can be extended to include a set of useful operations on relations. The chapter of these extentions is called REL, and it is assumed that all future definitions are in the scope of the constants defined this chapter. The chapter is generic with respect to S and T.

REL ——————————————————— S T —————————————————————

Let us first introduce the *Identity* function (relation) over a subset of any set, i.e.

S —————————————————————————

id : $P(S) \rightarrow (S \leftrightarrow S)$

$(\forall s : P(S))$
$id(s) = \{ (x,x) \mid x \in s \}$

396

This definition is *generic* in S, hence, we have several instances of the identity function. The use of different instances of a definition is illustrated in the next extention which is *generic* with respect to S and T. This extension defines two *domain* restriction operators and a *codomain* restriction operator.

$$S \quad T$$

```
op( ↾ )  :  (S↔T) × P(S)  → S↔T ;
op( ↓ )  :  (S↔T) × P(T)  → S↔T ;
op( \ )  :  (S↔T) × P(S)  → S↔T
```

$$(\forall \ r:S↔T; \ s:P(S); \ t:P(T))$$
$$(\ r \ ↾ \ s \ = r \circ id[S](s) \ \wedge$$
$$r \ ↓ \ t \ = id[T](t) \circ r \ \wedge$$
$$r \ \backslash \ s \ = r \ ↾ \ (S-s)) \qquad)$$

As for the identity function we have several instances of the domain-restriction operators, e.g.

$$↾ [N,N] \qquad \in \ (N↔N) \times P(N) \to N↔N$$
$$↾ [N,P(N)] \in \ (N↔P(N)) \times P(N) \to N↔P(N)$$

The 'parameter-list' of the instantiation of an operator is often omitted, since its 'type' can be determined from the context in which the operator appears, e.g.

let f, g, S be declared as follows

$$f,g : N \twoheadrightarrow N \ ;$$
$$S \quad : P(N)$$

then

$$g = f \ ↾ \ S$$

means

$$g = f \ ↾ [N,N] \ S$$

The nth iterate of a relation

$$R : S \leftrightarrow S$$

can informally can be written as

$$R^n = R \circ R \circ . . . \circ R$$
$$\underbrace{\qquad}_{n-times}$$

The following extensions define the *iteration* operators,

X
```
    op(^) : (X↔X) × N → (X↔X) ;
    op(*) : (X↔X) → (X↔X)
    ─────────────────────────────
    (∀ r:X↔X; n:N1)
         ( r^0 = id(X)        ∧
           r^n = r^(n-1) ∘ r )
    (∀ r:X↔X) r* = ∪{r^n | n : N}
```

NB, the *infix* operator ^ is implied (as usual) by writing the second operand as a superscrip to the first operand.

In the following we add the theory of functions.

FUNC   S T

The first extention define the function *overriding* operator.

S T
```
    op(⊕)  : ((S↛T) × (S↛T)) → (S↛T)
    ─────────────────────────────────
    (∀ g, f : S↛T)( g ⊕ f = (g\dom(f)) ∪ f )
```

The following define some wellknown subsets of the set of functions.

398

```
        par_inj : P(S ↠ T);

        inj, surj, bij : P(S → Y)

        ───────────

        par_inj = { f: S↠T | f⁻¹ ∈ T↠S };
        inj     = { f: S→T | f⁻¹ ● f = id[S] };
        surj    = { f: S→T | f ● f⁻¹ = id[T] };
        bij     = inj[S,T] ∩ surj[S,T]
```

B, functions and relations are sets to which the Set operations can be applied.

Operations on Sequences.

theory which is often used in the specification of systems is the theory of sequences. the following we will formalise *sequences* and some operations on them.

et us first formalise the well known 2-dots, as in

        3..m

```
        op(..) : N × N → P(N)

        ───────────

        (∀ n,m,p : N)( p ∈ n..m  ⟺  n⩽p ∧ p⩽m )
```

equences are then formalised as a subset of the partial functions, e.g. a *sequence* of length over a set

        {a, b, c, d, f, g}

ight be defined as,

        {1→a, 2→c, 3→b, 4→a}

his sequence will be denoted by

⟨ a c b a ⟩

The empty sequence is denoted by

⟨ ⟩

Sequences and their operations are 'formally' added to our theory by the following general extension.

SEQ ─────────────────────────────── X ──────────────────────────────────

    ┌──────────────────────── X ─────────────────────────────────────
    │
    │   seq,seq1 : $\mathbb{P}(\mathbf{N} \twoheadrightarrow X)$

    │   ($\forall$ s:seq)
    │   (dom(s) $\in$ $\mathbb{F}(\mathbf{N})$ $\wedge$
    │   dom(s) = 1..card(dom(s)))

    │   seq1 = seq - {⟨⟩}

In the following we add some wellknown operators to our 'theory of sequences'

┌──────────────────────────── X ─────────────────────────────────────
│
│   #   : seq[X] → $\mathbf{N}$;
│   first,last : seq1[X] → X;
│   ending,
│   beginning : seq1[X] → seq[X]

│   ($\forall$ s:seq) #(s) = card(s);

│   ($\forall$ s:seq1)
│   (first(s)   = s(1) $\wedge$
│   last(s)   = s(#(s)) $\wedge$
│   ending(s)   = s ∘ (succ\{0}) $\wedge$
│   beginning(s)= s ↾ (1..#(s)-1))

The function succ is the successor function over the Natural Numbers.

The *concatenation* operator for sequences is defined by,

X

$$op(*) : seq[X] \times seq[X] \rightarrow seq[X]$$

$$(\forall \ s,s':seq) \ \ s * s' = s \cup (s' \circ pred^{\#(s)})$$

The function pred is the predecessor function over the Natural Numbers.

NB, we have the following relationship the introduced operators.

Theorem _____ X

$$\vdash \ (\forall \ s: seq1[X])$$
$$(\ s = \langle first(s)\rangle * ending(s) \wedge$$
$$s = beginning * \langle last(s)\rangle \ )$$

A usefull operator is

X

$$next \qquad : seq[X] \ \rightarrow \ (X\leftrightarrow X);$$

$$(\forall \ s:seq) \ \ next(s) = s \circ succ \circ s^{-1}$$

NB, for

$$s = a \ b \ c$$

we have

$$next(s) = \{ \ a\leftrightarrow b, \ b\leftrightarrow c, \ c\leftrightarrow d\}$$

Reference.

[1]   B. Sufrin:
      'Formal Specification of a Display Editor'.
      Oxford University Computing Laboratory. PRG Monograph no 21, 1981.

TECTON: A LANGUAGE FOR MANIPULATING GENERIC OBJECTS

Deepak Kapur, David R. Musser, and Alexander A. Stepanov

General Electric Research and Development Center
Schenectady, New York   12345/USA

We will describe specification methods we are currently developing and illustrate their use on the workshop example of the communications network. The overall goal of our work is to develop formal
notation and methods that allow <u>conceptualization</u> of problems and
solutions at an appropriate level of abstraction. The kinds of problems we would like to be able to deal with range from the large
software systems developed for commercial and government customers, t
small "programs in products," i.e., microprocessor control programs
whose reliability is of critical economic importance because they are
duplicated in such large quantities. This implies that we must be abl
to deal with issues such as distributed computation, timing of real
time control, and the requirements placed on programs by their
hardware and application environments.

1. DESIGN PHILOSOPHY

The ability to reason abstractly, to see generality through the
particular, and then to particularize the general, are very useful fo
the development of high quality software. A central problem with most
current notations and methods of either specification or programming
is that they do not allow enough use of abstraction. We are thus
required to deal with too many details simultaneously. Most language
support a fixed set of abstraction mechanisms and ways to instantiate
them. They do not provide general purpose mechanisms for abstracting
a class of objects sharing common properties.

For example, most work on data abstraction has dealt only with
the notion of abstracting away from implementation details. This is
the important idea of expressing "what" operations are supposed to do
without getting into details of "how." But it is also often useful to

alk about a software module without knowing precisely "what" it does
that is, to abstract at the behavioral level also. For instance, it
may be desirable to describe abstractions such as "process control
system," "operating system," "transfer service," "electronic mail sys-
em," etc., without stating precisely what they do under all condi-
ions.

We need to be able to use abstraction and specialization of con-
epts for purposes of organization and understanding, irrespective of
he implementation question. The intention is to capture the general
properties of an abstract notion without having to specify too much
etail. When one wishes to describe a specialization of this abstract
otion, only details particular to the specialization are described,
hile whatever is known about the abstract notion based on its general
properties is also carried to the specialization.

It is also our goal that the notation and methods we develop
ltimately be usable as a programming language/system as well as a
pecification language/system. This seems to be a different philoso-
hy from most of the other participants in this workshop. In our view,
pecification and programming are not such distinct activities that
hey should be done in different frameworks. In many cases, the sim-
lest and clearest way to express "what" is to be done is to say "how"
t can be done, provided the "how" is expressed in terms of essential
oncepts rather than the irrelevant details required by most specifi-
ation languages and all existing programming languages. Conversely,
any of the tools that we are all finding useful for specification,
articularly abstraction and specialization, should also be available
o the programmer.

Having a unified framework for designing specifications and pro-
ramming enables us to view the development of software as a stepwise
nd systematic refinement of higher level concepts into lower level
achine (or programming system) supported primitives. In this way,
riting specifications becomes an integral part of the programming
ctivity and provides a way of recording higher level design deci-
ions. This is in contrast to the view that writing specifications
nd programming are totally distinct tasks, performed in different
rameworks and using different notations and styles – a scenario whose
ain consequence is that specification writing is regarded as burden-
ome activity.

In the proposed framework, a series of refinements constitute a set of design decisions leading to a program. It should be possible to backtrack to any stage of decision making and explore an alternate path of refinements. Different design decisions can thus be compared and evaluated.

A notion that seems to be particularly useful for achieving this kind of organization is that of "generic objects." A generic object is a notion for grouping objects sharing common syntactic structure and semantic __properties__. Informally, a generic object describes a whole class of non-isomorphic possibilities, unless a stage has been reached at which the described objects are fully defined. Adding properties to a generic object makes it more specific by narrowing the range of possibilities. Once we allow such genericity of objects, the way is open also to the development and use of "generic algorithms," which offer a way of organizing and extending our knowledge of algorithms and control.

We have begun developing a language called "Tecton" (Greek for "builder") for constructing generic objects and algorithms. Tecton will embody the above discussed design philosophy. It will provide a rich set of generic objects, and these objects will be built up and related by general description building constructs in Tecton. We will first discuss the constructs for building generic objects, then some of the different kinds of generic objects supported in Tecton. Later we discuss how the communication network example can be done in Tecton using these mechanisms.

2. __CONSTRUCTS IN TECTON__

The proposed set of mechanisms in Tecton includes:

(i) __create__, to define a class of objects by describing their syntactic structure and a set of properties relating their various components.

(ii) __refine__, to define a class of objects by refining an existing class by adding a set of properties, potentially to the level of detail where the objects in the resulting class are narrowed down precisely to what is desired in an implementation.

(iii) __abstract__, to define a class of objects by generalizing an existing class of objects. The generalization can be specified by generalizing a particular object(s) or class(es) of objects used in the description of the existing class or by forgetting some properties of the existing class.

(iv) instantiate, to identify commonalities among two classes of objects in order to transport the properties and algorithms of the class being instantiated to the other class.

(v) provide, to define new operations on a class of objects in terms of the existing ones.

(vi) inform, to add new properties to existing information about a class of objects.

(vii) implement, to give an algorithm for an already defined operations on a subclass of objects by making use of their specific properties.

(viii) represent, to relate a class of objects and its operations to another class of objects and associated operations as an aid to constructing implementations.

The create, refine and abstract constructs define new classes of objects. The abstract construct is roughly the inverse of the refine construct. The instantiate, provide, implement, and inform serve to include more knowledge about a class of objects, while represent is used to represent a class of objects in terms of another class. The instantiate construct records the information that a class of objects can be refined to another class; or, stated another way, a class of objects can be abstracted to another class. The latter could be obtained from the former by reversing the arguments to instantiate.

The use of these constructs is illustrated on structures (see below), a class of objects definable in Tecton, in [5]. (Except that abstract was not discussed and refine was called enrich in that paper.) In the next section, we will give examples of some of these constructs; their use is also illustrated in the discussion of the communication network example.

. OBJECTS IN TECTON

We discuss four different types of objects in Tecton which we have found useful in describing different kinds of activities of a complex software system: structures, entities, events, and environments. Some of these types of objects have appeared previously in

data base query languages, simulation languages and functional programming languages, though not in as general a form as in Tecton.

3.1 Structures

A structure is a representation of a time-independent object.
The language provides certain primitive structures, for instance
"set", "multisets", and "sequences", from which new structures are
built up step by step using constructs outlined in the previous section.   Each new structure is specified as a collection of other struc
tures and operations on these structures, which satisfy certain properties regarded as axioms; e.g.,

```
        create semigroup(S:set; +: S+S -> S)
           with  x + (y + z) = (x + y) + z;

        create monoid(S:semigroup; 0: -> S)
           with 0 + x = x;

        refine monoid into abelian monoid
           with commutativity: x + y = y + x;
```

If for some reason monoid was defined directly from set, then semigroup could be created using the abstract construct by dropping the
nullary operation 0 and the property that 0 is a left identity. Note
that the above definition of semigroup does not define a specific
semigroup, but a generic semigroup. Such a definition defines the
semigroup structure type. This is different from defining a specific
structure, such as natural numbers, which is called just a structure.

We define an operator to be a secondary operation associated wit
a structure type, that is expressed in terms of the (primary) operations on structures, e.g., we can define an operator "reduction" on
the structure type "sequences of monoid" by

```
        provide sequences of monoid
           with reduction:
           x -> if x = null then 0
                   else head(x) + reduction(tail(x)).
```

Such operators resemble those in APL [4] and in Backus's Functional

---

1. No distinction is made between structure and structure type
   syntactically in the examples discussed in [5], though the
   distinction is suggested in the discussion of the examples.
   The term generic structure is used there instead of structure
   type.

Programming Language [1]. They provide the same advantages of powerful, concise expression of computations, but differ in that they are
defined with respect to a structure type - one to which they naturally
belong. This is possible because Tecton permits description of structure types in terms of their properties.

In [5] an example is carried out of the development of several
generic algorithms for sorting in terms of the reduction operator.
The KWIC example can be done concisely in terms of a "closure" operator that gives a simple way of building the set of all rotations of a
title. Operators such as reduction and closure should be a part of
the standard vocabulary of both specifiers and programmers.

Structures types thus provide a method for abstracting a set of
operations and properties which can be applied to different time-
independent, unchangeable (also called immutable or constant) objects.
They enable us to abstract general properties of data and express
algorithms on that data in an abstract form. Structures are similar
in flavor to immutable data types as discussed by Liskov et al [6] and
Guttag [3], but they are more general and powerful. Structure types
are similar to "theories" of Burstall and Goguen [2] and "sypes" of
Nakajima et al [7], but we do not restrict ourselves to algebraic
structures. Using structures and structure types, it is possible to
define an abstract data type as well as a collection of abstract data
types and associate operators with the collection as a whole.

3.2 Entities

An entity is an object that exists and changes in time. An
entity type is a description of a collection of entities with common
attributes and properties. For example, "parcel" and "message" are
entity types in a transfer service and a mail service respectively, as
will be discussed later.

An entity is characterized by a collection of attributes, which
are functions from entities into structures. Examples of attributes
of the entity type "message" are signature, creation date, sender,
sending date, contents, etc. Attributes can have special properties,
such as unique, immutability, required. For example, the signature
attribute is immutable and required for every message. An entity type
can have properties, which specify consistency relations among the

attributes of each entity. For example, the sending date of a message
is always after its creation date.

Primitive updates on entities are create, which defines a new
entity with specified attributes; destroy, which gets rid of entities
with specified attributes; and change, which modifies attributes of
existing entities. An entity type can also include a list of user
defined updates, which have primitive updates as their building
blocks.

An entity type can contain a list of triggers, which are functions on the attributes of the entity type. along with associated
events. When a trigger changes its value, it activates an event.
(Events are discussed below.)

3.2.1 Classes and Classifications

It is often necessary to dynamically group different entities
based on their attributes or other properties. This is achieved using
the class and classification mechanisms.

A class is a collection of entities of the same type. The class
of all currently existing entities of some type is called the complete
class of that entity type. Thus any class of entities of a certain
type is a subset of the complete class of that type. Classes may be
described by attributes or properties of attributes; e.g., the class
of all messages with author "Jones," and the class of all messages
received after "June 30, 1980" with author "Smith." Classes may themselves be regarded as entities; they are called class entities. A
collection of class entities of the same type form another class; this
latter class is called a classification of the type. For example, a
classification of the message type can be based on the attribute
author. One class of this classification is the class of messages
that have author "Jones".

Classifications can have some special properties, such as being
complete, which means that every entity of its type must belong to at
least one class of the classification, or nonredundant, which means
that every entity of its type belongs to at most one class of the
classification. The classification on the message type based on
author is complete but redundant, as a message can have more than one

408

uthor.

In addition to standard primitive updates of entities, there are
wo primitive updates particular to class entities: the update _insert_
uts specified entities into the class, whereas _delete_ gets rid of
ntities.

There is a primitive update particular to classifications, called
ransfer, which moves specified entities from one class in the clas-
ification into another. In case of a mail service, for example,
ransfer on a classification on the message type can be used to
escribe the event of sending a message from A to B. Every classifi-
ation also has an associated binary relation, called a _transfer rela-
ion_, which specifies allowable transfers among classes in the clas-
ification. A transfer relation associated with a classification on
he message type would describe who can send messages to whom.

.2.2 Relations

A relation is a special kind of entity which establishes an asso-
iation among entities of several types. Primitive updates on rela-
ions are _link_ (which expands the relation by adding a tuple) and
eparate (which shrinks the relation by deleting a tuple). There are
lso special operations that build new relations, such as _union_,
ntersection, _product_, _closure_, etc.

.3 Events

An event is a representation of when and how certain objects are
hanged. One can define a specific event or a generic event. A generic
vent is defined using the event type mechanism. The description of
n event (specific or generic) includes an activation description, an
ction list, timing constraints, and an entity type which specifies
ttributes and properties of the event.

An _activation description_ specifies how the event can be invoked:
y another event, by time, or by a trigger.

An _action list_ is a list of invocations of different events and
pdates on different entities that are caused by the event invocation.

These actions are executed in arbitrary order if a precedence of actions is not explicitly specified.

Timing constraints specify constraints on the duration of an event invocation, such as minimum and maximum duration, as well as global constraints on the duration of all event invocations, such as frequency distribution and time precision.

The inclusion of an entity type in the description of an event provides for the notion of instances of an event corresponding to different invocations of the event. This also allows for classes and classifications of events.

3.4 Environments

Environments are a mechanism for grouping together different kinds of objects such as structures, entities, events and (sub-) environments. It is thus essentially an organizational tool, recording the structural relationship among various objects. A specific environment as well as a generic environment can be defined in the same way other specific and generic objects can be defined in Tecton.

Environments also contain interfaces to other environments. An interface describe the conditions under which the objects of an environment may be used by other environment. These interfaces are built with the help of the privilege relation.

If an object belongs to an environment, i.e. the object is in th class, the environment has an unlimited privilege to use the object. It also has a privilege to give a privilege to use this object to other environments, including the privilege to give a privilege. The privilege relation is a ternary relation among the classification of environments, the entity of objects, and the class of parameters of operations. It specifies whether an environment can use an object as a particular parameter of an operation.

COMMUNICATION NETWORK EXAMPLE

The statement of the workshop problem does not explicitly deal
with the question of what the network is to be used for. The presump-
tion is, of course, that some sort of message system will be implemented with the aid of the network. We will begin at the level of the
message system specification and refine it to the network level.
Thus, rather than just making up a list of properties that the network
should satisfy, the needs of the message system will place a natural
set of requirements on the network. (We had already chosen to specify
a message system, as a way of developing some of the features of the
Tecton language, before receiving the statement of the workshop problems.)

A key goal of our approach is to find ways of using abstraction
to break up the treatment of complex systems into natural components
that, when recombined, fully capture the essential properties of the
system. (This division into components may be unrelated to decompositions that are made in implementations of the system.) In specifying a
message system we have identified several main components. First, a
message system provides a "transfer service" for messages, and below
we shall concentrate on this part. Other components would be facilities for display and scanning, for composing and editing messages, and
for filing and retrieving messages.

In specifying a transfer service, we first observe that we can
view it more abstractly than just dealing with messages and passing
them around in the way that users of a message system typically do.
Instead of messages, our transfer service will deal with "parcels"
and will serve "clients." In a message system, parcels will be specialized to messages and clients to users, but parcels could also be
currency units and clients could be banks, for example, if the
transfer service specification were used as part of the specification
of an electronic funds transfer (EFT) service.

The question of who can send parcels to whom can also be dealt
with more generally than just adopting the discipline of a message
system. Both a message system and an EFT service have the same discipline, which might be called a "capitalistic" discipline - each
client can transfer his own, and only his own, parcels to any other
client. But a memory management subsystem of an operating system
could also be viewed as a transfer service in which the parcels are

memory blocks, the clients are jobs, and the discipline of transfer is
that there is a supervisor that has the privilege to transfer parcels
from any client to another.

We first create a new type of environment, called "Transfer Service." and provide it with an event for sending parcels among clients.

> create "Transfer Service"
> > from environment type,
> > > parcel: entity type,
> > > clients: complete nonredundant classification of parcels.

> provide Transfer Service with
> > an event type Sending "Send P to C",
> > > where P: parcel, C: client,
> > > with action:
> > > > transfer P into C.
> > > > {will transfer only if the transfer relation
> > > > of this classification allows it}

We ensure that each client can send parcels to every other client wit

> refine Transfer Service into "Complete Transfer Service" with
> > transfer relation of clients is complete.

Now, to make Sending available in a Mail Service, we can

> instantiate Complete Transfer Service in Mail Service as
> > Mail Transfer Service with parcel=message,
> > > > clients=message bins of users.

Now we give a refinement of Transfer Service into a network.

> create "Connected Static Network" from
> > Transfer Service,
> > a relation "C can route D to E", where C,D,E: clients
> with
> > transfer relation of clients is
> > > > connected immutable relation;
> > for every C,D there is an E such that C can route D to E
> > if C can route D to E then

                    C is related by transfer relation of clients to E
                       {making direct Send possible}
                    and E is related by
                       (closure of transfer relation of clients) to D.
                          {that is, D is reachable from E}

           provide Connected Static Network
              with
                 a functional relation "address" of parcel to client,
                    initially the client such that parcel is in client;

                 an event type "Start P on its way to C",
                    where P: parcel, C: client,
                    with action: change address of P to C;

                 an event type "Forward P from C", where P:
                    parcel, C: client,
                    activated by trigger:
                    P is in C and (address of P) is not C,
                    with action:
                          (Send P to E) for some E such that
                             C can route (address of P) to E;

                 an event type Network Sending "Network Send P to C",
                       where P: parcel, C: client;
                    with actions:
                    Start P on its way to C,
                    then collect
                          Forward P from any client.
                    {"collect" says that specified events constitute
                    actions which are parts of this event}

   he Network Sending event only actually performs the action of "Start
   on its way to C"; it then just "observes" the forwarding events that
   ccur because of activation by the indicated trigger. This is an
   bstract way of specifying a distributed implementation of an event.

      Having defined the network, it is now possible to

           instantiate Complete Transfer Service
              in Connected Static Network
                 by Sending = Network Sending.

with the result that this network refinement can be carried over to other instances of Complete Transfer Services, such as the Mail Service.

5. REFERENCES

1. Backus, J., "Can programming be liberated from the von Neumann Style? A functional style and its algebra of programs," CACM 21 (8), August 1978.

2. Burstall, R.M., Goguen, J.A., "Putting Theories Together to Make Specifications," Fifth International Joint Conference on Artificial Intelligence, Cambridge, MA, August 1977.

3. Guttag, J.V., "Abstract Data Types and the Development of Data Structures," CACM 20 (6), pp. 396-404, June 1977.

4. Iverson, K.E., "Operators," TOPLAS 2 (1), October 1979.

5. Kapur, D., Musser, D.R., Stepanov, A.A., "Operators and Algebraic Structures," Proceedings of the Conference on Functional Programming Languages and Computer Architecture, New Hampshire, Oct. 1981.

6. Liskov, B.H., Snyder, A., Atkinson, R., Schaffert, C., "Abstraction Mechanisms in CLU," CACM 20 (8), pp. 564-576, Aug. 1977.

7. Nakajima, R., Nakahara, H., Honda, M., "Hierarchical Program Specification and Verification - A Many Sorted Logical Approach, preprint RIMS 256, November 1978.

Leif Sandegaard Nielsen
Computer Science Department
Aarhus University

CONCURRENCY

This paper presents a conceptual framework for distributed
systems and discusses some techniques for specifying programs
with concurrency.

System characteristics

The system characteristics have been selected from an inspection of properties often found in resource scheduling systems
and communication networks.

A system is a static collection of named processes. A process
does one sequence of actions. A communication between two
processes takes place only when one process calls an entry-
operation in another process by "pr.op(...)" and the called
process explicitly allows the execution by an operation permission "op...".

Process description

In Path Processes [5] a process description consists of an
operation part and a control part. The control part is an
explicit and complete description of the possible sequences
of actions of the process. Every external operation call and
every operation permission must be done according to the control part. The control part consists of variable descriptions
and a number of paths. A path is a regular expression in conditional statements "condition → action". The operation part

consists of variable descriptions and operation descriptions. An operation may only access the variables of the operation part. We emphasize the control part in the following discussion.

An <u>action</u> is either an operation call (local "op(...)" or external "pr.op(...)"), an operation permission "op..." or an assignment. A <u>condition</u> is a boolean expression in constants, variables of the control part and counters. Each operation "op" has a return counter "op.r" (number of completed executions). The actions in the control part may use variables of the control part only.

The following path is the control of a process with two entry-operations "put" and "get" and a local operation "reorganize":

```
PATH (put.r-get.r>0 → get (* operation permission *)
      □ put.r-get.r<max → put; reorganize()
                           (* operation permission and
                              local operation call *)
      )*   (* indefinite repetition*)
END
```

An operation permission statement in its simplest form is just an operation name "op". However, the control part may use the value of a value parameter or may have a result to a result parameter. Presently we additionally allow the following two kinds of operation permissions:

"put=>x" : The value of the single value parameter of "put" is assigned to x before execution.

"get<=exp": After the execution of "get" the single result parameter is assigned the value of exp

The following path is the control of a process with one entry-operation "put" and a local operation "handle":

```
PATH (put=>x; handle(x); next.put(x) )* END
```

The presented process description technique has a sharp
distinction between the operation part and the control part.
The operation part describes an abstract data type with variables and with operations manipulating these variables, but
no synchronization . The control part has its own variables
and only through parameters to local operation calls and
through parameter manipulations is the necessary interface
between the operation part and the control part established.

Finite control graphs

The meaning of the control part is defined by help of finite
graphs. Each path (a regular expression) is transformed into
a finite graph with one start node and a conditional statement
on each arc. If the control part has more paths a combined
graph is defined from the path graphs. The nodes in the combined graph represent the cross product of the nodes in the
path graph. If an operation permission is given in more paths
the corresponding components all change in the combined graph.
Special care must be taken if parameter manipulation is used.

A simple example:

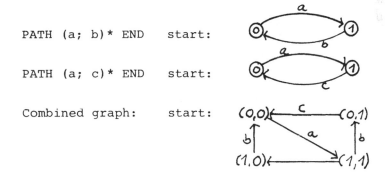

PATH (a; b)* END   start:

PATH (a; c)* END   start:

Combined graph: start:

The finite graphs are intuitively appealing specifications
of the process control. We now use the graphs as the basis
for the following techniques.

Control semantics

The process control may be defined precisely from the finite
(combined) control graph. The nodes represent the states and
the arcs represent the actions. In a state (node) the outgoing
arcs represent the possible actions. To choose an action the
condition on the arc has to be true. If the action is an
external operation call or an operation permission there must
be a partner willing to do the corresponding communication
action (synchronous communication): Though the naming convention is asymmetric (pr.op(...)" vs. "op...") the semantics
are symmetric. A process may wait for both external operation
calls and operation permissions.

We assume no fairness, neither between alternative actions in
a state nor when a communication partner is chosen. As an
example a process "A" with an entry-operation "op", which is
called by two processes "B" and "C" may be given a more explici
definition by the Petri Net:

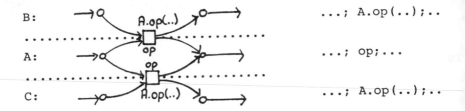

Any special scheduling strategy must either be explicitly
specified by the available tools (e.g. operation counters) or
by some new language constructs. A logical reason for aban-
doning fairness is that in a truely distributed system fairness
can only be demanded with regard to registration of external
communication requests. But the registration is implementation
dependent. Or to put it another way the non-fairness of our
model opens up the possibility of starvation of a process.
But starvation may be interpreted as a physical lack of interaction.

Related to control semantics is control equivalence between
two processes. Informally we define it to be the possibility
of two processes to do exactly the same actions (both communications and locally) and remain in equivalent states. A more
precise definition defines equivalence on two combined control
graphs by equivalence of the starting nodes in an equivalence
relation on all nodes in the two graphs (the idea of the formal
definition is found in (Milner[4]). The important thing about
this equivalence is that it is not equality on regular sets.
E.g.:

An interesting result is that there exist combinations of two
paths which give conbined control graphs not equivalent with
any single path control graph. As an example:

is the combined graph for:

        PATH (a; b)*; c END
        PATH a; (b; a)*; d END

But no single path control graph is equivalent with the graph.
Intuitively because the loop has two exits. A formal proof
may be given by use of infinite trees.

A more general result would be a characterization of the
combined control graphs corresponding to n paths (n≥1) under
equivalence. Possible techniques are reduction on graphs or
inhibited subgraphs. We have no general results. However the
use of more paths clearly gives a factorization of the control
restrictions, that is a more comprehensible description of
the process control.

Implementation

An implementation may be given by a language processor
turning the specification language into a programming
language or it may be a representation of a specification in
an available programming language. In both cases the use of
the finite graphs give a simple implementation. A single
comment on the complexity of the implementation: The size of
the combined graph grows exponentially with the number of
paths (the cross-product). However, it is possible to use the
individual path graphs. Then the process state is composed
of the path states and the possible actions in a state is
the union of the possible path actions (the only special case
is when an operation permission is given in more paths). The
growth of the size is now linear.

Verification

Two main techniques in handling concurrency are restrictions
on the possible interactions and verification within the
given framework. We have presented a system view where processes communicate by operation calls. A process description
includes an explicit and complete description of the control.
The finite graphs may be used in verification. One technique
is to connect a predicate to each node. These predicates may
use both control part variables and operation part variables.

The sorting array of the KWIC-example may be used to illustrate the technique. The following description is really a
full specification and may be understood alone. The control
graph of "sorti":

We introduce the four multisets (several occurrences allowed) of actual parameter values:

S1 = (x | put=>x)
S2 = (x | get<=x)
S3 = (x | sort<i+1>.put(x))
S4 = (x | sort<i+1>.get(x))

And two deduced sets:

Here = S1∖S2
Later = S3∖S4

Finally the two conditions may be defined as:

co1 ≡ (Later=∅)
co2 ≡ (Later≠∅)

The predicates are:

0: Later=Here=∅
1: ∃x: (Later∪(x)=Here)
   and (Later≠∅ => x≤min(Later))
2: ∃x,y: (Later∪(x,y)=Here)
   and (Later≠∅ => min(x,y)≤min(Later))
3: Later=Here≠∅

If we compare with the description of the sorting array in "KWIC-index generation" the only differences are: The bounded variables in the predicates (x,y) may be interpreted as the control part variables. And the extra state in the old description is a variant of state 1 (y instead of x).
With regard to external communication the new specification (the graph with the predicates) describe a system, which behaves exactly as the old.

Conclusion

The ideas in this paper are based on the Path Processes ideas
of [5] with some modifications. Path Processes has familiarity to Distributed Processes [2] (system structure, procedure communication), CSP [3] (communication primitives with
parameter manipulation) and Path Expressions [1] (the path
notation).

We have presented a distributed system view in which processes
communicate by operation calls and permissions. Each process
description has an operation part and a control part. We
emphasize the control part. Finite graphs are defined from
the paths (regular expressions) in the control part. The
control semantics are then defined from the graphs. Implementation and verification are naturally based on the graphs.

References

[1] A.N. Habermann, Path Expressions, Carnegie-Mellon
                    University, 1975.

[2] P. Brinch Hansen, Distributed Processes: A Concurrent
                    Programming Concept. CACM 21:11, 1978.

[3] C.A.R. Hoare, Communicating Sequential Processes.
                    CACM 21:8, 1978

[4] R. Milner, A Calculus of Communicating Systems,
                    Lecture Notes in Computer Science, vol. 92
                    Springer-Verlag, 1980.

[5] L.S. Nielsen, O.D. Nielsen, Specifikation af processsyn-
                    kronisering (in Danish),
                    Datalogisk Afdeling
                    Aarhus Universitet, 1980.

4.-7. August 1981

Material distributed during the workshop

ABRIAL, J.R.: Case Study 1: Specification of a KWIC Index.

BEST, E. & F. CHRISTIAN: Systematic Detection of Exception
        Occurrences.

BJØRNER, D.: The VDM Principles of Software Specification
        & Program Design.

BURSTALL, R.M. & J. GOGUEN: An Informal Introduction to
        Specification using CLEAR.

CRISTIAN, F.: Robust Data Types.

CRISTIAN, F.: Exception Handling and Software-Fault Tolerance.

CRISTIAN, F.: Robust Data Abstractions.

COLEMAN, D. & R.M. GALLIMORE: Partial Correctness of
        Distributed Programs.

EHRIG, H. & H.-J. KREOWSKI: Keywords in Context: An Algebraic
        Specification.

EHRIG, H., H.-J. KREOWSKI, B. MAHR & P. PADAWITZ:
        Algebraic Implementation of Abstract Data Types.

EHRIG, H.: Algebraic Theory of Parameterized Specifications with
        Requirements.

GALLIMORE, R.M. & D. COLEMAN: Specification of Distributed
        Programs.

GOGUEN, J.: Thoughts on Specification, Design and Verification.

GOGUEN, J. & K. PARSAYE-GHOMI: Algebraic Denotational Semantics
        using Parameterized Abstract Modules.

GOGUEN, J.: Research in Specification Languages.

GOGUEN, J. & J. MESEGUER: Completeness of Many-sorted Equational
        Logic.

GUTTAG, J.: Data Abstraction Grade Book.

HUGHES, J.W. & M.S. POWELL: Program Specification using DTL.

KAPUR, D., D.R. MUSSER, A.A. STEPANOV: Operators and Algebraic
          Structures (draft).

KLAEREN, H.A.: The SRDL Specification Experiment.

KLAEREN, H.A.: Recursive Definitions of Operations in Universal
          Algebras.

NIEVERGELT, J.: What is a "correct" behaviour of a file under
          concurrent access? (Draft).

NØRGAARD, P.C.: Letter to J. Nievergelt.

POWELL, M.S. & J.W. HUGHES: A Reduction Specification of DTL.

SANDEGAARD NIELSEN, L.: KWIC-index generation.

STAUNSTRUP, J.: Example 1: Geometrical Constructions.

STEENSGAARD-MADSEN, J.: KWIC-index specification.

STEENSGAARD-MADSEN, J.: Program Specification by Module Trees.

SUFRIN, B.: Behaviour of a "Smart Terminal" & A "Unix like"
          filing system.

SUFRIN, B.: Specification of a Display Editor.

SØRENSEN, I.H.: The Specification Language (informal overview).

SØRENSEN, I.H.: Non-deterministic Systems.

SØRENSEN, I.H.: A Specification of a Communication Network.

List of Participants

D.J. Andrews
Technical Communications Dept.
IBM UK Labs. Ltd.
Hursley Park, Winchester SO21 2JN
England

H. Barringer
Department of Computer Science
The University
Manchester M13 9PL
England

D. Bjørner
Department of Computer Science
Building 344
Technical University of Denmark
2800 Lyngby
Denmark

F. Cristian
Computing Laboratory
University of Newcastle upon Tyne
Newcastle NE1 7RU
England

T. Clement
Programming Research Group
Oxford University Comp. Lab.
45 Banbury Road
Oxford OX2 6PE
England

H. Ehrig
Fachbereich Informatik
TU Berlin
Otto-Suhr-Allee 18-20
D-1000 Berlin 10
Germany

K. Fischer
Comp. Research Centre
Bratislava
Czechoslovakia

R. Gallimore
Computation Department
UMIST P.O. Box 88
Sackville St.
Manchester M60 1QD
England

J. Goguen
SRI International
333 Ravenswood Ave
Menlo Park, CA 94025
USA

J. Guttag
Laboratory for Computer Science
MIT
545 Technology Square
Cambridge, MA 02139
USA

J.J. Horning
Computer Science Laboratory
Xerox Palo Alto Research Centers
3333 Coyote Hill Road
Palo Alto, CA 94304
USA

H. Klaeren
RWTH Aachen
Lehrstuhl Informatik II
D-5100 Aachen
West Germany

H.-J. Kreowski
TU Berlin
Fachbereich Informatik
Otto-Suhr-Allee 18-20
D-1000 Berlin 10
Germany

B. Løfstedt
Box 90
3900 Godthåb
Grønland

D. Musser
General Electric Research &
   Development Center
Bldg. K-1, Room 4C29
Schenectady, NY 12345
USA

P. Naur
Computer Science Institute
University of Copenhagen
Sigurdsgade 41
2200 København N
Denmark

J. Nievergelt
Institut für Informatik
ETH
Claussiusstrasse 55
CH-8092 Zürich
Schweiz

M. Powell
Computation Department
UMIST P.O. Box 88
Sackville St.
Manchester M60 1QD
England

J. Rushby
Computing Laboratory
The University
Newcastle upon Tyne
Newcastle NE1 7RU
England

J. Steensgaard-Madsen
Computer Science Institute
University of Copenhagen
Sigurdsgade 41
2200 København N
Denmark

I.H. Sørensen
Programming Research Group
Oxford University Comp. Lab.
45 Banbury Road
Oxford OX2 6PE
England

B. Sufrin
Programming Research Group
Oxford University Comp. Lab.
45 Banbury Road
Oxford OX2 6PE
England

P.V. Villumsen
Institut for elektroniske systemer
Badehusvej 9-13
9000 Aalborg

A. Wills
Department of Computer Science
The University
Manchester M13 9PL
England

107: International Colloquium on Formalization of Programming cepts. Proceedings. Edited by J. Diaz and I. Ramos. VII, 478 es. 1981.

108: Graph Theory and Algorithms. Edited by N. Saito and shizeki. VI, 216 pages. 1981.

109: Digital Image Processing Systems. Edited by L. Bolc and on Kulpa. V, 353 pages. 1981.

110: W. Dehning, H. Essig, S. Maass, The Adaptation of Virtual -Computer Interfaces to User Requirements in Dialogs. X, 142 es. 1981.

111: CONPAR 81. Edited by W. Händler. XI, 508 pages. 1981.

12: CAAP '81. Proceedings. Edited by G. Astesiano and C. Böhm. 64 pages. 1981.

113: E.-E. Doberkat, Stochastic Automata: Stability, Nondeter- m, and Prediction. IX, 135 pages. 1981.

14: B. Liskov, CLU, Reference Manual. VIII, 190 pages. 1981.

15: Automata, Languages and Programming. Edited by S. Even . Kariv. VIII, 552 pages. 1981.

116: M. A. Casanova, The Concurrency Control Problem for base Systems. VII, 175 pages. 1981.

17: Fundamentals of Computation Theory. Proceedings, 1981. d by F. Gécseg. XI, 471 pages. 1981.

118: Mathematical Foundations of Computer Science 1981. eedings, 1981. Edited by J. Gruska and M. Chytil. XI, 589 pages.

19: G. Hirst, Anaphora in Natural Language Understanding: vey. XIII, 128 pages. 1981.

20: L. B. Rall, Automatic Differentiation: Techniques and Appli- s. VIII, 165 pages. 1981.

21: Z. Zlatev, J. Wasniewski, and K. Schaumburg, Y12M So- of Large and Sparse Systems of Linear Algebraic Equations. 8 pages. 1981.

22: Algorithms in Modern Mathematics and Computer Science. edings, 1979. Edited by A. P. Ershov and D. E. Knuth. XI, 487 s. 1981.

23: Trends in Information Processing Systems. Proceedings, Edited by A. J. W. Duijvestijn and P. C. Lockemann. XI, 349 . 1981.

24: W. Polak, Compiler Specification and Verification. XIII, ages. 1981.

25: Logic of Programs. Proceedings, 1979. Edited by E. er. V, 245 pages. 1981.

26: Microcomputer System Design. Proceedings, 1981. Edited J. Flynn, N. R. Harris, and D. P. McCarthy. VII, 397 pages. 1982.

127: Y.Wallach, Alternating Sequential/Parallel Processing. 9 pages. 1982.

28: P. Branquart, G. Louis, P. Wodon, An Analytical Descrip- f CHILL, the CCITT High Level Language. VI, 277 pages. 1982.

29: B. T. Hailpern, Verifying Concurrent Processes Using oral Logic. VIII, 208 pages. 1982.

30: R. Goldblatt, Axiomatising the Logic of Computer Program- XI, 304 pages. 1982.

31: Logics of Programs. Proceedings, 1981. Edited by D. Kozen. 9 pages. 1982.

32: Data Base Design Techniques I: Requirements and Logical tures. Proceedings, 1978. Edited by S.B. Yao, S.B. Navathe, eldon, and T.L. Kunii. V, 227 pages. 1982.

33: Data Base Design Techniques II: Proceedings, 1979. by S.B. Yao and T.L. Kunii. V, 229–399 pages. 1982.

Vol. 134: Program Specification. Proceedings, 1981. Edited by J. Staunstrup. IV, 426 pages. 1982.

This series reports new developments in computer science research a
teaching – quickly, informally and at a high level. The type of mater
considered for publication includes:

1. Preliminary drafts of original papers and monographs
2. Lectures on a new field or presentations of a new angle in a classic
   field
3. Seminar work-outs
4. Reports of meetings, provided they are
   a) of exceptional interest and
   b) devoted to a single topic.

Texts which are out of print but still in demand may also be consider
if they fall within these categories.

The timeliness of a manuscript is more important than its form, whi
may be unfinished or tentative. Thus, in some instances, proofs may
merely outlined and results presented which have been or will la
be published elsewhere. If possible, a subject index should be include
Publication of Lecture Notes is intended as a service to the internatio
computer science community, in that a commercial publisher, Spring
Verlag, can offer a wide distribution of documents which would oth
wise have a restricted readership. Once published and copyright
they can be documented in the scientific literature.

Manuscripts

Manuscripts should be no less than 100 and preferably no more than 500 pages in length.
They are reproduced by a photographic process and therefore must be typed with extreme care. Sym
not on the typewriter should be inserted by hand in indelible black ink. Corrections to the types
should be made by pasting in the new text or painting out errors with white correction fluid. Authors rec
75 free copies and are free to use the material in other publications. The typescript is reduced sligh
size during reproduction; best results will not be obtained unless the text on any one page is kept w
the overall limit of 18 x 26.5 cm (7 x 10½ inches). On request, the publisher will supply special paper
the typing area outlined.
Manuscripts should be sent to Prof. G. Goos, Institut für Informatik, Universität Karlsruhe, Zirkel 2, 7500 K
ruhe/Germany, Prof. J. Hartmanis, Cornell University. Dept. of Computer-Science, Ithaca, NY/USA 14
or directly to Springer-Verlag Heidelberg.

Springer-Verlag, Heidelberger Platz 3, D-1000 Berlin 33
Springer-Verlag, Tiergartenstraße 17, D-6900 Heidelberg 1
Springer-Verlag, 175 Fifth Avenue, New York, NJ 10010/USA

ISBN 3-540-11490-4
ISBN 0-387-11490-4